D0560578

MY LIFE IN
WRITING

BY J. C. FURNAS

Nonfiction

How America Lives
Anatomy of Paradise
Voyage to Windward
Goodbye to Uncle Tom
The Road to Harpers Ferry
The Life and Times of the Late Demon Rum
The Americans
Great Times
Stormy Weather
Fanny Kemble

Fiction

The Prophet's Chamber
Many People Prize It
The Devil's Rainbow
Lightfoot Island

MY LIFE IN WRITING

Memoirs of a Maverick

J. C. FURNAS

WILLIAM MORROW AND COMPANY, INC.
New York

PS
3511
U85
Z465
1989

Chapter 17 was first published in a slightly different form in the Autumn 1988 issue of *The American Scholar*.

Library of Congress Cataloging-in-Publication Data

Furnas, J.C. (Joseph Chamberlain), 1905–
  My life in writing: memoirs of a maverick / J.C. Furnas.
    p. cm.
  ISBN 0-688-08842-2
  1. Furnas. J.C. (Joseph Chamberlain), 1905–   —Biography.
2. Authors, American—20th century—Biography. 3. Historians—
United States—Biography. I. Title
PS3511.U85Z465   1989
818'.5403—dc19   88-35694
[B]   CIP

Printed in the United States of America

First Edition

1 2 3 4 5 6 7 8 9 10

BOOK DESIGN BY BERNARD SCHLEIFER

For Anne and Anne,
neither of whom
ever asked that question,
and
with gratitude to
B&B = C.B.
B.B.
C.D.B.

Foreword

THAT A THING was there and is there no longer is both sad and stirring. Heraclitus said you can't step into the same river twice.

My impulse to try may reflect the large number of times I've been asked "How did you get to be a writer?" That question tends to be fourth in a series, like this:

"And . . . ah . . . what do you do, Mr. Furnas?"

"I'm a writer."

"Really? What do you write?"

"Books mostly."

"What kind of books?"

"Large ones usually." That *may* abort the conversation, but one can't count on it. In case of misfire, after a pause:

"Tell me, how did you get to be a writer?"

"I was never much good at anything else."

This large book is a discursive expansion of that churlish reply—necessarily autobiographical. When I was young and hungry I ghostwrote for a dozen or so persons whose experiences or opinions were thought worth printing: a couple of theatrical producers, a public-health pediatrician, a medical-lab technician, an important engineer-industrialist, a couple of bankers, a extremely English butler. . . . Most of them were easy to work with, less inclined to blow their own horns than might have been expected, and seemed pretty well satisfied with the results. At the time it never occurred to me that someday I'd ghost myself. Let the reader hope I do as well unto myself as I did unto others.

9

Contents

". . . and what is the use of a book," thought Alice, "without fictions or fornications?"

1

Such Interesting People

AUTOBIOGRAPHIES USUALLY ABOUND with celebrities-who-met-me. This one leads with celebrities-encountered-but-not-met-formally. For example, the Lord Mayor of London.

Some years ago my wife and I were creeping toward the taxi area of Gatrow airport—or was it Heathwick?—after an overnight flight from New York. We were short of sleep, stiff in the joints, groggy in the mind—all the physical and spiritual woes consequent on air travel. I was worse than usual because of rabbits. We had sat far forward under the movie screen. Preferring the chance of sleep to entertainment, we had eschewed sound-track earphones. But that did not altogether let me off the movie. Squeezed into my stuffy straitjacket of a seat, I often waked to savor my discomfort, and every time I opened my eyes there, ten feet away, menacingly looming, were rabbits, pastel-colored, anthropoid rabbits doing inexplicable things in dumb show, for that night's movie was the animated cartoon version of *Watership Down*. Big rabbits making sweeping gestures. It was a recurrent Technicolor nightmare.

At very long last the cockpit announced we were letting down to land and added that it "wished all success to the New Jersey trade delegation." That non sequitur was accounted for when, after formalities, we saw straggling ahead of us a clump of half a dozen people centered round Brendan Byrne, then governor of New Jersey. My wife, drowsily heedless, said: "Oh, there's our governor!" clearly enough for him to hear. Back

15

he came to shake hands with constituents. Though his accommodations in top class had been better than ours, he too looked pretty unbrisk. Just as he was blearily disengaging, there reared up beyond him a large man, broad and imposing in a dark suit and homburg hat, waving his arms and proclaiming: "Governor Byrne! Welcome to Britain, Governor Byrne! I am Lord Mayor of London, Governor Byrne!" Violently he shook the governor's hand, resoundingly he kissed Mrs. Byrne's and began to herd the party toward what, no doubt, was to be breakfast at the Guild Hall with Gog and Magog.

I was pushing our luggage on one of those supermarketish airport carts that, as usual, had a defective wheel. Bemused by His Worship's un-British flourishes on top of my surfeit of intermittent rabbits, I failed to steer hard-a-starboard to compensate for the cart's drift to leeward. So, in its slaunchwise fashion, it ran smartly into the Lord Mayor's left hind leg at about the level of the Achilles tendon. You could tell it hurt. He leapt and squawked and turned on me with a snarl the more impressive because he was twenty pounds heavier and twenty years younger than I was. I did my best to make my apology sound heartfelt, but he was having none of that. His mouth was working, he was flushed with mounting steam—all that saved me was his sudden recollection that members of the Byrne party were milling about like shepherdless sheep. Glowering, fuming, he limped off to resume charge. That, I devoutly hope, is the last I shall ever see of him. It's heavy odds he has never forgotten that damned clumsy American who crippled him so grisly early at the airport.

For that unrehearsed happening a psychiatrist might find an explanation in my equally informal encounter forty years ago with Mrs. Eleanor Roosevelt at a magazine promotion party. Making a rapid entrance as featured guest, for some reason she executed a sudden quarterturn and stepped on my foot. If she apologized as she took off on her new heading, I failed to hear. Indeed she may not have been aware of me at all. But I remained aware of her for she was tall and hefty and I was lame for a week, which impressed the matter on memory as well as my metatarsal region. Ah, says the psychiatrist, you maimed the lord mayor as surrogate compensation for trauma once inflicted by Mrs. Roosevelt, substituting one public figure for another. And there may be something in it, for just as His

Worship will always remember me, I think of my foot every time I see a picture of the creatrix of "My Day."

Those two notables are not seen there at their best. Now for one accidentally encountered in a favorable light: On July 1, 1945, the Seventh Australian Division supported by the Seventh Fleet of the U.S. Navy made the last amphibious attack of World War II on the Japanese-held oil port of Balikpapan in Borneo. I was one of the civilian correspondents going ashore after the first wave. Resistance was weaker than anticipated. I strolled into the half-burned settlement admiring the business-like way the Australians were moving up into action beyond the ridge back of town. Round a corner came a gaggle of twenty-odd men headed by General Douglas MacArthur—unmistakable; scrambled eggs on the visor of the floppy Air Force–style cap; actorishly handsome; long, limber stride; head high, eyes keen. Behind him came the Australian general and a U.S. Navy admiral, presumably in charge of the supporting squadron; then aides, orderlies, specialists lugging movie cameras and radio stuff, God knows who else—all hustling to keep up with the boss. He looked the part. Marlborough at Blenheim cannot have been better cast.

I had no special assignment, so, with nothing better to do, I seized this target of opportunity and fell in alongside MacArthur's Filipino orderly, who made no objection, just grinned at me amiably. On the fingers of one hand he had stuck the necks of some small Japanese sake jugs—souvenirs, I surmised. He saw me eyeing them and handed me one. MacArthur led us to the crest of the ridge, which had a good view of the valley beyond, where smoke and banging noises showed that something was still going on. There he stood silhouetted against the sky from both directions and with gestures delivered a lecture on the tactical situation. I'd have heard it had I stayed near, but zipping noises showed that the Japanese knew a target when they saw one and it would be safer back behind the crest. Most of the party had already moved back and down. I followed their example and watched as MacArthur went imperturbably on talking and pointing while the general and the admiral, honor-bound to stay beside him, did so like good men and true, only you could see their shoulders gradually hunching higher. Nobody got hit, heaven knows why. And eventually MacArthur finished his disquisition and

led us back down for a conducted tour of the town, where I
fell out without having a word with anybody.

It certainly did look as though he wished to get killed. But
I abandoned that notion after reflecting that the grand assault
on Japan was still to come—this was long before the *Enola Gay*
took off—and MacArthur surely hoped to be around when
the big game was played out. It had to be a simple matter of
an unflappable man being professionally, regardlessly brave if
bravery consists of disregarding danger when to do so is convenient. Some years ago William Manchester's responsible biography demolished the ill-natured tag "Dugout Doug" hung
on MacArthur. That was mere abuse of the generals-die-in-
bed cliché. There were ample reasons for mistrusting or dis-
approving of the man. But his skulking away from danger was
not one of them.

I still have that sake jug to confirm it.

At this point an encounter of more intellectual flavor is
probably indicated. Shift the formula to celebrity-whom-I-did-
meet-formally—the chess champion of Kiev, USSR (1935), a
brain indeed. We were going down the Volga in a steamboat
with a conducted tour of Americans chaperoned by a woman
guide from Intourist, the USSR's ubiquitous tourist agency.
Flora was demurely pretty in a Murillo-madonna way; spoke
French well and English very well; and having to ride herd on
tourists had not spoiled her sweet disposition. My wife and I
always traveled with a pocket chessboard. The second evening
we were whiling it away at chess in the boat's public room.
Flora spied us, smiled, and went away. Soon she was back all
in a cordial glow. The regional chess champion of Kiev was
on board and had consented to measure gambits with me.

It was abysmally absurd. Had I not existed, my wife would
have been the world's worst adult chess player, and vice versa.
We enjoyed matching ineptitudes and miscalculations; but
players of any competence used to moan when they saw the
board. I told Flora all that and more several times. She insisted that the match would be good for international goodwill
and I was just being modest. I held out for some twenty-four
hours, but when it was clear her feelings were really being
hurt, I caved in. She introduced the pride of Kiev.

To judge from his manner he liked my looks no better than I liked his. He could have been the glum cashier of a country bank or, say, Comrade Gromyko's nephew. I drew first move. I was determined to play as tight a defense as in me lay to stall off disaster for, with luck, maybe ten moves. He played fast, I doggedly slow, stripping my mental gears every move. At the sixth or seventh move I thought and thought and decided that to move that bishop four squares over there would give me a breath of air. I did so and saw I had misplaced it one square beyond what I had planned—a miscue typical of my normal chess game. It didn't matter this time. I was a gone goose anyway. *But* the pride of Kiev studied the board a while and resigned.

I managed to keep a straight face while he gestured eagerness to play again. Flora, round-eyed, abetted him. But I said no with patronizingly good humor, shook his hand, went on deck, and had my laugh out. He debarked next morning at some river port. That experience is high on my list of the things that persuade me that whatever else can be said for or against it, the universe, my universe anyway, does not make sense.

A more impressive item in that file involves that venerable and valuable figure John Dewey. My initial awareness of him was vaguely peripheral. Twenty years later repeated meetings occurred—he was a friend of my wife's family—and in a mouse-admiring-a-lion kind of way, we were friends. By 1940 he knew me well enough to enlist my assistance in his defense of Bertrand Russell against reactionary New York's attacks on his personal and intellectual integrity. Not long before John Dewey died, his new wife telephoned to say John wants to talk to you about something, let him know sometime you'll be coming to town; no hurry. Only he was gone before I ever learned what was on his mind. Years later, however, long after he had joined Pestalozzi and William James in Valhalla, I consulted one of his early books that, in the light of my childhood memories, utterly puzzled and confused me.

The matrix of this enigma calls for seventy-odd years of flashback to the corner of Park Avenue and Twenty-third Street in Indianapolis. The witness wears knickerbockers, high-laced shoes, and a "mackinaw" jacket and is feeling glum about just another day at Public School Number Forty-five.

2

Learning by Doing

NUMBER FORTY-FIVE'S WALLS were of brownish-yellow brick, its windows high and wide, its style, what little it had, the pseudo-Spanish that the Pan-American Exposition at Buffalo in 1901 had made fashionable. Circa 1911 its masking trees were still immature, but its small lawns and hedges were tidy and its graveled playgrounds—large for boys, smaller for girls—were free of trash. Indoors its gloomy halls smelled of the oil that kept down dust on its splintery wooden floors. But the rooms opening off them—principal's office and lower grades on the ground floor, higher grades on the second—smelled of only chalk dust and had ample daylight.

The vast hall that took up the whole third floor was lined with racks of wooden dumbbells, wands, and Indian clubs, the calisthenic paraphernalia that German zealots had wished on right-minded educationists in the mid-1800s. We pupils were unaware of those exotic details. We assumed that lining up regularly to twirl Indian clubs in unison one-two-three-and-down had always been as much part of schooling as the multiplication table. Whether that sort of thing went on in many American school systems of the day I do not know. Anyway, in Indianapolis seventy-odd years ago, though German influence was not as strong as in St. Louis and Milwaukee, it was considerable. German surnames such as Lieber and Vonnegut were weighty in the business community. Among my classmates were Kruse, Eckert, Schechter, Treuer, Fried, Mehrlich; among the teaching staff Scherf, Meyer, Neff, Duden.

German (optional) was the only foreign language taught; I can still sing right through "Die Lorelei" as learned under bulky, conscientious Fraulein Müller and read that staggering, sharp-cornered German handwriting. There was a Germanish feel about the way we marched down to the basement washrooms midmorning in columns of twos to the beat of a player piano pumping out not Sousa but a clamorous German march, "Under the Double Eagle."

On the piano bench labored Carl, a lanky pupil with longish, swept-back fair hair. I still see him swaying and half crouching as he put his back into pedaling. Number Forty-five already had electric light, but electric-powered player pianos, phonographs, coffee makers, and such were still to come. I recall wondering how Carl got chosen for the job and how he liked it. Not that I thought it desirable. It looked like hard work, dull too, for the tune never changed; but here was the school's one instance of a pupil doing something that no other pupil did.

Those stiff minor Germanisms were strangely at odds with the school's particular distinction as proving ground for some of John Dewey's then importantly innovative ideas on education. Under our supervising principal, an ungainly but ruggedly comely woman named Georgia Alexander,* Number Forty-five was one of three such guinea pigs in the city system. As noted above, years later I came to know and admire Mr. Dewey and his three remarkable daughters—all dead now, rest their shrewd and genial souls. In my knee pants days, however, his was only the name attached to an occasional silent presence in the back of the schoolroom, notable chiefly because normally the only men entering the school's gynocratic subculture were the manual-training teacher; Mr. Malloy, the grumpy janitor; and the black chore man. Among us, inculcating the three R's was as exclusively women's work as ironing shirts.

---

*The Indianapolis schools' speller was of Miss Alexander's compilation. The short literary extracts relieving its columns of words included bits from Mark Twain, George Borrow, Carlyle, Stevenson . . . showing, I now take it, that her level of cultivation was higher than that of her teaching staff. The extracts were not identified by either author or title of work. Gradually over the years I found them all: the Mississippi steamboats backing out from the New Orleans levee, Mr. Petulengro on "the wind on the heath, brother," . . .

We were unaware of the connection between Dewey's sporadic presence and the odd activities that sometimes sprouted
among our three R's. Nobody told us that we were testing the
theory and practice of Learning-by-Doing, the tactical axiom
of what came to be called "progressive education." Just as with
Indian clubs, for all we knew fifth-graders everywhere had always been given scissors, paste, and sheets of slimsy brown
cardboard and shown how to make toy bungalows. Later it
was knives, miniature smoothing planes, and jigsaws to make
flat-profile wooden figures of people and animals. That project cost me my left thumbnail; it grew back but is stiff and
ridgy to this day. We studied the Netherlands' struggle for
independence from Spain by writing and staging a play about
the siege of Leyden. Frank Callan, the class tough guy, was
Philip II; Justine Halliday was Duchess of Parma; I was bur-
gomaster of Leyden wearing a flat-crowned black beaver hat
that, in the belief it was appropriate, my mother borrowed
from a Quaker friend whose grandfather had worn it. She got
my sword, wearing which highly gratified me, from a neighbor who belonged to a fraternal order that went in for ceremonial swords. The best thing in the show was the homing
pigeon bringing news that relief was on the way; where we got
that stuffed pigeon I don't recall, but it whirred in on its taut
wire most effectively.

Some details of the agenda of Learning-by-Doing were thus
fun in a larkish way, but usually their chief virtue lay merely
in breaking the everyday irksomeness of the basic processes of
textbook, recitation, blackboard arithmetic. . . . We certainly
learned little from the above and other Doings that I recall
only vaguely or not at all. In my own case I did learn that light
cardboard is too sleazy to make passable toy houses of, but
that discovery taught nothing about architectural construction.
I learned that a school desk makes a poor workbench and toy
tools don't do well in all-thumbs hands like mine. From the
play I acquired only a hot prejudice against Spain (probably
heightened by cultural hangover from the rather recent Span-
ish-American War) as well as Catholics generally, a thing already rife in our WASP environment. God knows why that
particular episode in history was imposed on us. In Deweyite
theory, democratic discussions among the pupils should have

chosen the subject for dramatization. Yet though I was part-author of the script, I recall no such proceedings.

There were many such discrepancies between Deweyism and Number Forty-five's dabblings therein. But I did not grasp their extent until some years ago when, in connection with a book I was writing, I read for the first time *Schools of Tomorrow* (1915) by John and Evelyn Dewey (eldest daughter), an elaborate report on the success of Deweyism in several guinea-pig schools—Number Forty-five conspicuous among them and *at the very time when I was a pupil there.* In that book I learned to my great surprise that at Number Forty-five in my day "nearly all the schoolwork centered round activities which had intrinsic meaning and value for the pupils . . . most of the initiative for the work came from the children themselves. . . . In almost all grades . . . the pupils were conducting the recitations themselves," and even when that was temporarily inadvisable, they were "encouraged to ask each other questions, to make their objections and corrections aloud." I could recall no such collective experiences. I'd like to have seen Miss Conlon's face if some morning the front row of pupils had collectively suggested that they review subtraction that day instead of plunging deeper into long division.

Giving examples, *Schools of Tomorrow* tells of pupils setting up a parcel-post system—parcel-post was then a new, progressive anodyne for the express companies' semimonopoly—as a way to study English and arithmetic. To those same ends, it said, another class at Number Forty-five set up a retail shoe store. The fifth grade built a miniature model farmhouse that required scale drawings and nice calculation of board-feet of lumber, square yards of wallpaper, and so on (arithmetic and economics); planting the farm meant estimates of crop yields, cost of seed, and fertilizer (arithmetic and economics again); clothes and furniture for the farm family were designed, family life analyzed (sociology, writing, drawing). . . . Such doings—"projects" became the term—have long been imbedded in today's thinking about education. What startled me and still does was the old book's confident assertion that all these complicated, conspicuous, time-consuming, meant-to-be-stimulating things went on in my time at Number Forty-five—without my being aware of them.

I readily recognized the book's photograph of a typical classroom. The mural over the blackboard and the design of the desks were hauntingly familiar. Indeed the back of the head of one of the boy pupils—they look nine or ten years old—might well be mine. But in my recollection nothing more elaborate or stimulating than those cardboard bungalows and toy woodworkings was applied to us pupils. It is conceivable, if unlikely, that my particular class consistently missed out on those fancy projects. At most, however, that cannot account for the absence of teacher tactics encouraging us pupils to backchat and teach one another and choose our own lesson plans, such as the book described. And even if my class was the one that never set up a parcel-post system or designed a Panama Canal in case of war with Japan—another project that the book ascribed to Number Forty-five—we pupils down the hall would certainly have known of such matters.

I wish that sometimes I had talked with Evelyn and her father about their work in Indianapolis. Once, I think, I mentioned to him that I'd gone to school under Miss Alexander and he said something like "Yes, Georgia Alexander—able woman, wasn't she?"; nothing more. Since I had not yet seen *Schools of Tomorrow* I was unaware of Evelyn's share in describing those early experiments, so I did not take up old times with her.

Bewilderment persists. Here was a man of unimpeachable integrity and careful temperament who would never have allowed enthusiasm to tempt him to fabricate evidence. And Evelyn was searchingly honest and, though a warm friend, no enthusiast either. Father and daughter are long since gone, so to append this footnote to the history of education in America cannot distress them. I must assume anyway that somehow they could resolve the mystery of why my school so little resembled the one that they, in all good faith I'm sure, wrote about. I do wish they could come back and explain over a noggin of the rum that John Dewey was so temperately fond of.

Generally, as well as in "projects," Number Forty-five was as unstimulating an environment as I ever knew. Even its attempts to instill conventional skills were often ineffective. Every few days the soft drawing pencil and the Artgum eraser or the long tin box of blocks of watercolor were unlimbered and we did Art. There was no specialized art teacher. Miss Pedlow or Miss Arne or some other young woman with a pompadour and a Gibson Girl shirtwaist had to make do with skimpy normal-school training in the glories of shape and color. To create Art one took a piece of coarse, beige-colored paper, creased and tore it in half—scissors forbidden, why we never knew—swabbed it with a brush dipped in water, imbued the brush with black pigment, drew a smudgy-dark horizon across the wet paper, cleaned the brush, imbued it with green pigment, smudged a triangular green shape above the horizon (a tree). . . . Or teacher set on her desk a bulgy jug to be drawn in pencil. Had some budding Giotto been a member of the class, he might have immortalized that jug. Lacking him, our results, what with frequent erasures, were about as dismal as the watercolor tree.

Our music was better. Our teachers could sing recognizably and read music well enough to teach us the rudiments. And thanks to the prevalence of Sunday Schools, most of us were more or less broken to singing by ear. The large flat songbook provided half a dozen hymns (ah there, opponents of school prayer!); patriotic numbers—"America," "The Star Spangled Banner," "The Battle Hymn of the Republic," but neither "America the Beautiful" nor "God Bless America," for those had not yet watered down the national canon; a few operatic choruses; some blackface standards like "Old Black Joe"; but mostly dozens of examples of melodic milk toast with lame lyrics and music akin to the empty-calorie pieces with titles like "The Fairies' Tea Party" inflicted on me when I had to take piano lessons. I have a tenacious musical memory and a number of those songbook confections still run though my head, such as a nautical number about "My father's ship / With its rock and dip." Frank Callan sang "My father's shit," which went undetected under cover of the noise we three dozen ten-year-olds made when letting ourselves go. Always in unison. Sometimes a conscientious teacher tried introducing us to singing in parts, but the results were always so dauntingly hideous that the notion would be dropped.

Those half hours of song must have been a relief for teacher. With minimum drain on authority the little devils were enjoying themselves doing what they were supposed to do. There music stopped. The player piano in the lower hall and an upright in the gym were, as far as I recall, the school's only musical instruments. Once, expanding our horizon with a phonograph was tried. A large model with a tulip-shaped horn was wheeled in on a sort of tea cart and cranked up to regale 5B with half an hour of operatic highlights; I recall a hoarse, squawky sextet from *Lucia*. Whether we owed this to Deweyism or to an attempt to sell the school board phonographs we never knew, but the experiment was not repeated.

The less pretentious arts were, though not ignored, also stupidly handled. The elder girls had "domestic science"—elementary cooking, some sewing, I believe, and housekeeping hints. Neither then nor later did I hear a girl express gratitude for it. Maybe it was as feckless as "manual training," the elder boys' equivalent. The term has a history. In the same mid-1800s as the calisthenics cult, certain high-minded Swedes maintained that pupils and teachers would acquire intellectual and moral merit by including basic tool skills in the curriculum. The idea spread across the Atlantic along with Indian clubs. Eventually it grew sidewise into high schools such as Indianapolis's Manual Training High, set up to fit blue-collar youth for industrial jobs. But Number Forty-five's version was nearer the original in spirit. Persuaded that Manual Training was a Good Thing (for males), the school board had made it obligatory for boys in upper elementary grades.

Our large basement manual-training shop was a great improvement on those earlier handicraft fumblings. Its solid workbenches carried full-size, good-quality tools. It had ample woodworking raw material from the millions of chestnut trees killed by the calamitous blight of the early 1900s. Such favorable conditions should have left me with useful skills and maybe even spiritual satisfactions to match. But even with proper tools I was still all thumbs. To plane the edge of a board into the exact 90-degree angle needed for a glue joint I could manage only by chance after much waste of shavings; and by then the board was too narrow for its purpose. Eventually I did shape and cobble together the elements of a hexagonal-top tabouret that didn't fall apart on the way home. But nobody, least of all its creator, could have taken pride in the clumpy thing.

If any of the other twelve-year-olds developed aptitude enough to profit from twice a week of "shop," it was no doing of our instructor, a sulky young man as wooden as his pupils' materials, nothing like the joyously inspirational leader that those euphoric Swedes had in mind. His demonstrations in front of the class were too perfunctory to convey much; I think of him every time I see an airline flight attendant racing through the emergency routine. Most of the time he merely fidgeted from bench to bench grumbling, seldom taking the tool and saying better do it this way, I'll show you why. I really learned only two things: the difference between a screwdriver and a chisel; and that I'd probably go through life unable to make effective use of any tool subtler than axe, hoe, and spade.

I now appreciate indignantly—at the time no such feeling—how flagrant a waste of taxpayers' money this admirably equipped shop was. Otherwise public funds were not lavished on Number Forty-five, nor do I suppose any school in the system was better favored. In those primitive times no school nurse; once a year a functionary from the school board downtown lined us up to say ah and have our throats looked down; when I whittled my thumbnail off, Miss Neff just stopped the bleeding by sticking my thumb in a glass of cold water and then wrapped it in her handkerchief. No organized games. No lunchroom; we went home at noon and returned at one. No library; the only books were each desk's complement of arithmetic, speller, reader, songbook, small dictionary, and joggrify. Though Dewey-ism was strong on the virtues of such junkets, very few visits to museums, none to factories. No PTA; that virus had not yet reached Indianapolis. No busing; we all lived within fifteen minutes' walk. The most drastic shortage, however, probably persists in most schools today—lack of adequate teachers.

This needs careful stating: Miss Alexander; her sister, the assistant principal, who did some classroom work; and the sixteen rank-and-file, each handling a half grade, were all, I am confident, well meaning; certainly they were competent disciplinarians. Without needing the corporal punishment that was strictly taboo, they kept constructive order by brooding vigilance and moral ascendancy. Punishments, which were infrequent, began with exile to the cloakroom—bleakly dark, stinking of wet wool in winter—and progressed into "being kept after

school" for one-on-one exhortation to diligence and obedi-
ence; then to being "sent to the office"; then "a note to your
parents," the first step toward expulsion, which was rare indeed. Classrooms were typically quiet—not uncheerful—slightly
overheated except when, twice a day, the windows were thrown
open while we stood in the aisles doing minor calisthenics. One
reason it all worked out pretty well was, of course, the cultural
homogeneity of the neighborhood.

Further careful statement: Without losing their tempers
more often than was useful, these teachers got most of us reasonably skilled in the Three R's. At graduation we could add,
subtract, multiply, and divide with confidence, though few were
to be trusted with square roots. We could read the less demanding parts of the daily paper, though few of us did so
beyond the sports pages.* We could diagram a sentence on
the blackboard, write legibly, and turn out a coherent couple
of paragraphs on a given topic in the stiff-covered "composition book."

Note that all that came not of Deweyism but of conventional pedagogy: rote learning, rule following with small regard to the sort of momentum that might have resulted from
realized significance. When, hand duly raised, I asked Miss
Scherf why I had to place that number just there in long division, that ruddy-faced young woman replied briskly but not
ill naturedly: "Because you're supposed to, that's why." Her
normal-school instructor would have given her the same answer; only she'd never have asked, for the intellectual beauties
of the decimal system, whatever they may be, were no concern
of either party. Arithmetic was just something one had to acquire, an accepted and necessary routine like brushing one's
teeth. It can be taught that way and that's the way we were
taught it.

Penmanship (does even the word survive?) was inevitably
all drill to coordinate eye and hand. Ours was "the Palmer

---

*Comics are not taken into account because the morning paper, the *Star*, carried few,
and those feeble; and the evening paper, the *News*, none except Bud Fisher's "Mutt &
Jeff" and Kin Hubbard's inimitably pungent "Abe Martin." This near famine was
somewhat relieved by the Sunday *Chicago Tribune* comics that many Indianapolis
households enjoyed and passed round the neighborhood: "Happy Hooligan," "Old
Doc Yak," and so on.

Method"—thick, soft pencil in thumb and two fingers, wrist straight, underside of forearm flat on desk, circular sweepings making rows of capital O's and then gradual elaboration into insipidly cursive letters. The purpose was to enable clerks to write all day without disabling fatigue. That made less and less sense as typewriting took over. But Palmer—and who was he?—was then deeply entrenched in normal schools, and to this day my handwriting looks as though I were demonstrating his method while riding over potholes in a jeep at high speed.

Beyond that our teachers' devotion to duty, proper as it was, did us little good. It was not their fault that they didn't know enough about history or joggrify to handle them adequately; but they didn't. A certain amount of drawing and coloring maps did leave a valuable residue. I remain one of those lucky people who can divert themselves by the hour in a happy cartographical trance over a U.S. Geodetic Survey map of a township I never heard of or a detailed navigational chart of some godforsaken coastline. Of our studies in history, however, I recall only the preparation for that wheezy play and one other bit—and a map was involved in that. Miss Meyer (7B) explained that the Portuguese were the Europeans who colonized Brazil because it lay south of the line the pope had drawn to divide the overseas world between them and the Spanish. Yet the history book's outline map of the Line of Demarcation showed it running north and south down the middle of the Atlantic and cutting the eastward-thrust shoulder of South America off from the rest of the continent. Raising my hand, I maintained tactlessly—this was long before I began to understand what tact is and why—that the pope's line went north and south. She rejected the notion. I got out the book and showed her. She reacted strongly; I suppose that is why I remember the incident so well. There was born my suspicion that one could be a teacher without either knowing enough or being bright enough.

To be fair, several of Miss Meyer's colleagues were brighter than she. But the best were, as hinted above, no great thing. One would think that, since the school was a sort of showcase, Miss Alexander would have recruited a picked staff. If she had, what can the run-of-the-mine teachers elsewhere in the system have been like? Maybe one reason even that faint breath of Deweyism failed to lift us above rote-and-recite was that its instruments were these unimaginative women of little better than average intelligence and meager culture. Years after leaving Number Forty-five, I began to wonder whether any system of education can be better than those applying it; and, conversely, to surmise that a poor system with really good teachers, if that can be arranged, may be better than a good system, if such a thing is conceivable, with poor teachers. Consider, however, the depressing probability that the ratio of potentially adequate or even passable teachers to any population at any time is nothing like what extensive educational facilities should have. There can't be nearly enough good teachers anymore than there can be a plethora of big-league-quality baseball players—a point all too clear many evenings on TV.

3

World I Never Made

NOBODY CAN DEFINE or even describe himself. You've noticed how indecisive artists' self-portraits usually look? A college roommate let me know that his kid brother, and a crude young animal he was, said I was "droopy and skinny and talks like a book." In the 1930s I wore rimless glasses and had a thin mustache. When a snapshot caused me to notice that they made me resemble Heinrich Himmler, I shaved off the mustache, but resumed it in 1945 when rattling round among the armed forces in the Pacific theater entailed too much shaving of the upper lip in cold water.

For less somatic findings: Long ago the *Ladies' Home Journal* made much use of Dr. Paul Popenoe, a consulting psychologist with good credentials and wide reputation. Having been together on an assignment in Columbia, Missouri, he and I were trundling to St. Louis in a day coach. He was a friendly, relaxed sort, like the ideal dentist. I was sure he wouldn't mind being asked about his methods. How, for instance, did he size up patients or clients or whatever he called them?

Experience and mother wit, he said, could give rough but often sound notions offhand. For further probing he used formal tests, such as those for the narrow but useful dichotomy introvert/extrovert. Why not a demonstration? Out of his briefcase came a test questionnaire. I stipulated that he first write down the impression he had formed of me during our several days together. He thought a few minutes, jotted a finding down, folded the paper, put it on the windowsill, and handed me the test—pencil and paper, several dozen questions of the what-do-you-do-when-the-waiter-spills-soup-on-you kind, only of greater scope and shrewdness.

I played fair, answered each according to my best knowledge, and calculated the result according to the appended key-formula. I came out a marked though not pathologically recessive introvert. That was no news to me. Popenoe looked a little upset. He confirmed my calculation, then opened his note from the windowsill—it called me a well-adjusted extrovert. It was striking testimony to my success in papering over my temperamental handicaps in the interests of economic and social survival. I will say it for Popenoe that he took his miscue well. No reason to conclude, however, that the material he worked with—that is, me—was interesting, deep, or subtle, just off-beat. The reviews of my book on the 1930s (published 1977) made that clear again. The *Chicago Tribune* said: "So much that happened in the '30s was radical by Furnas' lights that one suspects he may be a knee-jerk conservative." The *Pittsburgh Press* said: "America's true course in the 1930s for Furnas . . . lay squarely within Arthur Schlesinger's 'vital center.' The reader will find few expressions of American liberal thinking that are more explicit than this volume."

Also skewed, though in a different context, was the description of me by the only royalty of my acquaintance. His name was Tugi (pronounced Toong-ee). He was Crown Prince of the small island kingdom of Tonga in the South Pacific; since we met he has succeeded to the throne. He probably still remembers me. He and the Lord Mayor would have that in common. Like most Polynesian patricians he was huge—well over six foot, broad and thick, mostly muscle, nothing gross about him. He was as quiet and well behaved as his teachers in the New Zealand schools, whence he learned his good English, would have wished.* He was the only other guest when my wife and I dined with the Chief Justice of Tonga, a white official from H.M. Colonial Office, which then administered Tonga as a protectorate. Local liquor control was caste-bound. Commoners could get only beer and not much of that; inter-

---

*I hope there was nothing in recent press dispatches stating that, as king, he was offering asylum to Ferdinand Marcos.

mediate family heads were limited to a bottle or two of hard stuff a month; but the highest chiefs and supervising whites were unlimited. So though spirits were scarce among the islands so soon after World War II, our host had plenty of Scotch and we were all fairly tiddly by the time we left late in the evening.

Next morning we felt poorly. Tugi, who had never been really tight before, apparently felt terrible, all 290 pounds of him. His reaction was logical and commendable—he turned in his liquor permit and swore off for life. I hope he stayed with it for the honor of his moral instincts. Though his hangover was primarily the Chief Justice's fault, my wife and I felt some responsibility. On reflection, however, I concluded that thus to make a teetotaler of a Polynesian chief of state—a class whom alcohol ravaged dreadfully in the past—partially offset our later direct responsibility for infecting the administration of the neighboring islands of Western Samoa with Manhattan cocktails.

I can't recall discussing religions at the Chief Justice's, but no doubt we did. For a few years later a conference of South Pacific governors and heads of state was held in Fiji. A good friend of ours, Colin Simpson, an Australian newspaperman, covered it for a Sydney paper. He sent us a snapshot of himself chatting with Tugi and jotted on its back Tugi's reply when asked if he remembered an American named Furnas: "Certainly, remember him very well. Drinks like a fish and claims to be a Quaker."

That first clause was not altogether justified, nor yet the implication of "claims" in the second. I am not only a Quaker, I am as far as I know a unique kind of Quaker. That distinction is among several things I owe my mother, though there resemblance between her and Nancy Hanks Lincoln ceases.

Most of the descendants of John Furnas, who left the north of England in the mid-1700s to join the Quaker settlement in South Carolina, have persisted in being Quakers. Among them, me. To be technical, I was born too late to qualify as a "birthright" member of the Religious Society of Friends. Until 1904 our segment of Society gave automatic membership to Friends' offspring as though their parents' intimacy with the Inner Light left a hereditary taint; but that custom was abrogated just before I arrived. My sister got under the wire, I did not. Instead

I was put through a watery equivalent of a confirmation class studying a stiff little Book of Discipline, and in due season was acknowledged a full-fledged Friend.

Now, among Friends divorce was a polluting disgrace. My mother remembered that with dismay when, in my mid-twenties, I told her I was to marry a divorcee. She took a dim view of my marrying anyway, and the added vexation of this special circumstance stirred her ingenuity. She envisioned my getting "read out of meeting" (Friends' equivalent of excommunication) at Indianapolis Monthly Meeting. The danger may not have been inevitable. The breach of discipline was clear, but I was domiciled eight hundred miles from home, had few connections there anymore, and in such matters Friends were getting slack. It had been a long time since John Greenleaf Whittier had refused to attend the marriage of Theodore Weld and Angelina Grimké because Weld was no Quaker, so she was "marrying out of Society." Even if word of my transgression did reach Indianapolis Quakers, it did not necessarily follow that they would bother to lower the boom. But my mother was taking no chances. She advised, indeed ordered me to apply for a "letter"—the Removal Certificate that transfers a Friend from his previous monthly meeting to the one covering the area to which he shifts residence. I was to act at once before Indianapolis could get the scent and then—fail to present the letter to any other monthly meeting. Thus I'd be off the Indianapolis roster and never registered on any other, so no monthly meeting would have the authority to read me out.

I obeyed to the letter, so to speak, not from filial duty but from delight in my mother's cleverness. I still have that certificate in my archives undelivered: "Joseph C. Furnas . . . having removed and settled within the limits of . . . meeting . . . upon due inquiry, no obstruction appears to . . . transferring his membership. . . . We therefore recommend him to your Christian Care. . . . In love we are your friends"—and the signatures of the two clerks of Indianapolis Monthly Meeting. Thus I am, as far as I know, the only free-floating Quaker—sole member in good or any other kind of standing of Limbo Monthly Meeting. Due inquiry indeed!

My mother was only formally a Friend. The tiny English Lutheran church near the Indiana farm where she was reared gave her what religion she had. On marrying my father she dutifully turned Quaker, but any hope she had of feeling and behaving as one availed little. The only Quaker trait of our household was the "silent grace" before meals—thirty seconds or so of sitting still and staring at one's lap. And happily for Isaiah Furnas's wife, Elizabeth, the meeting she attended at the First Friends Church at Thirteenth Street and Alabama was hardly more Quakerish than she. The building's being called a *church* not a *meetinghouse* marked how far it had fallen from the explicit and implicit standards of John Woolman and Levi Coffin. Instead of a soberly gaunt, clapboarded barn with separate entrances for the sexes and segregated seating, this was a frantically turreted, heavily gabled, stained-glass travesty of Victorian Gothic in red brick. Probably some Baptist or Methodist congregation had built it and, a generation later, moving uptown, sold it to the Quakers. I don't think it was altogether the trauma of having had to look at it for four Sundays out of five that makes me recall it as the ugliest building I ever laid eyes on.

Its auditorium had a fussily carved golden oak pulpit midships of a long triangular platform. No Quakerish plain benches with a "facing bench" for august member-leaders; instead 60-degree arcs of shiny golden oak pews with volute-turned ends and racks for hymnbooks and Bibles. Hymnbooks? The original Quakers deplored the heathenish vanity of music in worship. Worse, the purchase had included a pipe organ and choir gallery, in which a quartet led the congregation in pretty much the same hymns as other Protestant sects favored. The tunes and words of many of them haunt me and I still enjoy pumping out the simpler ones on my old-fashioned harmonium. The soprano, tenor, and bass of the quartet changed from time to time, but the contralto was a fixture. It wasn't her fault that she was strikingly homely, and for all I know she supported any number of ailing parents with such musical chores. But such considerations do not occur to children—at least the kind of child I was. She had a voice like a peevish Diesel locomotive and, while giving some interminable anthem her all, made such faces that I attribute primarily to her my intolerance of most conventional singing. The organ's offertories were little better, but at least the organist kept her back to the house.

Quaker custom was, and in some contexts may still be, for all in "meeting" to sit silent, presumably basking in the Inner Light, until "the Spirit moved" one of them, usually an occupant of the facing bench, to rise and pour forth a cross between rhapsodical prayer and a sermon for an indeterminate time. If no Spirit moving occurred at all, eventually a leader on the facing bench rose and shook his neighbor's hand in token that all should do so and depart. At Thirteenth and Alabama the only relic of that was some ten minutes of prescribed silence midway in the service; and the only Friend whom the Spirit ever moved was an unreconstructed old fellow whose occasional incoherent exhortings my mother found unbearable. She snorted and sneered about him all the way home.

Except for him, a stranger in the house would have seen no reason to believe that these behatted, bedizened women and their bare-headed (Quaker men always wore their hats in meeting and the women wore bonnets), benecktied menfolk weren't the congregation of "the world's people" (Quakerese for what Jews mean by *goyim*) who had built the place. Nor would the distinctly un-Quakerish presence of a salaried preacher, though with a good Quaker surname, have undeceived him. He had that look common in American pulpits, as of a Gay Nineties matinée idol *manqué*. His homiletic method, blending hog calling with tenor incantations, was consistent with such a tilted chin, heavy eyebrows, long-lashed eyes—and open mouth. The boredom I owed his sermons was not the suspended animation of school nor yet the leg ache induced by hanging about in a department store while my mother pondered size, pattern, and price. This boredom came of the man's heartless prolixity. Out of the simplest biblical text he would wring fantastic vain repetitions and farfetched applications. Of this weekly blather I recall one masterpiece so absurd that for a few lucid minutes it occurred to me at the age of nine or so that it was ridiculous. It concerned an obscure Hebrew who—implausible as it sounds, he's there in the Old Testament, I've looked it up—went down into a pit on a snowy day and slew a lion (2 Samuel 23:20). No further details. It took forty mortal minutes to smother that mideastern Davy Crockett in moral, social, and theological significances.

When my squirming and yawning grew too noticeable, I

was allowed to read the little leaflet-magazine that Sunday school gave us boys. It was unbelievably vapid except for a department called "The Order of the Silent Sphynx," which enlisted the susceptible in the use of an alphabet code based on Egyptian hieroglyphics. That was fun, but when deciphered the Sphynx's remarks would have made Chinese fortune cookies sound like trumpet calls. (Incidentally this inanity was another breach of Quaker principles, to which anything like a secret society is anathema.) The other permitted counterirritant was to slip a Bible out of the rack to read. Many such fidgety hours made me more at home than many parsons with the King James Version, an invaluable privilege for a writer. Most of it was not exactly enjoyable, too firmly associated with sitting on a smelly, varnished, and (in summer) sticky plank; with uneasiness lest a visit to the basement washroom grow necessary; and with gloomy resentment of the whole foolish business: balderdash from the pulpit, yowling and mooing from the choir, groans and whinnies from the organ. . . . Except for some of the parables, the gospels seemed flabby. The Old Testament prophets were, though vociferous, obscure and verbose. The Song of Songs was over my head. I was not yet up to the wonders of Job, the Proverbs, and Ecclesiastes. But those succinct accounts in the Old Testament of who did what to whom had vigorous merits.

The large Sunday School room next to the church proper was still another un-Quakerish aping of worldly churches. Platform up front; piano to accompany lightweight hymns; a blackboard, I think. The superintendent was a pink-faced gabbler who, my mother reminded us every few Sundays, had once had a brush with the law about fixing race bets. (She had a talent for knowing something discreditable about nine of every ten persons within range.) His son was one of eight or nine boys in my Sunday School class. At the age of sixteen he was leading the first live jazz combo I ever heard and, wearing a battered top hat like Ted Lewis's, doing a soft shoe between numbers—not in Sunday School, I probably should add in view of today's trendy churches. This holy kind of school was even duller than the secular. It amounted to sitting in a pew between 9:30 and 10:30 A.M. every Sunday swapping nudges and grunts between hymn singings and Bible readings. Very little attention was ever afforded whichever young or middle-aged matron tried to get some sense of piety into us.

For my mother, however, Sunday School was a pleasure. Toward church service she was somewhat aloof, did not sing the hymns, nor did my father; in view of his country Quaker rearing he probably did not know how. Yet in spite of her subliminal diffidence about being at home among Quakers, she had got herself recruited to teach the women's Bible class of the First Friends Church and gave it all she had. Proudly hatted, pince-nez gleaming and wobbling, she laid down the law, the prophets, and the gospel to some forty women concentrated in a certain block of pews. Neither they nor she had to rely on her interpretation of the snippet of the Bible that the national Sunday School guide to which the church subscribed specified for that week. What my mother taught came largely from a sort of encyclopedia of holy commentary compiled by a sage named Peloubet. There was nothing discreditable about this dependence. Peloubet was to many serious Sunday School teachers what a given state's Revised Statutes is to a minor law office. I heard none of her teaching, for her flock assembled too far away in the Sunday School room. It was probably workmanlike, for between college and marriage she had "taught school" at Amo, Indiana, a hamlet in Hendricks County just north of the National Road, and was presumably classroom-competent. As for the men's Bible Class, I recall of it only an occasional glimpse of my father sitting among his peers looking no more and no less thoughtful and clean-shaven than he had at breakfast and would later in church.

Maybe the incongruities of these un-Quakerish doings helped to warp me into mistrusting my Quaker heritage. I do not imply, however, that I'd have liked any better to have been reared in Quakerism undiluted—"the plain language" that my father used with his parents, unworldly clothes, dislike of surnames. Long ago I came to regard the whole Friendly Persuasion, even when they try to stay near what George Fox had in mind, as social freeloaders afflicted with amateur anarchism of rather pharisaical flavor.

I enjoy one of my persisting superstitions. When anxious about a chancy situation, I am likely to cross myself. I think I acquired that from seeing actors do so when going on stage;

by now it's a very stubborn, almost automatic habit. Only I don't do it properly—not up-down-left-right but up-left-right-down. When anybody tries to correct me, I say: "I was reared a Quaker and that's how Quakers cross themselves." Whereas, of course, that venerable gesture was in Quaker terms just as immoral as Christmas or brass buttons.

But one small vestige of the equation "Furnas = Quaker" stays with me gratefully. My great-grandfather, Isaiah George, was a farmer first in southwestern Ohio, then in Marion County, Indiana. The daguerrotype of him shows him even harsher and more formidable than daguerrotypes usually do. Well over six foot, spare-made, long arms, huge hands, bristly hair, reptilian mouth, he could be Andrew Jackson's homely brother in a rage. He was a renowned wrestler. Pugilism was taboo for him, of course, but anybody he picked up and threw down was likely to stay down. Once upon a time, says family lore, a local tough boy, probably half tight or he wouldn't have been so rash, sashayed up on a Saturday court day and said: "Isaiah, I hear you been telling it round I'm a scoundrel." "Friend," said Isaiah, "I have never called thee a scoundrel. But thee constrains me to confess that I have always thought that's what thee is." Then he got to his feet, hunched his shoulders, and flexed those bear-paw hands. End of story, tough boy melting away.

To contrast school boredom with church boredom does not mean the first was preferable. It weighed in five times a week, church only once. Indeed sometimes we came home after Sunday school, eschewing church; whereas there was no breaking the iron hold of school.

Truancy never occurred to me, nor, so far as I knew, to any of my classmates. "Playing hookey" was in our vocabulary, but this wasn't that kind of neighborhood. We pretty much took it for granted that school, rain or shine, nine months a year, 8:30 A.M. to 3:00 P.M., was the inevitable destiny of all between the ages of six and fourteen, no more to be avoided than having to grow two or three inches a year.

The pace of school doings fostered boredom in all but the slowest. Study assignments seldom required all the time allowed. One had to fidget through five or ten leftover minutes with no more fertile stimulus than the sourly foul smell of the ink in the desk inkwell and the banal view of a blackboard smeared with chalk dust. Booth Tarkington's fictional Penrod Schofield (presumably an Indianapolis boy only a few years in advance of me) relieved his school boredom by fantasies of levitation. I had no such resource. I tried to assuage the faint ache of it by reading textbooks over and over and prowling the little dictionary for unfamiliar words. I even copied in pencil many of the tiny engraved illustrations. That taught me nothing about drawing but did make me master, at the age of nine, of the Doric, Ionic, Corinthian, Composite, and Roman Doric classic architectural orders. To this day I feel let down on seeing instances of ignorant deviation from those shapes.

Otherwise those desultory porings left me no significant knowledge. The fact is—stated without apology—much of my boredom came of already knowing more of two of the three R's than school could teach. The cause was my intensive, wide home reading. From about the time I could wash my own hands I was a bookworm, and thank God for it.

God, and again my mother, for she had much to do with my chronic word-mindedness. Self-persuaded that her children were necessarily brilliant and deserved opportunity to show it, she took the only means that occurred to her and heaped books on us. Our playroom offered most of the period's accepted "children's books"—several versions of Mother Goose; fairy stories leaning heavily on Perrault and Grimm; *Peter Rabbit* (though no other Beatrix Potter); Andersen somewhat abridged; *The Arabian Nights* necessarily heavily abridged but affording us the King of the Black Isles and the garrulous fish in the frying pan and Morgiana's oil jars, also a mussy cut of the lady ghoul supping off a corpse; *Alice in Wonderland* (but not *Through the Looking Glass*); *The Water Babies;* Ernest Thompson Seton's animal stories. . . . Sound stuff but only a beginning, for we had rich supplemental nourishment from the glassed-in bookcases filling the far end of the living room with "sets" of books sold to my mother by door-to-door book agents—middle-aged women eking out slim resources by ringing doorbells to purvey literary culture.

Early among my mother's purchases was a ten-volume anthology, *Journeys Through Bookland,* bound in crimson and cream soon grimy from use. It began with the best of Edward Lear and *A Child's Garden of Verses;* went on into nonscandalous Greek legends; the basic Robin Hood ballads; passable redactions of the Round Table cycle; "The Gold Bug" and "Three Sundays in a Week"; solid extracts from Esquemeling's *Pirates, The Swiss Family Robinson, Moby Dick, Three Men in a Boat.* . . . A rival compilation, equally versatile, was *The After-School Library,* bound in red and green and stamped with a Robin Hoodish archer in gold. Either selection made our school readers look like thirty cents. Whatever my mother filched from the modest family income for those millions of words was a fine money's worth.

Better still, the agents also sold her library sets of Scott, Cooper, Dickens, George Eliot, Emerson, Victor Hugo (well enough translated), early Stevenson, early Kipling (probably some copyright hugger-mugger there). . . . At the age of eight I was well at home in several Scott items beginning with *Ivanhoe.* Late the next summer I took from a newly delivered set of Dickens *The Pickwick Papers,* rejoiced through it in a week, and went on with unchecked momentum through *Nicholas Nickleby.* That Dickens set now on my shelves still bears traces of a small boy's grimy paws. Then I was given *Huckleberry Finn* to read on a long train trip. The giver cannot have been my mother. She regarded Mark Twain as unacceptably vulgar. But she let me take the book along. Pullmaning southward, I encountered Pap's case agin the govment; the Grangerford establishment; Old Man Boggs. . . . I have never been the same since.

Had my mother read much in her catch-as-catch-can library she'd probably have forbidden Hugo because of certain interesting episodes in *Notre Dame de Paris* and *The Man Who Laughs;* and she knew nothing of the volume of Mérimée's short stories (in a set of five Continental writers) that told of King Candaules's bad judgment in hiding Gordius behind the bedroom door. I was already prepared for such doings in classic contexts. In a relative's bookcase I had explored Lemprière's *Classical Dictionary* with its brief summaries of home life among gods and goddesses. Yet prurient interest was hardly a factor in my omnivorous reading. I read for a general joy. To do so was a basic pleasure like eating, and luckily for me, what there was to read was highly nourishing—nimble narratives and striking things pithily set down, and laughter! When I found the whole volume of *Three Men in a Boat* in my aunt's bookcase, I lay on the floor and read and laughed till my belly muscles ached.

Omnivorous is the word. I read almost everything in every household to which I had access. In ours only Emerson and George Eliot had reason to feel neglected. I read all twelve volumes of *The New America in Romance,* a book agent's blockbuster that nobody has seen since, historical fiction by, of all people, Edwin ("The Man with the Hoe") Markham. He distilled into twelve segments the high-minded doings of a family named Stevens from Columbus's time to McKinley's. In each segment the hero Stevens fell in love with a beautiful, charming girl and won her in spite of hazards involving stock historical events and personages. I read a book agent's five-volume history of the world covering Charlemagne, Napoleon, et al., but what I chiefly recall is the halftone full-page of a painting of Cambyses in Egypt riding hell for leather swinging a cat by the tail, it didn't say why. I read the best-selling fiction of the day as I came across it. Some of it, such as Tarkington and *The Virginian,* had quality. But it was mostly easy-running junk. Indiana then prided herself on producing popular novelists and the junk supply was studded with Hoosier writers: Gene Stratton Porter, George Barr McCutcheon, Charles Major, Meredith Nicholson, and I expect nobody under the age of sixty ever to have heard of them. There was a special niche for James Whitcomb Riley, the Hoosier Poet. Today he needs identification as author of "When the frost is on the punkin" and "Little Orphan Annie"—no, not the reactionary comic-strip puppet with holes for eyes; her creator merely borrowed her moniker. Another Hoosier writer of the day was not entered. Two to one my mother never heard of Theodore Dreiser, nor, had she provided any of his works, would I have enjoyed them, then or now.

Dime novels still flourished, I understand, but I never saw one. My trash reading went no farther than *The Motor Boys* and a little Tom Swift borrowed from playmates. Farther afield I read Louisa May Alcott—girl's stuff, true, but a lot better than the pretentious *Little Colonel* series by another Hoosier writer, Annie Fellowes Johnston, thirteen volumes of it bound in beige cloth. I read a multivolume history of the Civil War with smudgily printed color pictures of horses and bayonets and forage caps. And thanks to my mother's zeal for the best, I read all fourteen of Jacob Abbott's Rollo books, the tone of which prepared me (as of twenty years later) to relish Arthur (Bugs) Baer's description of a bland dish that he disliked: "It tastes like my foot's asleep."

Rollo's sponsor was right out of Central Casting—Miss Prudence Lewis, a retired teacher living nearby, a gimlet-eyed, transplanted Yankee, essence of schoolmarm, whom my mother consulted as to what her children should read. Harking back to the mental and moral nourishment of two generations earlier, Miss Lewis prescribed Rollo. He was difficult to procure, for he was almost as obsolete as pantalettes on little girls, but finally Stewart's bookstore on Washington Street exhumed from some crumbling warehouse the whole damn series in mint condition: *Rollo at Home, Rollo at Play, Rollo's Travels, Rollo's Philosophy: Water* . . . imitations of Regency Britain's didactic stuff for children. Some of that, Maria Edgeworth's and Anna Letitia Barbauld's, had pace and style. Rollo did not. He was as smugly insipid as his pictured getup of round cap, big-buttoned roundabout, and loose pantaloons; or as his supporting cast, little brother Thady, dear little cousin Lucy, and Jonas, "hired man" of Rollo's gentleman farmer-father, who plied Rollo with moral lessons deriving from the shape of a cloud, the heinousness of not putting the wheelbarrow away . . .

The background—New England in Daniel Webster's time— was disconcertingly alien to my Old Northwest circa 1914. But I was used to printed contact with exotic spheres of reference, for instance, that of James Willard Schulz's books for boys glorifying the Blackfoot Indians and by implication the whole range of red men. I took both Mr. Schulz and Mr. Abbott to be authorities of weight. Somewhere, I assumed, was or had been an environment like Rollo's pa's where people lived such glib, dim, savorless lives. Ten years later I found myself in a position to check up in New England. Carryover from Miss Lewis and Rollo may have had something to do with the irksome lack of sympathy between me and the Land of the Pilgrims' Pride.

That full set of the Rollo books vanished long since. To

substantiate my memories of them I have only a copy of *Rollo's Travels* that I came across and bought a while ago. Its steel engraving of Mr. Halliday and Rollo boarding the steamboat is just as I recalled it.

Autobiographer's duty now returns us to Number Forty-five. That home diet of print and paper made my sister and me the only pupils thus enriched by such literary and historical supplement to the curriculum. For me—I cannot speak for her—that was unhealthy. It tempted me to deem myself brighter than my thrity-odd classmates. Today's schools, I understand, may provide special "learning tracks" for such cases. The wisdom of that is questionable. The child is likely to feel such distinctions as invidious. They must to some extent polarize the group into *select* and *run-of-the-mine*. That did not apply in my case but, though I never heard myself denounced as "teacher's pet," being uncrowned prize pupil was a social handicap. It denied me one thing that public elementary schools can give. Their first function, of course, basic if not widely acknowledged, is to keep the neighborhood's children off the streets during certain hours five days a week. The second, more broadly constructive, is to force the pupils spontaneously to develop the social skills of mutual adjustment and manipulation of one's peers in one's own interests. The third, which is pretext for the other two and yet does have some life of its own, is to teach the clerical skills needed in a literate society. No doubt most of my classmates got a fair share of the second. In that respect I was shortchanged—an unfortunate side effect of my mother's extravagant hopes for her offspring.

Not that she, or Number Forty-five, was altogether culpable. I may well have been born the shy puppy in the litter, destined to lagging adjustment. Yet, to some extent, circumstances did go out of their way to abet any such flaw. For instance, I was the only pupil who wore glasses. My eyes crossed when I was three years old; I remember seeing double. So between me and the world were set tiny lenses in easily bent gold frames. At intervals Mr. Werbe of Werbe & Miessen, opticians downtown, a large, pale, immaculate man, straightened those frames with delicate nippers, solemnly replaced them on my nose as I sat across from him at his little table, gazed hyp-

notically at me till satisfied, removed them, squirted a mysterious fluid on the lenses, polished them with a chamois pad,
replaced them, and let me go. In one form or another glasses
have now lived with me eighty years. An Adlerian psychiatrist,
if such still exists, would ascribe to that my bookishness—the
worse one's eyesight, the likelier one is to read and read. Too
pat to be valid, of course. My sister had no eye trouble and no
glasses, yet read about as avidly as I did. Nor were glasses
themselves a great emotional burden. Well before I entered
school they were as much part of me as the little nose they
straddled. Undeniably, however, they were a barrier between
me and my peers—occasionally got me called "Four Eyes"—all
the more because their connotations of pedantry fitted with
my unholy aptitude for knowing the answers.

Then I was youngest in the class. Enrolled when my sixth
birthday was imminent, I was "skipped" into 2B among seven-
and a few eight-year-olds when it was found I could read anything set before me. Had I done well in athletics, that would
hardly have mattered. Not that I was physically hopeless. I
grew as fast as my elder classmates, indeed reached five foot
eleven at age fifteen. I was handy as any on roller skates, rode
a bicycle better than most. But I could never throw a curve
and, when tolerated at baseball, was sent to right field, where
chances to muff something were few. At tennis, I was never
better than a dub in spite of much time trying to convince
myself to the contrary on the public courts at College Avenue
and Fall Creek Boulevard. Thus I got less than a healthy degree of the socializing effects of competitive sport.

Since too many children have the instincts of sadistic poultry, one would assume that Four Eyes, the Walking Encyclopedia, lacking even average schoolyard savvy, would have been
actively persecuted. Let me record it in my classmates' favor
that what actually happened was seldom worse than snubbing.
And after a while, the snubbing hurt less because obviously
that was the way things were in school; in a backhanded sense,
it was nothing personal.

So though Number Forty-five was a jejune wilderness that
I recall without the slightest nostalgic pleasure, it cannot be
dignified with the label "traumatic." The most positive thing
within those characterless walls was the whiff of elementary

Latin administered in the last semester to some of those entering the city's white-collar high school. If we had a commencement doings with parents beaming and songs sung, I don't
recall it. I recall only that in February 1919, along with a handful
of classmates—of whom I saw little from then on—Four Eyes
enrolled in Shortridge High School downtown at the corner
of North and Pennsylvania.

My mother's other enrichment of her children's futures was
inadvertent. That is, she cannot have planned to be born, to
begin with, nor given that, would she have chosen for herself
and offspring the environment vouchsafed her—Marion
County, Indiana. To it she would have much preferred Mason
County, Kentucky, whence came John and Sally Chamberlin,*
her paternal grandparents. Her girlhood visits to the blue-
grass kin they had left behind tainted her with a vicarious nostalgia. Those Mason County Chamberlins can hardly all have
been such gracious and flavorsome patricians as she described
them, but doubtless their ways and circumstances did differ
from mother's Hoosier native heath between Maywood and
Valley Mills. That difference warped her into defensive pretentiousness.

Why her grandfather John brought his Kentucky bride to
a middle-sized farm southwest of Indianapolis in the mid-1800s
I do not know. My mother sometimes hinted he had married
beneath him. It irked her that, when she joined the Daughters
of the American Revolution, her qualifying ancestor had to be
a New Jersey private from among her grandmother Sally's
forebears, not an officer from Virginian "quality" on the
Chamberlin side. She accused the British, how justly I'm unsure, of having destroyed the pertinent records when they
burned the local courthouse in the War of 1812. Anyway, both
her Chamberlin grandparents were dead before my time. Only

*This spelling differs significantly from the -lain ending of the name on my passport
and elsewhere. My mother made the change for a characteristic reason: She had a
tale about one of her Mason County kin, a flighty and probably loony Chamberlin,
calling on Joseph Chamberlain, the British statesman, when he visited America and
establishing grounds for believing that in spite of the discrepancy of spelling, he was
her kinsman and vice versa. Accepting this flimsy finding that she was related to
distinguished people, my mother thenceforth wrote me down as "Joseph Chamberlain
Furnas" to exploit it.

grassy bumps showed where their house had been. Nearby was a huge, untidy red cedar that my mother said was grown from a cutting from a cedar back in Kentucky grown from a cutting from the cedar back in Virginia under which George Washington proposed to Martha. That is horticulturally possible, but the witness was unreliable.

My sister and I knew as our "Grandmother Chamberlin's" a boxy, high-shouldered frame house built in "the east yard" for John's eldest son, Nelson, and his wife, Indiana (née Blue), my mother's parents. The place was a weighty focus in our lives, even more so than Indiana Blue's girlhood home a dozen miles northwest of Indianapolis. The two households were, so to speak, hereditary benefices enjoyed by us children by blood right. And in spite of my mother's occasional efforts to widen it, the world in which my sister and I were reared consisted mostly of blood relatives supporting, mistrusting, sometimes abusing, emulating one another, more from taken-for-granted custom than from affection.

As *machine à habiter* Grandmother Chamberlin's lacked a good deal. The only plumbing was the pipe from the pump on the kitchen sink down into the rainwater cistern. Baths were taken in a glavanized-iron washtub with hot water ladled from the reservoir of the wood-burning kitchen stove. Under the beds were the conventional thunder mugs, but use of them was discouraged because to service them was unpleasant. The privy, a two-and-a-half-holer, stood fifty yards from the house in the chicken yard; the accepted euphemism for visiting it was "going down below." My grandfather, whose standards were firm if narrow, seldom did so, preferring God's great outdoors on the undeniable grounds that the privy stunk.

No heat in bedrooms. To insert oneself between those augustly heavy linen sheets on a winter night was really to understand what *cold* meant. The cookstove kept the kitchen drowsily balmy in winter and hellishly hot in summer, even though the (screened) doors were kept open. The middle-sized, wood-fueled "base-burner" stove, all nickel trim and fancifully curled plates, overheated the small living room. The connecting parlor of the same size contained an upright piano and several ornate chairs, vintage 1880, but no stove, though a papered-over outlet for a stovepipe showed one had been allowed for. On the mantelpiece were plaster of paris statuettes airily costumed and vaguely classical, the base of one lettered "FLORA," of the other "POMONA." My sister and I were often in the parlor thumping out stuff on the piano regardless of its being far out of tune. All we wanted was rhythm and noise. Only once in our time did adults use the parlor—for the state and ceremonial occasion of the wedding of my mother's younger sister.

Those screens on doors and windows were indispensable because the stables were less than a hundred yards away and a hog pen, where the garbage was regularly administered to receptive snouts, was even closer. The broad veranda running round two sides of the house was unscreened, however, and flies by the thousand blackened its white clapboard walls. A national "Swat the fly!" campaign was then at its height and swatters lay ready to hand, but after a while further slaughter was obviously pointless. Make up the mind to flies, and a warm, shady afternoon could be enjoyable in a high-backed, cane-seated rocking chair or a camp chair, a long contraption of slats and sagging canvas, eating apples and reading while the quail went "Bobwhite! Bobwhite!" in the field across the road, the locusts turned their raucous buzz off and on like so many impatient doorbells, and the mourning doves moaned in the distance.

The apples came from the neglected orchard that the porch overlooked—several dozen trees long unpruned or sprayed, so worms were a hazard; but on finding a worm, one merely threw the apple away and chose another. The orchard meant playthings too. Tear off a long, limber shoot, impale a small green apple on it, and whip it far away sling fashion. Or climb up to a swaying seat on an outstretched limb. Or feed apples to the hogs in their triangular pen in the far corner and scratch their dirty white-yellowish backs with a long stick. Those straggly posts and rusty wire would never have held a normally enterprising hog. But my grandfather's were not enterprising, nor, as the whole place showed, was he.

Farms are seldom really tidy. This one was a welter of neglect and obsolescence. Much of the barn was still in reasonable condition. The floor across which the horses' hooves thundered as they tramped to their stalls was sound; the stalls were cleaned daily. Yet one element of the barn was a tumble-down log structure probably built by the first settler, whoever he was, and now, after eighty years, a mass of rotting timbers too far gone even to nourish fungi. On its sunny side grew a bed of horehound, that queer old-fashioned mint—do horehound drops still exist? We understood that the old ruin had once been a cow stable. Its successor in a corner of the barnyard was a flimsy frame structure that must have been cleaned out now and again, else the cows could never have got inside. But I never knew of any such purging. As the cows and I knew it, that stable would have made Augeus stare and gasp. In warm weather it smelled like the nth power of a Brie cheese ripened in hell. In spite of his squeamishness about the privy, my grandfather entered the place morning and evening, seated himself with a rheumatic grunt on the traditional three-legged stool, and milked his three cows. To the delight of us children, the incumbent cat got several squirts of milk into her open mouth.

Handling of the poultry was also casual. An underventilated henhouse provided pole roosts and nesting boxes. The hens used it for nighttime shelter. Their droppings, seldom scraped up, gave it a sneezy-rancid atmosphere. But they laid their eggs and "set" in the open. Was that because the outdoors smelled better or did it just feel more natural? Anyway, they created their own nesting places and hatched their chicks in them ad lib and al fresco. The household dog knew the locations well. To gather the day's eggs, one said "Eggs!" to Shep and followed as, nose down, beautiful plumy tail waving, he led the way to the pokeweed patch, the dark place under the woodshed, the discarded iron kettle behind the grape arbor—suave as a headwaiter, keen as a Geiger counter, he knew the hens' foibles as well as he knew everything else about the place.

His statutory jobs were watchdogging and fetching the cows. His hobby was lying in the grass on guard lest any heedless hen break the taboo marked by an intermittent fence between chicken yard and people country. He would let the feathered interloper come stepping and pecking a few forbidden yards and then rush her, snarling and snapping like a canine torpedo. The hen would take off squawking in a fifty-foot demonstration of what her wings had originally been meant for. And Shep would lounge back to his post until another transgression detonated him. Here "Shep" is a generic term. Several of him came and went in our time—all broad-nosed country types, yellow and reddish-brown with nice white shirt fronts, all courteously sagacious. None lasted more than a few years because a nearby interurban trolley bridge was convenient for nighttime forays. Sooner or later each got killed and was succeeded by a long-legged puppy to be the new Shep for us to roughhouse with.

Those anarchistic chickens contrasted sharply with the plump, conformist Plymouth Rocks or Rhode Island Reds that Hoosier farms usually stocked. This breed was "Indian Game," a race apart. The roosters were tall, high-stepping, sinewy-made. The hens, though more heavily built, lacked the matronliness of everyday hens. They had the steely, no-nonsense air of the spinster head nurse of an understaffed hospital. Both sexes were sheathed in dark-gleaming feathers with an iridescent sheen really stylish in a sinister way. The baby chicks following these impressive mamas were no dear little balls of fluff off an Easter card but vigorously scrawny and darkish-colored, as though they had been playing in wood ashes.

"Game" in the name of the breed implied cockfighting. The roosters were given to impromptu sparring of some vivacity though never to the death. But since my grandfather either paid no heed or perfunctorily kicked them apart and went his way, I doubt that "game" qualities accounted for his preferring this strain. Maybe he valued the creatures' independent attitudes. Likelier, in view of his great joy in eating and the fact that, because of age and profound deafness, that was about the only pleasure left him—he neither drank nor smoked—it was their savoriness he valued. The dark meat of the plump young cockerels that my grandmother fried in lard—the medium of choice—was sweet and yet richly heavy in a way I have never tasted in other poultry. That quality was partly genetic doubtless, but also environmental, due to the flavor-enhancing mixture of bugs, worms, weed seeds, and God knows what else they picked up foraging in addition to the scanty ration of cracked corn strewn among them on the ground after the summons: "Chick, chick, chick . . ." And apart from

toothsome fryers, what my grandmother did with tough old
Indian Game hens stewed with little dumplings and dried apples, Pennsylvania Dutch style, was just about as memorable.

The establishment was four-fifths autarkic. Beyond poultry
it relied for meat largely on the hogs processed in the November hog killing (a neighborhood collaboration), smoked as hams
and bacon in the smokehouse that flanked the vegetable patch—
what a pagan blast of pungency when its door opened! Vegetables from the garden patch—tomatoes, beets, cucumbers, and
so on—were variously canned* or pickled without benefit of
pressure cooker. Among vanished items on the cellar shelves
were tomato preserves as well as berry jams and pickled sweet
corn put down in brine in stone crocks, resulting in an eerie,
flyaway flavor like nothing else I have ever tasted. Berries,
cherries, and peaches were canned without sugar for winter
use in pies. Apples were peeled, cored, and quartered for
drying, a process that incidentally eliminated worms. From
outside, usually the Maywood general store, came only minimal essentials: salt, sugar, spices, kerosene for the half-dozen
lamps, matches, textiles for everyday wear. Tea and coffee came
to the door in high-built, light wagons making rounds for the
"tea companies" that grew into such chains as the A&P and
Grand Union. Fresh beef from the store was a treat. So were
lemons (for pie and, in summer, lemonade) and bananas. My
grandfather would appear silently with a bunch of them, share
them round, and go away; or with cantaloupes from the garden, a butcher knife, and salt and pepper shakers. I still pepper and salt melons and the waiter says: "That's salt, sir."

Ivory ("It Floats") soap from the store occupied the dish
on the kitchen sink. But though Fels Naphtha laundry soap
was plentiful and cheap, my grandmother made her own soft
soap for laundry and cleaning. She saved up waste fats, sifted
wood ash, and stewed the two into a redolent mess stirred with
a broken broomstick in a great iron kettle over an open fire in
the chicken yard. For half a mile to leeward one knew soap
boiling was going on. The product, looking like melted brown

---

*I think the glass Ball jars with screw-on lids were already available, but early in my
childhood my grandmother still literally "canned" things in shiny tin-plate quarts with
fit-in lids sealed with sealing wax.

sugar, was rich enough in unslaked lye to take the hide off a rhinoceros. Its rough rancidity was the household's dominant perfume. It wafted up from my bedroom sheets and my grandmother's work aprons. In another unnecessary anachronism, my grandfather sometimes took his own wheat from the bin in the barn to be ground at a gristmill then still operating somewhere over West Newton way; I often went along. Nor was Nelson Chamberlin alone in thus living near self-sufficient old times. Rural electrification, the pressure tank, and broadcasting had not yet revolutionized the American countryside. Barring the soft soap, most of his neighbors probably got along on a basis not much farther advanced, though a city of two hundred thousand people was just over the eastern horizon.

Those archaic details were consistent with my grandfather's personal old-timeyness. Part of it was certainly physical in origin. Arthritis and an undefined heart trouble were making full-time dirt farming inadvisable for him. It was understandable that he rented his more fertile fields to neighbors, usually a sturdy clan named Jay, on shares paying enough to get by on—little more. And his severe deafness cut him off from practically all oral communication, which deepened what had long been, I suspect, temperamental lonerness. My grandmother's high-pitched shriek often got key words across to him; with everybody else it was pretty much one-way. Beyond that I have a tenuous impression that the more strenuous and exacting glories of farming never appealed to him. He was not exactly lazy. Occasionally he plowed corn efficiently enough; but he was easily reconciled to inactivity. His world consisted of odd pottering, seldom with much result; reading the *Indianapolis News* and the *Rural New-Yorker* in a rocker by the marble-topped table by the west window; forays with his gun after squirrels or rabbits; though he needed glasses for reading, he was presbyopically as farsighted as a hawk and a good shot; those trips to Maywood; and relishing his victuals. My grandmother sometimes walked the mile or so to the miniature church at the crossroads; not he. Only twice a season could her remonstrances drive him into hitching a horse to the mowing machine and reducing what looked like a volunteer hayfield to something like a lawn. The yard was surrounded by a once elegant post-and-plank fence of the design demanding white paint; it never got it but grew grayer and grayer.

His remarkable appetite never modified the elegance of his person. Nearly six foot, narrow-made, long-boned, walking with a limber prowl in spite of arthritis, bright blue eyes under stern black eyebrows, black hair always sleekly combed; droopy mustache under a haughtily beaked nose between ruddy cheeks—he could have been d'Artagnan's uncle. One understood why Indiana Blue, a pretty, plump girl to judge from her early photographs, and softhearted to judge from her behavior toward us children, had viewed him favorably when he came riding so many miles to court her. For that purpose he probably wore his best clothes. I must sometimes have seen him dressed up but can't recall it. In my recollection he always wore his special version of farmer's work clothes: blue-jean bib overalls; a blue-jean jacket that he called a "blouse," with green-tarnished brass buttons. With these should have gone a by-gosh straw hat and a blue work shirt; only Nelson Chamberlin insisted on a low-crowned black felt with a wide brim that grew limper every year and a homemade white cotton shirt, neck-band-style with no collar, no collarstud, just a white button that gave a Russian effect. My mother often remarked proudly—it was one of the few things about her father that she approved of—that he was like her grandfather, idolized John Chamberlin, who took her visiting his people in Mason County, in that he never allowed himself to be seen in any but a white shirt. Another resemblance, I gathered, was that Great-grandfather Chamberlin was also disinclined to overexert himself. I inherited my grandfather's blue eyes—obviously a recessive trait since it appeared nowhere else among my immediate relatives—and appetite as of a pregnant wolf; maybe also his inability to regard work as intrinsically meritorious.

Grandfather Chamberlin liked me for my talent for eating and, I think, for my being undemanding company. He not only often took me along to mill or Maywood, he was first ever to call me "Joe" instead of the "Joseph" to which my mother's preference and Quaker notions limited me. Off we would set after breakfast with the butter and eggs in baskets in the rear tray of the buggy. The wheels rattled, their tires grated on the gravel road, and now and again a whiff of well-digested corn and grass escaped Dewey's large bay behind. To right and left the sun-ripened meadowlarks kept yelpingly insisting that "Laziness'll *kill* you!"—the traditional interpretation of their call that his deafness prevented my grandfather from taking personally. During the ensuing afternoon, picking cherries for my grandfather would put me straddling a limb with a tin pail hung on a wire hook and two eaten for every three picked. Or sitting on the great stone step by the woodshed with a heap of the previous fall's black walnuts, a hammer, a nutpick, and a flatiron upside down between the knees; for that my manual skills were adequate. Or wandering into the kitchen for a wedge of dried apple pie from the "safe"—the cupboard of perforated steel sheeting that kept out flies while admitting air. It was proper pie firm enough to hold shape when held in the hand and gradually bitten back beginning with the point. When Saint Peter, glancing through my file, asks whether I had a happy childhood, I shall reply: "I don't think so. But I spent a lot of time at Grandmother Chamberlin's."

It may best convey the antediluvian character of that environment to mention that so far as I was aware none of the neighbors as yet owned an automobile. When we arrived at the Stop Four shack on the interurban trolley-car line a mile and a half from the farm by road, my grandfather often drove to meet us in the buggy; if not, we walked and thought nothing of it. Yet drastic technological change was nudging in on an irregular front. Then rivaling Detroit in the growing automobile industry, Indianapolis manufactured ten or so makes of motor car and had set up in 1911 the brick-paved speedway that is still annual focus of "Indy 500" racing. The narrow gravel road that passed Grandmother Chamberlin's was a favorite among the begoggled mechanics who test-drove new cars—mere chassis, exposed motor, and noise, cutout always open. In the sun-heavy distance a quarrelsome grumble would rise into a roar. Shep would rush to the fence and bark himself into fits as the bellowing monster, throwing dust like a dry water cannon, whisked past with a screech of brakes at the right-angled jog in the road left long, long ago by a surveyor's compass correction. We children looked at each other delightedly, petted Shep as he returned panting, once again certain that his fierce demonstration had sent one of those things away with its tail between its legs, and decided that that "tester's" peak-topped radiator identified it as a National and not a Marmon or Stutz. We were unaware that this rousing cataclysm was the as yet youngish twentieth century asserting itself.

It was already present, of course, in the shape of the feeble local telephone, just one step above two tin cans and a string. Its varnished wooden box on the sitting room wall supported a gooseneck mouthpiece with a dumbbell receiver. The Chamberlin ring was two longs, two shorts, like a locomotive whistling for a grade crossing. To reach another subscriber on the party line one ground the little crank in the appropriate combination of short and long. A single long alerted the operator a few miles away in West Newton to connect one with some other party line or the Indianapolis phone complex. Rural Free Delivery of mail, a convenience then recent, brought the *News* six days a week, a triumph of governmental enterprise when roads were still so primitive. Before I was out of knickerbockers, an icebox appeared on the side porch and twice a week in summer the ice wagon serviced it. The incumbent Shep relished the chips of ice; I trained him to wait thirty feet away while I tossed them to him one by one and he would streak up into the air to catch them fountain fashion, all brown and yellow fur, fun and power. About the same time a hand-powered cream separator came to the woodshed—a strange contrivance of numberless metal cones fitting one over another like those Russian peasant dolls, a huge tank to pour milk into and a very low-geared crank to power the shrill-whining high gear of the centrifuge. Once my young arms got it going, it was amusing to keep it singing away like a persistent tea kettle. The hogs made no complaint about the higher efficiency with which the machine got the butterfat out of milk.

Cranking the separator and bringing in wood from the shed was about the extent of my usefulness, nor was I painfully conscientious about either chore. Practically all the time we children had the run of the whole hundred-odd acres. For peaceful, down-at-heels desuetude the place was like the Sleeping Beauty's castle without the elegance. Under an overgrown apple tree in the west yard was the wreck of an elaborate loom half again the size of a square piano. We poked and peered into its insides, full of spider webs and musty smells, but it never occurred to us to ask or even wonder what it was, let alone what it was for and who had used it and why it was left to disintegrate. It was just there, like the tree that shaded it, probably always had been there, always would be. It was the same with the dead farm machinery that crowded the tumbledown outbuildings. We knew the uses of the riding cultivators and hay tedders but again felt no need to ask what the rest were for. All were magnificently rusty, rust as rich as fudge, deep brown-red like a rotting cherry. Fooling about among such things might have been dangerous had their moving parts not been so firmly rusted together. As it was, however, suppose the prince had come and kissed the girl, those poor old contraptions, once the pride of John Deere and the Moline Plow Company, could never conceivably have resumed motion when the castle clocks resumed ticking. Equally decayed were the hundreds of yards of snake fence delimiting the lanes that led to the north woods and the south woods. Nothing looks as dismally ancient as the moldering, swaybacked panels of an elderly snake fence. Those remaining now are rare and considered quaint. Back then many still persisted, seven or eight rails high, cross-ended angles harboring a wealth of zoology and botany.

We had little to do with the north woods, being oriented toward the southerly, larger element of the farm. Downslope in the barnyard was a decaying wooden pump that filled the watering trough all padded with moss and small, wavery water grasses. It spouted "sulphur water" with a slight stench as of rotten eggs betokening pollution from a coal vein far below. The stuff was said to be "good for you" on the old principle that whatever is nasty and slightly mysterious must be therapeutic. Anyway it was marvelously clear and cold in the rusty tin cup that hung on a nail. The horses, lacking cups, made grateful splutterings, and bubblings as they dipped their muzzles into the trough. Our relations with them, though friendly, were more distant than with Shep and the odd cat or two. The plump bay gelding was named Dewey after, presumably, the hero of Manila Bay, but again, we never inquired about it. The black mare, Nell, was slighter and had the lighter end of the job, for the only operational double-harness rig on the place was the stout old farm wagon. For the spring wagon, the single-furrow plow and the buggy Dewey usually got the call. Now and then I was given the reins as we went to Maywood. Dewey seemed not to notice the change.

The watering trough drained into the "branch" that crossed the foot of the farmyard and the rolling pasture beyond, thence into a larger branch that bounded the south woods. Neither stream was deep enough to drown in, indeed could be jumped over in most places. Both offered natural stepping-stone riffles at handy intervals, tiny waterfalls, miniature cutbanks in the meandering stretches to complete the effect of baby rivers. Those two examples of water's insistence on running downhill were the finest playthings ever created. And the background of the larger branch, shady, lofty, and cool, could almost have been a plutocrat's estate park, for my grandfather, innocent of forestry, pastured his cows among those great oaks, ashes, elms and sycamores,—which kept underbrush down.

Follow the stream past the decrepit watergate that kept the cows where they belonged into another rolling pasture studded with shapely hawthorn. On its dominant knoll stood what was left of a classic log cabin, roof mostly gone, weeds masking the doorsill, no door. Today, of course, I wonder who built that relic of pioneering and when, and how his woman liked lugging water up that slope; there was no trace of a well. For us children, however, it was just another case of there-it-was-and-always-had-been. After exploring it we might revert to tossing twigs into the branch to watch them duck and dive-shooting miniature rapids; or building a dam by putting big stones among these that the good Lord had already set in the streambed; or walking the bank-to-bank tree trunk that held up the watergate, a feat wherein my sister's sense of balance was much more reliable than mine. I think I recall desultory fishing for the minnows that quivered in the dark pools. But suppose we fished, what tackle we used and with what success does not come through. Other aquatic wildlife consisted of crawdads, pale creatures the size of a medium shrimp to which we paid little attention; the busy, stylish dragonflies imitating airplanes over the shallows; and the waterbugs skating on surface tension as offhandedly as if they understood what that was. Flagrant hindsight: I had yet to see either a shrimp or an airplane;* and had no reason to think a waterbug's way of getting about either more or less notable than a bird's; and come to think of it, they *are* equally remarkable.

I associate the barnyard branch with sunshine and odors. We often usually went to the south woods along its course and dawdled along the way. Once, somewhere along there in the pasture, I was alone and first became aware of being an entity self-consciously experiencing things and finding in them intrinsic value. I cannot have been more than eight years old at the time. On the bank of the branch in a soaking sunshine I stood suddenly relishing the smells that the sun brought out— mint, mud, and cowflops. Sunshine was hot on my left hand and I raised it to my nose, why I don't know, which added to the mixture the minor effluvium that human skin gives off under direct sun. This olfactory nosegay triggered a powerful sense of: "Well, here I am. What do you know about that?" I have been more alive ever since.

Another smell that went with the old farm came with my first unflawed fear. I knew it only twice, for after the second time I gave it no further opportunity. Those days were long before Henry Wallace et al. endowed corn with gigantism, but even so the stuff grew a good six feet tall, dwarfing a small boy. From outside, a field of maturing corn looks as orderly as a battalion of Frederick the Great's grenadiers in green uniforms drawn up in perfect ranks for inspection. Walk into it, however, and it dissolves into a boundless succession of stiff green stalks that would stretch farther than the eye could see if the intervals weren't dauntingly obliterated by dangling, broad, and nastily sharp-edged leaves. Enter thus a little dreamily, as a child might, and all sense of direction, soon all hope of ever seeing the outside world again, vanish. It is hot in there, breathless, getting hotter, and with the smothering heat comes a high sweetish perfume sharp as the leaf edges but coarse too—the sort of thing young she-satyrs (are there any?) would dab behind their hairy ears. The sense of sight is

---

*Fairly soon both came along: My first airplane was a monoplane piloted by the pioneer avaitrix Ruth Law in an exhibition at the Indiana State Fair Grounds. My first shrimp was something pink and warm as first course at lunch in Indianapolis's Columbia Club. It so startled my sense of taste that I threw up; which understandably annoyed our host.

overwhelmed by that infinite mass of serried cornstalks. It takes a while for panic to subside to where one realizes that he has only to walk along any given row and eventually it will take him to the edge of the field—a blessed sight indeed.

Never get lost in a cornfield.

Over the incredible number of years since I knew the Old Northwest, it has probably forgotten about "buckeye snow." The buckeye is a scrubby, middle-sized forest tree of no particular value. The old folks had a pejorative saying: "I'd never go to a buckeye stump to find a hickory sprout." Its shiny brown nuts and showy spring bloom, however, identify it as a cousin of Europe's even showier horse chestnut. Beyond that it carries tingly little hints of special powers. Those nuts are seriously poisonous to anybody insisting on eating them in spite of their acrid flavor. Carrying a buckeye in the pocket is supposed to ward off or anyway mitigate arthritis. That Ohio should have chosen to call itself the Buckeye State is strange when you think of it. And a curious affinity with springtime weather is attributed to it. Twice certainly, maybe three times, I was crossing the Chamberlin pasture in early May, nothing particular on my mind, hardly aware of the gray overcast sky— and here came an uncertain breeze bringing a few snowflakes, the merest flurry, all over by the time I reached the woods. But sure enough, the buckeye just beyond the fence was showing the first of its annual bloom. Winter ended. Officially. These things are shy. Had I been expecting it, it never would have happened. I have sometimes thought of writing a novel entitled *Buckeye Snow* but never could whittle out a plot to match.

Now as to what my mother called "Grandmother Blue's"— the locus of Grandmother Chamberlin's girlhood and persisting siblings. My sister wrote a good first novel about that centripetal microcosm.

Its foundation was a large tract of land that Peter Blue, a Pennsylvania Dutchman from the Shenandoah Valley, acquired in early times northwest of raw young Indianapolis— how many acres I never knew, but he obviously followed the principle laid down by Old Mis' Means in *The Hoosier Schoolmaster:* "Git a plenty while ye'er gittin', 'twon't never be no cheaper'n 'tis now." In the hard times of the early 1870s Peter had financial troubles and died. But several thousand acres stuck to his widow, a formidable hypochondriac, and devolved through her to their nine offspring. Their portrait photographs, three up, three down, three crosswise, filled a large common frame that hung opposite the bed in "Great-aunt Rachel's room," where I slept when visiting. They did not look much like themselves as I knew them, but then one allowed for that thirty-year interval.

Great-grandmother Blue died just before my time. According to my mother's usually sour but sometimes accurate accounts, she had spent her latter years in armchair or wheelchair soaking up romantic novels and warping and shaping her children into two duties: obeying her and making the most of old Peter's remaining holdings. The three children who managed to break out of her gravitational field were, strangely, the less positive characters. Indiana, my grandmother, was often good-natured, sometimes opinionated, but lacked pungency. Great-aunt Kate, her sister, rotund and pop-eyed as an obese Boston terrier, married a lanky, carrot-bearded farmer splendidly named Lafayette Llewellyn and, so far as I was aware, merely vegetated—childless, charmless, appearing in her childhood home only as guest on seasonal holidays. Great-uncle Charlie, plump and quiet, lived in some obscure corner of Indianapolis with a wife whose name I have forgotten along with the rest of her. (The only other relative in my memory was some sort of cousin, a movie actor named Monte Blue, handsome and very successful in his day but now forgotten.) Blanche, prettiest of the girls, little older than my mother and a close friend of hers, died before my time. The remaining five of Peter's get—Romenta (presumably named after the heroine of one of the old lady's pet novels), Rachel, Albert, Cort (short for Cortez), and George (youngest and almost as good-looking as cousin Monte)—all played themselves as ably as members of a good stock company. Yet for all their marked qualities, none seemed ever to have tried to spread wings beyond the home Enchanted Ground. Once their mother was gone they carried on, collectively manipulating themselves and the land as though she were still laying down the strategy and tactics.

Old Peter would have approved. Not that they made the

handsome fortune that might have come of all that real estate right in the path of the city's inevitable growth. Some of the sales of land that they made were advantageous; for instance, the streetcar company bought their large wooded tract on White River for a take-the-trolley-and-picnic park; it is now the campus of Butler University. But I suspect that many other such lump-sum assets were dribbled away in minor, overingenious financing schemes. There was always much cryptic muttering among them about tax liens and appraisals and foreclosures and notes coming due, and hints of involvement in township or county politics. The chief concern, however—a large fruit farm focused on the house—was a model of efficiency. The profits from it alone would have supplied them the closed-ranks, plumply comfortable life they valued.

That makes them sound more selfish than they really were. Without ever having been told so explicitly, I am sure they paid for college for my mother and her two sisters. My grandfather Chamberlin could never have covered even their textbooks. The younger sister's position teaching school at Broad Ripple (a village on the river within the Blues' sphere of influence) she owed to Great-uncle George's being on the school board. Great-uncle Cort took me to baseball games at ramshackle Washington Park, home of the Indianapolis team of the American Association; I also owed him my first movie, a two-reeler western projected on a sheet stretched between trees in Fairview Park. Great-aunt Romenta was warmly if tacitly pleased with the zeal with which we children exploited her cookie jars—large crocks, one with rich, saddle-colored ginger cookies, the other with sunshine-yellow sugar cookies, delicately fragile. But their kindnesses were all in terms of blood kin. Though we children visited that house a dozen and more times a year, sometimes for several days or a week, I never saw a nonrelative within its doors. We might as well have been reared in an exogamic extended family in the Tarafu Islands.

Prima inter pares, eldest and ablest of the brood, Great-aunt Romenta was mainspring. Without anything like formal presiding, she half casually dominated the family councils, and her crucial suggestions made the skeleton of any consensus arrived at—a process that we children glimpsed only occasionally. She was starveling-thin, for she subsisted largely on black coffee and a cakelike whole wheat bread of her own baking. One understood that some unidentifiable gastric disorder made that ascetic diet necessary. In view of the toothsome miracles that she produced for three meals a day, her abstinence implied an ailment drastic indeed. What came out of her large coal range—its oven door carried a nickel-plated bas-relief of a smoke-belching oceanliner and the words GREAT MAJESTIC— would have made a graven image's mouth water. Yet all she knew of those delights was the occasional sniff or taste telling her all was as it should be.

Most of the ingredients came from within a hundred yards of the kitchen door. The place had its own cows, poultry— Plymouth Rocks and unexpectedly exotic, noisy guinea fowls— and generous expanses of green stuff and orchards. No hogs, probably because they are not only as untidy as cows and horses but also smellier. Great-aunt Romenta's cuisine, doubtless like her mother's before her, was based on the Pennsylvania Dutch tradition that was the glorious backbone of midwestern country cooking. (Years later, when I had a company dinner in a Pennsylvania Dutch farmhouse between Reading and Lancaster, I was right at home.) My grandmother Chamberlin's enjoyable table was a simpler, sisterly version of the same. Great-aunt Romenta supplemented that already admirable school into something at once robust and exquisite. The robustness of her Sunday dinners was formidable, the huge table paved with everything at once. Each dish—mashed potatoes studded with sautéed green onion tops, a dab of butter melting in the dimple on top; a symphony of savors in the cole slaw; a clove-studded ham as whet for the fried chicken and spareribs; fleets of little dishes of homemade pickles, jellies, relishes working up to open-faced green-apple pie rivaling red currant pie and peach cobbler—was memorable in its own right. This is no cliché nostalgia. I have thoroughly enjoyed eating here and there over much of the Western world but never yet found the match of that great woman's culinary magic.

Her excursions into the less traditional included topping an already brilliant potato salad with fine-chopped black walnuts and a three-layer cake with thin-sliced bananas in custard between the layers. Once or twice a year, maybe because we had been very good, likelier out of random family goodwill, she breakfasted us children on a delicacy I never heard of elsewhere—poached guinea-fowl eggs, each about the size of a silver dollar with a dark yolk stuck up in the middle like a large agate marble, the flavor both wild and refined. For that she had a special little pan. Some years before she died she went into confectioner-style candy, buying a book on the subject—the only cookbook that ever entered the house—and adding her own skills and refinements. In a few months she was turning out fancy bonbons that would have held their own in Paris or Vienna. The marble slabs to cool them on were already in place; the house was full of marble-top tables and dressers.

It was that kind of house, built (or massively remodeled to express growing affluence) circa 1860, I should judge; the rising ground it stood on had eventually become what the surveyor called the corner of North Illinois and Forty-sixth streets. As yet, neither was more than a wide, straight, dusty, or muddy country road. The Blues called Forty-sixth Street "the lane" because it had originally been the way into their properties and ran right by the side door. Across it was one of the finest stands of second-growth hardwood forest I have ever seen. But urban development was looming. The streetcar company, anticipating growth, had thrown a single-track line northward a quarter mile east of Illinois Street, all the way up Meridian Street to the old canal, and an oversanguine developer had bought up a large tract above Forty-sixth. Since the terrain was flat as a pancake, he had naturally christened it "Meridian Heights." The area teems with humanity now, but seventy years ago nobody was nibbling. All he had to show for his rashness was a majestic, and obviously costly, ornamental gatehouse of beige cobblestones built up peanut-brittle fashion with an archway between conical-top turrets. There it stood for years as solitary as Ozymandias. As we children got off the streetcar we sometimes peered within but never found more than weeds and feces presumably left by modest tramps.

Our leaving the streetcar, having been its only passengers, seemed to go to the motorman's head, for he pulled back on the control handle and sent her skittering and yawing vivaciously on while we trudged westward in the dust until there, high on the corner, was the Blues'. The big catalpa tree half masked the house, high-shouldered, mansard-crowned, embraced by wide verandas, buoyed up by a billowy, rich-green lawn. Far in the background were the barn-stable with its gilded-horse weathervane and its setting of huge, glossy-green chestnut trees. The ensemble embodied confident, long-established prosperity as smugly as a Currier and Ives print of a country gentleman's estate. Nothing could have contrasted more sharply with the frowsy slackness of Grandmother Chamberlin's. Here everything was perpetually, effortlessly, quietly shipshape.

Indoors too. The only thing ever verging on domestic irregularity was certain occasions when the room over the kitchen that harbored a black hired man was suspected of bedbugs. That detail, like hundreds of others, was Great-aunt Rachel's province, for while Great-aunt Romenta cooked and counseled, the subordinate sister tended to all the cleaning, furnishing, and refurbishing and management of six bedrooms, a third-story attic, four stairways, a front parlor, a living room behind it, a library (containing a desk, *Webster's Unabridged* on a stand, and a four-shelf, three-foot-wide bookcase), two dining rooms, a huge kitchen, a large screened-in kitchen porch. The farthest departure from Grandmother Chamberlin's was a cavernous bathroom, tub, toilet, and washstand looking lost in it, supplied with water from a horizontal pressure tank in the kitchen. Maintaining its pressure with its long-lever pump was the only domestic activity "the boys" ever engaged in. Great-aunt Rachel was not as lean as her sister, but plainly her daily chores, carried out at a sort of understated trot, kept her weight down even though she did the family table full justice. In family councils her voice was as querulous as her usual facial expression; but not toward us children; all the Blues treated us with unfailing benevolence.

"The boys" were a three-ply entity like the wise monkeys. Among them, parceling out responsibilities undiscussed, they supervised the fruit operation and looked after financial affairs. All three were sizable; all were zealous Masons, each wearing a heavy gold ring with a diamond nestling among Masonic symbols, and all involved in the arcane doings of the Ancient Accepted Order of Nobles of the Mystic Shrine—the social appendage of American Masonry that entailed red fezzes and high jinks; on their bedroom walls were group photographs of massed Nobles. My mother said all three were deep

in the Ku Klux Klan when, in the early 1920s, it infested Indiana politics to a shameful extent. By then I had gone East
to college, never effectively to return, so I cannot judge that
charge but see no reason to doubt it. "The boys" were given
to shabby politics and the family's views on Catholics, "the colored," Jews, immigrants, and white trash were splendidly intolerant.

Yet the boys were individuals too. Great-uncle George was
reputed to be a ladies' man, details vague. Great-uncle Cort,
curly-haired and plump, was the easiest-going and least articulate. Great-uncle Albert, gray and spare-made, had a close-
mouthed air that did not prevent his being a fine storyteller
of the cracker-barrel type; I wish I had a tape of his tale of
the old sow in the swill barrel. His person gave forth a pleasant, heavy odor that I came to associate with chewing tobacco;
yet he never chewed, probably because that would have entailed spitting, and "the girls" would never have put up with
that. Only in later years, pondering the matter long after he
had become the late Albert Blue, did I work out the probable
solution: He dipped snuff Down South fashion, tucked in between cheek and gum to absorb into the mucous membrane.
My mother must have deplored this low-down indulgence, but
she never mentioned it. Maybe she looked the other way because she tacitly approved of Great-uncle Albert's being the
only Blue who spent some of the family money frivolously—
by going to Florida to fish every winter. Otherwise she showed
little tolerance in their direction. Great-uncle George had bad
headaches, probably migraine, off and on, and aspirin, new
then, proved a reliable anodyne. From that my mother de-
duced he was hopelessly addicted to it opiate fashion, and enjoyed saying so.

The Blue living room got little wear. The only time I ever
saw the adjoining front parlor used was when Aunt Kate died
and was put on elegiac display in an elaborate casket—my first
corpse. Weekday meals were eaten in the smaller dining room
next to the kitchen. In the dining room proper the huge table
usually stood against a wall to make room for the odd chairs
that made this the actual family sitting room. On the table
were stacked thick accumulations of certain magazines not
available to us children at home, notably the weekly *Saturday
Evening Post* and the *World's Work,* a monthly of weighty arti-

cles on current affairs. Let me further illustrate my precocity by mentioning that at the age of six I was exploring such stuff. I can date it because I remember the piece about the *Titanic* disaster (April 1912); I was puzzled by the halftone of a photograph of passengers clambering up the side of the rescue ship *Carpathia* on a rope ladder; I did not understand why what they were climbing looked like a blank wall, no ship at all. A few years ago I was looking someting up in the *World's Work*, long since deceased, and took occasion to hunt for that article as well. Sure enough, there was that picture just as I remembered it.

I had no notion then that within twenty-odd years I'd owe my first modest prosperity to writing for the *Saturday Evening Post*. At that stage I did not find it very nourishing, except for, I am now ashamed to admit, its Octavus Roy Cohen stories about a fanciful black ghetto in Birmingham, Alabama, peopled by Florian Slappey and Lawyer Evans Chew and the Sons and Daughters of I Will Arise, extravagant caricatures of a black society depicted as farcically juicy; the stuff would be intolerable now. In that vein Cohen was inferior to Booth Tarkington's Genesis (in *Seventeen*) and Herman and Verman (in the *Penrod* stories), but I thought Cohen funny and always looked for his name on the cover. The world I was reared in lacked today's enlightenment in such matters, hence so did I.

On a great day for my sister and me there appeared in the Blues' living room an Edison phonograph almost as tall as we were, sheathed in a Roycrofterish cabinet as elegant as the Edison advertisements presaged. Its "diamond stylus" extracted music from a dozen or so thick records. We had no such thing at home, not because a modest wind-up Victrola would have been too costly, but because my mother thought phonographs "common." Movies too; I was approaching my eleventh birthday when the ballyhoo about the historical and religious importance of *Intolerance* persuaded her that she should countenance taking her offspring to see it—their first full-length movie. It was several years more before she relaxed further and began to take us Friday evenings to the little second-run movie house nearby at the corner of Illinois and Thirtieth. It took ten years to break her down about phonographs.

Back to the Edison: As in the case of *Huckleberry Finn,* my mother did not forbid us to use it once relatives saw fit to provide it. So we worked it pretty vigorously; whereas, to my knowledge, none of the Blues ever had anything to do with it, once it was installed. It was the same with the automobile they bought about that time. I think Great-uncle George learned to drive it but to my recollection it never moved out of the barn.

Besides eating, the other special enjoyment at the Blues' was berry-picking time. That centered around acres and acres of carefully tended strawberry plants stretched in serried rows to what looked like infinity. Come early summer they had to be harvested by a horde of whole families of local ne'er-do-wells trooping to their annual festival of cash income. Where they lived and how they made out the rest of the year I don't know and had no curiosity about then. Their ephemeral availability was just another *given* in the self-created world one was immersed in. As a later time of year would bring the katydids' monotonous evening clamor, so this earlier season brought these scrawny, shambling men, their scrawny or loosely obese, tight-lipped, sharp-jawed women, and scrawny, raggedy, slit-eyed children to fan out over the fields to fill quart boxes with strawberries as they came ripe. The Blues knew by sight and name and reputation, usually bad, those who turned up every year; scorn was implicit in each identification. For us children "berry pickers," like "Gypsies" or "Catholics," was a term of contempt for a disreputable mass. When I read Tarkington's *The Gentleman from Indiana* and met his mob of vicious "Cross-Roader" lynchers, I instantly identified them with berry pickers.*

We children would stroll into the picking area at our mid-morning leisure. If we wished, we could earn small change by picking and bringing berries to the ramshackle shed where they were crated for delivery to the commission house downtown. Or we could stay in the shed to help crate the little boxes that the pickers straggled in with, receiving for each a token good for cash at the end of the day. But the high point was prowling the fields seeking out the berries that the pickers had left on the vine because they were perfectly ripe, hence unsuited for market—likely to spoil before reaching the pur-

---

*Please accept frequent references to details from Tarkington. The Old Northwestern culture that he wove into most of his better works was, after all, exactly that in which this autobiography is necessarily set. I went to high school with Penrod Schofield, Willie Baxter, and Georgie Amberson.

chaser. Voluptuously sun-warmed, at once juicy and slightly chewy, so heavy with flavor that it went up the back of the nose—that is what strawberries can really taste like. The only equivalent I ever encountered came when my host on a Hawaiian pineapple plantation cut me a juicily dripping stick from a pineapple similarly left behind as too ripe for commerce.

Sixty years ago the blight caught up with the Blues' majestic chestnut trees. The last I heard the tall old house had been taken over by nuns—a peaceful end, but it would have outraged old Peter Blue's intolerant progeny. I hope the sisters were at least good cooks.

Grandmother Chamberlin's, but Grand*father* Furnas's. Grand*mother* Furnas, my father's tiny inarticulate mother, was (as I saw her) as much of a nonentity as one can be this side of the grave; whereas Isaac Furnas, her spouse, was calmly, almost negligently impressive in a Quakerish way of which my mother stood grudgingly in something like awe. His household was not her turf and she knew it. Her tone in addressing him was wary and our family visited there relatively infrequently.

"Father Furnas" was middle-sized, rosy, with large, alert but noncommittal brown eyes, a snow-white beard, and a good deal of soft white hair. Once he was persuaded to sit for a photographic portrait. He disapproved of the results because, he said, they made him look like a senator. Few senators look the part so well. But he was not emphatic about this repudiation. He never needed to go beyond a monosyllabic firmness. My father, who revered him, resembled him physically though lack of beard obscured the likeness. Had it been more than skin-deep, my father would have been a different person and I'd have had a different history, so I'm glad it was superficial. That may be selfish. My father's life would have been far happier had he inherited his father's quiet astuteness.

Isaac Furnas was a good if minor specimen of those well-integrated, word-is-his-bond Quakers combining pawky charm with the unemphatic shrewdness that accounts for the sleek well-to-doness traditionally associated with George Fox's spiritual get. I cannot doubt that his marrying Naomi George had much to do with her bringing with her sundry sizable assets derived from her father, old Isaiah George. North Country British Quaker stock was espousing Welsh Quaker stock because Isaiah approved of Isaac's quiet potential. His judgment was justified by the sequel—success, nothing flashy, of course. Looking back on scanty data most dimly realized at the time, I can now surmise that Isaac handled Naomi's woodenness with a quid-pro-quo sort of generosity that verged on kindness. Carrying out his side of the bargain, he kept the farm—in dairying when I knew it—producing properly and supplemented off and on by buying cattle for speculative feeding and, as occasion and others' needs served, lending money at stiff interest. He was able to contribute modestly to Earlham College at Richmond, Indiana, an Orthodox Friends' cultural focus, where his brother William was chief financial officer. I remember Great-uncle Will as a stately old gentleman retired to a chastely comfortable farmhouse over beyond Valley Mills with Great-aunt Debbie, his decorously decorative wife. I understand that one of the Earlham buildings is named after him.

Isaac's education probably stopped at a one-room schoolhouse. But he duly sent to Earlham four of the five children Naomi bore him. The fifth, given the non-Quakerish name of Elmer, mild and dutiful, was not taken beyond Valley Mills High School. He married a local girl, had no children, and under his father's eye handled the farm well enough. Actually none of Elmer's siblings lived up to the flavor of distinction and ability that emanated from Isaac there in his country backwater. The youngest, Joseph (a Quakerish and also a particularly Furnas name),* had a jockeylike charm, but it did not save him from being expelled from Earlham for some such crime as smoking. Edith, the one daughter, showed something of what racing writers call "early foot." Her father afforded her graduate study in Germany (then the Promised Land of American scholarship) whence she returned throatily well spoken and somewhat sternly handsome. Alone of the family she had light eyes; reading in The Heroes about "gray-eyed Athene" always made me think of Aunt Edith. The rest of her life

---

*I recently explored Dufton (Westmorland) in the North Country area that the Furnases came from, and sure enough in the parish church is a brass plate commemorating Joseph Furnas, a churchwarden in the early eighteenth century.

consisted of teaching at one Quaker college after another and looking very capably after her widowed mother, and eventually my father.

My father was eldest. Maybe because of that, maybe because of his emotional subordination to his father plus the physical resemblance, he was called "Zack"—a double anomaly, for that contraction did not fit Isaiah, and nobody dreamed of thus addressing Isaac Furnas. For some reason, maybe a patriarchal notion that the firstborn should emulate his father's successor in a different context, Zack got miscast. In his teens he seems to have daydreamed of raising horses in Argentina. I cannot picture him as a gaucho in wide breeches drinking maté. But he did like handling animals and was genuinely interested in farmerish concerns. His future should have lain among such things, as his father's foreman and eventual successor, probably with brother Elmer as lieutenant. Instead Isaac secured him a small stockholding interest in the growing ice cream business that my Great-uncle Rob, Isaac's brother, had set up in Indianapolis. For certain youths that would have been admirable: for Zack Furnas, disastrous. He proved to be, if possible, a worse businessman than his son would be.

Soon another kind of connection did him a different disservice. A young woman named Emma Doan—a good Quaker name and Doans and Furnases were allied—taught in the same school as Lizzy Chamberlin. Emma was engaged to Isaac's son Will. She introduced Lizzy to Will's brother Zack. Lizzy was on the dumpy side and wore pince-nez glasses, but Zack thought her pungently lively—as she could be—in enticing complement to his own diffidence. Eventually he popped the question. He was good-looking, respectfully undemanding, and had a prosperous father of whom she probably knew, for the Furnas and Chamberlin farms were only a few miles apart. She consented primarily at Zack's instance. The responsibility was his. Small blame attaches to her. But she was the last woman in the world to whom he should have entrusted his peace of mind, and vice versa.

Understand that since I was not on the ground at the time, the above is mostly speculation formed as bits and pieces swam up from the past and fused. It sounds like the bare bones of a glum novel that I leave for somebody else to write. By now I may feel a certain pity for my father. I did not at the time when we inhabited the same premises for eighteen years, and my pity may be false because I have so little notion of what he was actually like; whereas my acquaintance with my mother was copious and accurate.

That three-dimensional entity—"Grandfather Furnas's"— had its own aura like its owner's. Serene, immaculate, understated are the words that come to mind when I think of it. At the bend of a narrow gravel road running between fields and woods stood his retiringly situated small farmhouse, the kind with a dormered second story, an obviously seldom-used front door, and a narrow, slender-propped porch covering half its front elevation. Nobody ever sat on it; that was just the way the Old Northwest built modest farmhouses in the mid-1800s. I cannot recall ever going up the closed-in narrow stairs that led to the second floor, for we never stayed overnight. The small ground-floor rooms were all glistening white paint and black Holy Lord hinges and scatter-rugged floor whereon my sister and I fumbled with a few table games got out for our amusement; only nobody bothered to show us how they worked. More entertaining were two bound volumes of a British publication called *Chatterbox*, the essence of Victorian juvenilia. Their hard covers glowed with crudely colored, vulgarly elaborate artwork centering round pretty blond children cuddling bunny rabbits and such. Inside, however, they were worth attention while the grown-ups on their upper, sit-in-a-chair level talked slowly and dully about nothing in particular.

Early absorption in *Chatterbox* came in handy years later when I was handling Victorian literary materials. Every other number had a full-page steel engraving of how Lieutenant A.C.G. Hightower won the Victoria Cross in the Crimea; so at a strangely early age I knew what Redan and Malakoff stood for. There were stupidly written synopses of Dickens's later novels with full-page engravings of crucial scenes. I so disliked the artist's handling of Magwitch accosting Pip in the graveyard and Miss Havisham showing him "A bride-cake! Mine!" among the cobwebs that I put off reading *Great Expectations* for twenty years. A similar misbegotten illustration for the synopsis of *Les Misérables* so offended that though I already knew Hugo's other novels well, I have never yet tried the flagship of the squadron. But making up for all that was an enjoyable, interminable serial, *John Herrick, R.N.*, about a worthy youth of humble origin shanghaied by a Royal Navy press gang, who gallantly survived Cornish wreckers, French cruisers, Dahomeyan royal head collectors, and so on, usually in cahoots with a comic boatswain named Billy. The humor was lame and crude, but at the time I didn't know it.

The circumstances in which those valuable memories float were pretty juiceless but irreproachable in their own style, with a net effect as dry as Miss Havisham's cake. And what one ate at Grandfather Furnas's had an affinity with it. The stuff was not unpalatable but had no positive qualities either. The ingredients were of farm-fresh best, the quantities neither stinted nor lavish. But for anybody expecting enjoyment the effect was as though a heavy head cold were so fouling up one's taste zone that one couldn't be sure whether a given forkful was onions or turnips. The one item I recall gratefully was Naomi's salt-rising bread, then an already vanishing relic of pioneer times when yeast was hard to come by but the bacteria in the environment were willing to multiply pungently in dough. The flavor was once well defined by my sister as like distant dirty feet.* Provided one likes it, it is also exquisite, and was utterly out of keeping at that Quaker table. Insipid salt-rising bread is as much of a contradiction in terms as unfishy caviar.

The historical reason Quaker food is like that goes back to abolitionist times when Friends refused to use coffee, tea, spices, and other warm-climate products suspected of involving slave labor. Not unlikely a group temperamental hankering after amateur asceticism, the sort of thing that rejected bright colors and unnecessary buttons, also had something to do with it. Forty years ago my wife was staying in Honolulu while I was off on a post-Hiroshima look at Micronesia. A Quaker missionary couple, cousins of my father's, who had retired there somehow picked up her name and, correctly assuming a relationship, hospitably asked her to dinner. When she told me about it she described them as harmlessly well meaning. But when I asked what the food was like, she said unprompted that it gave her a new understanding of what "bland diet" might mean.

---

*In the mid-1930s a bakery on New York's Madison Avenue made a fair version of salt-rising bread for a while. But output stopped because the neighborhood objected to the ungodly odors emitted when a batch was baking.

4

Backwater

IN DIFFERENT DEGREES of depth all three of those kinship households helped to shape me. But the cocoon whence I emerged, rumpled and still damp behind the antennae, was the home environment.

The autobiographer's obligatory earliest memory: Mine was abnormally early. I can relive it now quite clearly: I am looking from a second-story window toward a back alley. (In central Indianapolis Philadelphia-style alleys for access to stables, garbage cans, and so on run between north-and-south streets.) I am standing on a cloth-covered storage box supported by the household "help" who is known to me as "Gay." (Her name was Gabrielle.) Coming along the alley is a horse and light wagon, the driver partly obscured by one of the huge fixed umbrellas that such vehicles then mounted. Gay says, "That's Gosney's wagon," and I am already aware that "Gosney's" means a nearby grocery. This can be no later than early fall 1907, when the family moved from that house. Born in late November 1905, I am not yet two years old. Otherwise that prosaic episode has no significance, no reason for being remembered when so many weightier impressions have obviously been lost.

There is my only memory of our Ashland Avenue premises. When we occasionally passed the place and the house was pointed out—an ungainly, neglectedly gray—I was always pleased that we had left it. My other earliest residues are rather unpleasant. I am sitting beside my mother in a streetcar. I must still be a baby, and it must be summer, for I am con-

75

scious of the white cotton-thread veil of the sort that was then stretched over babies' faces to keep off flies. The harsh threads pull and rasp at my nose. Offensively damp, from sweat I suppose, they give off a scorchy odor of wet cotton. I already have an inconveniently strong dislike of dampness—the trait that later made me so poor a swimmer. Lukewarm washcloths slopping on my face and boring into my ears are poignant recollections. As soon as I was allowed to wash my own face, I deposed washcloths in favor of the hands God gave me and eschewed soap on the face too, except for shaving; yet during the ensuing seventy-odd years I have been reasonably presentable. I was also irked by the lost, something-eerily-wrong feeling on the ends of my fingers after they pared my nails; because I still have some of that I tend to leave my nails longer than the statute allows. In this same infantile context a strong dislike of the warmed-over smell of heavily starched garments comes back to me, particularly in connection with the "Russian suits" that very small boys were then got up in. Over short, open cotton drawers went a belted cotton tunic the collar of which—this was the Russian part—was a high band buttoning under one ear. It occurs to me now that here was a foolishly remote reflection of the cult of things Russian that, consequent on the triumphs of Diaghilev's ballets, swept the Western world before World War I. My emphatic memories of these strong dislikes probably mean I was unusually finicky. Or are other inchoate human beings like that? Maybe Wordsworth's earliest retained memories were glorious, but I'm damned if mine were. Doubtless there were things I enjoyed at the age of two years. If so, they made no lasting impression.

The house the family shifted into from Ashland Avenue was better looking and its location, 2235 Broadway, was, though on a street no broader, a quarter mile nearer the prestige of Pennsylvania and Meridian streets farther westward. I never learned who built 2235, whether a speculative developer or a private person buying a vacant lot to build on. It was probably the latter, for its design differed from that of any other house on the block. But the lots were all alike, so narrow that there was barely room for walkways between the houses. Twenty years ago, when an assignment took me to Indianapolis, I went to look at the old place. It wasn't there. The Hacks' house to the north, 2237, and Mrs. Leachman's to the south, 2233, were surviving though rather the worse for the obvious down-go-ingness of the neighborhood. But 2235 was only a sordid, weed-grown cellar hole. Burned down? Torn down? I didn't ask. To have done so would have been hypocritical, for my mem-ories of life there are at best very mildly affectionate.

Its design was an amplification of the "California bunga-low" so popular all over America circa 1900—wide-fronted, hump-shouldered with an all-across front porch roof sup-ported on squatty columns. From its ceiling a porch swing usually hung on chains. The dormer window in the third (gar-ret) story gave the place the look of a dowager owl too help-lessly seated ever to get up again. The hot-air furnace in its cellar burned the soft coal of the region. In cold weather its register-circulation kept the house smelling slightly like the train shed of a railroad station. The same flavor permeated the bone-chilling, slightly foggy mornings of early spring and late fall, half water vapor and half Pocahantas coal smoke. In hot sum-mer weather 2235 sweltered even with all doors and windows (screened, of course) open. All through the night the bedroom second story was savagely hot, Merely to open the door of the third-story garret was to risk being smothered by a rush of superheated air. Grandmother Chamberlin's and the Blues' house had better shade and were cooler; and the aloof seren-ity of Grandfather Furnas's was such that one could hardly imagine anybody under that roof (except maybe in the kitchen when the salt-rising bread was baking) sweating a drop. But the only shade 2235 had was a middle-sized box elder in the front yard infested by tent caterpillars in season and another of the same size and failing in the larger back yard—neither near nor tall enough to be any use.

The far end of the back yard had a ramshackle stable used only for storage in the days before 1912, when our first auto-mobile came. But we had plenty of the budding motor age before that, for the stable across the alley was the garage of a family named Groff whose sons were already motor addicts, always tinkering with some proto-jalopy that plagued the neighborhood with the backfiring of its tortured engine. The backyards all up and down the block were separated by solid board fences too high for children to see over—unpainted, soot-blackened, dismal to look at when it rained, and oozing pine resin when the sun was hot. Our house, its cream-colored trim contrasting pleasantly with its chocolate-brown weather-boarding, was among the three or four most prepossessing; most of our neighbors lived in specimens of the older, mildly gingerbreaded school and stayed with the original grimly green or grisly gray paint. Had Broadway not been lined with well grown trees, mostly Norway maples, the general effect would have been pretty dismal.

We children were unaware of any right to complain about sweltering heat or smelly fogs. We even took in stride the further contrast between what we were fed elsewhere and what we got at home. My father's notion of a fitting dinner, true to Quaker simplicity, was chicken-fried round steak, mashed potatoes, and apples quartered and lightly stewed with a little sugar; *chez* Furnas "stewdapples" was just one word. (Weekdays he lunched at a counter near his office on a glass of milk and a piece of peach pie.) My mother had a wider range but small skill in, or feel for, cooking. Her strongest position in gastronomy was a deep aversion for poultry that she ascribed to having seen so many chickens beheaded, gutted, and plucked "down home." (Not pretty processes, of course, but in my own case observing them never put me off the good fried chicken that resulted.)

Of lunches I recall only a good deal of macaroni and cheese. Breakfast was stewed prunes—this was well before orange juice became an institution—overcooked oatmeal or corn flakes and cocoa, then thought particularly good for children; eggs seldom. "High on the hog" was not inscribed over the dining-room door at 2235. The quality of the cooking—actually even chicken-fried steak and mashed potatoes can be good eating if well handled—depended on whoever was hired to do it at the time, usually no great thing. During one memorable few months, however, a sweet-tempered "colored girl" named Estelle ornamented breakfast with delightfully delicate, right-out-of-the-oven hot biscuits. And during the long reign of Lulu Brooks in our kitchen somewhat more variety appeared than we were used to.

About her let me interpolate what I wrote thirty-odd years ago in *Goodbye to Uncle Tom,* a book on the American race-problem. Back then, the NAACP assured me, "Negro" was the acceptable term.

Born north of the Ohio forty years after Appomattox, I was late for acquaintance with former slaves. One I did know well, if children ever know adults well. Thought back upon, she seems to have been the most integrating influence in my childhood.

Her work was everything but laundry and dressmaking in our household. I recall little about her with police-court precision. She was not African-dark, but her face was broad Negro with bright little eyes, her build was stubby and sturdy; I have seen bush Liberians who might have been her sons. She must have been born soon after 1845, for she was old enough before Emancipation to have been set to iron the wash and mature enough to have tempted young master. Threats with a hot flatiron quelled him. By the time she came to us, she had been widowed of a husband of whom she always spoke with affectionate honor and, by working days, had been able to rear a large and self-respecting family in Louisville.

She had chronic arthritis, and her little bedroom off our kitchen was aromatic with liniment. Even her Bible smelled of it. But her creaky joints did not keep her from occasionally playing a shuffly little dance game that she called "Peep-O Rabbit" or from working doughtily, efficiently and with a huge good will that frayed only when she was to do something in a way other than her own. Ours was a household of monotonous fare. She had a free hand only in the children's breakfasts and delighted in ringing unexpected changes on prunes, oatmeal and eggs. Looming through the swinging door, with a flourish she would announce that this morning the Palace Hotel was serving pancakes and stand to watch us eat with the air of a horse-loving groom listening to a colt's feeding.

When gay she might gabble a wonderful rigmarole about how "They was Ringwood, Springwood, Dasher and Dan, the old bitch and nine pups, but the best ole dog I ever had, one night he et his belly full of mush and milk, turned his heels up to heb'n and died like a lamb," which we valued highly. It could have been an infiltration of minstrel-show material? No such suspicion was possible about her flavorsome but shapeless tales, of which I recall strangely little. There was one about a man who killed a booger, which should have been a head louse, of course, but its skin was unaccountably large enough to be hung to dry on a fence, and there were awesome complications when the booger returned and resumed its skin for some witchy purpose. At the time my mental picture of the booger was of something like a flayed ape.

On her afternoon off she usually visited the Idle Hour, a local movie theater that admitted Negroes. She called it the "Idle Hoover" because the name was lettered Roman style: IDLE HOVR. We knew what she saw only when the bill had included a Chaplin. Then we heard all about it. "Kickinest man I ever see!" she would crow and gasp between paroxysms of relish. She felt the same intimacy of gusto in Dickens whom, with an instinct that I still think shrewd, I set her to reading. *Nicholas Nickleby* was her favorite and Ralph Nickleby the character whom she discussed most. She would mutter and grumble about "That ole Nickle*by*!" until he acquired actuality greater than his creator ever gave him.

She drew us children by a sort of gravitation, the lighter attracted to the mass of higher density. We were always under her feet and she tolerated us with a good nature that astounds me when I recall her temper. Ah, she was a person. There was every bit as much thunder as butter in her. The whole family of us were, in a sense, afraid of her; only we children had the advantage of her sympathy. At a word, gesture or notion that she found unbecoming—and her standards were subtle and high—her mouth and eyes would lower, her skin actually darken, or so it seemed, her gestures grow extravagant and tense with power as she thumped the rolling pin or lashed her mop at the floor. The more she felt the less she said, but until the offense was corrected and the storm blown over, everybody in that house walked Spanish.

She never struck us, though a blow would often have been fair and from her we might well not have resented it. When she flourished that massive right arm and said, "Boy, I break the crystal yo' watch!" it was understood to mean merely "Calm down." But those earnest tempers of hers were formidable. She was formidable. One night when our parents were out and she was skylarking with us, I ran into a clothes closet and pulled the door shut after me. It jammed. She hauled on the outside knob and it came off in her hand. A neighbor was telephoned to for help. When he did not appear as soon as she thought reasonable, she fetched the crowbar-poker from the cellar and ripped that door out of the frame in about three seconds of powerful leverage. Coming upstairs a few minutes later, the rescuing neighbor met her with the poker still in her hand and the light of battle still in her little eyes. He said afterward that his first impulse had been to turn and run.

She died back home with her family in Louisville, God rest her soul. None of this conveys her pride, her strong sweetness, like wild dark honey, her scathing mother wit and the knotty richness of her speech. With ampler opportunity this woman could have commanded an army or founded a colony. There is no reason whatever to confuse her with the *Gone with the Wind* sort of "mammy." And she was only a fair-to-middling cook. It was the fun not the flavor that we valued in those breakfasts.

Our town then had the largest Negro-white ratio in the North. Southerners probably outnumbered Yankees among the forebears of local people, certainly among mine. The public schools that I attended had a few Negro pupils ignored even more completely than if they had been invisible. I knew of a Negro dentist in town but never saw a Negro with social or economic status above that of trusted servant until I was eighteen years old and away from home for good. Reared in this quasi-Dixie atmosphere, I had much to unlearn about Negroes. I cannot promise, I can only hope, that I have unlearned most of it. In the process I have met Negro chiefs of state, tribal emperors, scholars, soldiers, administrators and scientists. This was only a powerless and underpaid old woman able barely to read her Bible and get through the *Pickwick Papers* in the course of a year or so. But thanks to having known her I never needed telling, while unlearning, that a Negro can manifest superlative integrity, acumen and power of personality. *Uncle Tom's Cabin* contained nothing at all like her.

The 2200 block was no such social microcosm as a country hamlet of thirty-odd households would have been. I now marvel at how little I recall of the neighbors, which means we had little to do with them. Maybe my parents knew all the livelihoods represented, but I doubt it. Let me see—over the way, well toward Twenty-third Street, lived the Mansfields; Mr. Mansfield's tailor shop made my father's invariable medium-gray suits. Next door was Professor Dungan, a paunchy, elderly fraud who gave piano lessons at very low rates; as my sister and I learned, he was a slackly worthless teacher. Opposite him were the McMaths, solid, self-sufficient people; McMath had a high-up job with the streetcar company and the first automobile on the block, a chunky sidewinder. We played off and on with the younger McMath children. Assume that most of the breadwinners were, like my father, in some level of management in local enterprises. One neighbor lady defined the tone neatly: the kind of neighborhood, she said happily, where none of the men carried lunch boxes to work.

And we had celebrities. Opposite 2235 was the large, dark-green house of a widow named Hennessy with a red-haired schoolteacher daughter; a lanky, wary younger son, Dick; and an outgoing older son, Johnny, who rose to play Davis Cup tennis. Our immediate neighbors at 2237 were the Hacks. Was Hack a dentist? Anyway his wife, a pleasant, tallish lady, wrote under her maiden name (Elizabeth Miller) inconsequential novels that sold well enough for Bobbs-Merrill, Indianapolis's own publishing house, to keep on accepting them. She had nothing to do, however, with my sister's and my going into writing. The Furnases' relations with the Hacks were not uncordial but tenuous.

After old Mrs. Leachman's death the 2233 house on the other side was bought by a young architect named Daggett who rose in his profession and long after moving elsewhere was chief designer of the new Butler University campus that took over the streetcar company's park in old Peter Blue's woods. Jim Daggett, their elder son, was a fine playmate. But my point here is that as a girl art student in Paris Mrs. Daggett had shared lodgings with young Geraldine Farrar, who, of course, became a dashing opera star.

Davis Cup, lady novelist, operatic diva—who could say we lived in a backwater? Why, anybody with good sense. The scanty interaction among our neighbors, which seldom went farther than the proverbial borrowed cup of sugar, signified sluggishness. In the Furnases' case the lack of other Quakers at hand probably accentuated our problem, only we weren't aware we had one. Then, though the McMaths, Scotts, Winders's et al. played together more or less and attended Number Forty-five, none of the neighbor boys happened to be in my class. My sister and I were allowed, not encouraged, to let neighbors play in our yard but tacitly discouraged from doing so in theirs. Thus this numb little sub-subculture enhanced the Furnases' not exactly invidious but spontaneous standoffishness.

My mother's gestures toward interaction tended to be outside the neighborhood. She had that Sunday School class to don hat and gloves for and for a while women's clubbing took her farther. Regularly she read a "paper" at a Clio Club meeting and once a year or so the members met at our house—a grand occasion with refreshments and orders to us children to come in at the back door. Holed up in the kitchen, we got the rustle of genteel conversation every time the door opened. As to my mother's "papers" I remember only that one of them covered the Chinese Revolution of 1911, to explore which she laid in several books that stayed on the household shelves, so I explored them, not with much profit. (One was *Chinese Mother Goose*, a missionary's translation of what he represented as Chinese folk material, of which I remember one tag: "If I had found no chicken skin / I could not mend my breeches thin.") That my mother had much grasp of what Sun-Yat-Sen came to was unlikely. But she did know more about him than her club sisters and she did write her own papers, whereas certain other club members were suspected of hiring them done by half-educated widows or spinsters mining the public library to pick up needed dollars. A surviving piece of stationery tells me that around 1912 Mrs. I. G. Furnas was secretary of the Indianapolis branch of the National Federation of Women's Clubs. That must have lent her assurance when my father snorted about her "clubbing"—one of the few things about which he ever asserted himself even sporadically. By then her deafness, probably genetic, was hampering her and, I now surmise, gradually phased her out of what social life she had. That was, of course, hard on her; also hard on a family under the influence of an exacerbating personality pretty acid to begin with. If I wished to feel sorry for her, that would be a good place to begin.

Had my father kept in better touch with his household, he might have snorted oftener. But he had little time domestically. He rose at 6:00 A.M., breakfasted hastily, caught a College Avenue streetcar, got off where Massachusetts Avenue crosses Alabama Street, and arrived early at the ice cream factory (he called it "the creamery") where, as his Uncle Rob's nephew, very minor stockholder, and production manager— only he had no formal title—he struggled daily with the things that could and did go wrong with the refrigeration machinery, the horses that drew the delivery wagons, the milk supply, the flavor and texture of the ice cream that blobbed out of the battery of freezers. Getting home toward 7:00 P.M., he supped, read the *News*, and turned in to be up early again in the morning. That was six days a week. On the seventh he could seldom follow the Lord's example. Sunday School and church used up the morning. Often he had to drive us to Sunday dinner at the Blues' or for an afternoon visit to Grandmother Chamberlin's. When he had the luck to have a free Sunday afternoon it was even money something would go wrong at the creamery and he would spend the rest of the day there taking measures in collaboration with Lon—short for Alonzo, surname forgotten if I ever knew it—the loyal foreman of "the back room" who was in effect the only friend Zack Furnas had in his mature years.

He had once been good friends with two Earlham classmates—Elmer Stout, a lawyer who did well in Indianapolis banking, and Warren Barrett, also a lawyer, who went East and became president of the minor but economically important Lehigh Valley Railroad, the same that still (as part of Conrail) hauls piggyback trailers and tank cars up the South Branch valley a couple of miles from my hillside house in New Jersey. By my time my father saw little of either. As far as I know my mother never brought the contrast up directly, but

I can hardly be wrong, feeling back to subtleties that she exuded, in assuming that it rankled sore that both had left her husband far behind.

Somewhere I have a studio photograph of young Zack Furnas cheerful and handsome in an old-timey Quaker broadbrim hat—got up for some student doings at Earlham, I suppose—taken with a pretty girl in a correspondingly old-timey Quaker bonnet; I hope she was nice to him. His handwriting—unpropitiously crabbed, obviously laborious, nothing like my mother's teacherly cursive, highly legible script—was not a good omen for academic achievement. It fits that all I know of his college studies is that he occasionally growled his detestation of "old Doc Gerber," the German professor who, one gathered, had ridiculed him for mispronouncing the holy Deutsche Sprache. That gnawing memory probably helped him to accept Germany as enemy in World War I. His mind had a simplistic bent, as do most minds in one or another context. His social outlook was laissez-faire Republican with the usual alarmed contempt for labor unions and income tax. That latter monster had only recently come into being when his Uncle Rob sold the company branch in Birmingham, Alabama, and my father had to pay capital gains on his share of the proceeds. He fumed about that for years afterward, the more because as disaster crept up on him in the 1920s, it was bitter to remember those several thousand dollars that an unscrupulous government had forcibly extracted.

Beyond the vexing improvisations that kept the creamery producing, he did develop one imaginative scheme: A local ordinance required in ice cream at least 8 percent butterfat— a level more or less double what cows secrete in milk. So quantities of skim milk were run into the sewer system further to pollute White River, already rich enough with effluents from meat-packing plants—a consideration far from anybody's thoughts seventy years ago. But it did occur to my father, farmboy at heart, that here was good pig feed going to waste. The firm let him rent a farm near the village of Carmel* north of town, stock it with miscellaneous swine, and truck the skim

---

*Accent on the first syllable, please. To suit its having become a prosperous suburb, it is now, I understand, pronounced Car-*mel* as in California. I was greatly edified recently to see a newspaper picture of an elegant Hoosier girl winning a horse-show contest, with Car*mel* given as her provenance.

out there to become a profitable by-product. Father drove up there every few weeks to see how the hogs were doing and sometimes took us children along. I vividly recall fields full, extremely full, of black pigs, white pigs, striped pigs, red pigs, spotted pigs shoving and grunting and squealing in high excitement probably because the advent of us unusual persons might mean feeding time. It was an exhilarating sight, if smelly. My father relished it, for those vigorous, squint-eyed creatures represented his only instance of being a good businessman.

He garnished his dark gray suits with dark gray neckties and low-spreading stiff collars that left his neck defenselessly bare. His watch was a semiglobular Elgin with a nickel-plated case, the model on which railroad conductors relied. The conductor wore that watch on a gold chain across the vest. Much to my mother's distress, my father wore his on a thick black rubber band. It now hangs above my desk. When I bother to wind it, it keeps good time though it can't have been cleaned these fifty years.

Were I under oath with a judge adjuring me to tell all, I could add little of significance to the above. I. G. Furnas was not an easy man to know. How much was there to know? No gauge.

Sometimes my sister and I went with him to the creamery and stood around while he discussed the condenser's ailments with Lon in that "back room" full of complicated machinery, hissing noises, and a strong smell of ammonia. We usually escaped fairly soon into "the front room," where the other two minority stockholders, Mart Antrim (sales) and Will Griffith (accounts) had rolltop desks and telephones. No desk for Great-uncle Rob; as far as I know that handsome old gentleman —his un-Quakerish mustache made him look like the photographs of William Dean Howells—seldom appeared in the office. He spent summers in upper Michigan, winters in west coast Florida, and when at home frequented a local golf course. My mother wanted my father to take up golf, as so many important businessmen were doing, but he had no time for deliberate recreation and made his contempt for it tactlessly clear in the wrong company. She had small right to tax him with that, however, for she made little effort to conceal her disdain for Antrim's loud fatness and Griffith's demure sulkiness.

The archaic nature of the Furnas Ice Cream Company was obvious in its delivery equipment, which consisted of horse-drawn wagons until well past World War I. My father had a good deal to do with that, for he felt at home with horses and maintained, with some point, that they were better than gasoline engines for the frequent stops that deliveries entailed. The company's advertising consisted of occasional insertions in the *News* of four inches on two columns saying no more than "FURNAS ICE CREAM" with address and phone number. All business letters were still written by hand. The only typewriter was a primitive Oliver with a jump-up-and-down shift, dust-clogged insides, and a ribbon that printed only faintly however hard one hit the keys. We children alone ever tried to work it. Fortunately the other three ice cream companies in town, all smaller, were no more enterprising and Furnas Ice Cream, which was palatable enough, dominated local soda fountains, birthday parties, and weddings; hence Great-uncle Rob's conspicuous leisure. Eventually National Dairy bought the business, but for years they kept the Furnas brand name for its customer value.

When my sister and I tired of the typewriter and the glass case of beat-up plaster-of-paris models of the fancy shapes available for special occasions—turkeys for Thanksgiving, hearts for Valentine's Day, and so on—there was "the other room": once an ice cream parlor, presumably back when the neighborhood hadn't yet run down. It still retained two or three little wire-legged tables and lyre-backed wire chairs with small circular seats—high-ticket antiques now. More to our purposes, back of a counter was the original freezer box containing tall cans of vanilla, chocolate, and strawberry, even the original dipper, no stingy, hemispherical modern affair but generously cone-shaped with twice the capacity. No customers ever appeared; we were the only patrons. We seldom had ice cream at home, for my father had enough tasting of it to do on the job and my mother disliked milky things. It seems strange that with the free run of the place we children neglected to overdo our privileges. Now and again a classmate would half derisively prod me about getting all that ice cream free at will. I never tried to persuade anybody that it was something I could take or leave alone. Though true, to say so would have sounded ill-natured and implausible.

My appetite took special forms. Sweet stuff was very well but not worth going far out of one's way for. The virtues of certain flavors that I now find rewarding—of onions, for instance, asparagus, lima beans—were lost on me until I was well toward growing up. But I could put away the grocery's old-style "mouse cheese" (or "rat cheese" or "store cheese"), and pretty good it was in those days, by the quarter pound. It went great with the Grimes Golden apples of which our cellar acquired a barrelful each winter. Dried beef—"chipped beef," says the effete East—I gnawed at by fistfuls. Once at Grandmother Chamberlin's I ingested such a quantity of Kentucky Wonder green beans done with bacon that I had to go off by myself in the chicken yard and throw up. A curious palate for a boy in short pants. Several times I ate at one sitting most of a pint of stuffed green olives. I carefully saved the seeds of my apples for peeling and eating, a picayune process, but I vastly relished their cyanidish flavor; for the same reason peach pits were worth splitting open. To this day I find irresistible any comestible carrying that subsuicidal tang of "bitter almonds" that pervades detective fiction. It is the same that particularly attracts tent caterpillars to wild cherry trees. Maybe in a previous incarnation . . .

During World War I Great-uncle Rob died, leaving his dominant interest in the creamery to his married daughter, his sole heir. The consequence was my father's selling his interest to the estate and ceasing to be salaried manufacturing manager. His being in effect forced to do so outraged my mother, who, all along, on no sound grounds, had assumed that, as nephew, my father would take over command. I suspect that if there was any possibility of my father staying in his usual slot, it was her insistence that he stand up for what she considered his rights that made a complete break inevitable. Of the ethics of the matter I have no clear notion. But there certainly was no reason to cast my father as supervising executive over Antrim and Griffith, of whose functions he knew practically nothing, or as viceroy for his cousin Lelia, with whom our relations, though nominally friendly, were sparse and probably tainted by her awareness of my mother's crypto-jealousy.

My father did retain his interests in two of the branch crea-

meries elsewhere in the Midwest. Under his gingerly command a new Furnas Ice Cream Company also appeared in Des
Moines, and another in Louisville. The first managed to stay
strugglingly alive, the second petered out. Both had him
floundering among details of organization, finance, and sales-
manship for which he was unfit. Thus he gradually used up
what capital he could command. Once Zack Furnas was out of
the well-worn ruts of the Alabama Street back room, he had
nowhere to go but down, and thither he went.

Probably it was an early crisis in this slow-motion catastrophe that led to his selling 2235 in 1917. We rented a much
larger house farther north, 2717 College Avenue. Built on a
double lot half of which was a sizable lawn, it was one of those
many-roomed, pretentious, so-called "Queen Anne" wooden
mansions with multiple gables, a porte-cochère over the side
driveway, a candle-extinguisher tower on one corner, a cupo-
laed barn out back. The front-stair window was of stained glass,
the front parlor set off from the entrance hall by a spool-and-
spindle screen in golden oak. The third floor consisted of an
oak-floored ballroom. Off its corner in the third story of the
tower was a cylindrical room with generous windows that I
took over, with my stamp collection, some favored books, a
small desk—which went far to make up for new burdens that
also came with the place. For now, with my father away so
much pursuing his unpromising schemes, I was deemed old
and large enough to keep that lawn mown, that steam-heat
furnace stoked, those downtown errands run, and vegetables,
(which we had hardly bothered with at 2235) cultivated in the
paddock next to the barn.

To some extent I approved of horticulture, for it often
meant specially tasty eating. For forty-odd years I have earnestly grown green stuff. But I cannot yet be persuaded that
spading and hoeing and that much-admired smell of fresh-
worked soil are delightful in their own right. Back at 2235 a
gentle-voiced black man named Billy Davis had handled the
yard chores and fetching and carrying. I had a dim feeling
that it served the family right when, as inexperienced furnace
man, I failed to close the water intake on the boiler tightly
enough and the whole system filled with cold water up to the
second floor.

The house was only a few hundred yards from where the

College Avenue bridge crossed Fall Creek—a tributary of White River that would also be called a river anywhere but in the Old Northwest—and its steep, weedy, secluded, and heavily polluted bank was a good place for war games with garbage-can lids for shields and dead ironweed stalks for spears. Otherwise the new quarters had few virtues. For all its original pretentiousness the house was getting run-down. So was the neighborhood to south and east. That probably began when the streetcar company extended its College Avenue line and installed a turnaround loop in the triangle where College and Sutherland avenues met, right opposite the house. Several times an hour the schedule set a car grinding and screeching round that loop with the trolley slipping and the circuit breaker popping, noises that probably put prospective house buyers off. But one got used to it and it lowered rents; and having transport practically at one's door was handy. Even when I overdid leisurely collection of books, coat, and cap, and the car left without me, I could run it down a couple of blocks away and climb aboard the back platform, for what with overloading and stopping at every corner this was not the "rapid transit" that the franchise probably spoke of. In rush hours only females stood a chance of a seat inside. The underprivileged (or chivalrous) sex clung to the steps of the platforms so thickly that the conductor could not get at them to collect fares.

The fare was nominally a nickel, but it was usually paid with small cardboard tickets at six for a quarter printed with an engraving of "The Monument" that was, maybe still is, Indianapolis's distinctive architectural pride. An artificial capital, the town was laid out by admirers of L'Enfant's Washington with a circular central plaza as site for the governor's mansion. It was duly built there but eventually done away with because, legend said, governors' ladies objected to the goldfish-bowl life. Well before my time Indiana had erected in that focal circle a Soldiers' and Sailors' Monument that is probably the gaudiest tribute to the Union victors in the Civil War—a two-hundred-foot column that manages to be both prismatic and tapering, both majestic and jaunty, an effect combining Beaux Artsy ornateness with anticipation of Art Nouveau. On top is a wind-blown goddess known, of course, as Miss Indiana, whose magnificent view of the whole town has long since been ruined by high-rises. The column is melodramatically based on a splayed-out complex of broad waterfalls, interspersed stair-ways, and groups of double-life-size statuary honoring, respec-tively, the cavalry, the artillery, the infantry, and the navy more successfully than most such efforts. At intervals round the pe-riphery at sidewalk level are huge bronze buffalo heads, re-wardingly shaggy and morose, spouting water out of their mouths into ornate basins. (The state seal of Indiana shows a pioneer felling a tree while a buffalo scampers away toward the background.) The Statehouse two blocks west has been singled out by critics as America's most deplorable example of the dome-and-portico school of state capitols. But I find The Monument's impudent style exhilarating to think back on from sixty-odd years ago and eight hundred miles away.

How long ago is illustrated by the heavy bronze dippers that were chained to those bronze buffaloes so passers-by could slake their thirst. So germ-committed an arrangement would not be tolerated now. But when The Monument was designed, Pasteur's work had not yet widely affected public conscious-ness. Even in my time nobody regarded with misgivings the prevalence of horse dung—and consequent English spar-rows—fresh on the streets and in stables, dried and swirling in every breeze.

The ground-breaking automobiles were fumbly by any-thing like modern standards, a thing hard to appreciate when merely looking at some antique in a museum. The Indian-polis-made Pathfinder touring car that my father was finally chivied into buying had a powerful four-cylinder engine and a bronze bas-relief of General John C. Frémont on the radia-tor, but no self-starter. Acetylene headlights were fed from a tank on the running board—remember running boards? At dusk one's match lighted those headlights at some risk of blowing vehicle and self to kingdom come. The starting crank that dangled below the radiator had to be grasped in a partic-ular underhand fashion, else the engine's compression might make it "kick" and sprain or break the cranker's wrist.

Tires were abysmally untrustworthy. Even I, the all-thumbs mechanical moron, had to learn to get the casing off the de-mountable rim; take out the inner tube; find the leak; rough up that area with the grater; apply rubber cement; plaster a patch down on it; wait a while; pump up the tube; spit on the patch to see whether it bubbled, meaning the seal was imperfect; if it held, huddle the tube back inside the casing taking care to avoid wrinkles that would pinch under pressure; wangle the casing back on the rim, which required three different tools, infinite patience, and usually a finger or two mutilated; pump up to the statutory pressure; and ho for the open road! And another puncture twenty miles farther on. Whenever I feel gloomy about today's poor quality of goods and services, I remind myself that at least automobile tires and safety razor blades are most gratifyingly far better than they used to be.

Refrigeration was grotesquely primitive too. The kitchen "icebox" was a wooden cabinet with a large zinc-lined compartment for food preservation and a smaller one adjacent for ice from the local ice company. ("Tap-on-the-icebox" was the name of one of the hide-and-seekish games played on summer evenings after supper.) The ice was renewed daily by a large wagon full of hundred-pound cakes dissected by a large man with an ice pick and a pair of giant tongs. Each household on his route put in a front window a large square card with the

figure at the top indicating how many pounds were needed. The iceman split off a piece of roughly that weight, rushed it dripping round the house and into the back door and then the icebox. In summer, children badgered him for stray bits to suck, which he found irritating, and stole rides on the back step of the wagon, which he found more so, hence icemen were generally reputed to be bad-tempered. But some must have had charm, else why the persistent folk legends about neglected housewives regularly consoled during the iceman's morning call?

The icebox he serviced—not the housewife—is now, I understand, an item in antique shops. It was not very efficient at keeping things hygienically cool, and every day or two its melt-water pan had to be emptied. The pan was wide, shallow, and awkwardly situated on the floor beneath; getting it to the kitchen sink without drenching one's shoes and stockings took doing. Forgetting it meant a flooded kitchen floor. But it was an improvement on the old-timey springhouse or dark cellar and deserved well of the republic until mechanical refrigerators came along for home use soon after World War I.

I find it difficult to work up nostalgia for 2717 College Avenue, for 2235 Broadway almost as much so. The only saving grace there is grateful memory of summertime's occasional vendors. The popcorn man had a two-wheeled barrow crowned by a tall glass box half full of fresh-popped corn kept warm by a glimmering little lamp and resupplied as necessary by a kerosene-heated popper and a kettle of melted butter. The approach of this strange vehicle was heralded by its hot-air whistle of wistful tone that, though low-pitched, could be heard half a block away. In late summer twilight the sound enhanced the eeriness of flickering light behind the glass. In summer at irregular intervals, came spring wagons, one-horse, light affairs loaded with masses of bananas or watermelons, a specimen of the latter cut open to display bright magenta meat and shining black seeds—a fine sight in itself. But the special pleasure was vocal—the vendor, walking alongside the plodding horse, gave tongue every half minute: "Nan-n-n-n-n-*O*!" rising through half an octave with almost a whoop at the end. Or this in waltz time:

There is no getting away from my greediness. Those scattered pleasant details are inevitably concerned with things to eat.

5

War the First

ONE'S NOTION OF the history infiltrating one's childhood is necessarily fragmentary. That was particularly true in my day because we lacked broadcasting to heighten the sense of immediacy. No radio booming out you-are-there-while-it's-happening, no TV showing the restlessness of the black horse with JFK's boots reversed in the stirrups. Print and grown-ups' talk were the only channels of information. Personal observation was necessarily meager. I did know some details of the great flood of 1913 when Indianapolis, though not so badly off as Dayton, Ohio, was partly under water; Fall Creek was a sort of junior Wabash; and from its College Avenue bridge I saw an interurban trolley track hanging along the raw face of a newly undercut bluff like a half-mile necklace of rails and ties.

In my elders' discussions of politics and good or bad times I took little interest. I was aware that my father finally made up his mind to vote for Woodrow Wilson in 1912 but on what grounds I don't know; it cannot have meant a liberal loosening of ideas. Because of that presidential election I had a glimpse of the Republicans' William Howard Taft: Charles W. Fairbanks, the Hoosier who had been Theodore Roosevelt's vice-president,* put Taft up during the campaign in his Georgian

---

*Philip Dunne has a nice bit about Fairbanks in his book on Finley Peter Dunne, creator of "Mr. Dooley": Dunne was lunching at the White House in TR's time. The talk was about whether it was wise for TR to make a trial dive in an experimental new

95

mansion at the corner of Meridian and Thirtieth streets. That
sultry evening the Furnases happened to drive past—this was
long before air conditioning—and there were the unmistakably corpulent Taft and Fairbanks sitting in their shirt sleeves
on the retaining wall of the lawn, trying to cool off with palm-
leaf fans. During that same campaign Great-uncle George took
me to a Democratic rally in Tomlinson Hall and introduced
me to William H. McAdoo, who wore the stiffest, highest collar and gaudiest necktie I had ever seen. More on Democrats:
In Miami in the winter of 1915–16 at William Jennings Bryan's
renowned open-air shirt-sleeved men's Bible class in Royal Palm
Park my father had me shake hands with the Great Com-
moner, who, on a warm morning, was perspiring heavily.
Whatever its significance, the first two really famous men I
ever saw were swelteringly coatless.

No more personally acquired history. As to print, there was
the *Titanic* affair in a magazine, as aforesaid, but until I reached
the age of nine or so newspapers were good only for cartoons
of John Q. Public deploring the HCofL (high cost of living);
Abe Martin; the baseball box scores; and an occasional syndicated funny piece. No doubt the outbreak of World War I was
duly marked by newsboys hawking extra: "Wee-uxtry! Pay-puh!
European war! Read all about it!" Was I at Grandmother
Chamberlin's at the time? Not unlikely in August. Anyway,
either I didn't hear them or don't remember them or any adult
comment on the outbreak of hostilities.

It was some weeks before another magazine gave me some
sense of what was soon being called The Great War. The *Atlantic Monthly,* to which my mother subscribed, ran Richard
Harding Davis's impressive account of the German sweep
through Belgium. Until then for me Belgium was just the name
for a triangular splotch on the map between Holland and
France that issued queer postage stamps with perforated tails.
But this flooding of myriad irresistible gray-clad robots through
a helpless population thenceforth made me shiver whenever the presence of the German army over yonder came to

navy submarine, for eighty years ago, of course, all submarines were experimental.
Asked for his opinion, Dunne said: "Should be all right, Mr. President, provided you
take Fairbanks with you."

Soon another magazine, *St. Nicholas,* the high-prestige children's monthly of which survivors of my generation retain affectionate memory, supplied much more. Its current events department was so well done that I often read it. And no sooner had the Germans overrun Flanders than *St. Nicholas* went baldheaded for the Allied cause. No crude tub thumping; but its concise, sober accounts of the war as it took catastrophic shape—the bloody stalemate of trench warfare in the West, pendulum swings in the East, Gallipoli, poison gas—subtly transmuted the French and British, and off and on the Russians, into *our side.* That orientation reflected the magazine's cultural slot: upper-crust New England–formed, aimed at the offspring of good credit risks in the Back Bay, on the Main Line, and up and down Westchester County. Our best people were thus plumping for the Allied cause by a sort of temperamental gravitation. In parallel, *Life,* the original humorous weekly meant for the reading rooms of good clubs and library tables in literate households, began to fill up with savage-looking Kaiser Bills in spiked helmets, steady-eyed goddesses in liberty caps symbolizing France, doughtily majestic British lions, and a frowning Uncle Sam clenching his fists and studying an eastern horizon obscured by billowing black smoke. Even though it had a strong odor of vestigial colonial snobbery, the attitude did happen to make sense in the long run.

So the section of *St. Nicholas* showing how to make a raft or a dry-cell-powered telegraph outfit now carried pictures and descriptions of improved machine guns and new reconnaissance planes—only those of the Allies; the Central Powers' formidable siege artillery and all-too-effective submarines got no play. Ample coverage of the Royal Navy educated knickerbockered readers like me in armor-piercing projectiles and the pros and cons of battle cruisers. There was a stirring account of how a British battle cruiser lurking in ambush in the harbor of the Falkland Islands swooped out to annihilate the light German Pacific squadron that only a few weeks earlier had annihilated a British squadron off Chile. Recalling that seagoing melodrama made me one of the few members of the American general public who, when Argentina recently made that ill-advised descent, had any notion where or what the Falklands are.

The World's Work was similarly pro-Allies and dipping into it at Grandmother Blue's enhanced my partisan awareness of the Great War. Then early in 1915 the *National Geographic*, a monthly institution in our as in many households, carried an irresistible large map of the western front. I posted it on my bedroom wall, laid in a lot of colored map pins, and in much the same spirit as in following box scores, shifted them to match the news of discernible changes in the combatants' positions. All the while there was hell to pay in Galicia, in the Italian Alps, and so on; but for me the Great War was the trenches from Switzerland to the Channel. So when I came to read Ian Hay's *First Hundred Thousand* and *All in It*—ably written, utterly British, grimly amusing propaganda best-sellers nicely calculated to maintain morale at home and emotional support overseas—I was well prepared. I knew where Armentières was and still did some years ago when my wife and I visited World War I battlefields and their ancillary graveyards. Hay's books were far better than their rivals, such as Arthur Guy Empey's *Over the Top*; but I read them too. Good British humor—and Hay's had quality—has a way of persisting. I remember with great relish all about Private M'Splae's boots, the company on maneuvers that couldn't find Ghostly Bottom, and the shortcomings of field telephones.

Thus my awareness of Armageddon grew more or less in sync with that of older Americans through 1916 and Wilson's "He kept us out of war!" By then sheet music counters were thick with "It's a Long Way to Tipperary / The Song They Sing as They March Along" with a three-color Highlander in full uniform, kilt, sporran, pipes, and all. The administration's Preparedness program was doing a good deal to soften up popular reluctance to contemplate having to wage war. There were Preparedness parades and much attention paid Colonel Leonard Wood's Plattsburgh training camp for affluent volunteers readying themselves for not impossible commissions. The Indianapolis school system did its bit with a children's tribute to the Stars and Stripes at Washington Park. In preparation the whole population of Number Forty-five mustered daily in the gym for a calisthenics drill not with Indian clubs but with small flags—up, down, swirl, cross one way, cross the other way, swirl again—to march tunes on the piano. Then on the great day, boys in white shirts and blue knickerbockers, girls in white dresses, we were herded on chartered streetcars to the ballpark to line up on cross-barred chalk lines among thousands of our peers to do it all over again for admiring parents in the stands. A nice change from school; only it was hot out there near second base.

A mere mass flag drill was nothing compared to what overtook us when actual war was declared. What passed for education was subordinated to war-related doings. Encouraging us to plant "war gardens" made some sense. So did chivying us into selling War Savings Stamps to neighbors and relatives. For the rest of it, however, I suppose the purpose was to keep up war-mindedness in the households we lived in as we came home gabbling about our war activities. Quite possibly some of the socks the girls knitted proved useful on belligerent feet. But setting boys to knitting woolen scarves and squares to be assembled into blankets must have been largely a waste of scarce raw material. Certainly all I ever accomplished was to turn a ball of perfectly good yarn into a grayish tangle. Our teachers' efforts to keep us abreast of fighting in Palestine, the Balkans, and Russia—it was the year of the February and October Revolutions—as well as the Western Front and the Atlantic sea-lanes, were almost as fruitless for them as for us. They lacked the requisite background and so did most of the rewrite men on the newspapers they relied on.

Again the music was the best part of it. We were not, I am glad to say, asked to sing "Just a baby's prayer at twilight / For her daddy over there" or "Hello, Central give me No-Man's-Land." But the songbook in the desk was closed in favor of not only "Tipperary" but such other highly singable British imports as "Pack Up Your Troubles in Your Old Kit Bag," "The Long, Long Trail," and "Till We Meet Again." The domestic product, led by George M. Cohan's rousing "Over There," also included Irving Berlin's "Oh, How I Hate to Get Up in the Morning," "Oh Boy, Oh Joy, Where Do We Go from Here?"* and a tuneful tribute to Jonah Vark. I liked all those, and "Long Boy," a less popular number about a hayseed volunteer bidding his folks and the family mule good-bye

---

*Not a war song in origin, but like "Tipperary," so popular with the troops that it got embedded in the war songbook, maybe because of its reference to "a Jersey City pier."

and promising to bring home a kaiser or two as souvenirs even if he didn't know what the war was all about. ("Madelon" had to wait until demobilized brothers and cousins brought her over from France, along with assorted versions of "Mademoiselle from Armentières.") Those topical usurpers pretty well crowded out the nation's traditional patriotic numbers that one would have expected to be widely exploited. Instead we were taught an Englished version of "La Marseillaise," almost as difficult to sing as "The Star Spangled Banner." There was no thought, however, of playing up "Rule, Britannia."

German classes disappeared from the school system. The newspapers were recommending calling sauerkraut "liberty cabbage." In the boys' garment trade there was an epidemic of "trench buckles," that is, the rectangular clasps on the belts of British officers' waterproof "trench coats," a term that still survives among the TV spy set. The buckles proliferated on not only the belts of our overcoats but also on those of Norfolk suit jackets and useless straps across the tops of our peaked caps. They made us feel close participants in the Great War. Rather less widely girls and women took to berets like those of France's picturesque Chasseurs Alpins, a contingent of whom came over to tour the country with their Zouavelike drill carried out on the double. But the strangest side effect of all was that on the First Friends' Church.

The Quaker principle of categorical renunciation of war brought particular stress on Friends. Among the immediate family, if my father had doubts about the righteousness of belligerency against Germans, he kept them to himself. Uncle Joseph, a birthright Quaker, of course, volunteered ahead of the draft, I believe, anyway got into the army, was sent to France to train for intelligence work probably because he had spent some time in college, and wound up with a short stay in the stockade, why I'm not sure. Of other Furnases of military age Great-uncle Will's son Philip volunteered to drive an ambulance and did so inconspicuously but creditably in Macedonia. His brother Paul went the way of the conscientious objector on religious grounds. My father said nothing about that either. My mother deplored it, though it certainly was consistent with the teachings of the sect she had joined. Paul's case attracted the authorities' attention and approval from some liberal-minded spectators, but as far as I know he suffered no extreme penalties.

First Friends went far out of its way to countenance "the world's people" 's war. Conventional churches began displaying "service flags" of a white ground and red border with blue stars for members in the armed forces and gold stars for those dying there. Soon such a flag appeared behind our Quaker pulpit reasonably well starred. One of them was for our minister, Willard Trueblood. For, far from preaching Friends' anarchic reprehension of war, he took leave of absence to join the YMCA's auxiliary war service. I was there when he preached his leave-taking sermon all got up in the Y's quasi-military, forest-green uniform with Sam Browne belt, many buttons, and scarlet insignia. He looked handsome, but that would never have helped him in a Quaker meeting worthy of the name.

I think my parents had a long engagement. Had they married only a few years earlier I'd have been of military age in 1917 or 1918 and might well have enlisted, anyway been drafted. Not unlikely my lack of the qualities that make passable soldiers would have got me into the stockade; or I might have got killed. As it was I had to wait twenty-odd years for my war, and then the circumstances under which I saw it were not exacting. It may be disrespectful to say so, but I'm glad my parents weren't in a hurry.

Those of my generation may not need reminding that, on our side of the water anyway, World War I had a curiously anticlimactic ending. In mid-autumn 1918 the Western Front was obviously collapsing. So people were prepared for celebration when the United Press flashed it that all was over, the Germans had signed an armistice. Whooping crowds swarmed into the streets, men in uniform were smothered with kisses. . . . I saw nothing of it, only read about it after the fact, for my mother was not one for ecstatic exhibitions of civic hysteria. And she proved right, for the wrong reason. Immediate official denial of the story took the wind out of the demonstration's sails just as it was going good. False alarm. The United Press had treated as fact a probability so high that the temptation to score a beat had been irresistible. Two days later the genuine thing actually did come to pass. This time my mother poked my father into cranking up the Pathfinder and taking

us children downtown to witness history. It was fun—cars slowly
nosing through heedless, singing and shouting crowds, horns
honking, flags waving . . . but those who had been in the previous hullabaloo complained patronizingly that it lacked that
first fine careless rapture.

During World War II I made the acquaintance of the late
Frank Taylor, newspaperman turned eminent magazine reporter, who, as a young staffer for the United Press in Brest,
had had a principal hand in sending that jump-the-gun flash.
We became friends, but I never risked asking him what was
the most momentous bulletin he ever filed.

6

Learning in Limbo

SHORTRIDGE HIGH SCHOOL was named for a
Hoosier educationist-creator of the state's school system. I
learned that long after leaving home. In my time nobody connected with the place ever spoke of him or even speculated as
to what the name was all about. The ornamental escutcheons
on the balcony rail of the school's auditorium carried a mon-
ogram, "CM," because officially it was "Caleb Mills Hall." But
who or what Caleb Mills had been was never gone into; we
knew it only as "the auditorium." In its uncomfortable seats
during lunch periods Charlie Yott, a squatty and scruffy classmate, introduced me to the basic dirty stories.

Shortridge's nearest thing to a tutelary spirit was a grisly
green plaster statue of James Whitcomb Riley, "the Hoosier
Poet," rather like an incredibly bad Rodin. Its creator was Mrs.
Myra Richards, Indianapolis's sculptress-laureate; her son
Wallace Richards was a sharp and genial classmate who eventually had a large hand in building the New Deal's experimental Greenbelt model town and later in Pittsburgh's Golden
Triangle scheme. Riley had never got beyond plaster, one heard,
because his admirers who commissioned the job ran out of
money before he attained marble or bronze; so Mrs. Richards
found him weatherproof asylum in the New Building near the
entrance to the gym. For other statuary the school had only
gigantic plaster casts of Apollo Belvedere and Diana-with-a-
stag in the study hall; there were white scars where the beige
plaster had chipped and fly specks showed up shamelessly. Ri-

103

ley's lack of charm and those Olympians' insipid squalor may account for my inability to appreciate most of the sculpture I have ever seen.

Besides Shortridge, flagship of the system, there was also Emmerich (who was he?) Manual Training High School, previously mentioned, and Arsenal Technical High School, so called because its core building was a converted Civil War arsenal. Manual had a sizable minority of black boys, no girls. Tech was oriented toward vocational courses. Shortridge too had a "commercial department" (typing, bookkeeping, shorthand) but emphasized its original liberal-arts aspect: English, math, history, and languages. Its enrollment was disproportionately female; at graduation my class of 334 was 68 percent girls. Though only a minority of us planned on college, by and large Shortridge was usually the choice of the college-bound.

Our New Building, locus of most of the noncommercial classes, was a three-story, wide-windowed brick box much like Number Forty-five. Its banal simplicity contrasted sharply with the Old Building's mansarded tower, carved entrances, and ranges of high-shouldered, splay-framed windows that had close affinity with the Marion County Courthouse downtown and the Indiana State Insane Asylum to the west. All were sooty examples of the exotic Second Empire pretentiousness that trendy architects and greedy contractors had foisted on America fifty years previously. On my first sight of the Louvre I was right back home. Maybe for some years after completion those gussied-up tributes to bad taste and graft stayed clean enough to look worth the money. But by my time between weather and bituminous coal smoke the fuzzy, charcoal-gray coating over red brick and white limestone was so thick that it must seriously have hampered the job of demolition.

Withinsides the Old Building's wooden floors were precariously uneven and splintery beyond belief, its staircases ominously creaky, its narrow windows inadequate for natural lighting. Yet the old derelict had its place as historical token of our grandparents' time, when public high schools were innovative tokens of civic pride, their teachers were called "professor," their curricula, however near the elementary, allowing little or no elective nonsense; when even in cities so small a proportion of the young attended high school that its diploma carried social as well as academic leverage. Appropriately the Old Building and its upstart consort stood within the mile square of the original city plan. But city-center decay was already ominous in the seediness of nearby shops and dwellings. Undertakers and automobile dealers were taking over the spacious private mansions lining the near-downtown segments of Meridian and Pennsylvania streets. Only a few years after my graduation misguided civic enterprise demolished most of that area to create a huge War Memorial Plaza and built a new Shortridge two miles north in what was then the silk-stocking part of town, right opposite Great-uncle Rob's red-brick, tree-embowered mansion on North Pennsylvania.

A mere handful of my Number Forty-five classmates entered Shortridge in that February 1919. I saw little of any of them in this demanding new environment. The chief formal difference was that instead of one teacher handling all subjects, pupils migrated from one specialized teacher to another up stairs or down, whenever the bell rang on the hour. A grotesque but striking novelty was the basketball fever reaching its height in March soon after I entered. Johnny Hennessy, the eventual Davis Cup player, was a star forward. At the "sectional" tournament at Tomlinson Hall I, as neophyte freshman, first experienced something exuberantly collective—cheerleaders, school colors in pennants and sweaters, institutionalized mass enthusiasm. It was ungodly stimulating and I swallowed it whole.

Another mass strangeness was nowhere near as attractive—the, for God's sake, ROTC. World War I was barely three months over. Toward its close the War Department's training and indoctrination program for potential officers in college had extended into high schools because, I suppose, the more youngsters with some notion of the manual of arms and military courtesy, the better. And the thing persisted after the Armistice partly, for a guess, because postwar chaos still left a chance that fighting would recur; and partly because it provided occupation for officers not yet demobilized and a use for the immense surplus of olive-drab uniforms. Or maybe it was just that nobody had got round to calling high school ROTC off. Anyway, as a freshman each boy was issued a four-dinted campaign hat, two woolen shirts, a high-collared woolen tunic, a pair of woolen breeches, spiral puttees, and lump-toed army boots. Only the boots fit; we were kids, not full-grown recruits. Most of us wore our uniform only on drill days, and reluctantly then, for the hook-and-eye collars of the tunics dug into our tender chins; the shirts itched; the puttees, nuisances imitating the British, who had borrowed them from the benighted Hindu, were always coming embarrassingly unwound. A few of us, however, wore our uniform daily: the gung-ho types bucking to become cadet officers, and some whose parents' resources were so slim that daily use of free clothes was welcome. Nobody paid attention, still less commented, when Private X of B Company was seldom seen out of olive-drab. At high school age was some tincture of considerate manners seeping in?

For a couple of hours several days a week North Street between Pennsylvania and Meridian was roped off for maneuvers of the Shortridge ROTC at very weak battalion strength. Eventually we could creditably juggle our Springfield rifles through to "Port . . . *arms!*" from "Order . . . *arms!*" the slings whacking in unison against the stocks in a distinctly military manner. In close-order drill "Squads . . . *left!*" was not too fumbly, but we never quite got the hang of "Squads . . . *right!*" for, if I remember correctly, number two in the rear rank had to about-face, which I still don't understand, nor at the time did number two. Our officer-instructors changed from time to time as discharges caught up with them. I remember only a tall, pale, sad-faced Captain Willoughby who had been at Vladivostok (he did his best with us, though obviously bored); and a beefy Old Army sergeant right out of *What Price Glory*, temporarily promoted to lieutenant, who did his best to chew us out without using his native profanity, which was strictly forbidden.

More clearly I recall the corporal of my squad, Jabez Wood, grandson of the retired professor of divinity at local Butler College, one of the best friends I ever had—long-nosed, gray-eyed, instinctively shrewd. He took the ROTC program as something that had to be humored but with a minimum of fuss, like having your hair cut. On warm spring days, when the shirts were itchy and squad drill montonous, he would march us with due briskness into the shade of a distant building or tree and fall us out until authority approached; then he snapped us to in style enough to stand scrutiny. Sophomore year we were advanced into rifle practice in a range improvised in the Old Building basement. My marksmanship with a .22 bolt action on a Springfield stock was not improved by the sergeant's insisting that I aim righthanded, which meant sighting with my unreliably lazy right eye.

That is all the soldiering I ever did. It had one eventual dividend. Twenty-five years later, when I was a correspondent observing real soldiers in a real war, I had to wear a uniform that at some distance or in a bad light gave the illusion that I was an officer; so now and again I got saluted. It minimized mutual embarrassment that I could respond with the smartly snapped-off hand salute that I learned on North Street in 1919.

If junior high schools then existed, Indianapolis was unaware of it. It was freshman, sophomore, junior, senior, and out. Boys went in knickerbockered, shifting into long trousers as juniors; the blurring of age groups that puts preteens into longs had not yet come in. Simultaneously girls grew subtler in outline. Today's adolescents will not believe how high was the between-sexes wall on school premises, never mind what might go on outside—where, in today's terms, as a matter of fact, relatively little did. Any boy who walked down a corridor in Shortridge merely holding hands with a girl might just as well have kept right on walking out the front door, never bothering to return.

The best I can say for the place as an institution of learning is that it was somewhat better than Number Forty-five. Above the commercial department the curriculum was a misguided imitation of the mixture of required and optional courses then prevailing in colleges. We all had to take one or another number of courses in English, math (elementary algebra and plane geometry), American history, and, I think, a year of some elementary science. The rest of the time we chose optional subjects: music (playing in the orchestra under a puffy second-generation German); advanced algebra, solid geometry; Spanish, French, Latin, Greek . . . no German, for Luther's and Goethe's mother tongue disappeared from all our schools in 1917. A scattering among these presumably rounded

out the justification for the certificate granted at commencement that admitted one to most of the available colleges.

History was so poorly taught that, though I must have passed
it with high marks, else I'd never have been on the senior
"honor roll," the mere sound of "Compromise of 1850" still
revolts me. As to English our middle-aged-to-elderly women
teachers marked up our compositions more or less compe-
tently for spelling and punctuation, but their grasp of the language was as flabby as the literary materials presented. Had I
not already steeped myself in worthwhile reading, English as
Shortridge handled it would have put me off literature for
life. The prim, brown-bound anthology representing poetry
consisted largely of the more watery examples of Whittier,
Longfellow, Bryant, and Poe. It took me years to discover that
even those poetical Old Men of the Sea could occasionally sing
true and juicy; in that anthology about the only hint of such a
thing was "Skipper Ireson's Ride." In prose the item I most
resented was probably George William Curtis's "The Public Duty
of Educated Men."

Our Shakespeare was *Julius Caesar,* of course. Walter Dith-
mer (as Cassius) and I (as Brutus) were set enacting the quar-
rel scene before the class. Walter (his family owned the principal
ice plant) was a feisty Cassius. How my Brutus went I cannot
say, but most of his remarks have stuck in my head, and I
pored over the funeral scene until the bulk of Mark Antony's
speech has stuck too. That was nourishing stuff. So was *Mar-
mion,* which I absorbed so devotedly that even now, though I
haven't seen a copy of it for sixty-odd years, I can still spout
The Douglas's outraged farewell to his tactless guest. "The Pied
Piper of Hamelin" and Holmes's "One-Hoss Shay," privately
encountered, had already taught me that narrative verse could
hold plenty of possibilities; but the net result of school-admin-
istered poetry was to convince me that lyric and didactic verse
were necessarily, inevitably blah—a word that I then lacked
but would have welcomed. That highly erroneous judgment
was an understandable consequence of "The Deserted Schoolhouse," "The Village Blacksmith," and "Annabel Lee."

Shortridge's mathematics was not much better than Number Forty-five's. The purpose of algebra, whatever it may be,
was not gone into, nor yet any meaning it may have; how were

we to discern it on our own? For us algebra consisted of applying arbitrary formulae to artificial fictions about A's and B's
commercial and personal doings. Maybe a budding Leibnitz
would have divined the wider implications of it all, but none
of us was such a genius. So I still think of that multilayered
rigmarole for solving quadratic equations, learned by heart and
applied with no notion of what it was all about, not as a subtle
distillation of beautifully complicated relationships but as a gigantic typographical error gone mad. What makes a quadratic
equation quadratic or of what quadraticness consists was not
explained; maybe it can't be, I wouldn't know. Geometry was
better, for the reasoning behind demonstrations was out in the
open and the language employed was nearer human terms.
Euclid spoke in sentences and recognizable words; whereas to
the end, though I passed College Board math with flying colors, to me "ay" meant primarily not the interplay of two different quantities, a and y, but what a Scot said instead of yes;
and "ax" was nothing of greater abstract significance than the
name of the tool one fells a tree with.

I'd blame myself more for such numbness had any of the
three math teachers Shortridge afforded me shown apprecia-
tion of the alleged wonders and beauties of their subject. That
those several ladies (oddly enough, they were all women, one
brusquely clear about geometry, one sour and fuzzy about elementary algebra, one good-natured about advanced algebra)
failed to do so may mean that nobody had bothered to open
those vistas for them either. Had anybody tried, however, would
they have caught on? Toward the end of our tour of plane
geometry I strayed into the appendix of the textbook, which
was out of bounds, and came on *geometric* diagrams embodying the notorious facts that $(a+x)^2 = a^2 + 2ax + x^2$, while
$(a-x)^2 = a^2 - 2ax + x^2$. There it was, suddenly validated, comprehensible and yet abstract, expressing eternal relations among
a universal range of particular quantities and gratifyingly enabled to do so because suddenly freed from the clog of using
word-related symbols to convey nonverbal concepts. For maybe
thirty seconds I verged on feeling what mathematics might be
like. But it was no vision on the road to Damascus. Those glories could never have been my pidgin. My poor, puny flash of
enlightenment was mercifully suppressed. Miss Martha Hunt,

best of the three mistresses of math, strongly advised me to stop solving certain algebraic problems by concentration and dead reckoning—it can be done in some simple cases—and instead follow the formulae in the book.

As to living alien tongues, I had a semester of what was alleged to be elementary French taught by a blithe young woman in her late twenties who may have been exposed somewhere to the idiom of Molière and Alexandre Dumas but actually knew little more of it than can be acquired by two hours concentrating on the back pages of a tourist's phrase book. I am clever with languages (on the printed page), yet I came out of that fraud on the taxpayers barely able to guess what "Le garçon est sorti" might mean. The dead languages, however, were solidly if not inspiringly taught by a tall, handsome, middle-aged spinster, Miss Ella Marthens. If she relished the stylistic subtleties of Cicero and Vergil, she failed to convey it to others. For her "the stateliest measure ever molded by the lips of man" was just an exercise in grammar, syntax, and vocabulary. But her sense of language structure was sound and so was her persistence in inveigling an uninterested class into getting the hang of it. If it had to be got by rote, as in that list of prepositions illogically foisting the dative on compound verbs—I still know it: ad, ante, con, de, in, inter, ob—she saw to it that you not only learned it, you could apply it. She could even convey the natures of *zeugma*, *hendiadys*, and *oxymoron*. I'm weak on them now, but I wasn't then; and came out well enough in scansion to clear the hazard when the College Board sneakily rang in a dactylic line on the 1923 comprehensive exam. Thanks to her I can still wrestle my way through passages of classical Latin. In high school, of course, I was unaware that this getting inside the bones of a different, highly organized language—which Latin forces one to do—would be invaluable when word juggling in a disparate and simpler idiom would be my meal ticket. I only wish I had done myself the favor of allowing Shortridge to equip me with elementary Greek, which Miss Marthens also taught.

Number Forty-five had had nothing that satisfactory. Better still was Shortridge's science. Physics inhabited a laboratory-equipped room on the second floor of the Old Building as fusty and glum as the twitchy, elderly misfit who taught it.

But chemistry and biology had wide-windowed, uncluttered quarters high in the New Building and were enlightening to match. My chemistry came under Frank Wade, a transplanted Yankee (and member of First Friends' meeting) whose zest for the simplest experiments and what they meant was contagious. Indeed his approach to basic chemistry taught certain aspects of physics better than Mr. Clements did at the other end of the school. Wade led a class into discovering Boyle's Law as if for the first time. Incidentally he had a (I hope) profitable sideline of validating precious stones for local jewelers and occasionally fished up from where his suspenders met his waistband little packets containing some thousands of dollars worth of rubies, emeralds, or whatever with which he demonstrated the critical differences between natural and synthetic gems. I had no impulse to go scientific. It was just as well. My laboratory partner—Hiram Stout, years later a lieutenant colonel in the Office of Strategic Services (OSS) and then a professor of international relations—and I broke so much glass that our bill was the highest in the school's history. But the feel of science—its inquisitive harmonies, always losing focus, always groping toward another—was richly implicit in much of what went on in Shortridge's chem lab.

Elementary botany was also well taught by tall, fair, no-nonsense Miss Allardyce with the help of an unusually lucid textbook by somebody named Coulter. Between them one never lost sight of the truth that xylem and phloem, gametophytes and cotyledons, were not just engineering but interreacting parts of something alive. Zoology—which I eschewed because the prospect of dissecting frogs put me off—was the province of strong-minded Miss McClellan, chief of the biology department, who ran a taut ship without making it restive. The biology lab had pupil-assistants handling the aquarium, preparing slides, collecting specimens, and so on. Several of them—Howard Howe and Stanley Grey, for instance—made distinguished careers in medicine and biology. Around them (the team changed every year or two) clung a small group of boys—a few girls took biology but had no part in this—for whom under Miss Mac's shrewd auspices the lab was an informal club of which, discounting the local odor of dead-fish-informalin, I became a sort of associate member. Thus I encountered youngsters, only a year or two my elder, not only as bright as I was but also knowing more than I did about things that interested me. An unprecedented experience neither shocking nor disconcerting. And even better, the club drew me into a beginning of social adjustments that I needed.

My other hangout was the school print shop. Work on the school newspaper gave me access to its low-ceilinged seclusion. Shortridge's *Daily Echo* was a local pride, for few high schools had a daily and the commonsense judgment that no such thing was needed was never made. Publication on each of the five school days was managed by five separate staffs, one for each day, each with an editor, several staffers, and a faculty member candidly called a censor, who saw all copy before it went downstairs. Toward the end of junior year, when I was well used to long pants, I took over editorship of the Thursday *Echo,* which I had joined when still in knickerbockers. Why Thursday I don't recall; maybe because I had a good opinion of Miss Garber, the other chemistry teacher, its censor. I stand by my judgment that whereas until then Thursday's *Echo* had ranked below Dorothy McCullough's Tuesday and Herman Carrington's Wednesday, my management and energy, for I supplied three fourths of the copy, soon had it best of the five. My only frictions with Miss Garber came of the sometimes indecorous—how faintly indecorous!—cuts that I sometimes borrowed through a former Shortridgeite from the University of Wisconsin's undergraduate comic magazine. I didn't resent Miss Garber's ejecting the dubious ones. I knew that to print anything that she thought gamy would get her as well as me into trouble, and that if anything did slip past her, Mr. McKee, my very good friend in the print shop, would catch on. I wish I could recall some of the half-witted japes that she rejected. But all that comes back to me is the ghost of a grin with which, peering at me over her glasses, she would say: "Oh, no! No."

The horizontal-slot windows of the basement print shop were so grimy that electric light was needed, whatever the weather outside. Its equipment would today be hustled off to an industrial museum: massive waist-high tables encasing stones on which the steel frames of type were made up, a flatbed press, racks of various fonts of type awaiting the compositor's nimble fingers. Its only concessions to less archaic technology

were the electricity powering the press and the linotype machine that, though hand setting still had a place, set up most
of the jobs. Its reservoir of molten type metal kept the place
smelling like wash day; and the linotyper, whose name I forget, was harsh and unsavory to match. Mr. McKee was a dia-
metric contrast. Over seventy-odd years and two thirds of the
inhabited world I never met a kindlier person. Elderly, pink-
ish-plump in the face, hair scantily gray, movements slow but
well organized, speech slow but clear and laconic, seeming always about to smile but never quite that demonstrative about
the goodwill sustaining him as the heartbeat sustains an organ-
ism . . .

Every year he had to break in another cadre of five pupil-
editors to the juggling of headlines and makeup. He did it
with few words and no wasted motion. I, however, was the
only editor who, without explicit arrangement, spent much
spare time in the shop, doing odd studying, or just sitting and
pondering things, or holding proof for Mr. McKee—the shop
did some of the school system's printing—or hung at his elbow
while his wooden mallet hammered the quoins into a form, or
watched as he cajoled the press out of threatening to break
down. He never tried to involve me in anything mechanical,
sensing shrewdly that I lacked the requisite handiness. But when
I was editing the yearbook of the Class of 1922 I became a
sort of harassed production assistant as he and I struggled to
get the damn thing out in spite of lagging photoengravers and
the senile head of the art department. My reason for dwelling
on this is that, though we spent whole hours together without
exchanging a word, here was an adult *other person,* no kin of
mine, not imposed on me (or vice versa) by blood relation or
institutional function, spontaneously accepting me as a welcome entity in my own right. It was a gentle initiation into the
generalized human race.

The debating society, which regularly sent three-boy teams
to compete with well-known high schools elsewhere on one or
another "Resolved that . . . ," was coached by the rotund head
of the English department. Mr. Otto was as easygoing as he
looked but also had an able sense of logic. Elementary though
high school debating necessarily is, some of its structural requirements stayed with me usefully, and, in any case, im-

promptu rebuttals were valuable experience in rising on one's
hind legs in hopes of making sense out loud. I seldom make
speeches, but when I must, I always burn a candle for Mr.
Otto, shabbily dilute as his English department was.

Note that, except in science, all Shortridge's pluses were
extracurricular. The *Echo*, basketball fever, the sociable biology group—all were stimuli superior to anything at Number
Forty-five, true. But none of these resulted from the academic
facilities that Shortridge was built and staffed to supply.

Fortunately for my stumbly future I was soon in a manner
of speaking moonlighting at a better school, at least one that
supplied better cultural provender. After Number Forty-five
my sister went to Tudor Hall, the local high-chinned private
school that prepared girls for the august women's colleges in
the Northeast. Its school uniform was the "Peter Thompson"—navy blue worsted skirt and middy blouse with a white
dickey and a man-of-war-style black silk scarf, the whole provided at considerable expense by an eastern house of that name
holding a quasi monopoly on dressing the pupils of such
schools.* I recall little else about the place, which is ungrateful, for I owe much to its required textbooks brought home
by my sister.

For instance, a bulky ancient history rich in entertaining
and informative linecuts: "Fig. 32: Portrait-statue of fifth-dy-
nasty village headman"; Fig. 193: "Wine shop in Pompeii." The
text, though clumpy, opened vistas of long-vanished polities
and quarrels that struck me as more pungent than anything
that Mr. Muller, Shortridge's walrus-mustached fumbler at

---

*Firm and uniforms are probably now extinct, but they lasted at least into the 1930s.
For at that time I had dealings with the circus manager who had recruited those
giraffe-necked Burmese women who cut so odd a figure on the Ringling and Hag-
enbeck-Wallace posters—remember? He wintered them not at the regular winter
headquarters but for some reason, probably shady, in the attic of his house at Buck-
ingham, Pennsylvania, along with the male consorts (with normal necks) whom he
had recruited to keep the girls happy. They found the climate chilly until his wife
bought them Peter Thompson outfits at Wanamaker's, in which they went through
the winter as pseudo-able seamen in the Royal Navy; for that black scarf, which the
young U.S. Navy borrowed, betokened mourning for Lord Nelson. He had no photographs of them in that rig-out, which was a pity. They passed the time, he said, well
enough once he supplied them with plenty of chewing tobacco (in place of their accustomed betel nut), Four Roses whiskey, and playing cards. If I remember correctly,
hearts was their favorite game.

American history, ever worked up about the Mayflower Compact or the Gadsden Purchase. Still more fruitful was Tudor Hall's required *Golden Treasury.* Dips into it at the age of fifteen cured me of my low opinion of lyric verse. First to breach the barrier was Ben Jonson's hymn from *Cynthia's Revels:* "Queen and huntress, chaste and fair, / Now the sun is laid to sleep." Nothing like that in Miss Zelda O'Hare's classroom in the New Building. I now know anthologies far superior to the Reverend Francis Palgrave's. But in no currency could I ever repay him for arranging my passport to pure joy the more delightful because I was sulkily unprepared for it.

At about the same time my distaste for didactic verse was shaken by a paper company's advertisement in the *Century* magazine. The ad was a tasteful piece of "institutional" display—a simple black-and-white imitation of a Persian illumination of languishing, harem-style women accompanied by, boldly lettered, "I sometimes think that never blows so red / The rose as where some buried Caesar bled . . ." with attribution to Omar Khayyám, of whom I was only vaguely aware as source of a tag about verses underneath a bough. The way the thirty-one words of that quatrain jumped off the page into my spinal marrow made me buy the first book I ever spent my own money on—a skinny, brown-bound, murkily illustrated edition of FitzGerald's final and richest version, that miracle of inevitable monosyllables, pregnant rhyme, and insidious, hedonistic dismay. Once my dislike of significant discourse in verse vanished, my way was straight into "Dover Beach" and Shakespeare's sonnets. And to this day a spinal tap would show a dangerously high level of FitzGerald's Omar.

Then prose weighed in with effects just as durable. Noting Robert Louis Stevenson's admiration for a French writer named Montaigne, I bought for my sister's birthday one of those bad-paper, red-bound A. L. Burt editions: Montaigne's *Essays* in the Cotton translation. She found it unrewarding and neglected it. I retrieved and explored it and was captivated. That very volume, rather the worse for wear, is still on one of my shelves. The shrewd, pithy, leisurely voice of that marvelous text—I can read the original but, not being a Frenchman, can't believe it is any better—was part of the enchantment and still is. There was equal joy in the educational effect of the old gentleman's subtleties, as cogent as Omar's and of wider range. It is a pretty irony that I, who abominate translations as by definition distorting, misleading, and tending to corrupt the style of writers exposed to them, should owe so much to those two momentous translations. Lord mend the taste of those seeing in FitzGerald's Omar mere unctuous clichés or a sort of poetical Norman Rockwell in print. It was unnecessary for me to learn the thing by heart—a mistaken phrase, for if the heart is in it to the extent mine was, schoolroom- or greenroom-fashion memorizing has no place. To this day when I am shaving or spading those quatrains will come running through my head by the clustered dozen as wonderful as they were when Warren G. Harding had just been inaugurated. And what mind I have still floats in the "Apology for Raimond de Sébonde" as a moored lighter floats on an incoming tide, seeming to breathe and mutter.

Back to Shortridge as environment: Its ancillary facilities were either less than primitive makeshifts or nonexistent. No lockers. Hats and coats hung in the corridors, one's permanent desk in one's assigned "session room" took small stuff. No vocational or curricular counseling. It had not occurred to anybody that such solicitude might be advisable. The library was visible only as a hutch looking into the study hall and a squeaky little woman handing out assigned books on request. No reference books in the open, no pupil access to shelves of further reading. The gym had some equipment of the parallel bars–flying rings sort, but nobody ever used them, for basketball and track monopolized the place. In my senior year football, suppressed around 1910 during a national spasm of agitation against it as brutally dangerous, was reinstated. The squad had to practice on a vacant lot three miles away by streetcar and play scheduled games Fridays on the Butler College field just as far away in another direction.

Most of us boys would have been delighted to be deprived of what normal schools called phys ed. Gestures in that direction were made, however. The weedy young fellow paid to do us good regardless had no proper place to do it in. In bad weather he could only fall us in, forty or so at a time, in a large, stuffy basement room for elementary calisthenics, that dullest of human activities. Come spring he added a few track-and-field events—hundred-yard dash, shotput, high jump, broad jump—seeking not track-squad material but a gauge of our fitness. On a concrete sidewalk in shirt sleeves and street shoes I did the hundred in 11.4 much to my surprise; I think he punched the stopwatch a thought too soon. Between that and an impressive chest expansion my average of attainments was high enough to spare me remedial ordeals. But trouble awaited. We did our jumping in a graveled courtyard, landing not in the conventional sand pit but on thick-padded gymnasium mats. Somebody left a gap of a few inches between two mats.

My third or fourth high jump landed my right foot on that gap; it buckled disastrously. Today a school nurse would have recommended an orthopedist. No school nurse, and Mr. Phys Ed, seeing me limping away, merely told me to sit out the rest of the hour's program. In a week I could walk normally, but whatever happened to the small bones in that foot, it never altogether came right; to this day my right shoe sole develops a hole before the left does, and if I give it my attention, as I do while writing this, I can feel the faint beginning of twinginess. Sloppy place, Shortridge. As souvenir of it I prefer my memory of the print shop and Mr. McKee and the clank-whack, clank-whack, clank-whack of the old flatbed press.

The end of senior year meant commencement in Tomlinson Hall, boys in blue suits, girls in white dresses. The foolishness of graduating high school pupils in pseudo-mortarboards and gowns had not yet taken hold. Unlike most of my classmates I was not going straight on to college. Destined to take the College Board examinations required by the most respected northeastern colleges, I was advised to have another year of preparation—a tacit acknowledgment that Shortridge did not adequately fit pupils for such places. Pupils of private preparatory schools were allowed to take a group of exams each school year while Cicero or the Pythagorean proposition, were fresh in mind, gradually shaping a record admitting to Yale or Smith. Public high school pupils aspiring to such august colleges of the Ivy League or the Seven Sisters (both those labels are new since my time) were at much greater risk, committed to sudden-death "comprehensive" exams at the end of senior year covering several years' work in English, three years of Latin, geometry, advanced algebra in terms stiffer than anything Shortridge ever set. The other way was to enter a reasonably well-regarded college that admitted on certificate from well-regarded high schools and get freshman marks good enough for transfer into the sophomore class at Princeton, say, taking the place of a freshman who had flunked out. Unaware of that dodge, I stayed on for eight more months of low-key postgraduate cramming from teachers I already knew, plus desultory nibbling at odd electives, all dull, only one ever of any use to me—a semester of elementary bookkeeping. It was just as well I waited a year. I was only sixteen, not even beginning to dry behind the ears.

Most of the boys I knew went off to college, so I no longer had the society I had come to value, and my sister was gone to Vassar. Yet I could lunch with a few genial acquaintances at Powers' grocery across the alley or the drugstore at Pennsylvania and Market, home of excellent fried pork tenderloin on a bun; and Mr. McKee let me haunt the shop as much as ever. Largely because Wally Richards engineered it *faute de mieux,* I became president of the Corpse Club, the highest-ranked of the stupid little imitations of college fraternities that then infested large high schools and for all I know still do. Its chief purposes were shooting crap for small change—lack of capital kept me out of that—whacking aspirants with rolled-up *Saturday Evening Posts,* and giving an annual dance. The dance under my auspices was a gate-crasher-ruined catastrophe. I was also developing a knack of self-occupation. Extending my foothold in botany, I went prowling the world of trees, identifying as far as I could the diffidently varying varieties of black oaks and hickories, photographing bark, leaf, winter twig, habit of growth. No purpose in mind, just that I was interested. I remain an amateur of trees. Early in our marriage I found my wife looking at me with round-eyed respect when she said casually that that was a strange-looking tree a hundred yards away in a field we were passing and I, scarcely glancing at it, said "Hackberry."

And reading was and still is a prime, lone satisfaction. The Indianapolis Public Library, a stately new affair of authentic

Doric columns in Bedford stone, was near Shortridge. My father's spinster cousin, Marcia Furnas, was librarian. Spying me, she would nod at me brightly but never went into what I was browsing from. Had she breached Quaker reticence to do so, it might well have discouraged me. For I knew better than to let my addiction to reading show. Though it could not be concealed in my grandparents' and the Blues' households, they let it go charitably unremarked, and my sister and I talked books seldom. My friends, some of them close in a teen-agerish way, would have shied from such talk as a suspect aberration like taking voice lessons or teaching a Sunday School class. It recently amazed me to read in one of Malcolm Cowley's autobiographies how he and cronies in a Pittsburgh high school only a few years before my time at Shortridge eagerly talked Ibsen, Shaw, and Miniver Cheevy. In Indianapolis, which certainly thought itself more of a literary center than Pittsburgh, the brightest youth (as I knew them) didn't discuss even the Tom Swift books that were probably the extent of their voluntary reading. If there were dozens of crypto-bookworms like me, their protective disguises were even better than mine.

At the end of that postgraduate year, which worked out as a valuable cutting-off layer, came those stiff comprehensive College Board exams. I wrote them with a specially bought massive, orange-barreled fountain pen that Waterman had made fashionable.* Maybe the clumsy thing was good luck. It was early June and hellish hot, and maybe the exam readers were touched by the effect as of tears dropped on my bluebook pages—actually caused by sweat plopping off my nose. Maybe I owed something to the way Ivy League colleges were then self-consciously—and gingerly—seeking freshmen from sources other than the established prep schools and big-city private schools whence their students customarily came. Whatever the why of it, Harvard and Yale both accepted me.

The city editor of the *Indianapolis News* had offered me a

---

*In French class at Harvard, Mr. Herrick took grave exception to the number of such pens cropping up in class; he said one might as well try to write with the end of a policeman's nightstick. Mine has survived in a desk drawer, corroded beyond use. Not long ago the proprietor of a small hotel in Wales showed me his collection of antique fountain pens, including two specimens of this model. When I said I had one at home he offered me twenty pounds for it. No sale.

reporter's job on an upstate paper that the *News* owned. I thought I had better get past Harvard's door before the green light changed. I did not mention my refusal to my mother, but she most likely would have agreed with my decision—for different reasons, no doubt. Sometimes I wish I had had a couple of years' newspapering before I entered college. But that is unsound. I then lacked—to a considerable extent I still lack—the kind of savvy (an outmoded term, but there is no exact current equivalent) that city-room reporters need. On regular beats I'd have been a diffident failure and come home after a few months at loose ends—which would have been my fault, not the paper's, but not good for me anyway. In 1923 I was unfit even for the kind of reporting that I eventually did well for magazines. I lacked several kinds of shaping when, not yet eighteen, I boarded the Southwestern Limited at Indianapolis's Union Station, destination Boston and Cambridge. My temperament was cartilaginous, my fontenelle still visibly throbbed.

7

Alma Stepmater

HAD THE PRESIDENT and Fellows of Harvard University been aware of why I chose Harvard over Yale they'd have thought me frivolous. Indianapolis rated Yale higher partly because Johnny Joss, a hulking local patrician a few years my senior, went there via an eastern prep school and made the starting football lineup. About all I knew of Harvard was a popular boys' book about prep school football, *The Crimson Sweater* by Ralph Henry Barbour, that took the place very seriously. My choice had nothing to do with athletics. The sheaf of information accompanying Harvard's notice of acceptance said under some such heading as "Qualifications for the Degree of Bachelor of Arts" that one could substitute a year of philosophy for the year of mathematics otherwise required— a concession that Yale did not match. My distaste for what had passed for math at Shortridge told heavily. Any math courses that Yale provided for working off such a requirement were bound to be for me either inappropriately esoteric or drearily sterile. Philosophy, stuffy as it sounded, was undeniably preferable.

It was indeed. Harvard's undergraduate survey course in philosophy was rewardingly taught by Raphael Demos, already a remarkable and eventually a distinguished ornament of the department. He was good as well as intelligent. I have forgiven him for the farewell he tendered me. Suitcase in hand, as New York–bound graduate, I met him on Massachusetts Avenue. "You're on your way," he said. "Yes, sir." "You've learned one thing well," he said. "How not to work." I had no reply. He had reason for that severity (see later) and was unaware of extenuating circumstances.* But he was wrong. That was only one of dozens of things, few palatable but some highly so, that I had assimilated on Alma Mater's bony knee.

A few years ago I renewed acquaintance with Bill Wilson, a classmate whom I'd lost touch with, and unprompted he said what I had been thinking in the interval: "After Harvard, no later experience can shake or surprise you." The old lady may have weakened lately, I gather, but in Wilson's and my time she paid no heed to mutterings and squeakings under unnecessary stress. She behaved like not an Alma but a Magna Mater arbitrarily imposing mutilation and no more to be questioned than Job's Lord God. One felt that to consider dismantling or even modifying her would be as rash as melting the Arctic ice cap. Recall that TV commercial in which a tall, gaunt, elderly lady in Isadora Duncanish cheesecloth came on stagily intoning: "It isn't wise to fool with Mother Nature!" That is how I picture my Yankee preceptress.

Until then, as aforesaid, my New England had been all hearsay through Little Rollo, Miss Alcott, and "Snowbound." And I had hardly been anywhere outside Indiana except for a winter in Florida at the age of ten, visits to a Chicago suburb, and a summer in Des Moines. Such meager preparation may have heightened the outlandish effect of what swept past the windows as the train rushed beyond Albany. Eastport to Greenwich that impression has never left me. I have since been in Sierra Leone, the Palaus, Managua, Antikya, Paramaribo, North Bay, Kumasi, just recently St. Helena. As in the old song, I hope to travel more. But no such out-of-the-way place can give me so deep a feeling of immersion in alien dimensions as my first sight of Springfield, Massachusetts, did. And the subsequent scenery along the B&A right-of-way, all boulders and runty trees, was bare and pinched, a fitting complement to the gray-slovenly "three-decker" tenements that made so many New England towns look both smug and almost as dreary as Chicago's West Side.

---

*I learned recently that a while later, when there was an effort to get me a teaching job in some boys' school—which, thank God, came to nothing—he wrote a letter unreservedly recommending me.

My first trial of the Boston subway added misgivings. I asked a seedy, nervous Bostonian where to get off for a certain objective. After a frozen pause he made up his mind to risk speaking with a stranger and uttered oracularly, still reluctant to look at me, what sounded like "skuulyskwe-eh"—obviously a Finnish expletive—and hastily moved away. After some months of contact with Bostonese I divined that he had referred me to Scollay Square station. By then I was also aware that a dropped egg meant poached, a spa was a soda fountain, and carbonated soft drinks (I never had the courage to try the one named Moxie)* were collectively tonic. I have always had a dull ear for foreign languages. But might my inability to savor the virtues of the more thickly settled parts of New England be geographical/genetic? For so far as I know no ancestor of mine ever settled north of Manhattan Island. Nonsense, yes. But that such a thing ever entered my head shows how uneasy that part of the world made me, and still does. Consider, for instance, that among the good friends I made at college, where Yankees were out and away the largest group, only two were born east of Greenwich—and one of those was something of a maverick.

Add the slight churlishness of my first personal contact with Harvard. I had been accepted on condition that I arrive just before the academic year began for an oral examination in science—botany in my case—and show proof of competent laboratory work. By corollary if I failed either hurdle I could go ignominiously home again, an expensive eighteen-hundred-mile round trip. If a science exam was indicated, why wasn't it included in that series of sudden-death exams of the previous June? Cambridge looked dour and prim as I trudged to the Peabody Museum to seek out the indicated instructor in botany. He looked perfunctorily through my lab notebooks, ascertained that I knew what photosynthesis was and was sound on tropisms; and signed the certificate of proficiency. The whole arrangement had that lack of empathetic imagination that I grew so familiar with in the next several years.

Filing the certificate at University Hall floated me into full

---

*The hundredth anniversary of the creation of Moxie was celebrated in 1984 in Lisbon Falls, Maine. Like several other persisting "tonics" it was first concocted as a patient medicine for the nerves. One of the celebrants recommended it to alcoholics as killing the taste for booze (*New York Times,* July 16, 1984).

acceptance—and another of Alma Mater's inconsiderate bun-
glings. The new-built Freshman Halls on the Charlesbank were
meant to house all freshmen to create a mutually fertile com-
radeship.* How that worked out I never knew firsthand because more freshmen had been admitted than the halls had
room for. Assignment of quarters therein was theoretically first
come, first served modified by lot drawing and variations in
cost but no doubt further affected by the private leverage that,
unless the place has greatly changed, still shows how human
Alma Mater is. Freshmen from private schools, the large majority whose names had been on application lists for years, filled
the new halls, and the minority from high schools were mostly
squeezed out. For them, scattered accommodations in odd
University premises, or any private arrangements they cared
to make.

This tended to foster a caste system reflecting the Harvard
of final clubs and Gold Coast dormitories—see Owen Wister's
Philosophy Four and Charles Flandrau's *Harvard Episodes* and
Diary of a Freshman—what the Freshman Halls system was set
up to undermine. For thus to segregate the private school group
from the high school group, dispersing the latter round town,
tended toward a two-tier society. Indeed three-tier, for there
were also several dozen "commuters"—high school products
unable to afford quarters in Cambridge at all, living at home
in Boston or some three-decker suburb and subwaying back
and forth six days a week with book bag or briefcase and
sometimes lunchbox.† Most, not all, were Jewish, and with less
excuse from ethnic pressures, Alma Mater was, almost by definition, as unthinkingly anti-Semitic as the Boston she floated
on or the New York City of that day. The commuters typically
suffered under the illusion that, since Harvard was known as

---

*A decade or so later, when Harvard installed the "house system" emulating the Ox-
bridge colleges grouped within a university, the freshman halls became nuclei of separate "houses." They still look much the same, however. A classmate of mine took his
mid-teens son to Cambridge for the first time and showed him that array of white
cupolas—as though Massachusetts and Harvard Halls had mated and had triplets
afflicted with gigantism—and the boy said: "Why, Pop, it looks just like Howard Johnson's." *

†In his autobiography, *In Search of History*, the late Theodore H. White calls the three
tiers of his time, the mid-1930s, "white men, gray men and meatballs" (p. 34). He
identified himself as a meatball. His account sounds as if the "gray men" were more
numerous than in my day and more of them were upwardly mobile.

a distinguished institution of learning, one went there to learn all one could. They did so, outdoing practically all their nominal classmates and seemed content—italicize *seemed*—to have everybody but their instructors look right through them. We of the middle tier, however, were allowed, not too graciously, upward mobility in certain contexts, provided we had the talent, enterprise, and luck to cope.

One prevalent description of the place, taking account of its complexity and harsher traits, called it a spontaneous microcosm, a sort of spring practice fitting us for what we would encounter in the varsity season in the wider world beyond college; and there was something in it. The alternate description, not inconsistent with the first but woefully lyrical, was that at Harvard one became blithely acquainted with "the best that the past has thought and done." Those accepting that formula set great store by the inscription over one of the gates to the Yard: "Enter, to grow in wisdom." Or, in a good many cases, in savvy.

Correspondence during the summer made it clear that there was no room for me in the freshman halls. Tom Howe, a Shortridge friend in his sophomore year at Harvard, was to room with a transfer from Indianapolis in commodious quarters in Randolph Hall. I gratefully accepted his suggestion that I bunk with them. Randolph was one of the former Gold Coast dormitories on Mount Auburn Street that Harvard had recently taken over in another measure toward cozier relations among undergraduates. Those former nests of privilege had been built by private enterprise for sons of families able to pay high rents—hence "Gold Coast." The fanciest was Westmorly Hall, a pseudo-Tudor affair with a swimming pool in which, legend said, plausibly enough, Ann Pennington, half-pint, dimple-kneed darling of Ziegfeld shows, had once had a midnight dip. The whole complex, though now blended into "houses," still looks like an imitation of the decayed glories of New York's Riverside Drive, lacking only entrance awnings and doormen; even those synthetic, unkeyed labels—Westmorly, Randolph, Claverly—carried out the pretentious motif. Its now neutralized vulgarity contrasts with the wildly eclectic and yet austere character of the Yard only a five-minute walk away.

The Yard is dominated, functionally as well as visually, by Widener Library, that vast powerhouse without smokestacks. Its colonnade and stony cataract of steps remain almost as imposingly grim as, off to its right, the brooding scowl of Sever Hall, H. H. Richardson's early masterpiece that annually casts a shadow on participants and spectators at commencement. No doubt its lecture halls still enable the bulk of undergraduates to feel at least three times a week the emotional trauma of that overwide, underlofty entrance archway whence (as I wrote elsewhere) one expects to see a suicide's funeral emerge, stake and sledgehammer at the ready.

Just beyond the Yard in my time Memorial Hall, Harvard's monument to alumni killed in the Civil War, still had the great tower's wedge-shaped upper element that burned away a while ago and was not replaced—out of thrift, I suppose, not for aesthetic reasons, for nothing could alter the daunting ugliness of that Germanic pseudo-Gothic. The Yard's elder quadrangle, however, was then and remains as charming as its chief entranceway, the Johnston Gate between Harvard and Massachusetts Halls like Darby and Joan on either side of the hearth. The elder dormitories—Hollis, Stoughton, and Holworthy—may look like mere barracks, but after all, mass housing for groups of young men is what they were built for almost three hundred years ago, and the bricks have aged well; and across from them Charles Bulfinch's pilastered University Hall is as elegant as a Gilbert Stuart portrait. In front of it Daniel Chester French's seated statue of John Harvard—idealized, that is, utterly fictional—is equivocal. His attitude has a doubtless unintentional slump as though he were glad to sit down after viewing the irresponsible colossus that came of his bequest. Maybe that is why this capable example of Beaux Arts sculpture never became the symbol of either college or university; indeed Harvard has no such thing.

The point, however, is that not even the cotton-mill look of Thayer Hall's ranges of windows can seriously dilute the handsome dignity of the area. Only we freshmen had little truck with it. We entered University Hall only at the instance of the authorities. Most of our academic affairs centered in the Widener quadrangle, where only the great trees were gracious and for five months in the year even they were gauntly,

damply blackened and leafless. Harvard has succeeded probably better than any other university in inadvertently creating
an architectural museum, an edifyingly wide array of the mistakes of the past and a few of its triumphs. None could wish
the place otherwise, but in the 1920s at least it was a remarkably dismal environment on the whole. Under the night's sneaky
rain the snow melted into dirty slush. The slippery duckboards gave the effect of an abandoned construction site. The
bell of Harvard Hall came in querulous and muffled by the
damp air as if reluctantly tolling for an unpopular member of
the Board of Overseers; and it was still a quarter mile to the
New Lecture Hall. Under those conditions it was particularly
depressing hurriedly to glimpse those brownish-yellowy terracotta panels set into the face of Sever.

But the Harvard building memory of which most offends
me, was that housing the official swimming pool. In its day no
doubt it was a model of how such things were designed. The
swimming teams trained therein may well have covered themselves with glory, though, if they did, nobody paid any attention. Like the Hemenway Gymnasium and the Appleton Chapel,
this edifice of evil omen was named after its donor, I think,
but for reasons that would be obvious to any psychiatrist, I
cannot recall his name. For I loathed the damn place as the
locus of one of Alma Mater's most irksome breaches of common sense.

A hundred and more years ago well-meaning persons persuaded leading American colleges that *mens sana in corpore sano*
entailed athletics for all, no longer improvised by the boys
themselves but organized, supervised, and financed by their
preceptors. That was the misbegotten seed that sprouted into
the absurdities of intercollegiate football. Intramurally it led
Harvard and sister colleges into also setting up playing fields
for baseball, lacrosse, track and field; tennis courts; boathouses on the Charlesbank; an elaborate gymnasium, squash
courts—and the pool aforesaid. To make sure that no undergraduate inhabited a *corpus insanum*, every freshman was required to partake in some formal sport several times a week;
and a rigid requirement for a degree was to satisfy the swimming coach that one could swim fifty yards. The first could be
got round as one learned one's way; the second was another

matter. And ineffably asinine. A body could be as *sanum* as Gene Tunney's without ever having swum a stroke. Nor was there any conceivable connection between swimming and the attainments to which *baccalaureus in artibus* was supposed to apply. And why fifty yards? Too little to be of practical use in most emergencies.

Whatever it may be like now, Harvard was then, like many other societies, a place where a well-accepted person operating on behalf of the well connected could finagle practically anything, so the swimming requirement may have been got round now and again. Recently, however, my belief that I had been well advised to take it seriously was confirmed by a newspaper story showing that in the 1920s another Alma Mater had stuck sternly to it. In 1983 Dr. Mortimer Adler, pillar of conventional scholarship, augustly learned founder of the Great Books program, was finally, at the age of seventy-eight, getting his B.A. from Columbia. He had earned it sixty years earlier but had been unable to pass Columbia's swimming requirement. In view of what happened to him, only the rueful good nature of the Harvard swimming coach ever enabled me to hang on my office wall that bit of clumpy Latin certifying my admission to what Mr. Lowell called "the society of educated men." *Cum laude.* I hope they gave Adler a *summa*.*

That coach did his level best for me. Not caring to discourage him, I gave no warning of what he was up against. In Florida nine years earlier a startlingly sunburned Swedish swimming teacher had done all he could to earn what my mother paid him on my behalf. He failed because some degree of relaxation when immersed in water is necessary in swimming, let alone in floating on one's back, a feat for me as unthinkable as levitation. My vasomotor apparatus and epidermal tissues invariably combine in a simultaneous revolution against my getting wet all over. I drink water, shave with it, bathe in it. Heating it helps some but even so it takes resolution to apply that clammy, slippery stuff to my skin with or

---

Harvard magazine (Sept.–Oct. 1985, 10) carried a much later parallel: Roy Glauber, a brilliant physicist at the age of eighteen, was snatched out of the college to play a topnotch role in the Manhattan Project. On returning to Harvard after the war he took a few courses for fill-in credits for his S.B.; and learned it would be withheld until he passed his long-deferred swimming test.

without soap. There is an allergy to water, but this isn't it. Nor is it fear. Heavy weather at sea is one of my greatest delights. I can even grit my teeth, dive into a pool of reasonable length as the best way to get the ordeal over with, and fight my way to soundings at the other end. But it is about as much of a pleasure as sigmoidoscopy, which I don't fear but do find hellish unpleasant.

That Swede tried the breaststroke on me, then sidestroke, but both require relaxation. The Harvard coach got only slightly better results with the overhand crawl. Normally strong in the arms, I could reach forward, grab the water, and haul myself along vigorously enough to keep head and shoulders out and make floundery progress. I could hang on to the rim of the pool as instructed and frogkick or thresh my legs up and down like a bad child in a tantrum. But physiologically I so loathed the circumambient water that to coordinate arms and kicks was impossible because I could not relax. Once I cast off, my legs were no more use than if they were paralyzed. Since I have always been shortwinded, by the time I had threshed my way to the far end I was licked, could only climb out and sit there miserably, frustratedly dripping.

After weeks of that the coach contemplated me in that condition one afternoon and said something like: "Oh hell, I'll sign that certificate anyway." Kindhearted realism like that was rare *chez* Alma Mater. That same year, I heard, he had another such problem curiously solved: A classmate, even worse off than I, couldn't function at all in the pool, just struggled and sank. Somebody in the psychology department—the great William MacDougall?—heard of it and volunteered to hypnotize him. Given subliminal instructions, under hypnosis he swam like a porpoise. Snapped out from the influence, he gargled and went under. Yet while under hypnosis he had fulfilled the requirement. He was home free. Somebody should have rubbed the old lady's nose in that absurdity.

So the very sight of the swimming-pool building depressed me. Otherwise why Harvard's physical plant did so I don't understand as well. Nobody from Indianapolis, which John Gunther once ranked as the worst house-kept city in the country, had reason to take wintry grime so hard. Yankee slush was no worse to look at and walk in than Hoosier slush. But even now, when I find myself in Cambridge, I feel as I used to when getting the first whiffs of the dank, darkish, fungoid odor of the far reaches of my grandmother's cellar. It is unbecoming thus to be numb to the nostalgia recently recommended by the dean of the Princeton graduate schools: "Our student years constitute the paradise that all of us, first by geography and later by age, inevitably lose" (*Key Reporter,* spring 1983). Paradise indeed!

My jangling relationship with Harvard was probably the chief, though not the exclusive, ingredient in my lifelong academiphobia. Many a university library has hospitably afforded me privileges indispensable for putting together my half dozen significant books. Several professors of this or that have been among my very good friends, and on request many more have helped me on one or another problem. I recognize the eclectic charms of certain Ivy League campuses and appreciate the didactic trendiness, past or current, of campuses built all of a piece. But most of that is conscientiously objective. Put me in the shadow of any Old Main or Jones Lecture Hall or South Laboratory, and down among my emotional juices stirs a sense of being coldly at odds with my surroundings—nothing personal, mere awareness that it is inconsistent with my well-being. The analogy would be a mild version of what a saltwater fish would feel if suddenly tossed into fresh water.

So far this could be a British writer's whining about how miserable he was at public school. Let me admit that certain Harvard buildings afforded me good things. Though I described Hollis Hall as a barrack—in 1775 it really served that purpose for some of Washington's men—I retain a valid affection for its gritty, vine-hung walls. Senior year I inhabited its top floor. At the time my personal life was more miserably complicated than it has ever been since. Maybe the old building and its eccentric amenities were part of whatever—besides luck, nothing so dignified as fortitude can have entered in— enabled me to hold on until the darkness lightened. The very doorway of the lefthand entry was stolidly sustaining. Yet to the practical eye what lay within was somewhat unsettling. The clean-scrubbed, bare old flooring, the shaky wooden stairs, mingled the calm of a venerable tombstone with a quirky defiance of common sense, for Hollis and its two pre-Revolutionary sisters were firetraps, with antique chimneys, open fireplaces freely used, and outdated electric wiring. Why Hollis had not burned to the ground long before Ralph Waldo Emerson roomed there as student is hard to understand. In my day the fire escapes consisted only of stout ropes with a loop at one end rove through pulleys at windows in each two-room suite. A yellowed card thumbtacked nearby advised one to seat himself in the loop, climb out the window, and slowly let himself down. Once, legend said, a tipsy undergraduate tried it. Halfway down he was hailed by a "yard cop" (one of the college's plainclothes security men): "Git off thet, you young fool! Them things ain't safe."

On a recent visit to Cambridge—professional, not nostalgic—I found Hollis modified. On the top floor the cards on the door of Number Twelve carried female names. The makeshift shower-and-crapper cubicles in the hallways were gone. But the most striking evidence that Alma Mater had pulled up her crimson socks was replacement of the wooden stairs by fireproof composition and steel. It was no longer quite so likely as it was in 1926–27 that a wayward wire with worn insulation would put an end to not only me but also the future editor of the *Neue Zeitung* (the newspaper of the American occupying forces in Germany); the future best chairman that the National Labor Relations Board ever had; a brilliant teacher in traditional boys' schools; the future public relations chief of the early United Nations; *and* Charles Townsend Copeland, Boylston Professor of Oratory and Rhetoric, whose perquisites were said to include not only free quarters on the top floor of Hollis but also the privilege of keeping a cow in the Yard.

That fire hazard had furnished "Copey" another legend: At one of the informal symposia that he held Thursday evenings it was suggested that when It happened, the Boston press would headline: "COPELAND A CRISP." "No," he said, "COPELAND CRISPER THAN EVER." Maybe apocryphal but *ben trovato*, for the old gentleman, across the corridor from whom Kendall Foss and I spent our senior year, was a chronic self-dramatizer, doing his best to be as peppery as he looked. He was stumpy, sparsely made, with a bristly gray mustache and a habitual air of suppressed exasperation. As soon as we had moved in, he led Foss and me into the crapper cubicle, pointed into the bowl, and asked in his hoarse baritone: "What does it say there?" We saw in spidery blue lettering on the porcelain: "NIAGARA." "And that," he said, "*that* is what it sounds like. Thursday evenings I have people in my rooms, sometimes ladies.Thursday evenings this apparatus is not to be activated."

The Thursdays usually centered round an eminent friend from among his wide acquaintance or a visitor to Boston with a letter from an alumnus-disciple. I recall an affable, plumply blond young Englishwoman whom he talked up in advance as early among women called to the British bar; so, of course, the evening's talk had nothing to do with law. Felix Frankfurter came once; the Sacco-Vanzetti row was just then nearing white heat, with him ardently working the bellows. Copey and he got warmly into whether the issue of their guilt or innocence was damaging their legal prospects by obscuring the wider issue of whether they had had a fair trial. My memory is turning up lawyers: Late that spring the focal guest was the illustrious federal judge, Julian Mack. Lindbergh had just flown the Atlantic. Mack listened to the babble about it for a while and said: "The best thing that could happen to that young man is that he tries to fly back and doesn't make it."

Copey's minor raison d'être was a half course on "Johnson and His Circle," nothing profound, one was given to understand. His major aspect was a famous course for hand-picked seniors in what would now be called, God help the phrase, "creative writing." He was innocently proud of the callow talent he had taken over the rhetorical hurdles: John Reed, T. S. Eliot, Heywood Broun, Robert Benchley are the first among many names that come to mind. Boston loved his occasional readings and every year he staged one in the Harvard Club of New York City that was a sort of festival for his Manhattan-based disciples. Very well he read too, texts ranging from the King James Version to Finley Peter Dunne's superb "Mr. Dooley" pieces.

Foss had qualified for the famous writing course and valued it as well as its mentor. Since I did not apply, I don't know whether I'd have been tapped. Anyway, I never knew personally what members of the course described as the ordeal of reading one's deathless prose aloud as Copey lay back in his chair in semidarkness and moaned pitiably when he found a passage specially dreadful. Only now and again did he brush me with the skirt of his garment by grunting at me scornfully about one of the reviews I did for the *Crimson Bookshelf*. If he ever wondered why I did not apply for his course, since I was obviously self-doomed to write, he never hinted it. That he took a fancy to me was evident in his bothering about me at all. Every few weeks he warned me that I could never keep a job because, incapable of getting up early, I'd always report late. I did not dispute the point. I knew several other reasons I'd never be a likely job keeper. When he got wind of my financial woes, this way-down-East yankee, whose academic stipend was nothing lavish in those penurious times before Almae Matres began to pay decently, backed me diffidently into a corner and said in a booming whisper that he had funds laid away and could help me. Most gratefully I refused the offer while considering it a compliment—not so much to me as to his embarrassed goodwill. Bless his memory. The she-undergraduates who may now inhabit those rooms probably know little or nothing about him. A pity. He was always delighted when a lady visited one of his Thursdays.

He showed to special advantage in relation to our two kittens. Foss brought them back from a Cape Cod weekend saying that the parietal rules there on the wall prohibited dogs but said nothing about cats. What an official ruling might have been we never knew because the engaging little things never came to higher attention. As nominal proctor of Hollis, Copey probably should have gone into the matter. He rather disliked them. When he came into our rooms, they tried to climb his trouser legs. But he only shook them off, saying: "Drat these little cats!" and stayed formally unaware of their presence. Mrs. Seibert, our calm, elderly "goody" (Harvardese for chambermaid), was also lax about them, probably because she was already numb to undergraduates' vagaries and the kittens were conscientiously clean, even painfully so. In early autumn, wood fires burned in our fireplace only often enough to leave a layer of wood ash admirable for a kitten latrine. They never made deposits anywhere else. As it grew colder, however, and fires were going much of the time, they dutifully persisted, when the urge came, in using the accustomed place regardless. Fire or not, they backed in until their high-held little tails were singeing, dropped the load, and scampered away into cooler climes.

Such devotion touched us and we provided the conventional box of dirt. When changing it was necessary, we went out with the fire shovel at two or three in the morning and skulked over to the president's house, the flower beds round which afforded the nearest fresh earth. This very nearly brought the kittens to official notice. One night we were spooning up dirt when along came Mr. Lowell returning late indeed from some doubtless lawful occasion. Moonlight made him utterly recognizable—ample mustache, bearlike gait, and all. We froze. He slowed up, studied us at some length but not hostilely, said: "Good evening, gentlemen," and let himself in at his own door. That, since I did not attend my own commencement to receive a diploma from his hands, was my only personal contact with A. Lawrence Lowell. In the ensuing sixty years harsh things were said about him for his major role in the decision of Governor Fuller's commission not to recommend a new trial for Sacco and Vanzetti. In my view that position was wrong. A new trial would have been socially salutary and consistent with justice and good law. But in his defense note that he refused to be pressured into firing Harold Laski for supporting the Boston police strike—and very late one moonlight night let Foss and me roll to the outfield.

The kittens sometimes played games with the squirrels that swarmed up the vines and made faces at them through the window glass. Neither party had anything to gain. It was just interspecies pattycake for the hell of it. As Christmas vacation loomed the problem of what to do with them was insoluble, so somebody, Mrs. Siebert, I think, found them a good home. Wherever that was, I suppose they told the neighbor cats about the hell-hot latrines at Harvard and their misplaced affection for the famous Professor Copeland.

A different grateful memory involves another building— the Fogg Museum, a semicircular white stone affair looking as though strayed from a plutocrats' cemetery but actually containing a commodious lecture hall and sundry earnest students of the fine arts. Now who was Fogg? We had no more notion than of who Hollis was. Name and all, the institution is now housed in an angular sprawl of functionalist architecture. In 1923, in contrast to today's rich collections, the original Fogg's exhibition gallery offered only a few devoutly gaudy Italian primitives; an unfinished Tintoretto; a typical Ribera depicting—whom else?—Saint Jerome; but also, to my lasting immense benefit, a good display of Dürer engravings that initiated me into a new kind of joy.

My initial interest was, of course, bookish. From *The Light That Failed* I knew James Thomson's eery celebration of Dürer's *Melencolia*. Now here she was with all her props about her and well worth study. What I was not prepared for was a dozen or so sister engravings right and left in that waist-high glass case—graphic astonishments of varying import but all marvelous just to look at. Spontaneously I became aware how far these were beyond mere illustrations of a saint's life or a biblical parable or a medieval allegory. What they represented had its own intrinsic interest, yes; but what mattered differently and more was the lines and patterns so cleanly and cunningly handled by a master craftsman that a fourth dimension came glimmering into reach. Heady stuff. Strangely, incomprehensibly, the *Coat of Arms with a Skull* was just as pregnant as *The Knight, Death and the Devil* or *The Prodigal Son*. The experience was not unlike what Chapman's Homer did to Keats.

Only that is too literary a reference. This was practically visceral. As I think back on it, it reminds me of Henry and the cheese. In Liberia thirty years ago my wife and I borrowed from the U.S. Information Service for a trip up to the French Guinea border a station wagon equipped with a lanky, well-meaning local driver named Henry. For the first day's lunch we had bought in one of Monrovia's lunatic trading stores some picnickish items including a tall can of that wonderful thick, corpse-white French asparagus and a wedge of some French cheese. At noon by a stifling African roadside we broke out our supplies and Henry his couple of sandwiches. The contrast being great, we shared. Henry didn't think much of the asparagus but the expression on his face when he took his first nip of his chunk of cheese! Obviously he had not only never met cheese before, he had never even heard there was such a thing. A new universe spread before him.

In parallel my delight on straying into the Fogg's little gallery was the greater because until then my experience with graphic arts had been insipid. On the 2200 block in Indianapolis, Art consisted of muddy-brown photographic prints of a narrow range of paintings then as widely popular as van Gogh's sunflowers would be a generation later. Our house had Sir Galahad, tall and narrow, by some pre-Raphaelite; a Murillo madonna; Mme. Quelqu'un and girl child (by Ingres?); and (pre-Raphaelite again) that voluptuous lady in swirling robes precariously perched on a globe, title: *The Harp of the World*. In the Blues' living room was a four-foot color lithograph of Guido Reni's *Aurora*. Every couple of years some upper grade at Number Forty-five was herded through the John Herron Art Institute (and who was John Herron?), a handsome building at Sixteenth Street and Talbot Avenue that housed a number of paintings of which I recall (this is very hazy) only a portrait of the inevitable James Whitcomb Riley; in those days Indianapolis made as much of him as Brussels does of the *mannequin-pis*. I recall more vividly another painting from this time: Millet's *Song of the Lark* in the Chicago Art Institute. It was the most acclaimed item at the Chicago World's Fair of 1893, which my mother, I think, attended. That accounted for the respectful awareness of it that led her to take us children to see it when we'd much rather have gone to the Lincoln Park Zoo. Nevertheless I distinctly recalled what it looked like the rest of my life, even the location where it was hung. It was a queer twinge to come across it during a visit to the institute many years later, significantly hung much less conspicuously.*

Indeed, until the Fogg took my graphic-arts virginity, so to speak, my only nonliterary aesthetic tingle had come from the marginal sketches in Ernest Thompson Seton's books about animals. Seton wrote fairly well and drew very well. I now discern the flagrant anthropomorphism in his stuff; but there was none of that in his quickly slashed-down draftsmanship—in, for instance, a certain frieze of young cottontail rabbits that

---

*Please do not take this paragraph as meaning I endorse taking elementary schoolchildren to even the richest art museums in a shuffling troop laboriously talked at. On that same visit I treated myself to ten minutes' eavesdropping on what a conscientious young woman was instilling into a couple of dozen ten-year-olds about *La Grande Jatte*. Ten minutes was all I could take before stealing shudderingly away.

was hard to look away from. They not only conveyed essence of rabbit, the whole sequence was artfully composed and the drawing sang a special song—not as full and clear as Dürer's *Young Hare*, which I met much later, but delightful. And in some ways the sense of walking on air that Dürer's *St. Jerome in His Cell* produced in me was a higher power of the impulse to keep on looking at Seton's rabbits. Those early tingles may account for my lasting fixation on black-and-white graphic art and relative coolness toward so many paintings that carry a heavy charge for those of wider tastes. Is my relish for color defective? Well, not totally numb. Many van Goghs set me doing nip-ups; and the Chicago Art Institute has an early Monet of the Gare St. Lazare that, given the proper opportunity, I'd risk stealing. Such limited grasp makes me miss a good deal. No help for it. I'd rather pore over certain Rubens drawings than stand dutifully before any Rubens painting I ever encountered.

Very likely the hormones of late adolescence had me sickening for the graphic version of lust of the eye; that is, I might well have come down with something of the sort had I never gone near the Fogg. Anyway my gratitude to it is the warmer because the effect of its Dürers was so different from its other share in my contact with Art. For in that Fogg lecture hall for eight months of my sophomore year, three hours a week, I endured Fine Arts I and II, survey courses that took one from Luxor to Blenheim Palace, Fayum portraits to Degas. Nothing nearer our own time, nothing outside the Western tradition, nothing at all about American painting, architecture, or whatever. Maybe the primary purpose was a mental skeletal structure for potential museum curators and art dealers, for in that context the Fogg was almost as much of a professional seminary as the Medical School in Brookline. In view of the stodgy content of those lectures the purpose may have been selective, Gideon fashion—if a student's interest in Art survived them his call and election were, as Calvinism would say, sure enough to make him worth training.

There was little outside reading. We were as limited as medieval students to taking incoherent notes on Mr. Chase's lectures on matters classical, then Mr. Edgell's on matters medieval-to-recent. A slide showing the Erechtheum, say, came on the screen, quivering shyly as the pointer shifted here and there and the voice made sure we'd spell *caryatid* correctly. Homework consisted of long immersion in a set of what were called, I believe, the Copley Prints—several hundred brown-soaked halftones from photographs of the chief cultural monuments to be dealt with—and memorizing identifications so that in the frequent quizzes "Donatello—Gattamalata" would leap to the mind when the stimulus flashed on the screen, the Pavlovian method. I owe to George Weller's *Not to Eat, Not for Love,* a rewarding novel about the Harvard of my time, the student of Fine Arts II who identified cathedrals by associating their labels with the various times of day shown on their photographed clocks.

We worked over those dismal prints exactly as medical students work over rattling off the bones of the foot. How impertinent a dreariness! All those artifacts, whether basilicas or Tanagra figures, were reduced or enlarged to the same size, which ruined the element of scale, crucial in architecture and important everywhere. Small heed was paid to the abiding virtue of picture or statue, nothing but embalmed data and stagnant patter about stylistic cross-influences. No time—and only marginal inclination—to relish the quizzical charm of that Gothic saint or the stately loveliness of the Greek woman adjusting her sandal. I recall only one living touch: When the screen showed Watteau's (or is it Boucher's?) *The Swing,* with the natty young swain peering up under the lady's skirt, one of the Gates boys (we were always seated alphabetically) next to me called it "Moses Looking at the Promised Land."

For another building of happy memory: Nobody could feel affection for the Widener Library. One might as well purr over the River Rouge steel plant. The main reading room was a desert of cumbrous tables, squatty chairs, and largely perfunctory study. Its Sargent murals idealizing World War I in pastel colors were difficult to reconcile with the Sargent of brilliant charcoal portraits and zestful landscapes. I was not allowed in the stacks until thirty years later. But for a minor part of that complicated institution I retain warm affection. On the right of the main doorway at the head of those vainglorious steps was the Farnsworth Room—a memorial to a cultivated and affluent alumnus containing his private library augmented into an ideal reading-for-its-own-sake collection. It was handsomely and thoughtfully arranged. Every few yards round the walls was a large leather chair with a good reading light. The carpeted floor favored quiet; conversation, sleeping, and smoking were forbidden. The fourth taboo was an inspiration: A gentleman's agreement *never* to use these books for reading connected with an academic course. That was so genially imaginative that I always assumed, and a thousand to one rightly, that it was the Farnsworths' notion, not Alma Mater's. One entered, sauntered up to a shelf, took down a volume, sampled, replaced it, sauntered on, took another, sampled, sank into a chair . . .

A chair was always available because there were never more than two or three enjoying the place. There I greedily prowled toward filling the gaps in my wildly spotty acquaintance with Anglo-American literature and the chief pillars of wisdom circa 1910: Samuel Butler as well as Swift, Thoreau as well as *The Golden Bough*, Shaw, Ibsen, the major Russians . . . If the miscellaneous mental and aesthetic loot that I carried away from college was an education, I owed it primarily to the Farnsworth Room with an assist credited to the admirable upstairs library of the Harvard Union, where smoking was allowed and to the best of my recollection no other undergraduate ever intruded.

But then the Union was another of those self-frustrating, bland attempts to use bricks and mortar to dilute the college's natural set toward a vague but real caste system. Henry Lee Higginson, plutocratic Brahmin, created this imposing structure as a club for the unclubbed, open to all. Its dining room had tolerable, reasonably priced food charged on the term bill. Earnest minor-league undergraduates served on its committees. One such booked outside speakers, some worth hearing—I recall Donald Ogden Stewart and Clarence Darrow—and drummed up audiences for them in the big room graced with Major Higginson's portrait.* Except for my enjoyment of that

---

*I recall being invited, I forget why, to don a black tie as one of three undergraduates to dine at the Union with Francis Brett Young before he lectured there. Now forgotten, he was a conspicuous British novelist touring the States under the hidden auspices of Thomas S. Lamont of J. P. Morgan & Co. to say good words for Mussolini and fascism; the Morgan firm lent the New Italy a lot of money. Unaware of Young's mission—I hope I'd have done it anyway—I outraged him by saying Americans would never take seriously anybody who looked the way Mussolini did in newsreels. Soon

handy library, his good intentions accomplished little. He got
much farther as founder of the Boston Symphony Orchestra.

On a visit to Cambridge a while ago I had a look inside the
Union. Now a dining hall for freshmen, I believe, it was teem-
ing with young folks of both sexes. They so bewildered me
that I forgot to go upstairs to see whether all those snuffy old
calf-bound books were still there. Probably not. I understand
that long since the Farnsworth Room has been dismantled and
its books distributed among undergraduates' house libraries.

In my time most of what most college students got out of
"higher education"—"lower education" was not a recognized
concept—came of "extracurricular activities." As to whether
this is still true I lack, thank God, direct experience. It held
then, not only in secondary schools of all stripes but also
throughout the range of colleges from Old Siwash to the Big
Three (Harvard, Yale, Princeton). The chief reagents were the
national Greek letter fraternities and among the Big Three
unaffiliated social clubs with equivalently invidious policies of
recruitment; student publications (newspaper, funny monthly,
literary monthly); football with its associated rituals; dramatic
society with an annual production; glee club touring alumni-
infested cities during Christmas vacation. The time and energy
expended in such contexts by all but the grimmest knowledge
seekers or low-profile drones or misfits were often worthwhile.
The participant usually thus acquired social skills and, more
important, cordial acquaintance among those whose fathers,
uncles, or elder brothers could steer him toward post-
commencement careers.

At Harvard optimum use of those advantages might logi-
cally lead to graduate study in the medical, law, or architecture schools. But in 1925 the typical purpose of the typical
prep-school product growing in wisdom by the Charlesbank
was to acquire or enhance social leverage resulting in a berth
on Wall Street or State Street. (The School of Business Administration across the river was already flourishing, but it was
dominated not by Harvard graduates but by ambitious B.A.'s

afterward I heard on unimpeachable authority that the Lamonts had found Young a
very difficult house guest in New York. He behaved, I was told, as though in a hotel
that wasn't run to suit him.

from lesser Almae Matres.) That frame of mind was taken for granted like the local custom of turning up the overcoat collar, to which I still automatically adhere. The presumed end product was my class's good-looking, genial, brisk-spoken opportunist of, as it turned out, great native ability who married the eminent Wall Streeter's daughter and wound up chairman of the board of the billion-dollar corporation. And it was student-created and student-maintained doings that had shaped him and many of my successful, if not quite altogether as much so, classmates.

Words-in-print were necessarily my means of lubrication and assimilation as far as it occurred. I entered the freshman competition for the news staff of the *Crimson*, printed every weekday in its squatty, untidy red-brick lair on a side street off Massachusetts Avenue. At the time the Boston press was excited about an engagement of the great Anna Pavlova's ballet troupe. I went into Boston and persuaded the stage doorman to give Madame a note seeking an interview for the Harvard paper. It worked. Gaunt and gracious, she bade me sit down and in a samovar-flavored accent asked what she could do for me. I said Harvard would like her opinion of the fox-trot, or maybe it was the Charleston. She gave it, making the most of what English she had at command and filled in with fluid yet trenchant gestures. Those I could not reproduce but even without the accent her explosive remarks made an amusing feature that went on the front page of the "Crime," as the *Crimson* was called, and should have got me off to a flying start in the competition.

Only it didn't. It was soon clear that for my and the paper's purposes I lacked both the old-boy connections needed for momentum and the productive legman's savvy and persistence. After a few inept weeks I dropped out. Next year I tried again for the editorial-page staff, which required only gift-of-gab-on-paper, and won election, acquiring a glass-bottom pewter mug with my name on it—what did become of it?—and a tiny gold inkwell and quill pen for my watch chain. In spite of the rise of wristwatches during World War I, most of us still carried pocket watches on chains spreading from lefthand to righthand lower vest pockets. The vest too was necessary; and practically always a hat.

The "Crime's" editorial board was as low-key as the news

side was gung-ho. Its chairman when I joined, Edward Aswell, eventually became a prominent editor-midwife at Harper and Brothers and then at McGraw-Hill, and managed to stay sane while riding herd on Thomas Wolfe's late career. Ed banned typewriters not because of the noise but because he believed that only longhand copy would have proper quality; that was hard on the linotypers as well as his staff. He was just as firm and earnest about the university's educational obligations and covered such matters himself, only occasionally asking one of us helpers to "take the page." That may not have been wholly egocentric; he doubtless sensed that none of us was a budding Walter Lippmann. In fact, when he was to graduate and a replacement was needed, lack of chairman talent was so obvious that Wilder Foote was borrowed from the newsroom—a good thing too, for Wilder was out and away the most intelligent Crimsonite of my time.

Of what I wrote when "taking the page" I recall only likening a hot debate on high about some scholastic detail to the dispute between Bigendians and Littlendians in Lilliput. That was about as far as the *Crimson* of those days carried disrespect. It was in the administration's pocket to a degree that today's campus hot shots would think incredible. True, my two classmates who successively held the president's post eventually became running dogs of Communism. But that took time. The Class of 1927's version of put-upon youth's response to the world's ills consisted not of mobbing the dean of the college but of shouting "Rinehart!" out of windows in the Yard when blood grew hot in springtime.*

Even during the months when I edited the book review supplement, a chore I enjoyed and performed well, my relations with the "Crime" were not close. Too many of its pellucidly promising youths were too aware of their potential. Both the news and the business departments tended to look past you as though sensing no immediate advantage from the conversation. In that respect knowing them was good preparation for the outside world. Of the *Lampoon* one could say only that

---

*In memory of a legendary undergraduate who, having no friends, made up for it by shouting his name up at his own window after dark to give an illusion of popularity. That singularly hardhearted bit is Harvard College's only persistent folklore.

it wasn't quite as abject as the run of campus funny magazines. Its staff had a good time in their queer Dutch-towered house on Mt. Auburn Street. It was as much club as publication, and the one mark it left on my time was a breach of football relations between Harvard and Princeton consequent on Lampy's charge that Princeton played dirty. The *Advocate* student magazine was literary showcase for short stories, verse, essays. It eschewed avant-garde trendiness. Its desultory pace and eclectic flavor naturally attracted the fumbling writer that I was. Walter Edmonds, a born writer who later had a wide audience, was its guiding spirit. Nobody else involved went on to leave the Muses much in his debt. But it did enable one to get frequently into print—for reasons I am still unclear about actual print is the writer's touchstone—and made me several good friends.

The leaders of those three publications belonged to the Signet Society, an undergraduate club of vaguely cultivated flavor where one lunched and sometimes supped enjoyably in a hair-down atmosphere cordially celebrated by George Santayana in an autographed copy of verses that, I understand, still hangs on a Signet wall. Annually twenty-eight juniors were elected; sporadically membership was accorded congenial members of the faculty. Stir in some articulate graduate student members and the place had comfortable traits. On request I send the Signet a modest upkeep contribution every year, but I do not attend its annual dinner, which is something of a Harvard institution of note. I wouldn't dare work the secret catch and enter that demure little clapboard house with the elaborate carving over the door. Too many ghosts inside.

The slim entry under my picture in the 1927 senior classbook says: "*Crimson, Advocate,* Liberal Club." That last was a conscientious, incoherent bundle of undergraduates, graduates, and certain faculty bent on taking social problems seriously but mostly submilitant about it. Every few weeks the members met for a formal luncheon at which some pertinent mover or shaker held forth by invitation. I particularly remember Margaret Sanger looking bleak and yet strangely girlish in her mid-forties, chirping away about bluenoses and birth control. Once for broad-mindedness with a tinge of sadism our guest was the chief of Boston's Watch & Ward Society, who extolled the beauties of censorship and then submitted to scornful badgering for half an hour of questions. Somehow or other through the Liberal Club Foss and I got into the arrangements for H. L. Mencken to be arrested on Boston Common for selling a copy of the *American Mercury* containing "Hatrack," a smirking short story about a tank-town prostitute. We went to see Alfred A. Knopf about it in his office in the now-demolished Heckscher Building. We came out still zealous but taken aback by his taste in shirts and ties. He was the first publisher I had ever seen; even then I suspected he was atypical.

Harvard and Boston shared cultural circulatory systems like inextricable Siamese twins. The petit-bourgeois and blue-collar, still dominantly Irish, risingly Italian, increasingly Greek populations of both Boston and Cambridge were understandably prejudiced against Harvard and vice versa.* Upper-stratum Boston, of course, Louisburg Square Boston still only slightly diluted by miscegenation with Fifth Avenue New York and Main Line Philadelphia, sent its sons to Harvard, counted on its undergraduates to dance with and eventually marry its daughters, left it money, dabbled in its intramural cabals, treated it respectfully in its special newspaper, the *Boston Transcript.* Most of that, however, touched only the final-club minority. For the run of the College, Boston was merely the locus, twenty minutes away for a dime in a subway turnstile, of amenities that Cambridge lacked, such as good eating and formal amusements.

The only paid-for food of positively enjoyable quality that I ever encountered in Cambridge was the poached—sorry, dropped—eggs on toasted corn bread that the Georgian Cafeteria had Sunday mornings. In town, Boston's famous Durgin Park steak-and-seafood house did not enchant me, though

---

*Legend told in the Yard in my time: Harvard undergraduate seduces South Boston Irish girl. On learning she is with child, he decides he must do right by her, knocks at her door, and is confronted by her large father in a red flannel undershirt, instantly hostile at the sight of this obviously alien patrician. The youngster explains his trouble and makes it clear he'll marry the girl. Father says we'll see about that, slams the door, and leaves him jittering on the doorstep. In a few minutes the door reopens; father says: "Be off with ye! We'd rather have a bastard in the family than a Harvard man."

its fish chowder had great virtues. I couldn't afford Locke-
Ober's, the traditional superchophouse tucked away on Winter Place but went there anyway once or twice a year because
it was worth being broke for a month. It was far less disastrous
and pretty tasty to walk the few miles into Boston over the
Mass Avenue bridge to the Athens, a second-floor Greek place
providing for less than a dollar four courses, ending with excellent Turkish—sorry, Greek—coffee. I learned to admire
baklava and how to do eggs Polita. At home my only experience with pasta had been stodgy macaroni and cheese. At a
cordial little Mezzogiorno-style place tucked in behind the
Trinity Place railroad station I learned about good spaghetti
and ravioli, minestrone, and the ramifications of antipasto. I
had my first beer in an old-timey speakeasy somewhere in the
Stuart Street area.

Probably even more nourishing was the Boston theater, for
both tryouts and road companies of Broadway successes were
rife. One of the finest evenings I ever spent in a theater was
the Boston showing of *Beggar on Horseback* with the New York
cast intact: Roland Young, Greta Nissen, Spring Byington,
George Barbier, Osgood Perkins. What a moment when Young,
just come out of his expressionist nightmare, hunched his
shoulders, flexed his wrists, looked down, and said: "Hello,
feet!" Behind footlights Boston had to be itself, of course. When
the Watch and Ward element were feeling militant, which they
often did, the chorus girls in musical comedy or revue had to
wear "fleshings"—skintight, opaque long johns to keep naked
thighs from offending. From well back in the balcony, however, that made no difference, and the dancing, comic turns,
and production numbers were not otherwise affected. The
major effect of this cultural timidity was to inhibit the appearance of such overheated items as *Desire Under the Elms* and
those on ticklish subjects such as *The Captive* and *The Green Bay
Tree*. (Yes, Virginia, scripts dealing with homosexuality really
were produced on the Broadway stage fifty-odd years ago.)
And one could work them in during vacations in New York.

Beyond that version of bread and circuses, Boston and I
had small affinity. When I first encountered W. S. Gilbert's
line about "The bloom on cold gravy" I thought, Aha! Boston!
Its renowned symphony orchestra meant nothing to me. That

was settled my freshman year when kind people took me to one of its concerts in Memorial Hall's Sanders Theatre. Lacking previous experience of such treats, I perceived only that what came out of all those fiddles and blow-in things was dismally like the shuddery bleatings of the First Friends' organ and that my seat was almost as uncomfortable as one of its pews. Every time the orchestra lapsed into silence I hoped its stint was finished. Not until the third pause did I deduce that it merely marked another installment of the first item on the program, and there was a great deal more to come. And so there was—much more. I derived far greater pleasure from the first-class roller coaster at Revere Beach, reached by a marvelous narrow-gauge railroad, five cents a trip from the East Boston ferry slip.

In New York a few years later I walked all over, relishing whatever I saw from Castle Garden to Grant's Tomb. In Boston I was aware only impatiently of Faneuil Hall and Kings Chapel when passing them incidentally. Though I have spent only six or seven months there in total over forty years, I can find my way round London fairly well. To this day in no more difficult Boston I get lost within five minutes of quitting the Common. When I forget you, O Back Bay and South Station, maybe my right hand will forget her cunning but no matter—it's the back of my *left* hand for you. The same failure of rapport, doubtless mostly my fault, got between me and Cambridge. Is Somerville north or east of the place where, in my time, the Washington Elm, what was left of it, still stood? I wouldn't know. Tomorrow I'd have to ask a passing student how to get from Harvard Square to the Peabody Museum, a walk I took thrice a week for four months for Mr. Mather's half course in elementary geology.

Academic sterility must not be overstated. I was no autodidact freak. There was great profit in, for instance, Mr. Herrick's double (five hours a week) course in French—a prime example of teacher-to-pupil, rub-their-noses-in-it-till-they-squeal instruction that fulfilled in one concentrated dose the requirement for a degree of "a reading knowledge of French or German." Its very existence, of course, betrayed that the schools preparing us for learning had not supplied adequate training.

I often scold myself for not having taken Herrick's sister

course in German, so I could read it as well as I do French. But the slipshod college sought only "elementary knowledge" of the alternate tongue, and the elementary German I took was feeble about the farther reaches of grammar and so scamped vocabulary that it didn't prepare one to read a German newspaper. So what good was it? Well, it gave paying jobs to graduate students in German. Apple-cheeked, shy Herr Wünsch, under whom I qualified with an A—the easiest I ever got—was a nice fellow whom one didn't grudge a livelihood. But all I carried away from his year of flimsy instruction was a passage from a textbook that, for no sane reason, stuck in my head: "Doktor Luther sass in seinem Zimmer auf dem Wartburg und übersetzet die Bibel. Das war dem Teufel gar nicht recht und er kamm das heilige Werk zu stören." If the genders in that are incorrect, blame Wünsch. Under Herrick I'd have come out knowing them cold even now.

He did that superb job in spite of heavy physical handicap. Not that he looked handicapped—tallish, brawny, light-stepping, aggressively squared shoulders, bristly gray hair, high color—essence of hearty-ascetic Yankee, the kind that scorns overcoats and strides along at five miles an hour breathing out steam like a locomotive in homespun jacket and mittens. But he had the disability worst for teaching languages—he was very deaf. Probably otosclerosis had come over him gradually after he began his academic career and he had refused to let it frustrate him. He had resorted to a high-powered version of the primitive hearing aid of the day—a headset like a wireless operator's and a battery-powered box microphone the size and weight of a desk dictionary. Holding it out as though it were a Geiger counter (anachronism! no such thing as yet), he skipped up and down the aisle; stopped at random to put the mike in one's face: "Mr. Furnas—*devoir* in the subjunctive!" then listened, sharp as a bird hunting worms, while Mr. Furnas plowed ahead silently cursing the French Academy for not bothering to clean up irregular verbs. The vocabularies he showered on us! He wouldn't let us use French-English dictionaries but instead made us work it out by the definitions in the *Petit Larousse Illustré*. And he made the mysteries of *pas, point, y, dont,* and *en* so stringently clear that one almost believed they aren't unnecessary nonsense.

How to *speak* and hear French got small attention, however. To begin with, his deafness made it difficult to detect and modify the way we butchered it. With thirty-odd in class, even five days a week left little time for refining the soft palate and the relation between tongue and teeth. And Alma Mater said nothing about French as medium of audible communication; *reading knowledge* was all she specified. Herrick had proper skill in (to borrow from the late Kenneth Roberts) swallowing an *r* and breathing it out through the nose. But in class he so conscientiously cut up phrase or sentence into wide-spaced monosyllables, to make sure we understood, that the basic tune and rhythm—the be-all and end-all of practical comprehension—were lost. I ran head-on into this failing the first time I visited France and every time since, an experience common among American travelers. Yet honor where it's due: We came out of his linguistic greenhouse fluently reading French—fiction, newspaper, history, or whatever—without needing a dictionary more often than every twenty pages. It was superb teaching as far as he could take it.

In early 1947 I had a queer occasion gratefully to recall Radio Herrick, as his more graceless pupils called him because of the mike and headphones: The French governor of Tahiti was a pleasant and cultivated man who did his courteous best to understand my halting discourse—he had very little English. But my inability to make much of his replies—always my trouble—kept our relations, though cordial, elementary. Aware I was a writer, he suggested I do a little piece for the government newspaper about why I came to Tahiti—in English and he'd have it translated into French. Though deathless prose was not likely to come of the scheme, I mistrusted what Haumant's French civil servant secretary, who thought he knew English, would do with it. Clumsily I conveyed it to Haumant that I'd write in French and he could correct it. Obviously reluctant—how could anybody who spoke French so lamely write it even passably?—he consented. I did some thousand words about the crucial position of Tahiti in the South Seas legend, poking polite fun at the contrast between its actual beauties and the literature about them, etc., etc. And, praise God and Herrick, Haumant objected to only one word—he said my usage of *superlatif* was improper. But he left it in, dropping a footnote: "Nous n'avons pas voulu enlever sa saveur anglo-saxonne au texte de M. Furnas." Thus was added the *Bulletin de*

Presse des Etablissements Français de l'Océanie (13 Mars 1947) to the *Christian Herald*, the *New Statesman*, the *American Scholar*, *Plain Talk*, the *Virginia Quarterly*, the *Fortnightly Review*, the original (humorous) *Life*, and the dozen or so standard American monthlies and weeklies of yesteryear in which, at one time or another and in an extraordinary variety of contexts, my by-line has appeared.

In further justice to Mme. Academe, I should acknowledge that the reading incident to literature courses could be profitable. Thus the survey course in English (for lack of better advice, that was my "field of concentration") called for dipping into Chaucer. I became an addict. "Restoration Drama" under Mr. Greenough*—a pillar of Yankee rectitude anomalously deep in Aphra Behn and Shadwell—took me into the shapely, nimble dialogue of Congreve and Farquhar. The great or anyway eminent Irving Babbitt's "Rousseau and Romanticism" set me reading the titular subject's works and so admiring the terse grace of *Le contrat social* that I tried translating it.

Chaucer, Congreve, Rousseau . . . whom did the courses in contemporary literature include? Nobody. There were no such courses. A conscientious, unadventurous student whose sphere of reference was confined to what Harvard prescribed could have taken a good degree without ever having heard of T. S. Eliot, James Joyce, Marcel Proust, or Ezra Pound. For back then—my juniors will find this hard to believe—only the well-ripened past was offered. Now, of course, the shoe is so far on the other foot that every other page in the *New York Times Book Review* deploys an eminent professor discussing hot-off-the-griddle novels as respectfully as if they were newly exhumed sequels to *War and Peace* and as knowingly as if he were a literary agent. He is as eager as Saint Paul's Athenians to discuss any arriving new thing. And his course on "The Symbolic Future of Psychodramatic Charisma" is a chief ornament of Limbo University's curriculum.

Improvement? Not necessarily. It tends to neglect an im-

---

*The absence of "professor" from this account of Harvard may puzzle today's audience. The place teemed with professors, of course, identified as such in the annual outline of courses; but to call a faculty member professor was taboo. Indeed to do so would probably have earned one expulsion from the class. From the dean of the college down to the lowliest section man, all faculty were Mr. I hope that is still true in the Yard.

portant academic function. A man from Mars—only now we know there aren't any—might perceive that the primary utility of courses in literature is to keep today's culture aware of and valuing its gorgeous literary past, for no other agency will. In this view, overingenious as most of the lectures, seminars, and controversies about Melville or John Donne may be, at least they are pretexts for getting students to read them. Only thus will most students come to do so. Conversely every hour of academic attention devoted to John Updike is wasteful super-erogation, for students likely to savor literature for its own sake will read such contemporary writers anyway, whereas their college years are probably their only opportunity to gain lit-erary perspective. That sounds pedantic. What it means, how-ever, is that one's enjoyment of Updike is wonderfully enhanced if one has already vastly enjoyed "The Pardoner's Tale" and *Barry Lyndon.*

Having thus identified nontrendiness as a commendable trait of Academe in my day, I resume complaining—this time about the lecture system. Nowadays, I believe, the rise of seminars has modified it. And dilute as seminars probably are, that must be all to the good. Even in the case of Mr. Babbitt, a racy lecturer, a week's study of his corrosive books on the etiology and morphology of romanticism acquaints one with every-thing to be got from listening to him for two or three hours a week for half a year. When he went red in the face belaboring Rousseau it made a good show but it went on too long.

In some instances, of course, lecturers supplied matter un-available in print or added special flavor to familiar ground. Mr. Haskins, half crippled by a stroke but pluckily scrawling key names and phrases on the blackboard in Harvard Hall, was himself an indispensable element in his rich, pithy excur-sions into obscure corners of medieval France. Mr. Lake's half course on the Old Testament drew heavy enrollments because his histrionic talent and profound but light-footed scholarship made for remarkable entertainment. It was heightened by his appearance: angular-lean, eagerly stooping, jacket half again too large; pale blue, slightly grimy necktie clinging to scrawny neck; and the kind of face that Cruikshank might have cre-ated for a middle-aged Grandfather Smallweed. Eventually he grew a beard, but it was no help. Yet his confident charm and elegant stage presence sublimated his looks and, a transplant from England, he spoke the clearest, most flexible English-English I ever heard. His rendering of the last chapter of Ecclesiastes was what sent me exploring that area of the Bible in a receptive frame of mind.

I should have taken his other half course in the New Testament. Actually I did better. A classmate and I so relished him that we walked all the way to the Divinity School after lunch three days a week for his "Early Christian History." In it his style was less free-swinging, but the materials were keenly organized and brilliantly expounded. Later, when sharing an apartment with his son in New York, I came to know him personally and mentioned I had taken that course. He asked what I thought of it. I went into how much I'd enjoyed it, so he administered to me my first martini and showed me how to broil a steak French-fashion. I particularly remember him lying on our disreputable sofa whooping with joy over the pungencies of *Variety*, which, being on the fringes of show business, I always had around.

A few such exceptions could not reconcile me to lectures from lesser men repeating—indeed usually rereading—things they had been remumbling for years. Taking notes was advisable only because it was well to hand back at exam time the lecturer's limp notions. The meagerness of one's notes contrasting with the multiplication of page after page on the lectern showed to what little purpose one's time went down the drain. Occasional attempts to sparkle were usually ill advised; Lakes did not grow on every tree. The renowned George Lyman Kittredge, Harvard's august Shakespearean, tried too hard: a superb white beard; tweeds well tailored but too nattily pressed; a showy habit of pacing the platform, taking a piece of chalk from the blackboard ledge, breaking it into bits, and when reversing direction, tossing a bit across into the metal wastebasket—*clink!*—talking all the while. He never missed. He would hold forth vigorously until the first *bong* of the hour bell, then leap from the rostrum and lope up the center aisle finishing his sentence over his shoulder. It was not only silly, that bit of chalk meant distraction that was poor showmanship. I stayed away from his famous courses on Shakespeare. I needed no more of an elderly show-off who had the gall to contend—seriously—that Falstaff must have been brave at bottom, else he wouldn't have been funny. Such ingenuity was worse than forced, it was wrongheaded.

At least he laid down his law with energy and coherence. Much other lecturing was slack and watery. To complete my required year of science I took a half course in paleontology. The subject can be rewarding; but not as expounded by the pudgy man who stood there—it's significant that his name escapes me—droning away about implausible creatures with outlandish pseudo-Greek names. After some weeks of him I took full advantages of the Dean's List—a B average entitled one to cutting ad lib—and the Peabody Museum knew me no more until exam time. The night before I boned up in a couple of textbooks as shamelessly as though I were used to settling for a "gentleman's C" and passed going away. That is, in nine or ten hours of intense application, I learned enough of what would otherwise have taken some fifty hours of somniferous verbal dawdling.

A disinclination to get out of bed in time for an early class grew on me. No elective course that met before 10:00 A.M. could expect my patronage. That criterion drew no protest from my elders and betters because I had practically nothing to do with Harvard's then newish tutorial system. This was another symptom of the crypto-Anglophilia that had the College planning "houses" imitating the colleges of Oxbridge and smilingly deferring to prep schools imitating British public schools. It assigned each undergraduate a tutor from among minor faculty in his field of concentration to advise him in choosing courses, midwife him through difficulties with research or college rules, suggest special reading, discuss his work one-on-one, and if he looked promising, steer him toward going out for "distinction"—through arduous and more closely supervised study.

How it worked in my time I cannot say. It may be significant or mean mere indifference that I seldom heard a classmate mention his tutor. I certainly had no occasion to mention mine. I saw him only twice. Early in sophomore year he had me into his office to make acquaintance. He seemed bored with me. A while later he asked me to tea at his house somewhere off to the left going out Brattle Street. I drank his wife's tea and to the best of my recollection behaved myself. I never saw him again. I wouldn't have recognized him in the street, nor he me. I do recall his name—White. I was relieved that he stayed out of my hair. But he might at least have looked now and again into what I was doing. And my excellent scholastic record amassed with no help from him lends flagrance to his dereliction in the duty for which presumably the college paid him one way or another.

A good while later I had reason to regret missing the opportunity to take some anthropology. Mr. White could not have anticipated that. In view of the likelihood that somehow I'd take to writing he might have guided me into some American history. My distaste for the subject was strong, but he might have modified it. All I knew of that department was rumors of a bright new star named Samuel Eliot Morison, a course or two under whom might well have been advantageous as cultural compost. As it was, Mr. White's tutee, who eventually would publish half a dozen elaborate and well-received volumes on assorted aspects of American history, has never yet enrolled in a university-grade course in that field.

Backhandedly, however, Morison actually did do well by me. In New York soon after graduation I found among a friend's books—I often prowl others' bookshelves—Morison's recently published *Oxford History of the United States*, worked up from his visiting lectures at Oxford. I dipped in and found it was possible for a learned, intelligent, and urbane scholar to make American history march and sing. I was hooked. Most unmethodically I began to widen that opening, learned hand over fist, and was helped by the examples of such as Gilbert Seldes and Gerald Johnston to see that responsible journalism could be good training for nonacademic handling of history. In the Union Station in Washington in the middle of World War II, I happened to spy Morison, lean and sharp in navy uniform—only four stripes as yet, I think. I almost went up to thank him for what he had inadvertently done for me. He looked tired, however, and for all his incisive charm on the printed page, I feared lest this ornament of Brahminism give me that old in-group freeze. That probably did him injustice, but I preferred not to risk it.

Mr. White's masterly neglect lacked the pretext that light

did not show under my bushel. Certain artifacts attested my scholastic promise. In sophomore year I was summoned to the office of the dean of the college, Mr. Greenough. Wondering what obscure rule I had broken, I went. Solemnly the gray old gentleman shook my hand and said he was privileged to give me what I heard as "a detour." To me that meant only an irksome deviation from a blocked highway. As I puzzled over it he put in my hands an elderly three-volume edition of Percy's *Reliques* bound in polished calf with the Harvard "VE RI TAS" in gilt on the front covers. I thanked him, still puzzled, and went away. Only when I examined the books in my room did the gilded matter on the back covers solve the mystery. Under an elaborate coat of arms was "DETUR EX TESTAMENTO EDWARDI HOPKINS ARMIG" ("Let it be given under the will of Edward Hopkins, Esq."). Whoever Hopkins was, he had left a fund for prize books for high-achieving freshmen. As to "detour," Mr. Greenough used the British pronunciation, long *e* as in tree; whereas Shortridge taught the modern (and probably nearer Roman usage) way of long *e* as in tray. I'd have said "daytour." Nice books anyway. I still have them and value them for their own sakes as well as for a token of how even when she meant to be gracious, God save the mark, Alma Mater and I were doomed to frictions.

One morning my mail brought a richly engraved card like a wedding announcement taking pleasure in informing me that I was a John Harvard scholar. I assumed that it had something to do with high marks and might imply some financial advantage but curiously neglected to say so. I had no pressing reason to think my meager but workable money supply would dwindle, so I made no inquiries. Next year another such card dubbed me a Harvard College scholar, still no crass mention of money. It was not a mistake. John Harvard and Harvard College awards were then "assigned . . . primarily on the basis of high scholarship, but only to men of approved character and promise *who do not need scholarships with stipend*." Italics mine; the grin without the cat for sure. There weren't even jolly get-togethers of John Harvard scholars. Not that I'd have attended them, but this Barmecide honor mislabeled a scholarship was exasperating later on when I badly needed financial help and Alma Mater looked the other way.

A more substantial honor, though I had to pay for it myself, was my Phi Beta Kappa key acquired early senior year. It
went on my watch chain but by local custom was not left visible, instead was tucked into the righthand lower vest pocket.*
Only innocent graduate students from outer darkness dis-
played Phi Beta Kappa keys. Correction: The key I now have
put away for lack of watch chain is not the original but a replacement procured when my affairs looked up in the mid-
1930s. Its predecessor, solid gold like the present in cumbent,
was hocked in the spring of 1929 to finance my taking to dinner the girl I was to marry. The man behind the pawnshop
counter weighed it, saw the Greek letters, and said: "My boy
in college, he belongs to a fraternity too." When I was again
solvent, so far as I ever was those times, I went to redeem it.
The shop had disappeared, three balls and all, and I didn't
know how to trace the pledges that had been in its gripe when
liquidated. What do you suppose I could borrow on it now
with gold at three figures the Troy ounce?

Much of the foregoing may be skewed by strains incurred
in the final third of my Harvard career. With junior year my
niche in the College was feeling more commodious. I knew
my way about better, though I had been long learning it. I
was doing things I liked and enjoying some warm, stimulating
friendships. But even as junior year began came a small omen
hinting, had I realized it at the time, that Magna A. Mater was
unlikely to be anything but a balefully clumsy or ungracious
force in my horoscope.

That year Tom Howe and I were to room in Thayer Hall,
the least venerable of the Yard's red-brick barracks. During vacation the college duly moved our traps thither from Randolph
Hall. A few days before the fall term was to start that corner
of Thayer caught fire and when I arrived workmen were still
in the middle of putting the place back into habitable shape. Naturally it never occurred to the old lady to find me temporary
quarters or say go to a hotel and send me the bill. Philip John-

*In this world of wristwatches I wonder where the key is worn now. There seem to
be lots of them in circulation; is it dilution or inflation? Harvard College's class of
1984, 1,478 strong, contained 135 Phi Beta Kappas—a ratio of 9 percent, far higher
than in my day. (See *Harvard Gazette*, June 1984.)

son, whom I knew at the Liberal Club, had a roomy single in
Claverly Hall and put me up until Thayer was ready. When I
finally did take possession and unpacked my books, the firemen's
generous use of water had left a number of them stained and
damply smelly. I still have some of them. The smell is gone but
those stains on endpapers and upper edges remain to remind
me that any dealings with Her were bound to sour somehow.

Came spring and calamity. My term bill—charges from the
fall semester, tuition for the next—arrived and was sent home
as usual. Back came garbled word that home was stony broke.
Not even thin dimes would be coming my way any longer, let
alone the several hundred dollars of that bill. It was not altogether a surprise. There had been twitchy hints. I knew about
my father's affairs little more than that they had not pros-
pered after Great-uncle Rob died. But on the stupid if tempt-
ing principle of don't trouble trouble I had not asked questions
the answers to which might have been dismaying. Now the
answer came unsolicited.

In logic I should have resigned from college, let Alma Mater whistle for her money, and hitchhiked home to rally round
by finding a job. I had hitchhiked enough to know that was
practical; the few dollars in my pocket would feed me on the
way. Against that were sundry considerations: (1) My deep-
seated and not ill-founded belief that I was incapable of earning a steady minimum living; odd-jobbing was the best I could
hope for, so at home I'd be little more than another feckless
mouth to feed. (2) The contention of the few friends in whom
I confided that since I was two thirds of the way through to a
Harvard B.A.—an asset of value in some contexts—I'd better
stay the course if possible. And (3) in all honesty I was reluctant to go home with my tail between my legs—and to so little
purpose.

Deciding to play the hand as it lay, I determined to take
care of the term bill as preliminary to possibly staying on. I
took the matter to Mr. Bacon, the assistant dean in charge of
my class, the proper point of reference. Had I had any other
resource, I'd never have gone to him,* for he was a widely

*I can now see that my tactics were wrong. I not only knew Bacon's reputation, I had
some reason to believe he had taken a specific dislike to me. I could have gone to a
former Dean of the College who was friendly toward me and, though not a forceful

acknowledged administrative ulcer. His berth in University Hall was blatantly due to his august name. Only nicely pulled wires could account for his being there. Pudgy, sleepy-eyed, sluggish, peevish-spoken, indolent, he commanded no respect from the several hundred boys in his charge. I never heard anything but wary contempt for him.

My first experience of him was occasioned by the college rule that undergraduates going home for Christmas could have an extra day for travel if they lived more than four hundred miles away. But it had to be applied for specially since to miss one's first class after a vacation was a cardinal sin. So late in November I applied to Bacon. Was it my marked midwestern accent—still marked after sixty years in the alien corn, as I hear on tapes I make—that got me off on the wrong foot? Anyway as I told of my errand he squinted peevishly and said: "Oh, you're one of those. You really do live far away?" "Indianapolis." "And where is that?" I explained. "Well, I wouldn't know about such places," he said. "Never been west of Pittsfield."

During the next two years routine contacts with him had gone no better. Now that the stakes were high, he outdid himself. I described my situation: All money suddenly, irretrievably cut off; term bill due; hope of staying on somehow in order to get my degree; could the college help? He should, of course, have asked a few questions, looked up my record—those two Barmecide scholarships should have carried weight—arranged a moratorium, and stirred up whoever handled paying jobs for needy students. All he did was smirk at me and say: "Why, Mr. Furnas, you don't look poor!"*

It would have served him right had I gone across the desk and strangled him. A Cambridge jury, reflecting town-gown frictions, would probably have acquitted me. But I was feeling

---

personality, might have skirmished round and seen that I was afforded assistance, going over Bacon's head if necessary. That never occurred to me. In such affairs my judgment has never been good and at the time my tactical sense was no sharper for my feeling as though a load of wet gravel had been dumped on me.
*Puzzling detail: In my permanent record in Alma Mater's archives, which I was allowed to consult (and courteously too, without reference to the Freedom of Information Act) is a note about a temporary loan of fifty dollars arranged for me. Who arranged it I don't know, certainly not Bacon; nor did I ever receive any such sum from the college. Nor had I received it, would it have been any help on a term bill of several hundred dollars.

so utterly kicked in the belly that my adrenals were sluggish. In a sort of comatose incredulity I heard him say I'd have to work it out privately. And soon.

Without my knowledge friends passed word to a classmate who had a handsome income and sometimes helped undergraduates in hard luck. Just let him know from time to time how much I needed. Two conditions: Pay it back if, as, and when I could; and never say thanks or even mention the matter unnecessarily.* Whew! I could cover the term bill and resume eating and the rest of my thrifty normal activities.

But Bacon and the old lady weren't through with me. Oddjobbing in New York supported me during the summer of 1926 albeit precariously. Even so, as the end of the year loomed, my debt had reached a dismaying number of hundreds of dollars and though my helpful classmate evinced no uneasiness, I was again muttering about resigning and the hell with a B.A., I might as well take the plunge into pauperism without as with it. Enter friends again. I never knew just how it came to pass, but here was an offer of a job obviating the need for further borrowing.

The assistant dean of another class, whom I knew slightly, a fine fellow just right for the job, needed a combination tutor-nurse for a mentally disturbed freshman whose psychiatrist had advised his wealthy family that it would do him a world of good to get through a year of college. His first two months had shown he'd never make it on his own, but with a guide, philosopher, and friend at hand he might. For $175 a month and expenses I was to keep him afloat emotionally and scholastically from New Year's to early June. The notion of using Harvard College as occupational therapy struck nobody as curious. All, however, me included, assumed that the arrangement implied that the patient's family knew the right people. Anyway there it was. I was briefed by the dean, then by the psychiatrist, was looked over by the family during Christmas vacation in New York and launched on what a good faculty friend called "bear leading."

---

*Long afterward I learned—not from him—that of a number of such objects of his diffident generosity only two, of whom I am one, ever paid him back. Uncle Sam has been having the same trouble.

Scotty, my patient, was basically good-natured, luckily for me because he was six foot three and husky. We got on well, like an elder brother with an unstable sibling. The manners of his family, of whom I saw more than they or I contemplated, were considerate. And the psychiatrist in charge, whom I occasionally encountered in later years, was the late Dr. J.A.P. Millet, eventually president of the American Psychoanalytic Association, in my time on the staff of the Riggs Foundation in Stockbridge, Massachusetts, where Scotty had been a patient. Recently while awaiting sleep, I counted up the number of psychiatrists with whom I have had sizable personal—not professional—contact in a lifetime of elbow rubbing. It came to thirty-odd whom I remember well, and I'm sure there have been more, for psychiatrists in private practice, like architects and portrait painters, find it pays to get around. Of the lot— and some were eminent—Millet was one of only three to whom I would dream (sorry) of taking an emotional problem. Humorously thoughtful, with princely manners, he mingled common sense with an authoritative good nature. It was gratifying when, at the end of my assignment, he said he was grateful to me, I'd done Scotty much good.

Even so, those were as frantic a six months as I ever knew. Scotty had recurrent fits of galloping restlessness. "Wo ich nicht bin, dort ist das Glück" could have been his crumbling psyche's motto. Though I was never any good at it, I had the hang of squash rackets, a game new to him, well enough to head off some of his attacks of got-to-go-somewhere-else. After I'd run him ragged round a squash court for half an hour, he might simmer down. A huge Italian dinner—he was a mighty trencherman—might have the same effect. But all too often nothing helped and off we trundled to New York or to Stockbridge for a retread from Millet. The trainmen and dining-car help on the New Haven line and the Boston & Albany knew us well. His family were spending the winter at the Ambassador in New York. There I first met broccoli Hollandaise, beautifully handled too, and whitebait that must have been an overseas import. It caused comment in that dining room when Scotty, tired of fork work, picked up most of a plate of whitebait and poured a hundred or so little fishes down his throat in one gargantuan draft.

In Stockbridge Millet lodged us very comfortably in his fine old white clapboard Berkshire farmhouse. God knows what each of those several-day stays cost Scotty's family for room, board, and professional fees. Mrs. Millet, noncommitally hospitable, had been reared in India and for servants had an Indian mother and daughter whose curries, the first I ever had, were superb. The Indians had taken zealously to skiing, already a big thing in the Berkshires, and made a strange picture demurely streaking through the wintry landscape clad in sari and boots—with, I always hoped but never asked about it, woolies underneath.

Squash and eating were not the only sports garnishing this surrealistic interval. When Millet took us skiing in a local pasture, I was equipped with a pair of his favorite skis, unfastened for a tyro, of course. Naturally I fell down, naturally the skis came adrift and shot downslope into the stream at the bottom and no doubt were in Long Island Sound by morning. Millet merely talked on urbanely about other things, but I hope he put the price of replacements on the bill. In the spring my duty to Scotty got me into a Sunday afternoon softball game with some of the Foundation's young patients. Harking back to boyhood, I opted for right field. A high fly went over the fence behind me. I jumped the fence to get the ball and came down on a stone hidden in the long grass, tearing the ligaments in my right knee. Millet bandaged it and ordered up a chauffeured car to take me—and Scotty, we were due to leave that evening—to Harvard's Stillman Infirmary. I was there for a week, my knee softball size and colored blue, green, and yellow. Even though Mrs. Lowell twice spent five minutes at my bedside on her rounds of ailing undergraduates, every few years another orthopedist has told me that knee will never come right. Don't play softball with mental patients on Sunday.

While I was laid up, Scotty, who had certain commendable instincts, behaved with almost normal responsibility. And I had a week to get some academic work in. It hardly needs saying that between steering him through his freshman chores and those impromptu flights hither and yon my scholastic career necessarily suffered. Of my four courses, three required substantial climactic minitheses. With an ingenuity that still impresses me, I cooked up a topic that could be simultaneously submitted to Mr. Demos on ethics, Mr. Babbitt on romanticism, and Mr. Murray on drama. Each knew of and permitted this tripling in brass. But telescoping could go only so far and how I ever passed everything with credit was a frazzling miracle.

Midway in my six months of struggle, I had my reward from Her. I failed to get Scotty and me back for first classes from spring vacation. He wasn't nasty about it, he just couldn't be got into motion soon enough. His special status, whatever it was, exempted him from that most stringent of Harvard's requirements. For me—Bacon would hear no excuses about my livelihood being contingent on riding herd on Scotty in person. Disciplinary probation. One more false step and out.

My three-barreled final paper was a nice bit of prose, if I did think so myself. I submitted it for the annual Bowdoin Prize—$250 for the best piece of scholarly undergraduate writing, $100 second prize. Soon afterward I saw Paul Herzog's paper on Calvin's *Institutes*, beautifully handled; I suggested he put it into the Bowdoin competition. Since he didn't need $250 and I did, he won first, me second, and I'll say it for both of us that it amused me more than him. What did not amuse me was that, in view of how welcome even $100 was at the time, Alma Mater ruled me ineligible for the prize because I was on probation. I was to be swindled out of a badly needed just due because the College's refusal to help me had forced me to take a job that obliged me to break a College rule. It was the old lady's masterpiece.

I had the miniature last word, however. Adrenals firing this time, I assailed University Hall—not Bacon, I knew better than that, indeed he probably had a hand in it—but the temporary Dean of the College, Mr. Maynadier, whom I did not know at all. Bitterly I sang my song. He pondered a minute, then said: "I see, I'll look into it." And did. I got my hundred dollars and the accompanying artifact—a bronze medal carrying a rather foolish-looking bas-relief portrait head of pig-tailed James Bowdoin Armig, whoever he was.

Happy ending but disproportionate to all the precedent trauma. It occurs to me that She must have had ESP and been aware throughout of the wounding frivolity that had made me choose fair Harvard to begin with.

8

Makeshifts

FIFTY YEARS AGO the top echelon of the J. Walter Thompson advertising agency, already a giant, included Dr. John B. Watson, the psychologist whose "behaviorism" then rivaled Freud's more romantic doctrines in popular prestige. Watson was believed to have drawn up or sponsored the formidable questionnaire that the agency's personnel department inflicted on applicants. I came within its tentacles because I needed a job—I often did—and knew a man who knew a man who rated high at Thompson's.

The questionnaire began as usual: Age . . . sex . . . education . . . previous employment . . . then mousetrapish queries: Are you honest? . . . loyal? . . . truthful? . . . industrious? . . . and so on. Though those may not be the exact terms, they fairly represent the effect as of a catechism based on the Boy Scout oath. One could hardly afford to answer no to any. Yet to answer yes to all would sound like a priggish hypocrite lacking good sense. Then the boom was lowered: What qualities to you *lack*? Describe in full. . . . Thompson's people professed to believe that subtle scientific analysis of an applicant's try at squaring that circle could show whether he was worth hiring.

If I could recall how I handled it I wouldn't tell. I did not get a job at Thompson's. Maybe exasperation made me write that I lacked a sense of humor else I wouldn't be bothering to try to cope. Maybe I set down my job history at ill-advised length. One might well hesitate to hire anybody who already

163

by the age of twenty-three had been factotum in a hotel kitchen, spear carrier in a stock company, busboy in a big-city cafeteria; stock-issue clerk at AT&T, psychiatric nurse for a disturbed adolescent; gofer for a millionaire, gofer-copywriter for a Broadway flack; tutor for the son of an affluent surgeon; and lest any of that sound suitable, only one of those had lasted more than a few months.

Some ran concurrently—as is said of jail sentences—with schooling. Fifty years later I see them all as educational in a Henry Adamsy sense. But at the time that was not the point. Eating money was. Nor was any of it trial apprenticeship with eventual vocation in mind. No doubt many a footloose youngster today could match that miscellany of jobs. But there was an extra load behind my saddle: a conviction, which is still with me, that come right down to it, I'd never last in the organized activities—pimping, plumbing, or pizza tossing—that usually afford livelihoods. Hence in most jobs I felt like a tightrope walker whose mistrust of his sense of balance makes it all too likely he will fall off.

My first money from outside the family—whose slim resources supplied little—came from inheriting Jabez Wood's place doing Shortridge notes for the *Indianapolis News*. Those skinny few column-inches a week financed the odd movie and a typewriter—a primitive Corona with two shift keys, one for capitals, one for numerals and punctuation. It was sluggish and stuttery but well adapted to the hunt-and-peck method. Acquiring it made me typewriter-bound. Nothing I can set down with pen or pencil suits me at all until I regain access to good old *qwertyuiop* and type it out with drastic changes of pace and vocabulary. I cannot conceive how anybody ever wrote even a poor novel in longhand, no matter how clear the penmanship; or how a publisher's editor in pretypewriter times ever determined whether a manuscript was worth bothering with.

In freshman year at Harvard my only earnings consisted of a check for three dollars from *Life* for a laborious joke; and some six or seven five-dollar bills for going on as an extra in certain productions of the Copley Players, Boston's theatrical stock company. Five dollars for seven performances plus rehearsal time worked out to maybe two bits an hour diminished by ten-cent subway fare back and forth. But gain was not the primary purpose. Thus to enter the world of backstage was a bracing change from academic routine. Not that I was stage struck. Though later I rubbed elbows with Thespis pretty closely, that I never was. Just as well. Nobody with my diffidently stumbly temperament would have ever have made an actor.

The Copley Players were one of the few fall-and-winter stock companies then still surviving competition from the movies. They could not take advantage of the off-season Broadway talent that strengthened the Stuart Walker summer stock seasons that Indianapolis enjoyed in my time. The Copley people were, however, versatile, competent-or-better professionals, mostly British, who worked well together. Boston valued them as a local institution. Soon after my time they broke up. Some eventually made a fair to good thing of supporting roles in Hollywood. Now and then in an old movie on TV I reencounter the late Alan Mowbray, grainy voice, imperious nose, barrel chest, and watchful eyes; or demure, deft E. E. Clive, who was director-manager as well as a wheelhorse performer in the Copley troupe. He gave Boston solid fare. *The Devil's Disciple:* I carried a musket as a British lobsterback. *RUR:* I was chief of the robot rebels, stabbing Clive with a rubber dagger. And lest things get too cultivated, a knockabout fantasy, *When Knights Were Bold,* about a man dreaming himself back into medieval days, was a Christmas season fixture every year.

That one kept us extras busy. We posed upstage behind a scrim curtain with a stuffed deer on a pole and sang in jolly chorus: "The hunt is up! the hunt is up! / Sing merrily we the hunt is up!" In a later scene another extra and I haled Mowbray (in full armor) on stage as prisoner and threw him roughly down before the king or duke or whoever the ruling figure was. Mowbray probably remembered me as well as the Lord Mayor did, for, though the business went smoothly in rehearsal, in the first performance we varlets got carried away and handled him so vigorously that his feet shot from under him and with a crash he slid into the wings on his back. There was quite a wait while we went after him, got him back on his feet, escorted him round backstage to the previous entrance, and this time threw him no harder than required. Some actors would have been indignant, but Mowbray merely winked when he next encountered us. These were unflappable pros. *When Knights Were Bold* also had an abbess played by the middle-aged utility woman. Her several appearances were widely separated in time, so, piously dignified in starched white wimple and sweeping black habit, she spent the intervals playing poker with the stagehands under the stage. It made a striking picture.

Clive was a considerate but no-nonsense director, never raising his voice, never hesitating about the intonation or bit of business he wanted, blocking out stage movements decisively. These time- and energy-saving skills were essential, for the company not only did seven shows a week but had simultaneously to study and rehearse next week's play. This was no itinerant rep show seldom needing much rehearsal because they always played *Lady Audley's Secret, East Lynne,* and *Ten Nights in a Bar-Room* for each split-week stand. Nor yet a Broadway cast rehearsing three weeks and then trying out in Atlantic City and New Haven. Every Monday evening the Copley Players came up with a smooth handling of a script they might have seen for the first time maybe two weeks before. I have never regretted those idle hours in the half dark watching Clive and colleagues shaping things up. I vastly enjoyed playgoing anyway, but my pleasure has probably had a special edge from thus soaking in awareness of what it's like on the reverse side of the set beyond the magic boundary of the audience's line of sight—back there where one hears Juliet throbbing out her yearning rhapsody and relishes the anomalous flimsiness of the scaffolding that supports her balcony.

Late in my freshman year Jabez Wood wrote from home that he had a summer job as night clerk at a resort hotel in Port Huron, Michigan, and there was a berth for a youngster to do odd chores in the back of the house. That was my first job as such. Fifty dollars a month; free run of the menu; on duty seven days a week at 6:30 A.M., off round 9:00 P.M., two to three hours free afternoons. This Gratiot Inn was owned and managed by a rangy, gray-haired Cleveland woman, Mrs. Reese, who had a similar hotel for longer winter seasons in Florida. A clumsy, turreted, wooden affair, the Inn stood on the St. Clair River just below Lake Huron. Its dance pavilion and auxiliary shack colony were relics from what must have been a very minor amusement park. The wheel of chance, rifle range, and so on had been remodeled into quarters for the Inn's rank and file. The clientele were upper-middle-income couples and families coming back summer after summer, for the beach was adequate, the water clean, the nights cool, the sun bright, the food very good, and the daily parade of Great Lakes ships interesting. What the tariff was I never knew.

Mrs. Reese, her spinster bookkeeper-assistant, and the dauntingly corseted, exophthalmic headwaitress had individual rooms in the Inn proper. Next down the scale the four black cooks roomed over the kitchen. Mike, the engineer (by courtesy—he had spent most of his life stoking lake ore boats), had a cot in the boiler room. The dozen waitresses, three bellhops, Morris the handyman, the young black woman who kept the help's quarters more or less redd up, the night clerk, and the stockroom keeper—my official title—led an unorganized barracks life in the remodeled shacks.

They amounted to a blend of migrant labor camp and the first "tourist cabins." In a southern Michigan summer no more was needed than roofs that didn't leak, doors that shut (but not often), and bulbs dangling from the ceiling. No plumbing, instead basins and pitchers filled from a spigot in the yard, and two privies segregated by sex. Dips during the afternoon hour reserved for the help on the beach theoretically kept us clean. I think the cooks, who were certainly the most scrupulously groomed males on the staff, had their own bathroom upstairs. As for me, a few times I patronized the lake, but one afternoon I brashly threshed my way out to the diving float and when I tried to return, came so near not making it that Jabez had to tow me over the last ten no-footing yards. Embarrassed and angry with myself after that, I confined hygiene to illicit tubbing in one of the Inn's bathrooms late at night—easily arranged if one knew the night clerk.

The average age of our shack colony can't have been over twenty-two. No chaperonage; and if Mrs. Reese paid any heed to what went on across the road, she did it so secretively as to be unaware of it herself. In view of the standards of sixty years ago it still seems odd that her thus hiving up a number of young women, mostly comely, in close proximity to some half dozen he-youngsters for ten weeks of warm weather did not stir up the local Mrs. Grundy. But none of us came from Port Huron, so busybodies lacked immediate interest; Mrs. Reese actually was as respectable as she looked; and her bills from the local ice plant, milk company, and so on were promptly paid. Odder still was the actual lack of what scandal seekers would have had in mind. True, the arrangement offered little privacy. Also true, getting up at 6:00 A.M. and staying on one's feet for at least ten of the next fifteen hours seven days a week left a girl less energy for exploring primrose paths. The major guardian of virtue, however, probably was that almost all those putatively accessible waitresses were country schoolteachers using summer vacation to fatten their resources with the guests' tips; some were thus earning their expenses at teacher's college in Ypsilanti. For back then a country schoolteacher had to be farther above reproach than any wife any Caesar ever had, and that inhibiting caution tended to become solid habit. The theory is strengthened by the fact that the two who weren't teachers, instead coeds at Oberlin College, were those most given to strolling in the moonlight. And at that very little happened. My authority is good: the boys' gossip among themselves.

Daily observation of those girls somewhat reconciled me to the kind of teachers that Indianapolis had provided. These were good at waiting table—tireless, responsible, good-tempered, a quality essential in a large, blazing-hot kitchen with slathers of Sunday dinners reflecting an extensive bill of fare. No doubt the three or four most astute handled reading, writing, long division, and classroom discipline well. Yet their frames of reference were so limited and, worse, so likely to remain so that they made Number Forty-five's underqualified staff look like so many Margaret Fullers.

The cooks and their cooking were the Inn's strong point. The chef—only the office knew his name—was thick and African-dark, narrow-eyed, light-footed, consciously dominating the whole back of the house. Marshall, loosely fat, smiling, never hurried, did soups and vegetables. Frank, who did fish, short orders, and oddments, moved like a boxer and kept his white cap cocked over one eye with his handsome face skewed into a persistent grin. Nathan, the flatfooted pot-walloper, lean and pliable, did whatever his superiors told him to with pouncing zeal. All came from Maryland's Eastern Shore and had already worked together for Mrs. Reese winter and summer, with spring and fall at home. Their teamwork was as spontaneous as the way the interference formed up out of nowhere when one of Rockne's Four Horsemen recovered a fumble. Few or no words, each aware of what the others were at, each manipulating his segment of steam table or stove rank with the aplomb of a xylophone player. The waitresses came crowding up with shrill orders; the required item was instantly dished up or on the fire; Nathan skittered here and there apparently guided by twitches of the chef's eyebrows; Frank shouted to me for a quick can of something—which, to save time when the joint was really jumping, I hurled at him half the length of the kitchen.

Relations between these black craftsmen and the white personnel were easy though not positively cordial because neither party impinged much on the other. Even Morris, a shrewd little Florida cracker, never let white supremacy get the better of him; indeed he'd have been fired if he had, for Mrs. Reese and the chef were equally aware how much the hotel depended on its excellent table. I made some acquaintance with Frank, who taught me "Hot stuff!" as warning when approaching a swinging door; how to open a number-ten can not with a time-consuming can opener—electric openers were not yet available—but with four whacks of a cleaver; how to shoulder a hundred-pound sack of sugar to take up an incredibly long flight of stairs into the storeroom: and I laughed not too little, not too much, when, cleaning a promisingly sizable fish, he said: "Whe' I come from, boy, we'd use this fo' *bait!*"

Once I managed to understand Nathan's Eastern Shore patois I learned something about him. Lacking skill with pencil and paper, he asked me to compose for him letters to his girl friend about how much he missed her and the perils he faced here up North from bears and Indians. I complied—rather too effectively, for as the correspondence grew, she heated up and Nathan worried lest she insist on their marrying when he came home.* With Marshall, however, "Good morning" and "Thanks" were about it. With the chef it was only "Okay, will do" on, say, scrubbing the floor round the dishwasher first so it would dry soonest. One did not bother him with perfunctory passings of the time of day. There was a controlled ferocity about the way he sharpened his knives.

The staff eccentric was the baker, an elderly Swiss so gnarly that, without actually being so, he looked deformed. If Switzerland had trolls, his genetic origin would have been clear. He lived on soup, ingesting it by putting his mouth level with the bowl and sloshing the liquid in so cleverly that little escaped. The sugary juices of the canned fruit used for pies he accumulated in an empty butter firkin—peach, cherry, plum all mixed—put it in the cool cellar to ferment, and drank the results. The rancid remains of butter gave this tipple a notable tang; Tibet's yak-butter tea may be something like that. His bread, shaped French-style with tapered ends, did not meet what I later knew as French standards but was very good for America, and the guests valued it. It stands out in memory, however, because once, as he was kneading a batch, probably just after visiting his fruit juice, he lost his false teeth in the dough. The batch was vital to lunch and dinner. Frantic search inspecting every hunch cut failed to turn up those missing uppers. We waited miserably for some outraged guest to start up from table indignantly waving them. They never surfaced. Whoever found them—maybe a shy maiden lady—must have disposed of them clandestinely. Luckily it was near the end of the season and with his addiction to soup, Bill really didn't need teeth.

It was he who mixed the batter for breakfast hot cakes and, when he was too busy, I who baked them, a dozen or so at a

---

*My only other attempt at the role of Cyrano also turned out badly. A classmate was greatly struck by a girl he saw checking out of a hotel in Lyon. From the concierge he got her name and address (in England) and, on coming home, asked me to write letters for him to send her. I still recall her unusual surname and used to wonder what I'd do if, at tea somewhere in England, I met an attractive Miss Harplewich, only that is not the name. She wrote back gingerly if amusedly. She sounded cultivated, with more common sense than my friend. Next time he was over there he went to see her. She seems to have taken one look and made "Oh, dear!" politely but firmly clear. I never understood that too well. My Christian had manners and in his way he was good-looking enough.

time on a gas-fired steel plate lubricated with the traditional bacon rind. If batter ran low and Bill was still busy, I mixed more according to his directions. While flipping cakes I also kept an eye on the huge coffee urn and, when Frank was busy, refilled it; further renewed the supply of orange juice I had squeezed earlier—no electric squeezer yet, let alone frozen concentrate; dashed into the stockroom for another box of Shredded Wheat or cornflakes, all the time rather enjoying having to act like the proverbial one-armed paperhanger. When the guests were finally all replete, I relaxed over remaining orange juice, half a cantaloupe, a couple of poached eggs on hash, a stack of hot cakes. Round 11:00 A.M. I had to stop juggling supplies in the stockroom to get the pantry ready for lunch—wash lettuce, lay out salads, brew up the iced tea, restock the coffee urn. The pantry woman, a Grant Wood type, soon trained me into a not unwilling assistant. She was a stickler for homemade-from-scratch mayonnaise, which she elegantly pronounced "myonaze." I hope and believe that even now if given a well-chilled big bowl, a wire whisk eighteen inches long, two dozen eggs, olive oil, lemon juice, white pepper, salt, and dry mustard, I could still honor her tutelage with a mayonnaise that no electric blender could match.

At mealtimes I lent both hands and could have used three supplying everything that the waitresses demanded over the pantry rail. Eventually I lunched—copiously—and then mopped the kitchen floor, an area large enough to make me still a master mopper. I don't recall who assigned me to that—Mrs. Reese? the chef? In warm weather, under even minor exertion, I sweat heavily. Until the novelty palled, waitresses on their way to the shacks after resetting their tables for dinner would linger to watch Joe sweat. I helped the inn's rattletrap truck escort the garbage to a local piggery. It all left little time for the unpacking, shelving, stock taking, and reordering that maintained the stockroom's array of cans, bottles, bags, bins, and barrels. I lack that sort of efficiency anyway. The house never ran out of anything crucial like coffee, but minor crises kept warm my doubts of my ability to cope. Yet in view of my general, catch-as-catch-can usefulness in other respects, I was not quite sloppy enough to get fired.

It would be graceless not to celebrate the good eating that

my grandfather's grandson owed the chef and his crew. I fed joyfully and on a scale that they approved of and encouraged. I felt that Marshall hovered with special care over my poached eggs. Frank liked to choose me out that particular slab of whitefish. Indeed what he could do with fresh-out-of-coldwater Lake Huron whitefish left me addicted. Twenty years later, whenever I was in the area of the western Great Lakes, I sought out the best whitefish in town like an alcoholic seeking a bar. Once I had been working with a magazine crew in Chicago, then had parted with them to take an afternoon train to another assignment. The editor in charge wanted to check an afterthought with me and despaired of reaching me before it was too late. Martin Munkacsi, the renowned photographer on the story, with whom I had campaigned so long he knew my habits, said there was no problem; "He'll be in the Harvey restaurant in the Union Station eating whitefish for lunch." And so I was, doing just that, when the hostess came undulating up to say if I was Mr. Furnas, I was wanted on the telephone.

Port Huron's sole distinction in my time lay in having been the boyhood environment of Thomas A. Edison; his precocious chemical experiments once set fire to a baggage car, legend said, on the Port Huron & Detroit railroad.* For me its interest came of being across the river from Sarnia, Ontario—foreign soil, my first! And its shops sold British imports at duty-free prices. I bought a drop-stem Dunhill pipe, snobbishly valuing its tiny ivory-dot trademark, and smoked it stubbornly until my sore tongue made it clear I was too nervous a smoker ever to keep a pipe acceptably cool. In the ensuing sixty years I have lost and regret many things, including my great-grandfather's cherrywood walking stick, my admiration for the screen persona of Corinne Griffith, an inch in height. But I still have that pipe along with the Waterman pen. I didn't miss the pipe when a roommate borrowed it and returned it months later, possibly in a fit of conscience, with a hole in the mouthpiece worn by his righthand canine tooth. I

---

*In the early 1960s, of course, it acquired a possibly precarious slot as birthplace of the influential Port Huron manifesto of the proto-hippies. In 1924, however, its atmosphere was not visionary.

wouldn't miss it now if it disappeared from the lower lefthand desk drawer. Yet that is an ungrateful attitude toward a relic of one's first loot from a foreign strand.

The sense of Canada's being alien just over the way was enhanced early in July. While on an errand in what there was of downtown Port Huron I heard squeaky music—an elementary brass band was marching toward me leading a small straggle of men wearing orange-colored, horse-collarish regalia. Passersby had halted on the sidewalk and were looking on benignly. The band was playing a queer, dancy air new to me. I asked a man what it was. He stared at me strangely and said: "Why, Lillibulero!" A bell rang. That was the queer name of the tune that the pirates' boat keeper in *Treasure Island* whistled; but I was unaware of the political significance involved. When I still didn't understand the situation, my man, half angry, half incredulous, said: "It's the Orangemen. Have you never heard of Boyne Water?" Things fell into place. Harvard's required course in European history had briefed me on that. From Seton's *Two Little Savages* I also knew that because Scotch-Irish and Irish Catholic immigrants had brought along their quarrels to Canada, orange was a color almost as hot in Ontario as in Ulster. And the cultural osmosis between Sarnia and Port Huron was so pervasive that in this American small town it was emotionally incumbent on several score residents, doubtless Canadian-born, to celebrate the anniversary of Protestant King Billy's victory over Catholic King James II at the River Boyne 235 years previously and three thousand-odd miles across the sea.

Canada's nearness naturally led to rum running across the St. Clair River, though not on the scale prevalent in the Detroit area. Sometimes Jabez and I borrowed the skiff that a pair of local characters kept up the shore for occasional liquor smuggling. They stipulated only that we lay off it on cloudy nights and always have it back by 11:00 P.M. Ralph, the inn's bell captain, probably supplied certain guests with bootleg stuff; otherwise the inn was a dry ship. Except for Mr. Clark, who was Mrs. Reese's mistake. Seeking greater efficiency, I suppose, she hired as steward, on the same level as the chef, a twitchy, gabby wisenheimer named Clark who had been, or so he said, second in command of the back of the house at De-

troit's Book-Cadillac Hotel. To judge from the respectful nostalgia with which he dwelt on its glories, he might well have
had some job there. So before the Inn opened my second
summer, Clark was bustling about to install Book-Cadillac
methods and decry the primitive previous arrangements. He
didn't get far, but not for lack of explanation and expostulation. He scattered chatter about him like a wet dog shaking
itself. Bits about the petty rackets parasitical on his beloved
Book-Cadillac were perversely amusing and fascinated a lanky,
chuckle-headed bellhop named Walter who was always turning up with: "You know what Clark was telling me . . ."

With him came Mrs. Clark, billowy, tight-mouthed, Gypsy-
dark, fortyish. She stayed in their room most of the time, only
never missing meals. About 3:00 A.M. one night Jabez came
panting across the road to the shack: "You got to give me a
hand with Clark." We knew he had been getting potable alcohol and concocting his own gin and synthetic cordials. Apparently his latest batch had been highly potable and he had drunk
himself into convulsions; and Mrs. Clark had summoned Jabez from dozing at the desk. Clark couldn't have weighed over
130 pounds, but his threshings about, arms flailing and
snatching, spine and legs heaving, were so powerful that only
a straitjacket and bed straps would really have helped. Since
we had no such equipment, Mrs. Clark sat on his torso and
Jabez and I took a leg apiece. The three of us could barely
hold him down. Mrs. Clark began upbraiding the little wretch
in a slow, heavy flow of obscene and, I'll say it for her, imaginative abuse as if laying an interminable curse on him. I had
not previously known that a woman could know such words;
some were new to me. They made it indirectly clear that they
were not married but had been shacked up together long
enough for her to have seen him through several such episodes; only this, one gathered, was the worst yet.

Gradually, gradually he weakened and in an hour was in a
sleep so deep that it alarmed Jabez and me. Panting, "Mrs.
Clark" rolled off the bed and assured us that he would be
safely in a coma for hours. Happy to take her at her word, we
went away. So far as we knew, no knowledge of it all had
reached anybody else. But some notice had been taken, for
two days later—Clark didn't show at all the first day—the cou-

ple packed up and left, taking young Walter with them. God knows what happened to him under such auspices. Their leaving caused littler intramural comment. The Inn merely reverted to its informal way of getting to the end of the season.

For further education, down the shore was a frowsy little public hall used chiefly for Saturday night dances that we Inners seldom attended because Saturday was our most exacting evening. Once, however, in spite of the residual odor of sin attached to dancing, a team of pentecostal ("Holy Roller") evangelists held forth there for several days. I went to a midweek evening. Only forty or so local people came seeking the Lord. But those few worked up impressive response to the imperative rhythms of the portable harmonium, trombone, snare drum, and husky Mrs. Preacher with a voice like a soprano slide whistle; and her husband (I took it for granted *this* pair were married) was professionally rhapsodic. Their favorite number, "Look to the Lamb of God," a bouncy job that I never met anywhere else, still sometimes intervenes between me and sleep. It worked that handful of devotees into the traditional mass hysteria with all the trimmings: the jerks, the jumps, the whip-cracking hair, the speaking in tongues, the foaming at the mouth and rolling in holy joy. Neither the First Friends Church nor the First Presbyterian Church (Maywood, Illinois) had ever shown me anything like that plump girl in a mail-order white dress who, having looked merely adenoidally dreary through preliminaries, suddenly shrieked "Jesus!" leaped three feet in the air, and fell back on the floor rolling and twitching.

Later a touring *Uncle Tom's Cabin* troupe took over the hall for a one-night stand. It can't have numbered more than eight persons and one of them was tied to the piano throughout. But by innocently transparent doubling they worked through the basic characters: Uncle Tom (Yassuh, massa), Mr. and Mrs. Shelby, George and Eliza (Eliza's baby was a prop and looked it), Little Eva, Topsy, Mr. St. Clair, Miss Ophelia, Lawyer Marks, Simon Legree . . . The ice cakes in the crossing scene were packing boxes covered with white crepe paper. The bloodhounds were two elderly mastiffs who merely trotted once across the backdrop. The scenery had degenerated into token stuff of a simplicity that would have delighted the avant-garde stage of the day. The script was mere gabbling and gesturing through traditional motions as perfunctory as a losing tennis player's handshake.

That so dim an offering could earn a living for so many people and two large dogs was incredible. I knew vaguely of Tom shows, of course, but Indianapolis was too much the big town for them to try their luck there. Thirty years later, when writing at length about the Tommers' traditions, I learned from Wesley Stout's excellent article in the *Saturday Evening Post* (1924) that that very summer a dozen or so such troupes, with prospects dwindling toward the vanishing point, were still on the road—vestigial remnants of what was once a major segment of American show business. I am grateful to Port Huron for showing me that surviving specimen, however feeble and shrunken. It was like encountering one of the last passenger pigeons.

During our third college vacation summer Kendall Foss and I sought subsistence in New York. For him small difficulty. He was a licensed ship's radio operator who could ship out more or less at will as summer replacement in the Clyde Mallory service to Cuba and Mexico, returning with enough wages for a thrifty spell ashore. Our room in a dingy apartment on West Eighty-sixth Street had bedbugs but not unbearably many. Of our pudgy landlady, I recall only her indefinably loose, gray-bluish draperies and an air of being neither respectable nor ever quite sober.

For me subsistence was another matter. The residue from my friend's May subsidy was dwindling and I had little notion how to secure an odd job even in the boom times of 1926. My few personal leads petered out. For instance, Tom Howe's uncle, Will Howe, then a veteran editor at Scribner's, passed me on to the manager of Scribner's Book Store, who looked at me and suggested nothing. The day before Foss was to ship out the first time we blew ourselves to a despairingly hearty lunch at Bunn Brothers' cafeteria in a basement at Seventh Avenue and Forty-sixth Street. Nowadays "Times Square cafeteria" sounds squalid. Sixty years ago, however, a cafeteria could be in its own way elegant even on Times Square. Bunn Brothers' was handsomely carpeted, had white tablecloths and cloth napkins, a ladies' string quartet, and a presentable clientele of minor executives, accountants, and salesmen. The cooking was good, the prices moderate.

So we fed well while wondering how I'd manage eating a few days later. At the far end of the room there was a smashing crash. A tall busboy in a white jacket had dropped a loaded tray. Out of an adjacent door came a man in a business suit, presumably the manager. Into the door with him went the busboy. In five minutes he reappeared in shirt sleeves making angry gestures. The scenario was plain. I thought rapidly. Experience at the Gratiot Inn assured me that nobody got fired for dropping just one tray, for through isolated bad luck that might happen to anybody—deduct the cost from the next payday and that would be that. So this was probably the decisive item in a series of delinquencies and the culprit stood no chance of being rehired. In all logic and probability the coast was ethically clear.

The manager seemed harassed but pleasant and had a west-of-Pittsburgh accent. He asked where I came from and when I told him, said, Well, I'm from Fort Wayne myself. Hoosiers are not as clannish as Scots, but when they meet one another away from home, there is fellow feeling. I got the job: fifteen dollars a week, six days a week, two meals a day as square as one wished and, if I came early and helped ice and stock the salad counter, a bacon-and-eggs breakfast. The money would cover lodging and cigarettes (then fifteen cents for twenty) with a few dollars to spare. They found me a white jacket big enough, and Foss sailed aware I'd be eating better than he could expect in the *Siboney*.

Though I had never bussed dishes at the Gratiot Inn, I soon made a good busboy; indeed that is the only calling except writing in which I have been really at home. To this day, when I see a tray being loaded in a restaurant, I usually find much to deplore. The importance of saucer nesting and tumbler siting away from the edge to achieve balance and damage prevention is not always appreciated.

My colleagues were Diego, a young, squatty, good-natured Mexican who had little English and I no Spanish beyond "Buenos dias" and "Gracias"; and Heinrich, a young Alpine-type German of very gloomy disposition. My highly elementary German was already two years rusty, so our intercourse went no farther than: "Guten morgen, Heinrich; wie geht's," and his reply was always wearily, raspingly: "Schlecht! Schlecht!" But we three got on, possibly because we understood one another so little. We worked like robots too fully programmed to need back-and-forthing. That was just as well, for we had small attention from the chief busboy, Saul, a middle-aged Syrian with no Spanish or German and scanty English. Working with us during rush periods he was efficient. But the rest of his time was devoted to placing bets for the kitchen and counter help and the staffs of certain offices round the corner, which kept him in the lobby phone booth by the half hour. This moonlighting was probably why, after a couple of weeks, the manager fired him and offered me the job, with a ten-dollar raise.

Gratifying. I hope I made that clear when saying no. I did so because the day before Tom Howe's uncle's office had let me know that a job was waiting for me at the phone company's office downtown. It proved to be that of a stock-issue clerk (temporary) for the rest of the summer at twenty-five a week, nine to five, hour off for lunch. I did not regret the change. But it was true that for the ensuing couple of years I seldom ate as well or as healthily as during those few weeks of bussing. Even now when I pass that corner I recall with something like nostalgia the difficulty of polishing the tarnish out of the twisty crannies in Bunn Brothers' elaborately handsome, brass-grilled entrance doors, long since vanished, sold for scrap, I suppose.

The new job was at AT&T's stately headquarters building at 195 Broadway—tier on tier of classic columns topped off by the gilded statue of the Spirit of Enterprise, or whatever, that recently moved into the lobby of Philip Johnson's Chippendale masterpiece uptown. The old lobby downtown, chaste as a mausoleum, showed how to achieve impressiveness by not trying hard—a great change from crude Times Square. Just as impressive in its way was the room where I worked. "Room" does not convey its vastness. It was an interminable expanse of God knows how many girl typists hammering away like the myriad apes in Geoffrey Hellman's story. As far as I know none of them turned out *The Pilgrim's Progress.* What they did turn out was the paper work that I helped to process. No doubt the offices of New York's large insurance companies and banks had comparable aggregations of girls of all sizes and colors of hair all done the same way. I had never seen such a desert of femininity before. It daunted me.

The clatter of their typing was like a rising wind crossed with an electric buzzer. But they were more fragile than they sounded. We were high up from the street. Thunderstorms sometimes came up toward the end of the afternoon. The rain would lash at the windows, the thunder bellow overhead, and lightning strike down between our building and the one over the way. Then several girls—whether always the same ones I don't know—would faint and get carried down to the infirmary, a curiously Victorian touch in an otherwise no-nonsense environment. I'm sure they were well looked after. I once took a minor ailment to that infirmary and was admirably treated.

To regard fainting damsels as relief from clerical monotony would have been coldblooded. Besides, the job was not as dull as it sounds. AT&T had floated a large issue of common stock by giving its stockholders warrants to purchase at an attractive price—I think the ratio was one to ten—and the certificates for the new shares were being mailed out. No doubt computers handle that sort of thing now. Back then each individual mailing was checked by our crew of twenty-odd college boys, mostly from Yale and Columbia. It was a monumental task, for Telephone—as Wall Street then knew it; "Ma Bell" was a later invention—was very widely held, often in small lots, as with a shrewd view to the social leverage of widows and orphans, the company wished. And most of the holders had exercised their option to buy. The result was tray after tray after tray, thousands of trays of neatly packaged documents— in each package the new stock certificate, memo slip showing number of shares originally held, serial number of warrant, voucher for remittance received, original correspondence if any. When it all checked, as it usually did, fold certificate into the envelope provided, make sure name and address show through the transparent window, and put it in an outgoing tray.

Those addresses were a Whitmanesque romp through the U.S. Postal Guide: Box 7, Thirsty Gulch, Wyo.; RFD, Ephesus, Ark.; Rittenhouse Square, Philadelphia, Pa.; 1234 San Ananias Drive, Vista, Calif.; 321 Main Street, Gopher Prairie, Minn.; Harvard University, Cambridge, Mass., a certificate for several thousand shares. I was fresh from my trouble with Bacon and Alma Mater and when that piece of stiff paper came into my hands I was tempted to pocket it and try to work out some way to hold it for ransom.

When details did not match properly, the papers involved went to a small trouble-shooting crew to which I was assigned after a week or so. In such transactions dozens of things could misfire, of course, and working back to where the error had occurred and setting it right provided a sometimes vexing but often entertaining game. When the tangle appeared hopeless, one could unostentatiously pop it back into the hopper and wish luck to the next man encountering it. That dodge probably accounted for some of the cases in which the subscriber wrote in worried because the new certificate had not arrived. Even when it was simple nervousness or failure to understand that large institutions move slowly, we tried to take care of it. The typical letter would be like this on blue-lined paper in a spidery hand:

> Dear Mr. Blair-Smith:
> I think as treasurer you are the right man for me to let you know I dont yet have my two new shares of stock that I sent in about early this year. My daughter thinks I should ask you about it. Our mail-carrier says he is sure no envelope with your company on it come since you wrote me about the new stock. Not much news here. My youngest is out of high school now and got a pretty good job at the feed mill. He gives me four dollars a week out of his pay for board and it sure helps. But I reckon I better not get used to extra money like that. Like as not hell get married in a year or two. But no use borrowing trouble is there.
> Hoping you and yours are all keeping well.
> Yours truly . . .

My fellow clerks were genial enough in the give-and-take of the job, but their crony groups were well established before I cut in and I made no effort to get beyond "Good morning" and "See you tomorrow." I lunched alone and frugally at the

Automat across Broadway and snoozed the rest of the hour in the churchyard of St. Paul's Chapel, the serenely Wrennish affair next door for which I retain an affection. For some reason, its memorial to General Montgomery, killed in the assault on Quebec in 1775, sticks in my visual memory with gloomy vividness. Among our clerical crew was a nominal acquaintance—a classmate, son of the AT&T treasurer, putting in the summer with a supervisory post in the stock-issue project. I think we had been in a Crimson competition at the same time. Anyway he knew who I was as well as I knew who he was, but with true Harvard camaraderie he looked right through me when we met in a corridor. I knew the score and paid no heed.

This low-keyed windfall of a job, bless Mr. Will Howe for it, had a gratifying finale. As the project was winding down late in August, the rumpled personnel man who had hired me let me know that if I cared to stay on, AT&T had a permanent job for me. I now know that my reply should have been: "I'd better go get my degree; but how about a rain check for ten months from now?" That might well have secured me a basic living after commencement. But in such matters my presence of mind has never been good. I merely thanked him heartily and refused. And next year, when I badly needed employment, it did not occur to me to try to make use of my apparently good record at 195 Broadway. Just as well, however, that I let this opportunity slip. For those summer weeks, nine-to-five office routine had suited. But several years of it, probably as training for a minor executive post in a huge organization, would have ill fitted my sluggish habits and clumsiness in intramural relations. Not even Walter Mitty would ever have dreamed of me as a promising young credit to a great corporation's bureaucracy.

Strange that in two months or so, Furnas, the congenital economic misfit, should have had and turned down two offers of jobs. But even stranger that both, and several more to come in the next few years, usually but not always refused, so consistently involved activity for which he was egregiously ill fitted. Yet the people making the offers were normally shrewd and well meaning. How little even capable men are capable of understanding others!

9

Regards to Broadway

WHEN MY SUITCASE and I reached the South Station after Mr. Demos's blessing, we thought we knew where we were going. Paul Herzog had spoken about me to Messmore Kendall, his late father's law partner in New York. Among the lucrative pies in which Kendall had a well-manicured finger—and consequently a sizable fortune—was Metro-Goldwyn-Mayer. He was thick-eyebrowed, portly, well tailored; could have been understudy for J. P. Morgan and was never displeased when somebody mentioned the likeness. Midspring he had business in Boston, came out to Cambridge to see Paul, and looked me over at lunch. It went well. He definitely told me to come see him right after commencement for shipping off to Hollywood for some sort of berth in scripts or publicity. I have long been aware that I was no better fitted for that than for the post of lifeguard-instructor at the Beverly-Wilshire pool. At the time, however, it sounded fine, and was one reason— another was being dog-weary of bear leading—why I had said thanks, no, when Scotty's family asked me to come to Europe with them and go on looking after him. I turned that opening over to a classmate to whom extra money and a year abroad sounded good. His consequent close look at the life affluent nudged him into radicalism culminating in ardent fellow traveling, maybe even a party card. He was of an engagingly volatile temperament and, I suppose, might have gone that road anyway, but I still feel partly responsible.

Before leaving Cambridge I wrote Kendall that two days

later I'd report to him. His office was in the highly commodious owner's duplex on top of the Capitol Theater—neither largest nor gaudiest of picture palaces but the respected East Coast showcase for M-G-M movies. He received me kindly. I intimated tactfully that I was standing by for sailing orders. He leaned back and said in effect, Well, it hadn't worked out, nobody in Hollywood expected me; but he was prepared to put me on his office payroll to make myself useful until something appropriate came along, probably in the fall. I still suspect he had forgotten all about me until my note arrived. In that situation a good many big shots would have turned me loose with a brief apology or maybe a why-didn't-you-remind-me-sooner. His improvised solution might be attributed, of course, to reluctance to look bad in Paul's eyes. But the impressions that I eventually formed of him hint that his sense of personal behavior was better than that. Anyway I was in no position to refuse. With hardly a twitch of countenance, I hope, I became pro-tem fifth wheel of Kendall's private chariot.

It consisted of the boss and two women: an elderly, self-admiringly grumpy upper secretary, Miss Donnelly, who looked and acted like a role for Marie Dressler; and a youngish, red-headed under secretary, Miss McEvilly, who owed her job to being daughter of an early associate of Kendall's who had died leaving a struggling family. It was a question which of those two women handled and lubricated the less esoteric details of Kendall's affairs the better. Miss McEvilly's ironic turn of humor often lightened the day. And I still relish memories of how Miss Donnelly would give the business to a caller of whom the boss wanted no part. She would grunt scornfully when he gave his name, scrawl it disgustedly on the stylus-intercom connected with Kendall's desk, fix him with a gloomy stare until the machine clacked saying no, then snort at him and go back to some clerical chore as abruptly as though he not only didn't exist, he never had existed.

I knew Kendall's affairs only superficially, of course. He had that piece of M-G-M. He rode herd on the manager of the Capitol, Major Edward Bowes, later of radio fame. But he was also a one-man conglomerate: He was deep in Chilean copper. He occasionally angeled a theatrical production. He had a large piece of the newborn Farrar & Rinehart publishing house. He owned tenement-clogged real estate northwest of the Capitol. On one of his block-through plots on Eighth Avenue he was building New York's first general-traffic bus terminal. He had the American rights to a trick British all-weather top for open touring cars; a sample was mounted on a British-made Buick in which I ran office errands, cursing its righthand drive in lefthand-oriented traffic. No doubt I never knew of a dozen other of his concerns. Yet he stayed pretty clear, I believe, of the stock market fever then rising to hysterical heights.

He also neglected to go splashy on the scale into which his order of wealth would have tempted many thus risen from small-town Michigan or wherever it was. The extensive apartment under the office was his only town domicile. No Rolls-Royce or Isotta-Fraschini; the other car was a discreetly dark green Cadillac coupe. No Long Island manor house down the shore from Gatsby's; Kendall's stronghold was a fine old rambling white clapboard antique up the river at Dobbs Ferry. A genuine Washington's headquarters, it had a gratifying but tasteful prestige; therein he collected Federalist antiques and Washington memorabilia including a set of George's false teeth. No occasion—well, not much—for appearing in the newly booming gossip columns. He had sloughed off his first wife, who had given him a handsome daughter, and apparently without friction maintained them expensively somewhere on the Upper East Side. His new wife, chatelaine of Dobbs Ferry, where she bred Pekinese, had come out of a Ziegfeld chorus. That sounds splashy, but actually Kitty, though pretty as a little red wagon, dressed and behaved, so far as I saw, most discreetly. Occasionally she asked me to drive her on shopping trips in that damn Buick and after getting her fill of Fifty-seventh Street, she'd blow me to lunch and tell me all about her purchases.

My stipend was eighteen dollars a week. Since I had free lodging at Paul's family house on West Sixty-seventh Street while he was in Europe, at 1927 prices that was adequate if not ample. And the Pennsylvania Dutch housekeeper made very fine pies; I often found a sample in my room. Kendall had been sketchy about my duties. One definite assignment was to catalogue Harry Houdini's collection of books on show business he had recently bought; a professional librarian had quit the job, why I never knew. Even now, after I've sired a number of large books stiff with scholarly references, such library chores are not my long suit. What I managed in this one was meager and sloppy. But much of the material was fascinating, particularly many early nineteenth-century memoirs gorgeously bound and lavishly extra-illustrated, from which I soaked in a familiarity with Covent Garden and Drury Lane very useful fifty years later for my definitive biography of Fanny Kemble. Kendall never checked up on my cataloguing. I think he just liked owning the stuff and occasionally taking down a book to caress the binding and look at the pictures; and it had been a happy thought that if he had to employ me to salve his conscience, my college degree was the solution to getting that catalogue completed.

Even had he wondered how I was doing, however, it soon didn't matter, for I became a free-floating factotum doing most things well enough, some badly, seldom the same thing twice. At collecting overdue rents among the tenements I was ineffective, but trying took up a lot of time. I arranged and hung in one of the spare offices Houdini's large collection of autographed theatrical photographs from Edwin Booth to George M. Cohan. When it was all nicely arranged chronologically, Kendall came in and said no, not that way, I want them higgledy-piggledy; so I did it again, all higgledy-piggledy. I typed out the actors' parts from the script of Somerset Maugham's *The Letter*, which Kendall was producing in the fall. Transatlantic phone service was splinter-new then; when Maugham telephoned from London about some detail it was I who picked up the phone, and I almost dropped it. When Dobbs Ferry needed a new butler I prowled the best employment agencies and hired a solemn German in a pince-nez that wobbled precariously when he leaned over to hand a dish. Emil assumed I was a power in the household to be propitiated. At the opening-night party for *The Letter* he plied me mercilessly with champagne; then Fania Marinoff, actress-wife of Carl van Vechten, I believe, insisted on my drinking gin with her toward the end of the evening—result, the worst hangover I ever had. If I ever saw her again, I had every excuse for not recognizing her. When Kendall wanted a high-ticket cigarette case in the shape of an envelope to give Katharine Cornell, star of *The Letter,* I actually found such a thing already made up in solid silver at Cartier's. I still recall my amazement when, just because I said I came from Messmore Kendall's office, the salesman casually handed it over to be taken away on approval.

This bits-and-pieces career culminated when a ward of Kendall's, a smoldery girl of Russian extraction, was to marry a fine young man of impeccable background whom nobody paid any attention to. Kendall told me to handle arrangements—not the guest list or the wedding party, those were women's concern, but the unsentimental logistics. The Dobbs Ferry house was an ideal setting. Up to then I had attended only one wedding that could ever have been called formal, but with amused hints from Miss Donnelly I plunged in. I stirred up the chief florist in Yonkers, saying don't foolishly overdo but shoot the works as far as good taste allows. I consulted lengthily with a caterer. The Dobbs Ferry cellar already contained more champagne and varied hard stuff than George Washington ever saw in one place; I needed no bootlegger. As far as I was aware, nobody involved had any religious affiliation, so, going for class, I phoned the Archdiocese of New York (Episcopalian) to ask what hymenotectonic talent they had on hand. In five minutes I had salt on the tail of the Reverend Dr. Somebody who lived upriver and would be delighted. And to judge from the fervency of his handshake when it was all over, Kendall's fee gave him reason for delight.

Everything was falling into place. When the Cadillac and I reached Dobbs Ferry that morning, the groom was already on deck, dim but presentable; the flowers were chastely gorgeous; the caterer was well on the way to being set up. In his who-giveth-this-woman-to-this-man morning coat and ascot, Kendall was downright distinguished and as matron of honor, Kitty, very short-skirted and dripping chiffon, was delicious. But then wailing hell broke out upstairs. The wedding gown, having needed adjustments late the day before, was to come out on an early train from Grand Central—only it hadn't. And Olga/Tanya/Sonya was up there in step-ins and bra having fits and it was hard to blame her. Over the phone one learned that the dressmaker's assistant, the chosen messenger, had missed her train but was already on the next one and would arrive, gown in hand, at 10:58 or some such cliff-hanging time—nobody had thought to have it rushed out in a taxi. So I—who else?—met the train and the gown, and the substantial black woman carrying it scolded *me* all the way to the house.

At something like 11:15 the telephone rang. The dear schoolmate of Olga/Sonya/Tanya's who was to play the wedding march had fallen over the dog or come down with smallpox or something—anyway was out of the running. Such a no-show was specially awkward back then when, among our best people, a wedding without Wagner was hardly legal. Kendall looked at me.

"Joe, can you play the piano?"

I should have said I had a hereditary phobia about pianos and fainted if I touched one even accidentally. But it was true that at a defenseless age I had been exposed to "piano lessons" acquainting me to some extent with the instrument's simplest ways. So I said I'd see what I could do. Out in a summerhouse was a half-ruined upright abysmally out of tune but the keyboard still worked. No sheet music available: all I had to go on was rough memory of Dee-dee-di-*dum!* and some notion of octaves with the left hand and primitive chords in the key of G, the only one with which I had ever felt at all at home. It was a good thing I didn't have to cope with that vivacious Mendelssohn recessional. Once Wagner had hummed his tune over a few times it probably took even him a while to work it out in sharps and flats. It took me too long to cobble up a faintly recognizable version of the first seventeen notes of the melody—through what might transcribe as dee-dumty-*dum*. As I reached that point they came running from the house to hurry me up. In I went, sat down at the grand piano in the lower hall and gave it my first thump. It was in good tune and would make me sound better if anything could.

It worked—kind of. Down George's elegant staircase came Tanya/Sonya/Olga doing that damn wedding dress proud, keeping good stately time, cuddling her flowers charmingly. The trouble was that when I reached the end of my seventeen notes I had nowhere to go. Even had I had time to try, I could never have worked out anything like the twiddly bit that Wagner wrote in to follow. So, doing the only possible thing, I went back and started over again and Olga/Tanya/Sonya, who either had no ear for music or was too keyed up to notice, kept on coming. Kendall joined her at the foot of the stairs and several more reprises wafted them into the drawing room. Afterward, as I was having a well-deserved second drink amid the babble round the buffet, a gaunt, gray-haired lady guest asked me: "I thought you played well but why didn't you go on?" I just mumbled and went away.

The Cadillac and I took the happy couple to the Plaza, where I had reserved them a cozy suite. Sonya/Olga/Tanya kissed me good-bye, which was certainly the least she could do. Two days later the office got a notice from the police that a dark green Cadillac, license plate thus-and-so, had been observed at excessive speed in Central Park. Kendall told Miss Donnelly to take care of it with an indicated phone call to the right person downtown—and raised my pay three dollars.

This story should go on, slick-magazine style, into my remaining Kendall's protégé-henchman, marrying his daughter, who was pleasant as well as handsome, and living happily ever after. Only there were flaws, usually of my doing. Miss Cornell was returning from Europe to rehearse *The Letter;* Kendall sent me to meet her on the pier and make myself solicitously useful. I could find nobody resembling her under the custom letter "C," so I missed her clean. It did not occur to me that she might be under "M" for McClintock, her director-husband's name, of which I was imperfectly aware. Kendall said nothing but had no reason to be pleased. Then he staged a party at the apartment and gave me the key to the liquor lockup, telling me to fetch up four cases of champagne and whiskey, gin and so forth, to match. That lockup was something to see: stacks and stacks of genuine, pre-Prohibition booze thoughtfully laid in circa 1919. Maybe just looking at it went to my head. Anyway the champagne, good California stuff, carried the same vineyard's name and style of label as the dry vermouth. Next morning I learned that I had sent up four cases, all right, but of vermouth not champagne. There was a certain bleakness. And toward the end of summer I was to leave the keys of the Buick on Kendall's desk so he could drive himself home to Dobbs Ferry late in the evening. Miss McEvilly had two passes to *Seventh Heaven* at the Roxy; after work she and I used them. Janet Gaynor's pixieish charm—that picture plus

Sunrise and *Street Angel* won her the first best-actress Oscar ever
awarded—so bemused me that I forgot about leaving the keys.
Next day I had nothing to say in my defense. That was all I
said, just handed over the keys and reached for my hat. I should
have been fired but wasn't.

In view of my string of bobbles that was much to Kendall's
credit. He was in no position to know or care that I'd done
that sort of thing all my life and would probably keep on. Sixty
years later I still like him for his forbearance. Yet I cannot
pretend that I ever found him generally likable. He was too
walled away behind good tactical footwork, good tailoring, good
living; too suavely impressed with himself as, in some ways, he
had a right to be. And there were hitches in his tactical machine. Once he took me into his private box on the Capitol's
mezzanine to study the between-showings stage show—a pretentious and expensive wallow in production numbers of the
sort that the Roxy did twice as big and three times as flashy.
When the pit orchestra and the ballet number and the hot-
diggety number and the winsome soprano and so on had
worked all through the light plot—I forgot the adagio team—
and the movie had come on, he said that in view of the high
average drawing power of M-G-M's product it was ominous
that attendance was slacking off. What could I suggest that
might step up the stage show's supplementary drawing power?

Had I been a trusted henchman of long standing and experience, useful as catalyst and sounding board, the discussion
thus sought might have been useful to him. But I felt only
"Who, me?" and may well have left him feeling that in turning
to me he had been guilty of an absurdity. It was even more
awkward when he tried to pump me about Paul's private affairs. His approach was skillful, but it forced me to respond
so meagerly that he knew he was being snubbed by his twenty-
one-dollar-a-week, only marginally useful hanger-on. That
cannot have set well. Even so, after decades of to some extent
rubbing elbows with a number of the affluent and important,
I consider him a creditable specimen.

Anyway, I think he had come to feel, at least subliminally,
that it would be more comfortable to slough me off—decently,
of course, by finding me other livelihood. Among potential
employers to whom he sent me was John Farrar, editorial pil-

lar of Farrar & Rinehart. All he did was send me to Burton Rascoe, editor of the *Bookman;* it came to nothing. Two years later I was doing odd editorial chores for Farrar & Rinehart, but I never mentioned our previous interview nor did Farrar show signs of recalling it. In the end, however, Kendall's solution arrived in the shape of a brisk and personable young theatrical press agent, Lynn Farnol, who, with a recently acquired partner, Howard Benedict, was handling publicity for *The Letter.* In what terms Kendall recommended me I don't know. But after the play had been running a couple of weeks—creakily, for it was half a flop—Farnol was in the office one afternoon, said hello, and went on: "Did the boss tell you you'll be working for me next week?"

Lying fast, I said indeed he had and I was looking forward to it. I asked no questions about payment or duties. On Saturday I bade farewell: chipperly to Miss McEvilly, respectfully to Miss Donnelly, who snorted less emphatically than I expected, gratefully to Kendall, for gratitude I did have reason to feel.

When going into New York from the country these days, I usually walk from the Port Authority bus terminal across Forty-second Street to my midtown appointment. The block between Eighth and Seventh avenues is, of course, focus—or say central abscess—of the town's cut-rate lewdness. Much of New York has changed since I first saw the Public Library lions, no other bit of it has changed quite so strikingly into something scruffy and strange. In 1927 its half dozen large theaters glittered with high-powered, expensive shows embodying the go-for-broke, brashly synthetic spirit of the Great White Way. Their flagship was the New Amsterdam Theatre, where the annual editions of the *Ziegfeld Follies* had long been a national institution. Now, those shows were no Sunday School stuff. Their prime asset was lovely girls wearing very little; the showcase was often trimmed with bluish jokes; but for change of pace the *Follies* and its rivals also recruited the great comics and vaudeville songbirds of the day. So, though just as vulgar as their typical patrons, in their own terms those productions had class. Now those same houses serve up triple bills of XXX pornography. The shops between their marquees, formerly

lunchrooms, tobacconists, drugstores, were, granted, sometimes fronts for bookmakers or bootleggers. Those relatively
innocent rackets have given way to two-bit peepshows, anthro-
pomorphic rubber goods, and books and magazines that would
make a goat blush. The sidewalks seethe with cruising no-goods
spelling prostitution and drugs. The degeneration is the more
striking because it has not meant demolitions. Behind that in-
crustation of both literal and metaphorical filth are the same
old bricks and mortar. And right there next to the New Amsterdam's half-obliterated lobby is the slender Candler Building, chastely new in 1927, wherein I served Farnol & Benedict.
God knows what now goes on in those two rooms on the ninth
floor. Anybody who wants me to look into that must provide
a police escort.

Farnol was sizable but shortlegged, which, added to his
broadly confident smile, put one in mind of Maurice Chevalier. Fairly new in New York, he had already upgraded himself into handling well-considered legit productions. When I
weighed in, the office's chief concerns were *Burlesque,** a solid
success produced by the widely respected Arthur Hopkins, and
the several irons in the fire of George C. Tyler, once a giant
in the American theater, now fading though still taken seriously, particularly as specialist in touring revivals of old favorites like *Jim the Penman* and *Trelawney of the Wells* with all-star
casts. Benedict was a Baltimore newspaperman trying his luck
in New York—solidly handsome, easygoing, taciturn, taking
his lead from Farnol. The office had a gofer-factotum, Harry
Davis, a Bronxite about my age of globular body but sharp
above the neck, who answered the phone, fetched the sandwiches—functions that I covered when he was out on prolonged errands. Twenty years later, needing an interview with
Laurette Taylor for my book on the South Pacific, I phoned
the office of the producer of *The Glass Menagerie,* asked for

---

*Hopkins was no Minsky. The title derived from the background of the heroine, a
dancing soubrette who rises out of "burleycue" to Broadway stardom while her former partner goes downhill via drink. The only thing the show really had to do with
burlesque was the past of Hal Skelly, playing the hoofer, who actually was a veteran
of the Columbia (burlesque) Wheel. Oscar Levant did the piano player in a pungent
supporting role. As the heroine, Barbara Stanwick made her first headline-causing
success, thence off to Hollywood.

the press agent, and when I gave my name: "Furnas! How you been?" and it was Harry blossomed into a big-time press agent. Both of us were going baldish. I got the interview with a pair of ducats to match.

Farnol & Benedict's strangest client was a creepy little man, Myron C. Fagan, author and producer of a meant-to-be-gamy farce, *Jimmy's Women*, starring Fagan's wife, Minna Gombell—plump, not so young as she had been, but personable behind footlights and professional enough. Her footlights were those of the small theater on the New Amsterdam roof that had originally housed a glittersome, Ziegfeld-begotten cabaret. No doubt it is still there gathering cobwebs and cherishing gaudy memories. In 1927 it had been turned into the Frolic Theater, or some such name, seating several hundred. I never knew what Fagan paid for our services rendered, but it can't have been the standard two hundred dollars a week, for the show hardly *grossed* that at the box office. A larger dribble of revenue came through Gray's Drug Store, in which a cut-rate ticket agency sold seats for shows failing to sell out. Depth of discount reflected relative popularity; in such cases as Fagan's, a nominal $2.20 seat went for 55 cents whenever some penurious hopeful felt what-have-I-got-to-lose.

Even so, plenty of seats were left empty. So it was the job of the press agent—meaning me—to "paper the house": give away tickets to those who would use them to fill out the audience. One telephoned a big employer of white-collar help, say AT&T or the great insurance companies, and asked the personnel people to spread the word that anybody applying at the *Jimmy's Women* box office for seats held for Mr. Thompson would see a free show. I never pass that location now without recalling the trouble sometimes thus occasioned. The third or fourth applicant in line, hearing Mr. Thompson's seats called for and handed out, objected violently, and it could take dangerously long to persuade all those in line to understand they were all Thompsons.

A crony of Fagan's was somehow connected with an embryonic radio station in the substratum of nascent broadcasting. Hence a half hour of free radio time to plug *Jimmy's Women*. Strange as it now sounds, at the time I not only didn't own a radio, I knew few who did and had heard few broadcasts of any sort. Yet here I was seated in a dingy office somewhere on Broadway facing a table mike and sentenced to talk for half an hour about that dismal show to the satisfaction of at least Fagan, who was likely to listen in. It occurred to me afterward that I should have read from the script of the play. But that a coherent script existed was improbable—it had certainly eroded drastically in rehearsal and nightly ad-libbing—and anyway putting out on the air such lines as were available was certain to make people stay away. If it's true that all broadcasts go out into space forever and ever and that somewhere, sometime, sophisticated technology out there among the galaxies will pick them up, someday my disembodied spirit will play back for me this, my first broadcast.

Fagan never mentioned the matter. Either he was content or hadn't listened in after all. If the former, it showed he was incapable of making sense, but that was already clear in his keeping that appalling turkey running. After a while, of course, it disintegrated and the Fagans disappeared from my cosmos. Years later, however, the lady, still not uncomely, occasionally turned up in minor parts in Hollywood movies; today's movie buffs should identify her as Mimi, the crass and dangerous bitch in *The Thin Man*. Fagan's only surfacing, as far as I know, consisted of being mixed up in one of those amateur Fascist movements that infested Hollywood in the late 1930s.

Routine at Farnol & Benedict: write letters for the bosses; concoct releases for the daily papers and the dramatic editors of magazines; peddle photographs of leading performers in both crucial stage moments and fancy portraits; juggle requests for free tickets. The great FPA, supernal columnist of the *New York World*, nearly had a fit when he phoned, saying: "This is Adams. I want a pair for *Burlesque* tonight," and I, unaware that FPA stood for Franklin P. Adams, said: "I'll have to check with Mr. Farnol. Let me have a number to call you back." Arrange testimonials: In those innocent days a big-name actress, say Madge Kennedy in Hopkins's production of Philip Barry's *Paris Bound*, would shill for Lux soap for a consideration no more valuable than a case of the stuff and the publicity value of her picture smiling in next month's national advertising along with the gurgly quote about her and the show supplied by guess who.

Farnol soon learned I could write sizable pieces of copy that didn't read so much like plugs that the editors of the Sunday amusement sections wouldn't print them. I also did much interviewing. Had I ever felt awe of stage stars, I now lost it. Some were nice, most weren't, none was more than life-size, that is, much like other people. Among the nice ones were the leading women of the Abbey Theater company that, in a disastrous effort to recover prestige, Tyler brought over from Dublin. He couldn't pay well, so the Abbey's leading women, Sara Allgood and Maire O'Neill, matter-of-fact and unpretentious as well as distinguished, took a kitchenette apartment somewhere in the West Forties and kept house. I recall helping Miss O'Neill shell the peas for dinner while, with a publicity piece in mind, she talked about old days at the Abbey.

Their repertory was three plays by Sean O'Casey, then just developing international renown. The newest was *The Plough and the Stars*, about the 1916 revolutionary troubles. Though the acting was first rate, I thought the play too topical for audiences who had forgotten whatever they had ever heard about its subject. Among Irish-Americans, however, "Abbey Theatre" was a potential buzzword. In pre–World War I times the Abbey's original company had brought to America Synge's *The Playboy of the Western World*, which hypersensitives considered a lampoon on the Ould Sod. In Dublin and later in New York they expressed that view in riotous attempts to close the production down. Both veteran theatergoers and New York's Irish might well be expected to remember. And when produced in Dublin, *The Plough* had set off similar rioting, for it was pretty candid about its material, though never questioning the validity of the Sinn Fein cause.

Farnol deputed me to find out what were the odds on riots to match in New York. Among other sources I tried the Irish-American papers. The editor of one of them fixed me with a stormy-dark but opportunistic eye and said in effect that while he knew of no plans to mob the Abbey troupe this time, if anybody thought it worth anybody's while for publicity (as indeed it might be) he was prepared, for a consideration, to arrange turmoil C.O.D. I reported this to Farnol with amusement. I think he was tempted, but by then Tyler's resources were so slim that such a deal was out of the question. My chat with the

helpful editor remained merely one of the educational details
of press agentry.

By spring 1928 the waning theatrical season was giving us
little to do. I had an offer of a two-month job on a sheep
ranch in Wyoming tutoring a kid for College Board exams.
Farnol granted me leave of absence with alacrity. On my return I found both partnership and my job dissolved. Benedict
had gone to Hollywood on some sort of publicity deal—he became a minor but well-thought-of director—and Farnol was
doing East Coast publicity for Samuel Goldwyn's New York
office at 729 Seventh Avenue. During that summer my odd
pickings were most inconveniently slim, but toward fall I found
myself again working for Farnol as his nominal secretary on
the Goldwyn payroll at twenty-five a week plus ten from his
own pocket. I was then sharing a fifth-floor walkup, two rooms
and a bath, at sixty a month among three of us. At 1928 prices
life could be maintained, though not lavishly.

Among Goldwyn's talent properties at the time was Vilma
Banky, a recently imported Hungarian pretty as a Gabor if
somewhat plumper, profitable then, forgotten now. She got
off to a flying start in America by delighting the press with
complaints in a stumbly accent that Mr. Goldwyn would let
her eat nossing but pineapple and lamb chops—a reducing
diet then popular. We planted any number of stills of her
looking soulful and toothsome in blouse-slipping-off-the-
shoulder roles. Her only American incarnation was that of a
fetching waitress in one of the Childs chain of restaurants then
prospering as New York institutions. It was shot in Hollywood, but the producer wanted some footage of actual customers going into the Childs at Fifth Avenue and Forty-ninth
Street, where one went late in the evening for butter cakes
and scrambled eggs. We sought permission to set up there and
dwelt enticingly on nationwide publicity. The notoriously cranky
Childs management would have none of it. So we arranged
for a cadre of construction men with rolls of cable, tool kits,
pickaxes, welding masks, and large MEN AT WORK signs to plant
a public-utility-style tarpaulin tent on the sidewalk at the restaurant door with a movie camera hidden in its depths.

To plug a Banky picture called *Two Lovers* Farnol wanted
an attention-attracting automobile to run up and down Broad-

way. I hired a 1910-vintage struggle-buggy, installed in it the owner and his girl friend in suitable dustcoats and goggles, and set them driving slowly along between Columbus Circle and Times Square with *Two Lovers* three-sheets on both flanks of the car and in the rear a large placard: TWO LOVERS / PLEASE EXCUSE OUR LUST.* As an attention caller it had points, but in about half an hour the police phoned saying get that thing off the street, people were outraged. It was Farnol who took the call. Since he hadn't seen the thing in action, he just told me to get down there and kill it, which I did, much to the relief of my two stooges. That the gag shocked people shows how drastically the Times Square area has changed.

For the opening of *Two Lovers* in Pittsburgh I was sent there to drape a huge banner over the theater, make the usual advance-man gestures, and particularly turn out a week's worth of daily advice for lovelorn columns to be signed Vilma Banky; I forget which of the local papers held still for that. The first two days had to be concocted out of whole cloth, but then real pleas for help began to come in. Nathanael West had yet to write *Miss Lonelyhearts,* so I had no better focus for the assignment than to wonder whether these hapless people could really have got into such troubles as they described. The editor was no such sadist as West's Shrike, and I was allowed to ignore the most lurid letters. After all, responses to only three or four a day was all the traffic would bear. And it's at least conceivable that in a couple of cases the advice that Vilma supplied made some helpful sense.

She was probably unaware of these shenanigans in her behalf. At the time whatever mind she had should have been dwelling on what the effect of dialogue on movies would do to her future, for eventually she was one of the stars whom talkies' requirements extinguished. How many seats for *Two Lovers* those columns sold nobody worried about. The point was that they fattened up the sheaf of clippings sent to the head office on the coast. An even better showing was the front-page splash in the *New York Evening Post*—then an unsplashy

---

*By now this needs explanation: In the 1920s many minor roads were still so dusty that in summer a fast driver passing a slow one would smother him in an unpleasant cloud of dust. Heavy-footed showoffs went in for rear-end lettered signs: PLEASE ECXUSE MY DUST!

afternoon paper owned by the Curtis interests. It was cam-
paigning for readers' contributions to a fund to cheer up needy
old folks' Thanksgiving (or was it Christmas?). Norman Klein,
the *Post*'s star reporter in charge of the project, took me up to
the Bronx to visit a nice old couple in hard luck on the basis
of whom I wrote a really affecting five hundred words signed
by Miss Banky, all about how she had gone to see them and
though her heart was wrung by their difficulties, grim as things
were, at least their Thanksgiving would be all that heart could
wish. Klein liked it so much he persuaded his boss to run it
on the front page with a lovely shot of Miss Banky. What the
old folks thought of it I never knew. At worst they did get the
ingredients of a bang-up Thanksgiving dinner and a cash
sweetener to boot, so what conscience might feel about the
matter was somewhat assuaged.

Now and again Mr. Goldwyn would come east on the Su-
perchief and the Twentieth Century—flying coast to coast was
still as primitive as in *The Last Tycoon*—and spent ten minutes
in the chair by my desk while I disappeared and he told Farnol whatever was on his mind. My memories of so weighty a
phenomenon are shamefully slim. I retain an impression that
he was intensely deadpanned and his clothes, though the fab-
rics were regrettable, were exquisitely tailored. But from the
few remarks I ever heard him make I can supply no new
Goldwynisms or old ones either.* Invariably, as soon as he left,
Farnol would be on the phone to the *Times:* "Sam's in town
and says he wants to talk." And next morning that part of the
public that cared learned, on Samuel Goldwyn's expert word,
that the new sound-track techniques were invaluable for mood-
music accompaniments and establishing theme songs, but the
screen was basically different from the stage and would never

---

*William Safire ("Mr. Bonaprop," *New York Times Magazine*, February 15, 1987) wrote
that Goldwynisms were concocted as publicity for Goldwyn "by the press agent Lynn
Farnol." Since they are part of the language, I must point that this is erroneous. Lynn
did no such thing during my tenure with him in New York in the late 1920s, and in
any case that sort of thing was not at all his style. Further I checked with my good
old friend Robert J. Landry, retired managing editor of *Variety*, who was in the *Variety*
office in Los Angeles during Lynn's tour of duty for Goldwyn on the coast; Bob never
had reason to attribute the Goldwynisms to Lynn. He referred me to another *Variety*
veteran of that day, Tom Pryor, who corroborated all of that and said he always had
the impression that it was Howard Dietz who created the Goldwynisms.

go in for give-and-take dialogue stage fashion. Within a few months, of course, he was producing Ronald Colman's first "all-talking" movie, *Bulldog Drummond*. Mr. Goldwyn was not the only big shot in show business or elsewhere whose motto should have been: "Never mind what I say, watch what I do."

As Goldwyn's first talkie, *Bulldog Drummond* was accorded a double springboard—a Hollywood-style world premiere but *in New York*. Colman was to come east for it. Farnol told me to get hold of a covey of bulldogs to meet him at Grand Central for the photographers. The American Kennel Club found me a Westchester breeder of the old-fashioned, bowlegged, undershot-jawed, bug-eyed kind, insufferably ugly but, as I was to learn, ineffably good-natured. I hired five for the arrival morning. The kennel man buzzed my door early; here he was with a station wagon bursting and boiling with bulldogs, mostly brindle, all powerful. Though he assured me they were friendly, it took resolution to get into the same vehicle as that whining, bouncing mass of gargoyle-faced monsters. But in thirty seconds we were all the best of friends and I rode down to Grand Central half smothered by two hundredweight of demonstrative affection.

At the station the kennel man took three on leads, I took two. Those beasts pulled like Percheron plow teams at a county fair. In we charged at ten miles an hour, commuters panicking and scattering right and left. A number of people were already waiting at the gate to meet passengers on the incoming Century, but I had to get the dogs through to the platform for pictures as Colman disembarked. The gate man said no. So did a railroad security man who came to see what went on. I expostulated, waving Colman's name at them. Nothing doing without the stationmaster's okay. Off we trooped to get that, causing more panic along the way. For a miracle the stationmaster listened and I persuaded him to pet one of the dogs, who licked his hand and gazed at him adoringly. That so softened him that he sent his man Friday along with us to make sure we were passed in.

There were the photographers for me to round up, there was the red carpet that the New York Central always rolled out for the Century and, in a few minutes, for we had cut it pretty fine, here was the train sleeking in behind its nonchalantly humming electric locomotive. I had the car number and position taped, my dogs were lined up just right grinning ear to ear, the photographers' flash guns were loaded . . . no Colman. He had got off at 125th Street. I had nothing to show for all that scramble but a strong ambition—which I never got round to satisfying—to own a dog like those.

Rags to riches, however. That evening I was a hero, albeit unsung. The doings at the theater were Hollywood-style more or less—sky-sweeping searchlights, floodlights under the marquee, radio announcer's yapping and gurgling about arriving big names, police barriers, mounted policemen riding herd on traffic. . . . But this was Broadway, not Hollywood, and New York's Finest lacked experience in handling the kind of mob that such goings-on attract. My assignment was to lurk outside and take action if anything was needed. It soon was. For a while the long black cars duly rolled up to disgorge elegant silken legs topped by mink jackets and escorted by black ties, even some white ones. But informally a great deal of hey-look-ut! whutzgoanonhyuh . . . was being created and an inquisitive crowd of unhousebroken New Yorkers was building up. Ten minutes before the houselights were due to dim, the ill-placed and poorly manned police barriers gave way. From right and left what seemed like half the chronic frequenters of Times Square surged into my post between curb and lobby and the meeting of the two waves created a sort of human tide rip shoving, squalling, swearing, giggling, simultaneously seeking celebrities and bucking obstacles.

The bulk of our fat-cat audience was already safe indoors. But that was the moment when a limousine disgorged Will H. Hays. For all his clout as former Postmaster-General, former national chairman of the Republican Party, incumbent president of the Motion Picture Producers and Distributors of America (Hollywood's indispensable false front), Hays was physically tiny, only a thought too large to have made a professional career as a midget. In that overblown Rugby scrum he stood no more chance than a burnt match in a flushing toilet bowl. I recognized his squinchy little face just as he was going down and got there in time, gathered him to me like a mother kangaroo, hunched my shoulders, stuck out my behind, and shoved backward toward the lobby with more power than I knew I was capable of. I did have the advantage, as the members of the mob did not, of knowing where I was going and why. It took doing, but we made it. I shot Hayes, tousled and gasping, into the lobby door and know nothing more about what kind of evening he had. For a few minutes, as I caught my breath, I observed the floundering efforts of the police to clear the sidewalk, then went in to watch the picture from the back of the house. I said nothing to Farnol about my heroism. But now, if Hays left any great-grandchildren who may feel grateful for my saving him from what might have been at least serious injury . . . *Bulldog Drummond*, by the way, was a solid success and Colman's grainy British accent—he had had an early stage career—showed he had nothing to fear from the new demands of talkies.

Stray bits from that period keep floating up through my synapses. (Note to proofreader: Spelling correct. All right, go look it up!) I have forgotten the name and raison d'être of the temporary she-client to take a picture of whom Hearst's *Evening Journal* sent a curly-headed photographer under my chaperonage; but I haven't forgotten that he was so tight he set his hair on fire with flash powder. Nor have I forgotten Lily Damita, Goldwyn's French-imported siren. She cut a minor swath in Hollywood because casting her was a problem. The role of Irma la Douce was still to be created. Goldwyn finessed her accent by starting her off as the aloof British heroine of a silent movie made from Conrad's *The Rescue;* nothing could have been less suitable. A recent TV movie about Errol Flynn, to whom she was married for a while, had Lily played by a small, scrawny brunette with a mail-order French accent. It saddened me. Lily was not large, but none could have dared call her scrawny.

She disapproved of me. Whenever she came into the office she scolded me in what English she could muster: "For why you look so? You seeck or somsin?" Possibly she sensed that I had never seen anything like her and couldn't believe it. She got Farnol into a jam when he took her for a "personal appearance" in Detroit and she insisted on going shopping for duty-free British bargains across the river in Canada. When they tried to return, the Immigration men, spotting her as not only exotic and lacking a passport but, I surmise, suspicious about her walk in life, refused reentry. I wish I'd been there for the fireworks.

Then there was the warlocks' Sabbath of Groucho Marx's dressing room as the four brothers huddled before curtain time. Farnol was moonlighting on Goldwyn by handling *Animal Crackers*, the Marxes' great stage show. He came down with erysipelas and lay for weeks at Roosevelt Hospital inadvertently growing a beard because they didn't dare shave him. I had to cover both Goldwyn's and the Marxes' needs. Every morning I went to the hospital and got orders for the day, as far as the harried convalescent could improvise them, but it was a poor way to run a railroad. Fortunately nothing important was then pending and *Animal Crackers* generated its own publicity and to spare. About all I had to do was dole out press seats to the right people and visit the theater before curtain time every evening to see that the press list was taken care of and to show the flag by passing the time of day with the Marxes.

It was a harsh but rewarding experience. The four were individuals as distinct offstage as on, indeed not far from their stage personae. Harpo was least like, not at all frenetic, saying little but at least talking. Zeppo chattered brittlely as chorus for the others. Chico had that predatory smile and deliberate speech, though it lacked the Gorgonzola accent. Those three would be already dressed and made up, their wildly disparate costumes lending a Halloweenish effect as background for Groucho at his dressing table finishing off his black greasepaint mustache and throwing over his shoulder a nonstop, ad lib monologue of wisecracks and double entendres—often unblushing singles—that should have been taped and rented out for stag parties. He was even more brilliant than I ever saw him on stage or screen. He and his brothers were as memorable—and off-putting—a Comus's crew as ever romped through the thickets.

As Captain Spalding donned his beat-up cork helmet, I withdrew and went to hang over the rail at the back of the house to laugh myself bowlegged for the fourth, fourteenth, fortieth time when Groucho as Louis XV leered at Madame Dubarry and asked swooningly: "May I call you Du?" and Chico and Zeppo entered, audience right, in lockstep singing, "Du, du liegst mir im Herzen." If *Animal Crackers* were in its millionth performance, my spirit would still be there laughing its ectoplasm loose.

Yet maybe Groucho's best laugh was a one-time affair. A U.S. Lines ship made a most seamanlike rescue of the crew of a freighter foundering away out in the Atlantic. The ship's captain had been too ill to take charge, but his first officer had filled in admirably and the newspapers played him for a hero, deservedly enough. In those days George Washington Hill, hardboot president of the American Tobacco Company, was pulling out all advertising stops for Lucky Strike cigarettes. While the ship was still several days from port, the first officer was propositioned by radio and for a most substantial consideration said yes. So the day before she arrived, the newspapers carried full-page advertisements with a fulsome testimonial from the hero ascribing his and his men's courage and skill to their having smoked Lucky Strikes to sustain them in the emergency.

The flagrancy of it caused unfavorable comment, lots of it. But the management of *Animal Crackers* stayed with an already completed arrangement to make the hero and his boat's crew guests of honor the evening after they landed. They arrived late, during Captain Spalding's bombastic entrance. The music stopped, the whole cast froze, a spotlight played on the stage box as the seamen filed in. To moderate applause they stood grouped while the orchestra played "The Star Spangled Banner." Then Groucho held up a hand for silence, went over to the box, took out a pack of cigarettes: "Have a Lucky, Cap?" The house had hysterics. It was probably his finest moment, comparable to Babe Ruth's lashing that home run into the stands just where he had pointed.

Once Farnol turned over to me another moonlighting job for an anemic comedy, *Young Love*, that had gone unable to pay his full fee; all they could get up was fifty a week. The good parts of that were the producer, Kenneth Macgowan, then still a name for his share in the catalytic Provincetown Playhouse sort of thing, a pleasant and cultivated gentleman, and its star, Dorothy Gish, a charmingly salty lady. The bad part was that as an independent flack I proved so inept that I was fired even before the poor thing had a chance to close— two weeks' pay was all I ever got. Have no illusions about my skills as press agent. The few ideas I had usually backfired, like the *Two Lovers* stunt. My typing was sketchy and still is. My absentmindedness was a persistent hazard. Farnol once knocked himself out getting seats for some runaway smash hit as a favor to Mordaunt Hall, movie reviewer of the *Times*, and I was to take them to him personally. I forgot all about it and Hall's important visiting firemen, whoever they were, went without. I braced myself for a firing but had only to apologize to Hall—and he was every bit as shirty about it as he had every right to be. Humble pie is not healthy as a steady diet, but now and again it can be good for the soul.

Anyway my days with Farnol were numbered. The poor man developed pulmonary TB and was sent west to a sanitarium; then, on his recovery, to the Goldwyn office in Hollywood for a year or two. That severed my connection with 729 Seventh Avenue. When Farnol eventually returned to New York, we were on only an occasional-chore basis, some piece of writing he needed, a few dollars from which were, of course, welcome. Once—oh, joy!—he gave me the $250 advance from Grosset & Dunlap for making a novel out of the script of a forthcoming Goldwyn movie, *One Heavenly Night*, a hurry-up job because it had to be published simultaneously with release to theaters. The story was good-natured fluff set in a musical-comedy Hungary, original by Louis Bromfield, shooting script by no less a talent than Sidney Howard, then working for Goldwyn on a six-months-a-year basis. I loosened up my elbow and did forty-five thousand words in a week. Thus it happened that the spine of my first-published book says in now half-obliterated red letters: *One Heavenly Night* by Lynn Farnol. Years ago I found a surviving copy in a bin of twenty-five-cent oddments on Fourth Avenue. I did get some sense of sprightly fun into its tinselly doings.

Several slimsy magazines then specialized in novelizations of movie scripts. Valuing that $250, the most money I had ever seen in one place, I applied for more such jobs to the editor of *Screen Romances*, I believe it was, impressively mentioning that I had knocked off forty-five thousand words in a week. "The writers we use," he said, "do that in two days."

The summer of 1929 brought a brief taste of prosperity. The great bull stock market had drawn Paramount Pictures into a prospective merger. It was far enough along for an arrangement to give the new outfit's advertising to Hanff-Metzger, a smallish New York agency that already handled much for Paramount—and sometimes oddments for Goldwyn. I had done copy and layout in that connection. And a man I knew at Paramount now showed he could blunder as well as anybody by offering me the job of copywriter for the consolidated account. It paid seventy-five a week, then enough to marry and rear a family on in a modest way. By Labor Day I was installed in Hanff-Metzger's offices in the spandy-new Paramount Building on Times Square, the one with the globe on top that, wags said, made it look like a seal balancing a ball on its nose.

For weeks I drew pay for doing just about nothing. My sole duty was to frequent the Paramount projection room as the new crop of fall movies came in, so I'd know what I would be plugging. I had no objections. I saw Maurice Chevalier's first Hollywood venture and Gary Cooper in *The Virginian,* a fair job that I recall gratefully because it introduced me to Eugene Pallette's bronchitic-bullfrog croak. Otherwise, day after day, I merely watched the gradual creation of the Chrysler Building half a mile across town.

Had I been a savvy type, I'd have got somehow into sync with the organization, absorbed its ways of working, developed personal relationships, constructively exploited having a foot in the door. But to work, that sort of thing must be instinctively spontaneous. All I did was pester the copy chief every week or so with a protest against inactivity. He always said take it easy, any day now things will jell.

How right he was! The last week of October my perplexity was assuaged by a disproportionately big wind—the great stock market crash. The Paramount merger was immediately dead in the water. So was I. I must have been one of the earliest cases of Depression-related unemployment. It sometimes makes me feel downright historic. A durable distinction too, for that was almost sixty years ago and never since have I drawn regular salary or wages.

10

Ways and Means

As DESCRIBED, my private hard times preceded the nation's. Beginning in 1926, three years early, they persisted, with a few upward fluctuations (Farnol, Hanff-Metzger) into 1933. During the last four of Joseph's seven lean years, times were hard all over and far more disastrously for many than for me. I now know I was lucky again to have failed to find another job in advertising, or in teaching, indeed in anything entailing meshing into an organization. That is no pretense to anarchic virtue. Had I known how, I'd readily have sought to learn my way into an intradependent, layer-organized complex of people manipulating institutional ends five days a week. Only I was no more made that way than I was gifted with absolute pitch or the ability to wiggle my ears.

So for a good while it was minor-oddments-or-die. I reviewed a few books for the evanescent *New Freeman* at fees so small I cannot recall what they were. Publishing houses occasionally gave me manuscripts to read at three to five dollars according to size, as French bills of fare say of fish. Sometimes it was an already accepted manuscript to process for spelling, punctuation, and sense. That might pay twenty-five dollars for a couple of days' work. Clifton Fadiman at Simon & Schuster (then smallish but fast-stepping) wafted a good deal of that sort of thing my way, bless him; and bless him doubly for recommending my article on phrenology to Stringfellow Barr at the *Virginia Quarterly;* it was my first blush of auctorial respectability. One editorial chore had a queerly disconcerting end-

207

ing: Farrar & Rinehart called me in: The text of Upton Sinclair's autobiography was, Sinclair himself acknowledged, very rough. He'd make it worth the while of whomever the publishers chose to put it in shape. It was not only rough, it was dull and flabby. Few best-selling authors have ever written worse than he; see that dreadful Lanny Budd series. I did what I could and sent it to Sinclair in California. Back came a letter that I wish I had saved: He was delighted with my plastic surgery. In grateful recompense he'd like to send me an autographed copy of one of his books; which would I like? No check!

There was more satisfaction in a developing offshoot from Farnoling: The editor of the Sunday amusement section of the *New York Herald-Tribune,* Arthur Folwell, a sweet-tempered old-timer rather like Shortridge's Mr. McKee, liked the kind of copy I did for Farnol and several times invited me to do him a free-lance piece on some bit of theatrical history. Thence I moved into an occasional criticism of a Broadway production that had run long enough to justify another look. (Late on the Saturday evening when I first met my wife-to-be I stopped with her at a grim little newsstand where Thompson Street meets Washington Square to buy a Sunday *Trib* to see whether Folwell had run my thoughts on World War I–based plays; there it was on the front page and I hoped she found it impressive.) Then I worked up to Sunday pieces on movie trends—at ten dollars a column. Since I usually held forth for a column and a half, that was something like fifty dollars a month. Only subway fare now. Then it took care of basic nourishment.

Some of my stuff on movies actually got read. C. A. LeJeune, eminent movie critic of the London *Observer*, wrote to me cordially. A man called in to shore up the faltering *Vanity Fair* approached me about doing its movie reviews. When samples were shown to Frank Crowninshield, the publisher, however, he said he didn't want another Aldous Huxley—disheartening but at least backhandedly flattering. When Bruce Gould tapped me for a series in the *Ladies' Home Journal* in the late 1930s, he confessed to having made an enjoyable habit of Furnas-on-movies in the Sunday *Trib*. Once I wrote in print that W. C. Fields was the six funniest things ever created, or some such temperate statement, and for several years afterward, no matter how often I changed addresses, I got a

Christmas telegram signed by a grateful reader alleged to dislike both children and dogs. Otherwise my assiduous riding herd on Hollywood was a dead end. It was annoying when the paper called me in to be photographed for promotional advertising along with the salaried theatrical and movie reviewers—no mention of even a few more dollars per column. I bet the *Trib*'s files survive somewhere with that mug shot in them.

By and large my odd pickings may have come to twelve hundred dollars a year average. Averages include wide swings. Yet thin as the ice, not to mention shoe soles, could get, I never went actually hungry, could even finance the far too many Fatima cigarettes without which the typewriter keys wouldn't work. When down to pocket change, I dined on Campbell's vegetable soup heated up with milk—not unpalatable and sure to stick to the ribs for a while; lunch on a pot of baked beans, ten cents at the Automat; breakfast on peanut butter, crackers, and tea. A diet low on Vitamin C, but I seemed proof against scurvy, and usually in the next few days dollars would somehow materialize. There were frugally zestful dinners for say seventy-five cents in the Levantine restaurants on Lexington Avenue, three nutritious, spicy courses. For a quarter or so more, large, garish Zucca's between Sixth and Broadway in the low Forties had a well-cooked several courses with pasta and excellent bread that would nourish one for days.

In flush times—and there were some, relatively—a dollar more covered Broad's mellowly old-timey, sawdust-floored place in a cellar south of Washington Square. The fatherly waiters' white aprons came down to the tops of their lace-up shoes; the Manhattan clam chowder was the only specimen I ever met that rated evenly with the New England version; my wife-to-be was instantly addicted to the scallop broil with bacon in a ten-inch pie dish; the fish were broiled with as much respect as if Polycrates' ring had just been found in each. It was literally a belly blow when one evening we went to dine at Broad's and found it dark and shuttered, a victim of hard times and its quixotically low price policy. But we had an almost adequate second string to our bow: Dick the Oysterman's on Eighth Street over toward Wanamaker's—not Jimmy the Oysterman's behind the Flatiron Building, much better known—*Dick's*, much less expensive. Dick's fish were very, very good; the house specialty was oysters sautéd with many thin bits of Smithfield ham, just as memorable as it sounds. On Thursdays the kitchen cooked for the help's supper a lordly mess of Smithfield ham hocks with spinach, and a waiter whom you knew would cut you it on it. . . . Zucca's, Broad's, Dick's—all one with Nineveh and Tyre.

Alcohol was no great part of those pre-Repeal experiences. My apartment mates and I couldn't afford much and expected more or less protracted dry spells. I knew only a few speakeasies, most notably Julius's at Tenth Street and Greenwich Avenue, where the whiskey sours were palatable but the atmosphere noisy and self-conscious. Things were more relaxed at the grappa cellar on the west side of McDougall Street not far south of Washington Square. Down eight or nine steps into a basement furnished with two long tables and benches refectory style; at the far end a tall counter displaying a glass jug of white wine, another of red, a third of grappa—Italy's explosive peasant brandy distilled from what's left in the cask when the wine is drawn off. A smallish man skipped about retrieving glasses to be washed, but it was strictly self-service; the bar was tended by an incredibly solid Italian lady.

A regular shot glass of grappa and a chaser of red or white cost a quarter: no further choices. The red was awful, the white more or less potable. Even if the place did look like a stage thieves' kitchen, the miscellaneous clientele, both sexes, were mostly orderly, low-spoken, minding their own business as they chatted and slowly absorbed the jocund grape. When somebody did get noisy or otherwise obstreperous, the lady would come bulging out from behind her fortification, lift him classically by the seat of the pants and the scruff of the neck, and heave him up the stairs into the street. The other customers hardly bothered to look round. Sometimes we bought a bottle of grappa to take home and drank too much of it, but the only consequence next morning was a raging thirst for water. Whatever the Italian for hangover may be did not result.

On Eighty-sixth Street east of Lexington, focus of German-American Yorkville, several beer halls ran wide open. One's first two steins were "near beer"—legal because de-alcoholized—spiked with a dash of grain alcohol to restore its nourishing quality or with ether, then still used as an anaesthetic. I always suspected that after two or three such the customer was served further rounds of unspiked near beer on the principle that he could no longer tell the difference. At the smaller German beer joints downtown on Third Avenue, however, particularly Allaire's Scheffelhall, the beer was honestly—if that's the word—needled all evening and greatly enhanced one's delight in singing "Ja, das ist ein Gartenhaus."

The ethnic-exotic note was most rewarding and authentic at a Hungarian place on a side street in the East Nineties opposite the corpse of the Ruppert Brewery. It was almost as simple as the grappa cellar though more extensive—a lofty, warehouselike room sparsely set with small round tables; on one side a small dance floor and a narrow dais for three Gypsy musicians. Out of the kitchen came at generously low prices excellent goulash, of course, and a heavily seasoned, thick, cerise-pink cabbage soup said to be the Hungarian cure for the morning after; it was certainly wonderful the evening before. At thriftier moments two or three persons could spend a pleasant couple of hours there with a bottle of reasonably potable bootleg white wine and a quart of soda water to make *spritzels* at a total cost of, say, three dollars, fifty cents for the waiter.

Now and again the combo played a fox-trot for outsiders wanting to dance, but the soul of the place was the traditional Gypsy things, two fiddles and the *zymbalon* weaving straightforward and yet involved wizardry for the largely Hungarian clientele. Timing and timbre were visceral like hunger. The message of the fiddles as pursued by the *zymbalon* player—I can see him yet, all beaked nose, thick mustache, swarthy cheeks, and gloomily rapt expression, reaching his hammers across the strings to make them throb like weeping—was exultantly personal. Some evenings they were joined by Mme. Ilona Thury, whom I recall with grateful awe. She was a five-by-five, black-eyed, poker-faced genius at exploiting a deep contralto that, when she turned it loose, would have made Ethel Merman—only Miss Merman had not yet come to fame—sound like a discouraged canary: yet no hint of squalling, just pure, sure richness. Even without that majestic sound, her obviously fierce delight in what she sang was formidable, most of all when, in spite of being the shape of an oversize owl, she'd wind up a wildly accelerating number with a frenzy of dance steps as though the context and rhythms were irresistible—as indeed they were. Periodically the Hungarian patrons would feel the same urge and flood the dance floor with the half strut, half bounce of the czardas. I was never tempted to join in. It was better than good enough merely to listen and watch.

None of those places took any notice of Prohibition except, one can safely assume, paying protection to the police. The folklore of Prohibition, as later generations envisage it, needs modifying. True, the classic speakeasy—and there were many— gave out admission cards and inspected arriving customers through a peephole in the door. But in Hoboken across the North River, just as in Yorkville, beer flowed openly, and on a hot day West Fourth Street in Greenwich Village was practically foggy with beer fumes from the open windows and door of basement after basement. Even at Julius's one just walked in off the street. The tidy little French restaurant on Fifty-third Street under the Ninth Avenue El had the peephole ceremony; but on our first visit my wife and I gained admission without a shadow of introduction merely by wishing the eye in the peephole "Bon jour" with some assurance. Within was good bourgeois cooking, a passable imitation of absinthe, and half a dozen friendly cats and dogs, usually pregnant.

Just as free and easy was the rooming house on West Eighth between Fifth and Sixth—I forget the number but old-timers will locate it as just east of Alice MCollister's, where the Village often ate Sunday brunch—the top floor of which housed Donald Gibbs, then a cub on the old *New York World*, and me the winter of 1927–28. Our large, scantily furnished room and sketchy bathroom cost eighty dollars a month. In view of the primitive heating and raffish ambience that was high, but the landlord, a creepy little creature with no name other than Celestin, justified it on the grounds that in it Martha Ostenso had written her great novel, *Wild Geese*, then well known, though I've never yet read it. That was our landlord's only sign of cultivation; he was probably a pimp, certainly a small-time bootlegger. So far as was discernible through his sordid ambiguity he was French, likely out of the Marseilles waterfront. Every week or two a couple of stewards from the French Line would appear with a consignment of miscellaneous booze from the ships' stores and Celestin would ask Gibbs and me down to sample, for some quirk of his devious mind had persuaded him that we were gentleman-connoisseurs. Thus I had my first taste of cognac. The stewards were pleasant fellows, but my efforts to converse with them showed me for the first time that, no matter how well Mr. Herrick had grounded me, French would never afford me two-way discourse. I couldn't understand a word they said. Pity the French are so poor at pronouncing their own stylish tongue.

The bootlegger who had the franchise at Hanff-Metzger stocked a candidly nongenuine gin in unlabeled square-face bottles faintly yellow to match a touch of orange flavor. It had no ill effects during the five or six weeks I was there. Most bootleggers used admirably faked Gilbey's, Gordon's, and so on labels—too admirably, in fact; once we acquired a bottle of genuine Gordon's from a friend's uncle's pre-Volstead cellar and noted with amusement that its label, juniper berries and all, was not as good a print job as the forgeries we were used to. "Bathtub gin" was strictly amateur, home-created, and a misnomer, for nobody would have used a bathtub for mixing vat; draining would have been awkward. For domestic production one bought from a bootlegger a gallon of what one hoped was diverted "hospital alcohol," and sometimes may actually have been so; from the drugstore "gin drops" (essence of juniper) and glycerine; from the Croton Reservoir system water was free. One part alky, two parts water, tablespoon of glycerine per quart to take off the rough edge, dash of gin drops; shake violently and, if possible, let stand a few days, but actually it was already as potable as it ever would be.

The alcohol was probably more dilute than represented and even in theory the end product was little above 60-proof, so it packed less wallop than today's legal 80- or 90-proof gin. And it was usually drunk in high dilution with ginger ale—*gingingerale* was all one word like *damyankee*—or with orange juice shaken with ice to make the omnipresent "orange blossom" cocktail that nobody has ever asked for since Repeal. When Repeal arrived, my wife and I had a pint or so of homemade gin left. With a fine sense of historical duty we put it into a glass flask, sealed it elaborately, and told ourselves we'd exhume it after twenty years. By now the Smithsonian would be glad to have it. Only it got broken during one of our many shifts of quarters and the contents were forever lost, as

irretrievable as prephylloxera Burgundy and the song the si-
rens sang.

Prohibition inspired many dodges. De-alcoholized vermouth was advertised in smart magazines; on the neck of each
bottle hung a tiny booklet warning that it would be strictly
illegal to add to it grain alcohol in proportions of one to six.
Drugstores freely sold several brands of dreadful sherry slightly
spiked with quinine or some other pharmaceutical enabling
them to be sold as tonics.

In spring 1928 Gibbs and I shifted into two rooms and
bath on the top floor of a venerably rickety brick house on
Jane Street just west of Hudson, a few doors from the house
where they brought Alexander Hamilton to die of Aaron Burr's
pistol bullet. Our rooms were painted a pistachio green so violent than living there should have impaired our psyches; but
the only actual risk was concrete—bricks and mortar rather,
for all too near to west and south ran the Ninth Avenue El's
right-angle northward turn. When motormen took that curve
a little too fast, as they usually did, the vibration and grinding
roar made the old house behave as though calling the whole
thing off and falling down. Only it never did—the El is gone
now, but the old dump still stands or did a few years ago when
an interview took me into that still obscure neighborhood.

Its luck has been better luck than that of the next super-
annuated walls to house me. For a guess they went back to the
1860s, anyway long before Park Avenue was built over the
New York Central's open-cut tracks. When the developers
bought up sites for the ladylike, elegantly corniced, high-rise
apartment houses that still command Park Avenue well uptown, the owner of this ugly job on the corner of Eightieth
Street must have held out for too much too long, for they left
his building standing, only five forlorn stories. Its top-floor
apartment of one small and one smaller room with a minimum bathroom went unfurnished for sixty dollars a month.
Gerard Lake, then breaking into the textile industry at thirty-
five dollars a week, had inherited the place from a friend
working at the nearby Metropolitan Museum. When Gibbs
moved to Jackson Heights—then new and highly regarded—
to join his mother, Lake recruited me and John Kormendi, a
good-natured Hungarian (a classmate) who was breaking into

Wall Street. Both of the other two were paid regularly, though some weeks Kormendi's twenty-five-a-week drawing account was all he came up with. Whenever I acquired some cash, I paid up arrears on my third of the rent. Somehow even the phone bills got paid.

Now, 920 Park Avenue was—still is—a high-ticket address. That had disadvantages: Kormendi had to have an ailing kidney removed, and when the fee was fixed, the address was damning. Job on Wall Street, living in the Eighties on Park Avenue? What's this nonsense about reduced charge? One morning the mail included a notice from City Hall that personal property in apartment #4, 920 Park, was assessed at fifty thousand dollars, proportionate taxes now due. I went down to the Municipal Building and told the man behind the counter that if he could find five hundred dollars worth of personal property in that apartment, I'd push a peanut round City Hall Park with my nose—or words to that effect. To calm me down, he explained that it saved the city energy to make an arbitrary guess without inspection as to the contents of fat-cat addresses, assuming that if the shoe fit pretty well, there would be no protest; if it was too high, the degree of adjustment could be gauged by the fervor of the protest. So he tore the paper up and we parted friends.

Life at 920 was a sort of central-heated camping out. Lake and Kormendi had army cots in the small bedroom. I slept in the living room on a contraption we called *stupor mundi* because to see it for the first time was to disbelieve in it—an antediluvian, turn-into-a-bed, backless, black horsehair sofa all springs and metal braces as though designed for Mr. Hyde. It took twenty minutes to unfold it, twenty more to reassemble it, and in either phase it bit one's fingers savagely. Lake had no notion of its origin; it had probably been disgustedly exiled to the top floor in the house's early days. Other furnishings were a small wobbly desk for my typewriter and the telephone; three rickety odd chairs, two very odd; a battered chest of drawers for what spare shirts and socks we had; an electric hot plate on top of it; and a crippled but operational wind-up phonograph.

I owe it gratitude, for it flawed my indifference to what was known as "longhair music." One Monday morning Lake returned from a Cambridge weekend on the New Haven's dis-

mal Owl train with a new recording of Bach's Toccato and
Fugue in D Minor to give a musical girl he was interested in.
Finding me still asleep, he put it on the phonograph as a duly
tactless way to wake me. I was coming to before consciousness
could revert to type. The music sneaked into me subliminally
and, to my astonishment, delighted me. I said: "In God's name
what's that?" and, being told: "I be damned!" The breach then
made never widened far. The symphony orchestra sort of thing
still bores me as cruelly as grand opera. But I do genuinely if
ignorantly enjoy some eighteenth-century chamber music, notably Bach and some Handel, no less for my persisting amazement at experiencing any such thing. The analogy would be
the semiliterate who gets obsessively entangled in Shakespeare
without ever developing further feeling for literature.

Since my co-tenants had nine-to-five jobs and I usually did
not, I was in the apartment much of the time and answered
the phone. Its ringing might portend potential revenue—an
editor with a five-dollar reading, say. Irksomely often, however, the call was another reflection of our gilded address—
somebody assuming it meant affluence. A professionally clear
voice, often vaguely British, usually male: "Good morning, this
is Reginald Blatherskite. Miss Anne Morgan has asked me to
see if you'd care to take a box at her benefit for heedless virgins. . ." and so on until I told Reggie what to do and hung
up. The more it happened, the more annoyed I got and began
taking countermeasures, risking lèse majesté with: "Anne
Morgan? Who's that? Never heard of her. And who had the
presumption to give her my name?" Or I'd let the voice go all
the way through its pitch: "Awfully sorry but this is a bad connection. Would you mind repeating?" and at the finish again:
"No use, I get only a few words here and there. Is English
your native tongue?" Or—this was the best—"Let me have your
name again. . . . Yes, I thought so. Mr. Blatherskite, this is a
fortunate coincidence. I was lunching with John Jacob Astor
yesterday and he asked me to invite you to be a sponsor for
his dinner to raise funds for the Rehabilitation of Unwed Fathers.* Only five hundred dollars a plate . . ." None of it mit-
igated the nuisance, but it made one feel better—until the phone

---

*Note that sixty years ago this sounded like an absurdity.

rang again and it was Mrs. Marmaduke Suydam's committee for alleviating the distress of English sparrows consequent on the disuse of horse-drawn vehicles.

On the poor old house's ground floor was a florist's shop with which the tenants had nothing to do; its entrance was highly-chinnedly on Park Avenue, ignoring the grimy high stoop on the Eightieth Street side that served our street door. The second-floor tenant was a harassed-looking blonde implausibly named Blizzard, or so the card on her mailbox said. Above her lived and practiced psychiatry Dr. Florence Powdermaker, just beginning a prosperous career, with whom we were on hello-maybe-drop-in terms. Some years later my wife and I came to know her fairly well. I vividly recall the party she gave in, by then, a much more eligible apartment the evening FDR wiped the floor with Alf Landon. The iris bed that I weeded this spring at my place in Jersey was of Florence's planting fifty years ago. That was the weekend she came out all over poison ivy because she had been playing with her previous hostess's shaggy dog that had been romping among the local flora.

Our encampment at Eightieth and Park would have fit well enough on Bank Street, but this was in the middle of New York's best try at plutocratic elegance. For years whenever something took me that far uptown I made sure that the old wreck was still there on its squeezed-in corner like a chewed cigar butt on Mrs. Vandequist's breakfast tray. Late in the 1960s I had a shock. Some rash developer had demolished 920 and built on the site a slender, glass-glossy, twelve-story apartment house. Its expensive tenants' address is still 920 Park Avenue, but they wouldn't know what that signifies. If they did, a bronze plaque on the Eightieth Street side would say that on this spot in 1928 it was definitively demonstrated that if one puts sugar, raisins, diced carrots, rice, yeast, and water in a large crock, lets it all ferment for a week at room temperature, and pours off the liquid, it won't be potable.

The one thing we had in common with our gilt-edged neighbors was bedbugs. The superintendent of the huge apartment house next door, nominally in charge of 920, admitted that it too was infested. And so was every building in

sight up and down the avenue. Not all the time in all apartments, you understand, but off and on and more or less at
random, for New York's breed of *cunex lectularius* was no re-
specter of persons, prestige, or high rentals. In the imposing
old Fish mansion on Gramercy Park, in the annex of which
my wife and I lived in 1932, we and all other tenants were
ordered out twice a year for one night so the exterminators
could weave their spells with sulphur candles and gas bombs.
Setting the bed legs in cans of kerosene was supposed to thwart
the little devils. When Doc Lewis tried that in a charming old
house on the west side of the Park, the bugs learned to climb
the walls to the ceiling, crawl across, and when right over the
bed, let go.

At 3 Rutherford Place on Stuyvesant Square my wife and
I lived above a quiet, old, strikingly emaciated lady known to
our landlord and the white-aproned delivery boys from the
James Butler chain store as the countess because her husband,
father of an eminent politician in Queens, had been created a
papal count. Why, in view of son's position, was she relegated
to a floor-through in that raffish neighborhood?* Anyway there
she was. Glimpses through her opened door showed a wealth
of jigsawed Victorian furniture and walls dripping with fancifully framed pictures, elaborate fans, tasseled scarves—a bedbugs' paradise. When she died, rest her harmless old soul, it
was clear why she had been such a case of skin and bones.
After her effects were moved out and the walls stripped for
redecorating, we on the floor above were eaten alive. Deprived
of shelter and accustomed nourishment, all that wildlife migrated. On every wall in our bedroom, platoons of skirmishers
deployed in open order and advanced. It availed nothing to
swat them. Replacements gallantly took their places and thousands more lay in reserve. We moved out.

That was less of a hardship because it was early fall and in

---

*It had been most respectable once, witness the presence of the Friends' Seminary
and St. George's Church, "Morgan's church," because the great banker was reputed
to be its chief support. Long since, however, it had become center of the abortion
industry, in which our landlord was a leader. As relic of past elegance, the building
had a dumbwaiter shaft up through all stories, long inactive, but the shaft was still
there and the doors fit loosely, so we often dined to the accompaniment of strong
whiffs of ether, meaning that the doctor had a patient.

those times most people we knew moved every September–October. In our ten years in New York we inhabited eight different apartments, all but one south of Fourteenth Street: West Fourth, East Tenth, Waverly Place, West Eleventh . . . each time fleeing one set of inconveniences and hoping the next set would be less irksome—which it seldom was. My wife developed a precaution against the bug hazard: When we inspected an apartment with a view to renting it, she gleaned two or three names from the mailboxes in the entry and made phone calls: "This is the Entomology Exterminating Service. We make regular checks for your landlord. Are you having bedbug trouble?" And if the voice at the other end said, "God, yes," we wrote that building off.

I understand—and hope it is true—that modern insecticides have pretty well rid New York of bugs. If so, that is one of the few ways in which the town was not better in our time. Yes, it was noisy, expensive, sour-tempered, dirty, overcrowded; but in each of those respects it is now far more so. Our subway was, though never clean in a housewifely sense, relatively tidier and, though horrible at rush hours, far more reliable and offered much lower risk of being robbed, mugged, or both. It was possible to get mugged in the street, but in most neighborhoods the odds against it were so high as to be negligible. My wife and I would dine thriftily in the West Forties, buy at Gray's half-price tickets to some play we had long been wishing to see, and walk home to the Village through scantily frequented streets with no reason for a tense feeling between the shoulders. By day I walked all over the southern two thirds of the island, not only along the conventional avenues but into the Hell's Kitchen waterfront; the strangely lifeless world of Avenues A, B, C; the convolutions of the Lower East Side and Washington Street's Middle Eastern bazaar—encountering actual danger only once, when curiosity set me mingling with a Communist-led demonstration in Union Square just when the mounted police decided to break it up. Those horses looked double normal size and their mostly Irish riders seemed to resent being called Cossacks—which certainly does sound insulting even when you aren't sure just what it means.

For a city then as now deservedly accused of a frantic atmosphere, New York had certain low-key opportunities and amenities. Five cents took one across the North River* on the Hoboken Ferry to walk up the Stevens Institute bluff for the priceless view of Manhattan from the Battery to the steelwork of the George Washington Bridge, then under construction. When they painted those shapely piers with red lead as undercoating for gray, they were so Japanesy-handsome that there was a movement, with which the engineers had no sympathy, to keep them that color. Ten cents inserted in the conductor's fare-collecting gadget gained one access to the upper deck of a Fifth Avenue bus, a lumbersome affair affording views of mile after mile of Bedford stone mansions or Riverside Drive apartment houses (still impressive though the ensemble was already decaying) with the Palisades across the shimmering river. Drive, with decay dominant, and water are still there, but no double-deckers.

A generation ago they dismantled the Els—Third Avenue, Sixth Avenue, Ninth Avenue—that roared and vibrated the length of the island over majestic track-viaducts of piers and girders that kept the streets below in perpetual variegated shadow. In some stretches trolley cars clanged, whirred, and rattled along under the El trains at street level. The inhabitants of the tenements lining the routes and the owners and customers of the small shops on the ground floors went about their lives heedless of a racket that would daunt the foreman of an old-time boiler factory. Five cents passed one through the turnstiles of the really remarkably dingy El stations—bogus Swiss chalets on stilts. They were like implausibly enlarged cuckoo clocks—all stained glass, perforated bargeboards, filigreed wrought-iron railings, jigsawed screens encrusted with such grime as will never be seen again now that the Els are gone and New York heats with oil. On a warm summer evening it was almost as exhilarating as a trip on a roller coaster and much more satisfactorily prolonged to stand in the rush

---

*This dates me. New Yorkers now say "the Hudson." In my time that meant the whole navigable stream from the Narrows to Troy; whereas "North River" meant its terminal reach from the Battery to, say, Spuyten Duyvil. That disregarded the stream's position west of Manhattan because it is a survival from Dutch times, which distinguished the Hudson from the Delaware as "the South River" on which the Dutch also had early interests. "East River" for the tidal strait between Manhattan and Long Island survives in spite of its inadequacy; though the *east* part is all right, it is not a river but a saltwater strait.

of air through the open front door of an El train swooping and rattling and (on curves) squealing ever onward through the night between streaking vistas of lighted windows. Today's Third and Sixth avenues are banal, glass-lined canyons with all the charm of superhighway toll booths.

The relative ease of car parking would be inconceivable now. *Relative*, mind—there were already complaints about traffic jams and scarcity of curb space. Farnol had a secondhand, open, baby-blue Pierce-Arrow—yes, the car with those frog-eyed lights on the fenders—and often drove it to work though he lived only half a mile away. Round 9:00 A.M. he seldom had trouble parking on our 700 block of Seventh Avenue. It might be more difficult midmorning when I brought the car back from some distant errand, but I always found room round the corner of Forty-eighth Street. I recall that car affectionately, particularly for the Saturday when I used it to put the Farnols' dog, a hyperkinetic wirehair named Rabbit, into a kennel far up in Westchester and took along Lake and his chief interest at the time, a brawnily handsome Brahmin girl whose imposing voice had got her into the chorus of Winthrop Ames's lovely productions of Gilbert and Sullivan. All the way along the Boston Post Road she sang highlights from the *Mikado*, the *Pirates*, and *Iolanthe* while Lake provided a surprisingly able second and Rabbit yipped joyfully in the back seat. It was a good afternoon.

I assume it was Saturday afternoon because otherwise Lake would have been juggling textiles down on Worth Street and I cleaning out the files of stills of dead-and-gone movies, for in most jobs in the 1920s working Saturday mornings was taken for granted. In the Kendall office we assumed the boss would disappear late Friday until Monday, but Miss Donelly, Miss McEvilly, and I were there knitting up loose ends. Those three hours or so cannot have contributed much to the Gross National Product* (a statistical convention then not yet invented), for the desk was hardly cleared for action or the machine warmed up before noon arrived. But that was the custom of the country.

---

*A phrase I deplore because it betrayed me. A newspaper story recently mentioned that pornographic stuff was still Denmark's traditional export. "That," said I, "must be what is meant by Gross National Product." Nobody but me thought it a good joke.

11

Breaking In

WHEN DAVID HUME analyzed causality into an inscrutable fusion of contiguity and succession, he illuminated and yet further darkened the bewilderment that comes of tracing back how cleverly in the past one thing led to another—that crucial, specific another, *not* something else that might have led into a different succession of contiguities. My case: No doubt genetic quirks and environmental warpings programmed me into thralldom to reading and writing. But that fails to account for the way profit-seeking organizations have seen fit to print my writings at their expense. The woods have always been full of mute, inglorious Miltons, as vanity publishers well know. And only seldom does one of them—usually posthumously—prove worth publishing; whereas during most of my lifetime I have been paid well for the pleasure of seeing my words in print.

All that is probably an elaborate way to say I have been lucky. Or that my escape from mute, inglorious frustration was a matter of chance—a shamelessly personified, capitalized Chance pursuing heads or tails like a computer skittering through choices to a solution. Thus my choosing Harvard instead of Yale meant I often lunched at the Signet. There I came to know a law student whose New York acquaintances included G. D. Eaton, waspish editor of *Plain Talk*, a monthly magazine emulating Mencken and Nathan's *American Mercury*. Through my friend's good offices Eaton saw and bought my first professional publication—an article pillorying the Reverend Dr. Frank Buchman, pudgy Savonarola of the Ivy League, later founder of "Moral Rearmament" (remember it?). His "Oxford Movement," so called without Oxford's leave, was an elm-shaded crusade against undergraduate sin. Its "house parties" for mass confessions, anticipating today's group therapy, were a cross between early Christian agape and dormitory bull sessions. They had grown so warm and sticky that Princeton barred Buchman and his well-tailored young apostles from the campus.

Bob Lamb and I knew some lapsed Buchmanites at Harvard from whom we had gathered data for an article without quite knowing what to do about it. During spring vacation I arranged to interview Buchman in the New York office supplied him by the Rockefellers, prominent among his fat-cat supporters, in their town house stronghold on West Fifty-fourth Street. He said he never had to worry about financing his forays into academe. He had only to mention need of cash in his daily "quiet time" of communion with God and in a day or two or an ample check from some well-wisher was sure to be in the mail. As he explained this he absently picked up a copy of the New York Social Register that lay on his desk and stroked its spine as though it had been a feline familiar spirit. Scholastic pressures forced Lamb to bow out. So I did the writing and months later Eaton paid me fifty dollars—I think Bob was finally persuaded to take twenty—and I was an author while still in college.

Now backtrack: Had I not chosen Harvard I'd never have been in Kendall's office typing those parts for *The Letter*. That whiff of inside-a-play structure (and maybe residues from rehearsals at the Copley Theatre) set me hankering to write for the stage. A minor producer named Robert Milton had an office in the Kendall suite and an affable, Dutch-bobbed young secretary. Soon after I left Kendall, she moved on to a similar berth at Brandt & Brandt, already an eminent literary agency. And bless her heart, she told Janet Cohn, number two in B&B's dramatic department, that a youngster she knew might reward attention. Miss Cohn, bless her heart too, read my one-acter making wisecracking farce out of Pocahontas and Captain John Smith and got it staged by an amateur group in Westchester. They were a set of loud-mouthed cutups, but they did learn their lines and business, and thin as the script was, the laughs were there and Miss Cohn concluded I could write dialogue. A good while later I worked out a three-act comedy about a stage star having her autobiography ghosted. Miss Cohn was thinking well of it when S. N. Behrman, no less, announced his new play would be on a similar theme and starring—no less again—Ina Claire. Signals over. Here was luck again of a backhanded sort. Had I ever met Behrman, I'd have thanked him for thus inadvertently steering me away from footlights. For had my script actually got produced, success or flop, I might well have been hooked and gone on committing plays, a field for which, with all those rehearsal crises and personality conflicts, I'd have been abjectly ill suited.

Changing the idiom, I cobbled up a short story about a chorus girl and a press agent; its bouncy patter was modeled on J. P. McEvoy's clever *Show Girl*. Miss Cohn showed it to Erdman Brandt, then handling magazine fiction for the agency, and first crack out of the box it sold to *Red Book* for $400. Even less 10 percent that was half again as large as the $250 for *One Heavenly Night*. I bought the first good suit I had had for seven years and, multiplying 360 times 12, assumed that at the easy pace of a story a month, economic comfort was just around the corner. Only it wasn't. For a long while I wrote one story after another and Erd Brandt advised me solicitously and wisely, change this, step up that—nothing sold. Erd was a remarkably patient man and willing as ever to keep trying. It was I who, with all due gratitude, called it off. Short fiction was obviously not my line of country. Every four or five years the impulse to spin a yarn comes over me so strongly that I succumb and sometimes the result sells. One—about a Timid Soul character who kept finding snakes in his bathtub—got reprinted in several anthologies. But beyond that I retain the good sense to leave Ambrose Bierce, O. Henry, and Katherine Mansfield unchallenged.

While I was turning my back on plays and fiction, a third avenue to solvency was opening up. George C. Tyler, the veteran producer whose affairs were already deteriorating during my time with Farnol, had gone irretrievably bust. Booth Tarkington, his close friend and professional ally in several successful plays, rallied round—as many of Tyler's other associates did not—and persuaded the *Saturday Evening Post*, where Tarkington's stories were most welcome, to pay well for Tyler's reminiscences, proceeds to go into a trust fund for a modest maintenance beyond the reach of creditors. Carl Brandt, Sr., of B&B, a friend of Tarkington's, was enlisted to make arrangements, including finding the ghost-writer who, it was taken for granted, would be needed. By then those in the B&B office were more or less aware of me as knowing how to work a typewriter and somewhat acquainted with matters theatrical. Carl Brandt—my first dealing with him in an association that lasted over thirty years—asked me to see Tyler and work out a sample installment to show the *Post*.

As it happened, my wife and I were soon to visit her family at their summer place at Kennebunk Beach, Maine, not far from Tarkington's at Kennebunkport. Though he was a sporadic resident of Indianapolis and a most successful Hoosier writer, I had never met him, indeed knew of him only gossip about his problem with alcohol and severe eye troubles. None of it fitted with his nimble light fictions—*Seventeen* and the Penrod cycle, which I knew by heart—and the shrewd ironies of his best serious work, *Alice Adams* and *The Magnificent Ambersons*. Neither way was I prepared for the person with whom I dealt in re Tyler. Visually formidable—flanneled and jacketed, necktied and hatted on a mild afternoon, seated apparently immovably in a big wicker chair on a veranda, very dark glasses adding grimness to a strongly featured but corpselike face, he was as near as next door to an elderly version of Claude Raines in *The Invisible Man*. But the dry yet flexible voice that came out of the mask was cordially helpful without a hint of condescension from veteran to cub. The project was shaky, for Tyler rather mistrusted me at first, probably thinking me too cubbish, and the *Post* was uncertain about the sample. But Tarkington wrote to Carl to stay with me: "The youngster has humor, get him to exercise it," and advised me, in terms pertinent to writers' subliminal approaches, to—I don't recall exactly what he said, but it meant loosen up your wrist and distance yourself from the dispiriting nuances of Tyler's situation.

I did not actively like him, and his political bent was certainly regrettable. He had a wonderful big black poodle that, when asked "Did you vote for Roosevelt?" yelped pitiably, laid his head on the coffee table, put his paws over his ears, and whined. That could have been mere high-bracket politics; only Tarkington's closest friend in the Kennebunks was Kenneth Roberts, whose reactionary-minded historical novels were best-sellers and whose fairly recent magazine pieces about Musso-lini's trains running on time had glowed with fervor. Conso-nantly Tarkington's *Claire Ambler* (1928) presented a high-minded young henchman of Musso's as hero struggling against the bad guys of the Sicilian Mafia. Yet as the Tyler project progressed, I came away from each visit to Tarkington as mid-wife with heightened respect. Yes, he wrote too many potboil-ers in his later years. Yet, though my acquaintance with novelists has included several whose works are properly ranked more highly than anything Tarkington ever did, he floats in my memory as somehow more professional than most of them. His better writings, however short on profound depths, em-body a loving skill with our language of the same order as Ring Lardner's and Mark Twain's.

Tyler showed no sign of recognizing me as the kid who had run errands for Lynn Farnol a few years earlier, nor did I recall myself. Even back in those days his setting had been depressing. That low-ceilinged office behind the wide-arch window over the lobby doors of the New Amsterdam looked as though the cleaning woman were still away on vacation. The skinny bookkeeper and scowling secretary-assistant were al-ready exuding gloom because the boss had fallen from being chief of Liebler & Company, that major force in show busi-ness, down to where the phone bill had to be carefully watched. The dust and depression were far thicker now; and though he was still outwardly rosy and plump, Tyler's once mellow voice and what it said had gone shrilly querulous. Most explicitly he resented his deplorable situation. He punctuated our work with complaints about what he considered Brandt's stupidity and interfering clumsiness; one gathered that his relations with agents had always been *de haut en bas*. And inevitably he blamed his hard times on the disgraceful falling off in the quality and integrity of actors and rival producers, the degeneration of public taste, the rise of the movies. . . . Time and again he told me and wanted it put into print once more that when a woman's virtue was no longer a trenchant issue, plays worth producing could no longer be written.

Yet when I'd steered him back on track developing the ups and downs of his break-in days, there was something pathetic about the relief that change of subject matter obviously brought. Even during his snarlings at me about things I had nothing to do with, I could feel sorry for him. I once said so to Tarkington and added that I wished I could think of something to do about it. His reply—that I was doing about all anybody could— made handling the old man easier. It also helped that his yarns were usually lively and eloquent of his feisty, egocentric, and yet self-measuring personality; doubtless athletes in such solo sports as tennis and golf develop that quality. If boxing were pertinent, Tyler would have been a nippy lightweight, for he was only five foot six, or so he said; I never saw him erect, he was always seated in his desk chair as squarely as an articulate little Buddha. Tarkington's generous introduction to the eventual hardcover book, *Whatever Goes Up. . .* , mentions a facial resemblance to Napoleon. This had not betrayed Tyler into equipping his office with a bust of the emperor. But though he was much better looking, he did candidly admire Mussolini.

More harmoniously than all this sounds, Tyler and I gaily set down his story from stagestruck boyhood in Chillicothe, Ohio, into coast-to-coast wanderings as young tramp-printer, then as frenetic, never-say-die advance agent, and soon manager of barnstorming troupes. He financed his first independent production with flagrant check kiting that would jail him in a week nowadays; then onward and upward by fits and starts into becoming an exultingly affluent and importantly catalytic focus between the Chicago World's Fair of 1893 and Lindbergh's flight in 1927. One way or another he was deep in the careers of dozens of performers who still meant something to many *Post* readers: James O'Neill, Frank Mayo, William Faversham, Nat Goodwin, Eleanor Robson, Julia Marlowe, Viola Allen, Laurette Taylor . . . Even today the names of the promising youngsters in his Washington stock company trying out new scripts in 1918 are impressive: Helen Hayes, Lynn Fontanne, Alfred Lunt, Cornelia Otis Skinner . . . He was instrumental in the early progress of such playwrights as George

Bernard Shaw, Tarkington, Maugham, George Kaufman . . .
The index of the book ran to eight hundred-odd entries, about
60 percent proper names, for his nontheatrical acquaintance
ranged from Theodore Roosevelt through Samuel Gompers
to Tod Sloan, the great jockey. And it wasn't mere name dropping. Most of those references led to something that sparkled
or chuckled.

He talked usefully well too, if loosely, picking up speed
with eyes brightening. I had only to tighten up the flow and
sharpen high points while not losing the effect of spontaneity
garnished with peppery comment. He was less exacting than I
anticipated about the rough drafts; I attributed that, and still
do, to his professional recognition of good lines when he saw
them. For it was a good job. Recently I read it for the first
time in fifty years and thought: "M-m-m-m, the kid had it."
After their first hesitation, the *Post* lapped it up. I never asked
what they paid into the Tyler trust fund. I got $250 an install-
ment less 10 percent—in 1930s dollars, mind. In a matter of
months I could actually consider taking my wife to Europe as
escort on what would be my first transatlantic venture. As to
the quality of my ghosting: Soon the *Post* put me on a similar
job for William A. Brady, a rugged, old-timey competitor of
Tyler's. Reviewing the consequent book, *Showman*, Richard
Lockridge, dramatic critic of the *New York Sun*, who certainly
knew Brady personally, wrote: "Told in a manner grandly un-
apologetic and gives every evidence, oddly enough, of having
been written by Mr. Brady himself." Heh-heh.

Sandwiched between these emeritus impresarios, the *Post*
wanted a series of articles on eating and cooking under the
by-line of George Rector—a name that then still connoted the
hot-bird-and-cold-bottle school of stay-up-late, high-ticket restaurant. George's father had been guiding spirit of the famous
Rector's on Broadway where, during the turn-of-the-century
decade, big spenders took their expensive girls, sometimes their
expensive wives, for lobster Newburg and champagne. By all
accounts, some trustworthy, Rector's cooking was actually as
elaborate and toothsome as the prices were high. Many of the
patrons had been exhaustively around and were as knowl-
edgeable about recognizing quality as George's father had been
in supplying it.

Son George was keeping the publicity value of the name lucratively alive. He was fresh from fronting for the A&P grocery chain at the Century of Progress, where millions had encountered his elegant snowy hair, waxed mustache, blooming pink cheeks, twinkly eyes, knowing smile—a cross between Santa Claus and a white cockatoo wearing a chef's toque at a jaunty angle. Its implication was valid. His father had sent him to Paris to learn, and he came back a very good if limited cook. Most of the rest of him was phony, but food he knew.

Two years or so previously George Horace Lorimer, formidable editor of the *Post*, who took eating seriously, had sent Rector to Europe to do international dining articles ghosted by Arthur ("Bugs") Baer, a widely syndicated newspaper humorist. The series had been popular. Now, provided I could supply lively enough copy, Rector was to get comparable entertainment out of American-flavored gastronomy. Baer, a tirelessly clever old-timer, was a hard act to follow, but Rector, my wife, and I managed to keep the patter going and the aromas wafting in from the kitchen for nine or ten articles before we ran out of material. Deduce the tone from the titles I supplied: "You Know Me, Al Fresco" (about outdoor cooking); "A Touch of Eggomania"; "Salad Daze" . . .

Before an audience George could palaver ingratiatingly, and many of his stock anecdotes and name droppings proved useful. The Furnases supplied the bulk of the patter, however, and a good half of the culinary lore. I could draw on memories of my sainted Great-aunt Romenta and the Gratiot Inn, and my wife occasionally came up with Down East ideas from many summers in Maine. For precautionary hints and helpful sidelights, we relied on Sheila Hibben's utterly authentic *National Cookbook* and Mrs. Simon Kander's richly midwestern *Settlement Cookbook*. And we kept things simple partly in order not to daunt readers, partly to insure against controversy with regional experts—no Brunswick stew, no pit barbecues.

George had the good sense to welcome what must sometimes have seemed to him outlandish notions. He tried them out in the A&P's test kitchen, of which he was nominal supervisor. That was not only useful but essential, for the A&P had him tied hand and foot by contract, and though they allowed him to enhance his publicity value by writing for that unimpeachable national institution, the *Saturday Evening Post,* they insisted on vetting every word before the *Post* saw copy—which might have irritated Lorimer had he known of it. He took special interest in the series; once, in fact, he fell foul of our method of scrambling eggs and imposed his own—it was far better, if tricky, and I still follow it to universal admiration. But neither Lorimer nor the A&P staff nor George nor my wife nor I nor the *Post*'s copy staff picked it up when we told all about how to make the perfect Welsh rarebit and failed to mention cheese.

Dealing with George was eased by his awareness that he was getting very good value for the money the *Post* paid us; also by our skill in disguising how often his behavior seemed to us misbegotten. Thursday mornings (the *Post* appeared on Thursdays not Saturdays) he would hover round one or another newsstand in Grand Central and accost customers with his best Century of Progress beaming smile: "Hello, I'm George Rector. I have an article about good cooking in the new *Saturday Evening Post.* Buy one and I'll autograph it for you." The newsstand men never objected, the circulation department might not have, but it was just as well Lorimer never heard of that either. On some special gastronomic quest we went to Washington with George and his loosely upholstered, rather foolishly good-natured wife. As we were driving back to the hotel, George suddenly turned his LaSalle into the driveway of the White House—security was not yet a major industry— and addressed the functionary who appeared: "Please give my card to the president. I'm George Rector of the Great Atlantic & Pacific Tea Company and the *Saturday Evening Post,* and my friends and I would like to pay our respects for a moment. The president's never met me but tell him I used to help look after his father in the old days at my father's restaurant on Broadway. He'll remember." It was summer, my wife was wearing sandals, I could see her toes curling. The functionary returned: The president was all tied up but would be given the card; good afternoon, sir. Far from feeling snubbed, over his second drink that evening George maundered happily on over whether it was a Golden Buck or Welsh rarebit that FDR's pa liked for supper. Anyway, something involving poached eggs.

Yet the deepest embarrassment he caused us was not directly his or anybody's fault but ours. The end of our overseas trip found us in Paris with our funds running distinctly low. Only with care could we reach shipside with enough money for tips and bar bill during the homeward voyage. Rector had given us a letter of introduction to a good friend who had risen to become managing chef of the group of elegant restaurants including the Café de Paris. We must look up good old Pierre-Jacques or whatever his name was. Happy to do so, we sent the letter and a deferential covering note. Prompt reply: Come the following day, 1:00 p.m., to the Café dé Paris. We too were prompt, gastric juices stirring. The maître d' said that unfortunately M. Tournebroche or whatever his surname was could not greet us personally, he had been called on an emergency to another restaurant in the chain . . . and by that time we were seated at a table for two in not the worst but not a prime location and a sommelier was seeking my approval of a bottle labeled Veuve Clicquot or something just as dire. I was too jittery—this was before credit cards existed—to consider precautionary measures. Amid an odor of burning bridges I nodded. *Pop!* went our peace of mind. The ensuing dialogue went something like this:

HE: Did he say anything about on the house?

SHE: No. What on earth will we do?

HE: My God, look at these prices!

SHE: I could fake *mal de* something and run out.

HE: We'd still have to pay for the champagne . . .

We should have had the courage to plunge, not ordering caviar, of course, that would have been bad manners, but something we'd never have a chance at again, like squab nightingale *sous cloche*. Instead we cravenly searched out the cheapest item. I believe what we settled on was omelette *fines herbes*, and I don't doubt it was exquisitely cooked but I can't say we enjoyed it. And when I gritted my teeth and asked for the check—there was none, of course. The waiter, mighty puzzled, I'm sure, made it clear it was all compliments of M. Tournebroche, who was desolate *de ne pas faire la connaissance de madame et monsieur*. My relief was so great that I tipped so generously all round that the hole in the bankroll would have dined us twice over in the nice little restaurant across from our hotel.

Tyler had given us a letter to an expatriate friend from his great days—Mrs. Brown-Potter. Oblivion swallowed her up long ago, but in the late 1880s, when Tyler was breaking into the big time, she had come to fame as a New York society beauty ostracized because, at a staid upper-crust reception, she had recited a poem about a fallen woman. Then instead of repining, she had squared the offense by capitalizing on it by going on the stage—and then cubed it by proving to be an able actress. After some years of success she moved to England and became a much sought-after hostess with an elegant country place where Tyler, among many gratified others, had been entertained. By my time she had shifted to a villa on the French Riviera, where we presented our letter and were duly asked to lunch.

Our hostess was unmistakably stricken in years but regally cordial. Unwittingly she had done us a favor by adding us to a luncheon party of half a dozen elderly, gilt-edged Americans from the local expatriate colony. The ensuing two hours of conversation were unbroken peevishness rising into shrill exasperation because that man Roosevelt had taken the United States off the gold standard, the exchange value of the dollar had slumped, and these people, long accustomed to very comfortably doing nothing at bargain rates in a beautiful environment, no longer knew where their next case of Montrachet was coming from. They were repetitiously, obsessively vocal about what that traitor to his class had done to them. Mrs. Brown-Potter said little, merely looked vaguely sympathetic; maybe fewer of her resources were tied to the dollar or, likelier, she had the good taste to keep her dismay to herself. Anyway the others needed no encouragement. They carried on with a bitterness that, though understandable, could have been so much more responsibly expressed.

This was handy for us. We were hoping to pay part of our traveling expenses by doing an article to be called "The Vanished American"* about the effect of the fall of the dollar on Americans in Europe. Here was an unsought laboratory sam-

---

*The popular novelist Zane Grey wrote *The Vanishing American*, that is the Indian.

ple spontaneously filling us in on the fat-cat stratum of same. My wife had had some experience of the aesthetic-alcoholic stratum in Montparnasse and during our earlier stay in Paris had guided me knowledgeably into the half-deserted Ritz Bar, la Rotonde, the Closerie des Lilas, and so on—all sluggishly dismal because most of the Montparnassians dependent on money from home had used their last remittances to repatriate themselves. The run-of-the-mine seasonal tourists who thought that Harry's Bar and the Folies Bergère added up to heaven had stopped coming, whereas the victims of economic frightfulness we had lunched with apparently decided to stay put. What became of them I don't know. We honorably disguised them beyond personal recognition and worked them into a good article that the *Post* bought. And there I was with my by-line in *the* national slick magazine.

Actually I had had a putative, miniature hand in the dollar affair. Late in 1933 Carl Brandt involved me with my third millionaire (after Scotty's stepfather and Kendall): Frank A. Vanderlip, retired president of the National City Bank, acknowledged economist–elder statesman. He approved of the proposals to stem the Depression by modifying the gold standard. The editor of the *Forum*, a well-considered public affairs magazine, asked him to write about it. Years earlier Vanderlip had been financial editor of the *Chicago Tribune*. He was still all there mentally and presumably capable of doing his own writing. But he was pushing seventy and no doubt busy with other elder-statesmanlike doings. He asked Carl Brandt, at the Union League, I suppose, to find him a ghost.

He worked with me daily at his house in the East Fifties, a huge stuccoed affair dwarfing its merely affluent brownstone neighbors. Whoever built it must have been a mighty hunter before the Lord, for the walls of its drawing room, which had the dimensions of a large basketball court, were disconcertingly thick with trophy heads of the African elephant–warthog–Kodiak bear–moose school; presumably Vanderlip had bought the place "as is." The other rooms were mostly furnished with blatantly genuine French antiques doubtless reflecting the taste of the hunter's wife. (A few years later I used that house in my second novel, *Many People Prize It*.) That furniture presented me with a problem: Vanderlip set me up in an upper room full of voluptuously august Louis XV stuff. The frivolous little writing table took my typewriter safely—in those days portables were still acceptably light—but the chairs were a ghastly risk. When writing, if I pause to think—which is often advisable—I lean back in my chair, the front legs come off the floor, and the strain on the chair back is heavy. And when I leaned back *chez* Vanderlip the chair of the deputy mistress of Louis XV or maybe only the Duc de Richelieu would creak and wriggle threateningly.

I suggested to Vanderlip that something sturdier, say, the conventional kitchen chair, be substituted. He said he'd see to it. Next morning, however, I learned that his wife, who at lunch the day before had seemed a sensible woman, refused to allow a kitchen or any other inappropriate kind of chair upstairs. When Mr. Furnas wanted to think, he could get up and walk about. I did my best to remember to do so. No chair actually collapsed, for each time one showed signs of impending disaster, I discarded it and chose another. But whoever bought the furniture in that room in whatever sale of the Vanderlip effects eventually took place must have found his purchases ungodly wobbly.

Otherwise Mrs. V. and I got along. Her lunches were elegant, the butler hovering at one's elbow with Scotch and Appolinaris, the only time I have ever had highballs to wash down lunch. There were sometimes special guests. I particularly remember Anna Louise Strong, already riding high as crypto-flack for the USSR, explaining with coldblooded charm the dialectical necessity for Stalin's ruthless way with peasant and poet alike. I think her presence meant not that Vanderlip leaned toward radical chic—he struck me as a pretty levelheaded old boy—merely that he liked to explore people of all stripes and significances.

He liked my work; I retained from Economics A enough of the quantity theory of money to know what he was talking about. Indeed he offered me an apprentice's berth in the City Bank. Once more puzzled by the way people suggested jobs for which I was unsuited, I thanked him and said no, for the Tyler project had made eating money less of a problem. I suppose that the article on the gold question with his name on it carried some weight in high quarters. If so, my faint scratch on history was made. Anyway it was one of the few exceptions to my formula when asked: "What do you write about?" "Anything but politics and economics."

What with half a dozen other ghostings in the next few years a good deal of Furnas's copy got into print—only without his by-line. That bothered him not at all. It was interesting work, it was a developing livelihood, and it left time for some travel and writing two novels published to good reviews and poor sales. Gradually, however, under B&B's expert auspices, reporting articles signed "J. C. Furnas" came along until he was one of several dozen free lances on whom the national slicks relied for weekly or monthly fodder. Yet two successful magazine series that he wrote still carried no by-line:

DeWitt Wallace, founder-editor-publisher of the *Reader's Digest,* asked me to write both sides of printed debates on public issues of the day—capital punishment, compulsory sterilization, fair-price laws, intercollegiate football, that sort of thing—anonymously. We created Mr. Pro and Mr. Con, both of them my alter egos, without mentioning they were identical twins or, in today's terms, clones. It would have spoiled all to let readers know what was going on, just as it would spoil it for children to let them see the man manipulating both Punch and Judy. And with well-chosen issues it was easier to play fair than one might expect. My own opinions—which, of course, I either started with or developed along the way—never showed. That was apparent when a reader's letter would say Mr. Pro sure told it like it is, but why print that imbecilic Mr. Con's nonsense—and the next letter would say the same vice versa.

On top of more or less regular jobs for the *Saturday Evening Post* came occasional assignments from the Curtis Publishing Company's *Ladies' Home Journal,* a national institution then picking up speed under guidance of an able husband-and-wife team, Bruce and Beatrice Gould. They planned a monthly feature covering a single American family from a representative segment of the population, detailing their finances, tastes, ambitions, problems, foibles, and so on, backed up by departmental articles discussing, advising, warning—the indicated department would even replant the flower beds (with color photographs, of course) or install a more efficient kitchen for

free. Basic illustration came from Martin Munkacsi, interna-
tionally renowned for both photoreportage and fashion work;
mine was the central descriptive piece, for which my wife's
interviewing skill and general diplomacy, as well as the usual
midwifing of copy, were indispensable. Yet to maintain the institutional feeling—the *Journal* as America's concerned friend
and good neighbor—my piece was not signed.

The series proved very popular. I wrote its first five years,
seventy-odd families ranging from black sharecroppers to Chicago stockyards millionaires, entailing monthly travel, usually
with my wife, into some four fifths of the forty-eight states.
(In my basement is a huge map of the United States. I once
put a map pin into every place where one or another assignment took me; it looks as though sprayed with birdshot.) My
leaving the series, which went on for years and years, was, I
think, due to conjunction of two factors: I was hankering to
get closer to World War II; and a subtle, never impolite chill
had developed. Mid-1944 Beatrice Gould told me that the November issue, due just before the election, would be two-ply—
the Roosevelts and the Deweys. We had already done the Harold Stassens and the William O. Douglases. Stassen was most
intelligently rewarding, but Douglas had been a headache,
keeping Munkacsi freezing on the steps of the Supreme Court
Building for a couple of hours and letting his wife persuade
him to try to back out of the thing halfway through. Partly in
view of that, partly because I had a rather poor opinion of
both the candidates, I evinced doubts about the presidential
scheme and told Beatrice she had better get another boy—
though I stated it more suavely, of course. It was tactless of
me to be, for once, right: Mrs. Roosevelt, a valued contributor
to the *Journal*, cooperated cordially but not FDR; and Munkacsi and Dewey signally failed to get along.

Back to 1935—a really eventful year: The Moscow Trials
were not yet occasioning uneasiness among admirers of the
USSR, and Miss Strong's co-workers in the propaganda vineyard, both paid and amateur, were ubiquitously vocal, far outdoing their counterparts putting their hearts into shilling for
Hitler and Mussolini. Conducted tours of the Future-That-
Works arranged by Intourist, the USSR's travel agency, were
as fashionable among little groups of serious thinkers as sup-

port of the Spanish Loyalists would be a few years later. My wife and I had been at still another large party full of people babbling about either their meaningful experiences during their previous summer's visit to Russia or their plans for making the pilgrimage in the coming summer. On our way home we stopped for a pitcher of beer at the Brevoort's sidewalk café. Under its influence we decided to join one of those wide-eyed tours and do an article about American sociological sightseers. We could afford the venture: The *Reader's Digest* had just bought two pieces, one on what to do when burglars come calling, one on the ghastly consequences of automobile accidents.

We booked ourselves through the Bureau of University Travel, a well-considered outfit that worked with Intourist, for Leningrad, Moscow, down to Volga by steamboat, and so on under guidance of a Harvard professor of Slavic languages, Samuel Cross. On a sweltering June morning we sailed tourist–third class in White Star's old *Britannic.* Our particular party consisted of a professor of economics (and wife) from Colorado; a professor of English from California; a member of a Wisconsin school board; a high school teacher from innermost Pennsylvania; two of Cross's students; and an elderly Kansas housewife who had yearned to visit the Kremlin ever since she saw a picture of it in her school geography. Third class also contained a score or so Irish-Americans booked for the Ould Sod. But they were swamped by a hundred-odd college students, mostly from the Northeast quadrant, headed for a month of Moscow University's summer school. As we cast off, their leaders massed them forward to sing the "Internationale," fists duly clenched, then in lighter vein "There's a Chain Gang Down in Georgia"* to the tune of "A Rainbow Round My Shoulder."

The *Britannic* was a nine-day plodder. Plenty of time for Party-lining lectures and on-deck seminars led by half-acknowledged Party members including Bob Brown, head of a Party-lining college in Arkansas; Lem Harris, whom I recalled from Cambridge, now a Party-lining expert in organizing farmers; a yappy little British exchange student; an impressive black understood to be going to Moscow for retread

*Reflecting the wide impact of a book and movie called *I Was a Fugitive from a Georgia Chain Gang.*

because he was given to heresies; John Bovingdon, who celebrated the joys of collective farming with writhing dances and
hard-breathing monologues; witty little Ray Rabinowitz (pseu-
donym), professedly on a visit to her grandmother in Byelo-
russia but working hard for the Party en route—one of the
few Communists we ever liked well enough to make friends
with. The lower echelon included Dick Lauterbach, who later
became a prominent journalist-apologist for the USSR, and a
fulsome blonde who scolded me for selling my soul to the cap-
italist press; she was bucking for a Party card. Most of our
pilgrims, however, were earnest small fry each spending a few
hundred hard-earned dollars for the privilege of dipping into
the sacred springs of Red Square.* Because of the strong academic flavor we decided to call our piece "Leningraduates."

We carefully eschewed analyzing the USSR's symptoms or
attempting prognosis. When asked whether I planned a book
on such topics, I would reply: "No, we were there five weeks.
I leave that sort of thing to people who had three." Our angle
was the absurdities created when that pack of wishful thinkers
encountered the grim, sordid, twitchy reality that, when they
saw it, they could not bear to recognize. Their will to believe—
or, in certain contexts, not to believe—was extraordinary. Our
schoolteacher looked about her as our bus crossed the bridge
over the Moscow River on the way to our hotel and said with
a triumphant snort: "Well! I don't see any starving people, do
you?" A few of the pilgrims' leaders had the grace to warn
them that it was inadvisable to drink unboiled water or eat raw
vegetables or soups heavily loaded with dill to disguise their
corrupt ingredients. Most of them paid no heed, for to do so
would imply that in the Promised Land all was not necessarily
better than anywhere else. In consequence many came down
with what we called "Russky complaint," which they stoutly
denied even when frantically hastening to the washroom. It
was specially inconvenient because the toilets so seldom flushed
and the only toilet paper was newspaper cut in six-inch squares.
Pravda was no better than *Izvestia*.

---

*A while ago a magazine writer following the same trail decades later put on his
article a title I'd never have dared try: "Down the Volga with a Pack of Fools." Things
as he described them didn't seem to have changed much in the intervening forty
years.

We were to stay with Cross's party down the Volga, leave it at Stalingrad, and work back to Moscow by ourselves. That did not mean "on our own." Inevitably Intourist sheepdogged us all the way, meeting our trains, taking us to stations, arranging where we went and when to see what. This was taken for granted and indeed, since we had only two hundred odd words of the language and wished to follow the tourist routine, we preferred that. In Moscow a staff foulup sent us not to the specified Nova Mokovskaya all-tourist hotel but to the once elegant, now run-down, turn-of-the-century Metropole, much frequented by American newspapermen. The food was better than we had been getting, the drinks adequate: Caucasian wines were good and there was a bar cocktail made of one third vodka, one third Russian gin, one third Russian cointreau garnished with a salt-pickled wild black cherry streaking its depths with astringent pink. On getting home I tried to reproduce it with American gin, vodka, and real cointreau with Indian chutney juice batting for the cherry flavor, but it never attained the flyaway tingle of the original.

All that is by the way. The point is that we were in the Metropole bar when Ralph Barnes (*New York Herald-Tribune*) came in with word that the University summer school was summarily canceled. The official pretext was that its professor-lecturers had been called into the field in a social emergency. The press corps saw it as just another Byzantine symptom of turbulence on high, consequent on the assassination of Kirov earlier that year, bringing on mass exiles and executions. Overnight several hundred foreign students, including our *Britannic* shipmates, were denied what they had spent their money on and come so far to get. No refund, merely permission for an equivalent in third-class group travel on the Intourist trail of collective farms, hydroelectric dams, antireligious museums, Parks of Culture and Rest, and reformatories for whores. The pilgrims did mill about in some dismay but essentially took it lying down, never a word sounding resentful. The USSR could do no wrong.

Booking our trip in New York had required tourist visas. I went to the USSR consulate in its Bedford stone mansion in the East Sixties; when filling out the applications, feeling whimsical, I suppose, I gave "ghost-writer" as my occupation.

Either *ghost* or *writer* did not set well, for in spite of the auspices of the Bureau of University Travel, it took me twenty minutes to persuade a stony-faced vice-consul to clear our visas. Maybe that resulted in our eventual discovery that we were under special observation over there—being tailed. On our first day in Moscow appeared a ferally handsome blond youth shaking hands with Cross as an old acquaintance and being introduced round as Bill Kulagin. He stayed to dinner. He proved to have been born in Jersey City of Latvian parents, trained as a die-cutter, come to the USSR to help build socialism, and was now studying Chinese to prepare for a consular career—or so he said. His hobby, he allowed, was hobnobbing with Americans to keep up his English. He took specially to the Furnases, often coming round at lunchtime for the advantage of their spare meal tickets, in return steering them to shops that had the best old-regime antiques; we bought little, but nobody seemed to mind. In time Bill grew fatuously confidential, bragging about his good friends in the GPU (successor to Lenin's Cheka, predecessor of the KGB) and advising us to discount stories about torture of dissidents; torture wasn't necessary—just keep a man on salt fish and no water for a week and he'll talk. Bill was a strange kind of tame reptile.

He saw us off for Gorky and the Volga boat, dwelling on how he looked forward to our return to Moscow. We did not then know that we'd come back a day early and to the wrong hotel. Neither did he. Yet within half an hour of our arrival at the Metropole here was Bill all smiles, staying underfoot during most of our subsequent stay. This clairvoyance left little room for doubt. Somebody among his GPU cronies . . . When he saw us off on the train for Leningrad and the Russian ship for London, he gave us a letter to take to his wife in Leningrad. Mails were slow and unreliable, he said; address on the envelope, just show it to a taxi driver. Next day we sat on a bench in a Leningrad park out of earshot of passersby to discuss what to do about the letter. The toilet in our bathroom in the Astoria Hotel actually flushed efficiently. I have never doubted that we arrived at the right decision.

Next morning when the *Felix Dzershinsky* cast off, London-bound, my enteric tract made a scatological comment. We had been careful of what we ate and drank and until then I had

had no difficulties. When a ship sails, I make a point of being on deck: "All clear forward? . . . All clear aft?" This time I was absent. All was *not* clear aft. As the parting whistle blared I was darting belowside to pay (excuse the expression) arrears to Russky complaint. It was a fitting and well-timed purgative symbol of how we felt about the Future-That-Works.

Some weeks after getting home I ran into Sam Cross in the Harvard Club. We had a drink. After awhile, looking slightly queer, he reproached me with having neglected to tell him I planned to write about the trip. I said I'd made no secret of my being a writer and reproached him with not warning us about Bill. I think I had the better of the exchange. The other sequela of "Leningraduates" was the cover of the *New Masses* of November 19, 1935, featuring "Saturday Evening Liar" by Bob Brown, a diatribe consisting largely of parallel columns headed respectively "FACT" and "FURNAS." A crumbling copy of that issue is one of my most prized possessions. I never understood why the Party took it so big. The readers of the *New Masses* never read the *Post* and vice versa. It was welcome, however. I hoped that this disproportionate reaction on high meant that Bill's bungling of his mission got him shipped to Outer Kamchatka.

Now and again somebody learning that I visited Russia fifty years ago asks whether I ever consider going back to see what it's like now. No. Neither would I return to incredibly hopeless Haiti or the cold-drawn rigor of New Caledonia. I lack the clinical mind that would inflict on me the further stages of a pathology I have once inspected. True, nothing is *all* bad. Bela Low, a very good friend and a staunch Social Democrat, was once lecturing on the USSR—as caustically as usual—and a heckler asked: "Mr. Low, isn't there a single good thing to say about the Soviet Union?" Bela considered a moment and answered: "Yes. They cut two letters out of that impossible Cyrillic alphabet." To such a question I'd answer that Haitian rum was palatable and ingratiatingly cheap; that in New Cal the giant sea snails in garlic sauce at that Polish exile's place down the shore from Nouméa were excellent; and that in the Soviet Union fifty years ago, in addition to those surrealistic cocktails, the equivalent of fifty cents secured a deep saucer heaped with pale-gray, lumpy fresh caviar—the only caviar I

ever really liked. Nowadays, I understand, caviar is as ob-
scenely expensive in Moscow as anywhere else. Go back?
What for?

Late in August 1935 the motherly *Scythia* landed us in Boston on our way to the family place in Maine. My wife's young
half-brother John and a crony of his drove down to fetch us.
Once we were clear of Boston's even then calamitous traffic,
the crony said shyly that he was honored to meet me. "Yeah,
now you've gone and got famous," said young John. I couldn't
imagine what he was talking about. Neither of the boys could
believe I didn't know. It took a while to clear up what they
meant and what had happened.

Late in July, while we had been five thousand miles away,
the August *Reader's Digest* had appeared with my article about
highway accidents titled "—And Sudden Death," a no-holds-
barred account of blood-and-bones, lethal mutilations and
screaming agonies. Overnight the thing had snowballed into a
national sensation. Coast to coast the newspapers had reprinted it accompanied by approving comment; the *March of
Time* did an installment about it—my only appearance in a
movie; judges were sentencing speeders to copy it out fifty
times or go to jail; insurance companies were handing out free
copies to their customers; oil companies were distributing it at
gas pumps; the Sunday full page of H. T. Webter's "The Timid
Soul," a widely beloved comic strip, showed Casper Milque-
toast pushing the family car back into the garage because, having read "—And Sudden Death," he was afraid to start the
engine. The *Digest's* offer of unlimited reprints at cost was
swamping printing presses. It remains true today, I believe,
that it had the widest circulation of any article in the history
of magazines. Unprepared for any such hullabaloo, I came
down with shingles, which often attacks those under heavy stress
who had chicken pox in childhood.

I can describe this success without blushing because (a) it
was genuine and (b) it was no more than 50 percent my doing.
To write about such a thing was not my idea but Wallace's. At
a Westchester filling station he had seen a total wreck waiting
to be scrapped. As he shook his head over it, the gas-pumper
said: "You should of seen it before we got the bodies out."

Wallace had already been sensing a rising tide of public outrage over the skyrocketing highway death toll. This casual cue stirred him into the editorial ten-strike of his generation. (Dick Berlin, chief of the Hearst stable of magazines, told me that, as the furor grew, he asked one of his editors: "Why didn't you think of that?" and the editor replied: "If I had, you wouldn't have let me print it.") And it was my good luck at the time to be on Wallace's mind as a useful writer. We both were lucky to have on tap Charles W. Ferguson, the staff editor who midwifed the job. Fergy's dogged insistence on getting pace and idiom just right by rewriting and rewriting had a great deal to do with the eventual impact. The title was mine, out of the Book of Common Prayer. But beyond that, given the ground-breaking idea and Fergy to ride herd on it, any one of a dozen free lances of the day could have achieved the same success.

Wallace paid me four hundred dollars, equivalent to say two thousand dollars now. Ten years later he ran it again, paying another thousand dollars; again, paying the same, on its twentieth birthday. He also had a pleasant habit of sizable Christmas bonuses for frequent contributors. We put together a sequel that I called "Better Off Dead" about crash victims who survived but had ghastly good reason to wish they hadn't. In a way it was even more disquieting, but Wallace finally decided against it. It was included with "—And Sudden Death," however, in a paperback that Simon & Schuster published with a good advance; Paramount Pictures bought the title for five thousand dollars. I had no reason to complain. But next spring I had trouble convincing the Internal Revenue Service that, believe it or not, I never got a dime from the sale of those millions on millions of reprints. They really were sold at or below cost.

The chief dividends were intangible. The *Digest* had already been doing well; this inspiration of Wallace's now boosted it into a far higher orbit. In parallel my free-lancing had been coming along nicely; now, thanks to "—And Sudden Death," I was far better known and for the next few years particularly in demand for articles on highway safety. It was not a good slot for somebody with no background in engineering who never bothered even to own a car while living in New York.

But between help from the National Safety Council and common sense, I think I gave a fair money's worth. Indeed one such assignment was wonderfully rewarding. For a piece for the *Post* on grade-crossing accidents I arranged to ride in the cabs of four or five New York Central locomotives hauling fast passenger trains. *Steam* not diesel. Nobody who has never ridden like that can have any notion of what it was like at eighty-odd miles an hour as those massive tons of steel roared, rushed, yawed, rattled, and cavorted through the night as though on the verge of leaving the rails and taking off for outer space. I've been driven faster than that on automobile test tracks and gone a lot faster in open-cockpit planes. But that, gentlemen hush, was *speed*. And they let me blow the whistle for grade crossings: Whe-e-e-e-e . . . Whe-e-e-e-e . . . Whe-e- . . . Wh-e-e-e-e-e! That was living.

All the while I was developing a semispecialty of lay-medical articles mostly for the Curtis magazines: the advent of sulfa drugs; ophthalmological problems; the first general-magazine warning of the hazards of the sun cult; hearing aids (developing deafness eventually forced me into that); athlete's foot (the *Post* rejected my title "Ain't We Got Fungus!"). For *Collier's* I combined both my specialties by spending New Year's night in the New York medical examiner's morgue watching autopsies on the holiday's quota of heedless drinkers. Once is enough on that one.

There was a medical angle, sort of, to a job for the *Post* that I think as highly of as of "Leningraduates." They wanted a piece on "Dr." John A. Brinkley, the amazing quack who first extensively used radio to drum up business, particularly for his practice in Kansas promising to restore potency to aging men by implanting goat testicles. His radio-borne medical advice for the half-witted made him so popular in his area in the late 1920s that when he ran for governor of Kansas with the slogan "Let's pasture the goats on the Statehouse lawn"— and almost made it—he carried four counties in neighboring Oklahoma, where he wasn't a candidate. Eventually Kansas ran him out and the federal authorities lifted his license to broadcast; but he merely moved down to the Mexican border, bought the hotel in Del Rio, Texas, for a hospital, and took over a couple of Mexican broadcasting stations to spread his gospel.

Their signals were powerful enough to favor most of the States and some of Canada with his outrageous flimflamming.

My wife went to Chicago to prowl the files of the American Medical Association, which had successfully defended itself against Brinkley's libel suit a few years previously. I went to Texas to interview Brinkley's radio-commercial clients plugging love charms, occult amulets, miraculously anointed prayer handkerchiefs, genuine simulated diamond rings, $3.95 typewriters guaranteed to print all twenty-six letters . . . The rest of his broadcasting revenue came from viciously reactionary old-time gospel preachers making straight the way for Jerry Falwell and Pat Robertson. Then on to Del Rio to meet "Doctor," as his indispensable helpmeet—wife—deputy broadcaster called him. The upper five stories of the hotel were the hospital where daily, off the Southern Pacific trains, came the elderly hopefuls ensnared by Doctor's folksy-sincere broadcasts, often having mortgaged the farm to pay for renewed libido. Grapevine from their broadcasters had warned the Brinkleys of our coming, of course. The atmosphere was highly charged. The first time we left our room in the lower half of the hotel, I so arranged my briefcase that I'd know if it had been frisked in our absence. It had been. To squire us round, Brinkley assigned his bodyguard-assistant, a huge goon whom Hollywood would have jumped at for a movie about the Abominable Snowman. Several times while we lunched with him he went glazedly dreamy and growled apropos of nothing, raising his enormous paws: "Anybody does my boss dirt, I strangle him with these bare hands."

The Brinkleys made themselves amply available, however, in their mansion-retreat. The swimming pool was half-Olympic size with "Dr. Brinkley" spelled out in blue-and-white tile all round the edge; the grounds were ornamented with Carrara marble statues of mythical deities that Doctor had picked up in Italy and a ponderous tortoise shanghaied from the Galapagos islands. When we left, Doctor told us that if we ever found ourselves in a port where his yacht lay, we must come on board for champagne.

Wesley Stout, editor of the *Post,* had us clear our copy for libel with Curtis's lawyers. We toned down a word here and there; even so the effect was murderous. Yet this time Doctor had no intention of suing. He put his wife on the air off and on for a week: "Dear friends, do read the beautiful article about Doctor in this week's *Saturday Evening Post*." Correctly he assumed that his public consisted of either people who were aware of the *Post*'s prestige but never read it or, if they tried to, would miss the implications or couldn't read well enough to get halfway down the first column. Stout telephoned me in a rage: "Damn all lawyers! I didn't want not to get sued! I just wanted not to lose the case."

Brinkley died during the war, but his radio stations went on under the Abominable Snowman's management. Soon after the war my wife and I did a follow-up on bootleg broadcasting across the border, which was still flooding the nation with sucker come-ons, religious quackery, and folksy gospel choirs. Texas was still Texas. With one of the most active of those advertisers, I led off with: "They tell me in Washington you're one of the biggest fake jewelry operations in the Southwest." "Man," he said, "I'll have you know I got me *the* biggest thing in fake jewelry in these whole United States." In Houston I went to see the Abominable's local representative, asked him how was business, and said I was going on to Del Rio and wanted to see his boss. In one sense that was true: interviewing him was highly indicated for my story. In another sense, no; Abominable was certainly aware that my previous effort had been poison and on hearing my name he was very likely to draw a long breath and clear for action. His man said he'd arrange it. Next day I had a firm date in Del Rio for the end of the week. Only an hour later he was on the phone again: He had just been advised that Abominable had dropped dead of a heart attack. Very strange. So soon after hearing I was there? Contiguity and succession? Or mere Pavlovian stimulus and reaction? Or random coincidence? Anyway I was really grateful.

My presumably nonviolent profession sometimes led to anomalous risks. A generation ago I wrote a novel about the early Mormons that the Church of Jesus Christ of the Latter Day Saints (Salt Lake variety) denounced as disrespectful, which it was, and blasphemous, which it wasn't. Some years later my wife and I were driving to the Coast. I had been in Salt Lake City several times, but she hadn't, so I swerved south at Ogden to give her a glimpse of what Joseph Smith's God hath wrought, particularly the central square with its tabernacle and temple—the Kaaba of the Mormon Mecca. Then we regained the car and took off westward. I switched on the radio for a weather report. A newsmanly voice, very sober, announced that a sharp earthquake had just shaken the temple area. I said: "My God, we were there ten minutes ago!" "Ten minutes," said my wife thoughtfully. "Missed you by a hair." We laughed halfway to Winnemucca.

I had already had a brush with another side effect of religion. In 1955 a plethora of movies with biblical themes caused me to write a brisk attack on that school of celluloid showmanship. Deduce its tone from my concluding paragraph about how Hollywood would soon handle the New Testament's parable of the wise and foolish virgins: "Like this, see, these five foolish virgins and their five wise sisters get snatched by some Mediterranean pirates and sold as slaves to Nero and you know what that means, only the five wise ones are Christians on the side and they don't go for the orgy routine, so it's the lions for them. But the other five, they don't care. I can see them now dancing away like crazy in five different colors of gauze while Nero fiddles." Though I adduced examples of the genre outside the De Mille oeuvre, I justly treated Cecil B. De Mille throughout as archetype of the whole gold-plated shoddy tradition of pseudoreligious, prurient vulgarity.

In an inspired moment Carl Brandt sold it to the *Christian Herald*, a conspicuous Protestant religious organ. They headlined it "'LOOK WHAT HOLLYWOOD'S DOING TO YOUR BIBLE!'" along with a juicy selection of sexy, Scripture-based stills. Mrs. Katherine St. George, freewheeling congresswoman from New York, inserted it whole into the *Congressional Record*. It caused other ripples, for a Paramount publicity man fired off to the Reverend Dr. Daniel Poling, editor of the *Herald*, a two-hundred-word telegram shouting "Foul!" and reminding him that only three years previously he (Poling) had fulsomely endorsed the *Samson and Delilah* movie (a juicy still from which was one of the exhibits) as even more commendable than De Mille's earlier masterpiece, *The King of Kings. Variety*, the oracle-newspaper of show business, ran a column and a half about it all. Poling, his tail twitching pitiably in the crack, could only reply in an editorial that though he approved of most of my strictures, De Mille's Bible stuff should not be tarred with the same brush as his imitators' doing, "those major menaces to all that Christian people stand for"—a distinction without a difference if there ever was one.

Reactions to print among those whose oxen are gored may not always be an enjoyable as that. My *Post* article about eye doctors warned that though optometrists are trained to test and do lenses for errors of refraction (such as astigmatism), they are not qualified to diagnose diseases of the eye, which are the province of the M.D.-ophthalmologist. That statement, still sound, exasperated optometrists. The article appeared while my wife and I were creeping round the Caribbean in an elderly cargo liner. At Port of Spain the mail coming aboard included a large green canvas mailbag bursting with letters from furious optometrists mostly addressed to the *Post*'s editors, of course, for the angry reader usually squawks to the editor; the favorable reader writes to the author, so the editor never sees the letter unless the author cooks up some pretext for passing it on.

A while later I risked many more such letters by doing for *Look* magazine an exposé of unscrupulous undertakers. Every few years somebody writes that piece, and though the profession seems to have effected some improvement, it always needs doing. A cousin of mine had just had a hard time arranging the funeral of an aunt of ours in California, so I had my heart in my work, even though well aware that the industry's reaction would be an avalanche crossed with an earthquake. At the same time I was risking another lynching by a *Look* piece that took astrology apart. There are a lot more star-struck people than there are undertakers. Payment for both back-to-back bombshells was in the bank, galleys imminent, when—sorry about this anticlimax—*Look* had a sweeping change of editorial guard and the new boss decreed a clean sweep. Everything in the stockpile of accepted articles was thrown away. My skin was saved. No longer did I have to envisage the undertakers' shock troops swarming up the hill to my house with syringes of embalming fluid at the ready while flights of astrologers saturated the premises with baleful influences from Saturn and Cancer. Note again how lucky I was. The only penalty I paid was, if prolonged, light. For the astrology job I subscribed to dozens of astrological magazines, financial advice services, newsletters, and so on; so for the next couple of years my mail was clogged with weird junk that I hadn't even asked for. I had not foreseen that astrology swaps mailing lists with spiritualism, neowitchcraft, self-hypnotism, metempsychotics et al.

Much earlier Providence had spared me a grave risk in a rarefied context. In the late 1930s the Duchess of Windsor wished to do an autobiography and the Goulds wanted it for the *Ladies' Home Journal,* Furnas to ghost it—not the sort of thing one turns down if only from curiosity. The Duke was then governor of the Bahamas. My wife—thrice indispensable for this—and I were to be the Windsors' guests at Government House in Nassau while doing the work. I lunched in New York with an affable Lady Betty Somebody of the Duchess's suite who presumably reported on me favorably. My wife was deep in planning the right clothes. . . . World War II broke out. All bets off. The one good thing about that grisly cataclysm was its saving us from what all too likely would have been a journalistic abortion, frantically frustrating for all involved. From what one now knows about the subjects, the scheme could never have satisfied the Windsors or the Goulds, or the Furnases trying dismayedly to cope in between.

In thirty years of magazine free-lancing a wild variety of curious situations developed. Assisting (in the French sense) while a black-and-white nanny goat in a below-zero Wisconsin barn gave birth; I recall my wonder at the businesslike air with which she chomped down the afterbirth as though she had read the instructions coming with it. Standing on the front platform of Oliva Dionne's rattletrap house in northern Ontario while he gleefully showed me how he had loosened its planking so that reporters daring to approach the front door would get slammed in the face. Sitting in the boiler room of Henry Ford's private lab in his Dearborn compound while he whammed a sledgehammer on a sheet of black plastic reenforced with silk grass to show me how sturdy it would be in automobile bodies . . . introspectively smiling, nimble as a squirrel and, at God knows what age, hellishly energetic, much like Walter Huston playing Daniel Webster's Devil in the movies. In my judgment he was certifiably far round the bend. On my previous visit to Dearborn, Ford's staff had treated me to a memorable lunch: At the time he was obsessed with the manifold uses of soybeans—for plastics, incidental soil enrichment, substitutes for costlier, conventional foods, and so on. The menu was: appetizer of soybean cheese; soybean soup with soybean crackers; salad of soybean sprouts, dressing of soybean oil; soybean hamburger steak with soybean puree; ice cream made of soybeans with soybean cookies; soybean coffee. It hadn't the positive quality to make it the worst meal I ever choked down but did succeed in being even more blah than Grandmother Furnas's well-intended Quaker cuisine.

Eventually the end of World War II unleashed American television and the ensuing competition for advertising dollars undermined the national slick magazines that were the free lance's mainstay. *Collier's* foundered. Piece by piece the Curtis empire was sold off. *Look* succumbed. Lucky again, I was already shifting into books. In 1956 I had my first Book-of-the-Month Club selection. By 1965 I was pretty well out of the magazine field, such as it had become, which was just as well, for it was suffering heavily from what I thought of as mastheaditis.

In the 1930s a staff of only seven or eight, plus secretaries and office boys, of course, got out the brilliantly edited *Saturday Evening Post* each week. A free lance's suggestion of a subject he'd like to cover was okayed or rejected with brisk promptness. I recall once presenting three ideas to Lorimer in his office after lunch. I was in there six minutes: ninety seconds per idea for me; ten seconds for each yes or no; one minute for a thank you and handshake. Score: two okay, one no, both of the approved items bought on delivery, no revisions asked. For when the *Post* bought from an established writer, it was assumed that further fussing was unnecessary. On the galleys maybe three or four minor queries in four to five thousand words; a spelling correction; practically never editorial tinkering with the text. By the 1960s, however, every magazine's masthead was clogged with dozens and scores of senior editors, associate editors, contributing editors, "researchers"—it looked like the roster of a destroyer's crew, all sending one another memos and attending staff meetings and brainstormings in an orgy of dispersed responsibility and chronic nervousness. More and more articles were staff-written. The free lance was up against rewriting, rewriting, rewriting as still another editor developed another shift of approach. Once I finished the fifth or sixth version of a job and gave it to our secretary to retype and send off while I was away on some new assignment. "Same title?" she asked. "Oh hell," I said, "call it Penelope's Web." She was an ideal secretary but insufficiently mindful of Homer. A week later an editor phoned: "Piece okay now, only what's this new title? Penelope's Web? Penelope who?"

12

War the Second

MANY VIEW THE Spanish Civil War as dress rehearsal for World War II—a cliché sounder than most because of the Germans' and Italians' use of Spain's agony to test new tactics in the air and on the ground for wider use a few years later. Beyond that, other alleged affinities are more ingenious than sound. Yet very generally the war was a sort of psychological and political preparation for the way the Germans went through Western Europe's defenses like a booted foot through a rotting watermelon. I insisted to my wife that, in long-run terms, the fall of Paris meant not a permanent Nazi triumph but somehow eventual redress. That was no strategist's sound judgment, merely a sneaking, half-superstitious sense that all that goes up comes down; that any situation so grotesquely far out of equilibrium would eventually prove friable. Meanwhile, of course, what one felt was a disgusted dismay. Civilization had blown it again. And things like the Spanish affair made it easier to believe that Dunkirk was really happening.

I associate that frame of mind with a white-knuckle plane trip in April 1940, when people stopped talking about "phony war." I had been out in the corn belt on a piece for the *Country Gentleman* and was flying home TWA from Kansas City. Those pre-jet prop planes were more comfortable than today's jets. They had two-by-two seating, better leg room, and for a fancy touch, radio speakers embedded in the upholstery at ear level, so a flick of a switch would bring in broadcasts without disturbing one's seatmate. The weather was ominous. As we neared

New York, the cockpit announced that LaGuardia was socked in, we'd circle over Newark and wait our turn to land there. We circled and circled—and soon Newark too was ineligible, we were off to Philadelphia. By then air traffic for hundreds of miles round was a mess and heaven only knew how many homeless aircraft were up there circling in competition. And long before our turn came at Philadelphia, she too was socked in and we were on our way, the cockpit said, to Harrisburg, whence TWA would put us on a train for New York.

The stewardess—they were still called that in 1940—tried to cheer us up by exhuming a quantity of stale chicken sandwiches. We needed cheering up. Though nobody in my hearing was tactless enough to mention it, we had been airborne so long it was a question of whether there was fuel enough to make Harrisburg. I had had the bad judgment to consult the brochure in the seat pocket and multiply our fuel consumption per hour by hours in the air relative to stated fuel capacity. Worse, those of us using the radio for distraction were learning what was happening to Norway—detail after detail in Elmer Davis's slow, deep, no-nonsense voice. Between our personal difficulty and the world's, that planeload of several score people made up a mighty quiet environment.

Had anybody asked, I'd have said our situation could hardly be worse. I'd have been wrong. Through our squinchy little windows we were welcoming the lights of Harrisburg—a lovely sight, all clear. Only that was the moment Harrisburg chose for a power failure. Its lights were wiped out as though by a magician's trick. So were its airport's runway lights. No landing place down there.

On we went into the blue-black yonder. The cockpit, still pluckily noncommittal, said we'd go on to a WPA emergency landing field near Altoona, high up in the mountains. We made it. The runway was theoretically much too short for us, but our pilot, bless his nerve and reflexes, managed—barely. As we trooped down to solid ground we, shuddering, saw that the plane's uptilted nose was within yards of a high-tension power cable beyond the end of the runway. And we had ten minutes' worth of fuel left.

Waiting buses took us in to Altoona's hotel, where the management had thoughtfully kept the bar open. The lobby had a battery of telephone booths. It was like watching bees performing ritual to see passenger after passenger pop into a booth, talk with many gestures for two minutes, and then pop out again to seek refreshment. Henry Fonda, our only notable passenger, beat me into a booth by some six inches. Had I ever met him, I'd certainly have asked him if he remembered that April night. We were a tiddly lot by the time a Pennsylvania Railroad overnight train from Chicago was whisking us off to Philadelphia, Newark, New York.

The way things had looked, I was probably justified in having reflected, as I did, that if the news got any worse, at least I wouldn't be around to brood over it.

Where were you when you heard about Pearl Harbor? The question dates one. I was driving into New York to interview Nathan Straus, Administrator of the U.S. Housing Authority. That incredible radio bulletin exploded about halfway and I nearly drove the little red Studebaker Champion off the road. I should have got to a phone, called Straus at his hotel, and said all bets would now be off as to housing and a hundred other matters, no point in our meeting. Not being skilled in international crises, however, I drove on and found him as dithery as I was. Both of us were confusedly polite and all at sea. Then I drove the sixty miles home again to begin adjustment to my country's last—probably only—really popular war. Adjustment was difficult but only in practical matters, not emotion—I never doubted, nor do I yet, that it was as good a cause as ever was fought for.

The practical hitches developed only gradually. Since midsummer 1939 I had been doing that "How America Lives" series for the Goulds. The first twelve pieces, all in pre–Pearl Harbor contexts, were eventually collected into a book that the Office of War Information had translated into eight or nine languages for propaganda among Allied peoples. I still have the Greek version, of which I can't read a word. "How America Lives" gradually, properly shifted into How-America-Lives-with-Its-War. Soon my articles for the *Post* were also largely on war doings: emergency shipbuilding on the Ohio River; iron mining in the wilds of western Ontario; rehabilitation of 4F draftees; a newly created shell-loading plant in the economic wilds of western Tennessee; women's dwindling readiness to take war-supply industrial jobs—Rosie the Riveter was a fine girl but there weren't too many of her. Between *Post* and *Journal* I was all over the country briefing readers as to what went on in the home-front aspects of this war so abruptly wished on us. In the process the only even inconvenient thing I encountered was a security check at the border on my way to Mexico City. I had in my pocket Darwin's *Voyage of the Beagle,* which I was reading for my projected postwar book on the South Pacific—reading *and* liberally underlining. Officials took several hours to determine no spy code was involved. Its text is fascinating as well as educational, but they seemed only resentfully bored with it.

Inevitably it made me uneasy that man after man among my friends was in uniform, mostly naval. One in procurement diligently snapping stuff up before the army got to it; one lubricating the navy's labor relations; one in training movies; one juggling ships for the Maritime Commission; one headed for an admiral's staff and a bomb splinter in the behind—all exiled from normal life, as I was not, and getting less every payday, as I was not. My brother-in-law, who had already been in World War I, was a scientific consultant for the military. My young half-brother-in-law was in the marines.

I had registered for what was tactfully called Selective Service. I was married, thirty-seven, had only one useful eye, and was hard-of-hearing—unlikely to be drafted. Conceivably a medical examiner might overlook all that if I insisted that a volunteer college graduate like me should have a couple of bars on his collar and some formal, at least noncombatant share in the war effort after the manner of his friends. But I knew where that would probably lead. On a magazine story, I had dealt with the former city editor of a western newspaper who had been in the National Guard and got taken off the desk to train a new-forming battalion of black recruits. He had made them, he assured me with tears in his voice, the best damn combat battalion an enemy ever would come up against. In return for that service, a paper shuffler in Washington had come on· the file that identified him as journalist and had snatched him away from his black command for a post as public-relations-officer. Now in a god forsaken, snow-clogged corner of Wisconsin, he was juggling the small-time local press, making speeches at local Rotary lunches. Much as he hated the job, he did it well. But by then I had seen in action a number of PROs of all degrees of intelligence and ability and was certain that if Uncle Sam made me one—as it would be superficially logical to do—it would be a sort of favor to the Germans and Japanese and a minor disaster for whatever outfit, commanding officer, and community I was inflicted on.

Several times I mentioned my uneasiness to Bruce Gould, who had been in the air force in World War I. Each time he said more emphatically that the sort of thing I was doing in the magazines helped the war effort better than anything I'd do in uniform. It was probably true; but that tingle of troubled mind remained. I looked around for something to assuage it. For the same reasons that would have made me a poor City Hall reporter, I was no full-time war correspondent *in posse*. But . . . somewhere I read something about the good antisubmarine work the Royal Canadian Navy was doing in the North Atlantic. It took a lot of finagling, but I eventually persuaded the *Reader's Digest,* the U.S. Navy (to vouch for me), and Ottawa (various agencies) to let me do a piece about it.

The timing was hazardously good: In that winter of 1942–43 the German submarines still had things far too much their own way. My project was two-ply: briefing from the naval command in Ottawa and then—the part that would help assuage my conscience—an antisubmarine cruise out of Halifax. Well aware of what it would be like off Newfoundland in January, I broke out the long underwear and woolen shirts and boarded the train for Montreal in the heavy, pile-lined gabardine overcoat and earmuffed fur cap that I occasionally needed at home in the Jersey countryside. Strictly a civilian getup; but I was to learn that when on watch the personnel of my hostess corvette would look even less warlike. Canada had zealously besought the public for old fur coats to brave the North Atlantic in. Affluent Canadian ladies had responded generously. Persian lamb was useless, of course, and I saw no chinchilla, though probably some was turned in; but mink, sable, fisher, and seal were largely available and remodeled parka-style. No ship's crew had ever been so luxuriously turned out since Cleopatra sailed down the Nile. Those furry makeshifts did look strange when worn over heavy pants and seaboots.

The whole operation had that sort of ironic realism. As we

sailed from Halifax, the vessels opening and closing the anti-submarine net at the harbor mouth were middle-sized private yachts* signed on for the duration and looking innocently fragile in that grim context. More vessels came into commission in time; but at that early stage, Canada's bluewater navy consisted of a number of hastily built corvettes and a few of the elderly four-piper destroyers that FDR had swapped for West Indian bases with the British.

My corvette was, up to then, the smallest craft I had ever voyaged in—modeled on the North Sea fishing trawler, round-bottomed, highly seaworthy, but given to rolling like mad in any kind of beam sea and in a head sea pitching like a child's rocking horse. Her shallow draft had the advantage that a torpedo fired at her was likely to slide harmlessly underneath. The depth charges racked aft would be as effective in use as if dropped from a more formidable ship. But her single gun mounted forward was hopelessly outranged by what German U-boats carried, and her speed, though enough to keep up with most convoys, was critically slower than the submarines'. Just as undashing as her prosaic ancestry, she managed to look both gaunt and tubby. But her white ensign was grimy, meaning she had already done her share, and her crew, well aware that their country was, for lack of better equipment, sending a boy to do a man's job, didn't even bother to joke about it—they just went ahead with their assignment as casually as if it made perfect sense.

Officers and ratings were mostly Coast Guardsmen from Canada's west coast. I was their first experience with the press, but they accepted me with no sense of strain, neither Britishly stuffy nor suspicious nor impressed. For quarters the best they could do for me was the wardroom "sofa"—a skinny bench between table and bulkhead with half an inch of mashed-down upholstery; it was barely five feet long, so the steward fetched a camp stool to prop my feet on. I was given the run of the

---

*Some years later I reencountered one of them. The Port of New Orleans had bought her and fetched her down, along with her wartime skipper, to take visiting firemen on tours of the port. While making the tour for an article for *Holiday*, I learned of her past and the skipper and I discussed old times. He said yes, they had mounted a three-inch gun forward. I asked had they ever fired it. "Once," he said, "for testing. It knocked her half a mile back from where she started."

ship with the sole stipulation that when "action stations" sounded, I stay put for five minutes to keep out of the way of those sprinting to their posts. I was also advised that the water was so cold that, if the worst happened, it was better not to bother with lifebelts or rafts; just jump overboard carrying something heavy. That sounded sensible, particularly for so hapless a swimmer as I am.

Cold was the prevailing motif. Whether that vibrating bucket of steel had some sort of heating system I don't remember, but if so it hardly took the edge off the cooling effect of below-freezing seawater under us and half gales straight from Greenland. Long underwear and sweaters were almost pointless. I have seldom realized cold as stridently as when the first action-stations gong sounded—it reverberated through the ship's naked metal surfaces like a fire alarm in Pandemonium—and I followed the pounding feet to the bridge. We were making a turn to investigate whatever the listening equipment had detected, and there was starlight enough to dramatize the way that, with the helm to help, she rolled God knows how many degrees. One could look straight down into the privacy of the school of fish or sounding whale that had fooled the instruments into suspecting a submarine.

Cold as I was, I knew I was in a good place to be. Meals were large and dullish but not ill cooked. It wouldn't have mattered had they been inedible, for I was utterly enjoying myself. As aforesaid, I rejoice in being at sea; I scorn large ships and cotton to small ones; I prefer lively weather. And here I was in weather that my old shipmate, the Atlantic Ocean, could have been saving up for me in a vessel small enough to remind me every minute that I was at sea; working at my own pace on my article—every line or two I had to retrieve the typewriter when, in spite of its rubber feet, it slid to the other end of the wardroom table; going aft whenever I chose to relish the wind and the great hulking swells. Add the piquant possibility that at any moment the horizon might sprout the dark gray hump of a U-boat lobbing a shell in our direction.

In a perverse way I even enjoyed a demonstration that, though I had always been notoriously immune to seasickness even in weather rougher than this, I was not ironclad immune. It was another of those false alarms. After an hour or so on the bridge I decided to go below. The violent motion and blasts of cold air up there were poor preparation for the reek of fuel oil prevading belowside. And as I passed the galley, the door opened and a blast of hot mutton fat and onions from the stew the cook had on the fire filled my lungs. For a flash of retching, I thought I was gone. But it proved untrue that there's a first time for everything. I made it to the wardroom, lay down, prayed . . . and the emergency flickered out. My semicircular canals were still virgin and for the next forty-odd years have succeeded in defying anything saltwater can do. Granted, I have never been afloat on the Great Lakes in heavy weather.

Evenings the captain used toothpicks and paperbook matches on the wardroom table to give me lessons in antisubmarine tactics. He and his officers were monosyllabically grateful to America for those destroyers and impressed by the relative elaborateness of their fitting out when handed over, right down to a new ribbon in the captain's typewriter. They also groped toward apology for not finding me a genuine alarm so I could see what it was like dropping depth charges and playing tag with an invisible enemy.

By the time the luck grew worse, we were well acquainted. The bad luck was an ailing engine that seriously reduced our already inadequate speed and could not be repaired at sea. The radio ordered us back to the nearest repair facility—Louisburg out on the easternmost point of Cape Breton Island. Thither we limped and learned it would be at least two weeks before we got to sea again.

That probably made little difference to Hitler's admirals, but it affected my plans. I was soon due home on a "How America Lives" job—I believe that one involved the marine general known in the Corps as Howlin' Mad Smith—and though I had seen no fireworks, I had all I needed for a sound article to show Ottawa's censors. After dinner the evening we came alongside at Louisburg, out of the wardroom locker came a jug of Booker's rum, the Royal Navy's traditional tipple—legend ascribed its distinctively pungent bouquet to having old seaboots and Cayenne pepper soaked in it—and I got out my fifth of Myers' Jamaica and we had a good evening. Next morning when I went ashore rather the worse for wear, the captain paid me as high a compliment as I ever had: "Please, Mr. Furnas, persuade Ottawa to let you try another cruise with us."

I never saw him again. But I did see the ship again. Some ten years later I was eastbound through the narrow pre-Seaway canals of the St. Lawrence in a beautiful little Dutch freighter. As we nosed into a lock, there she was, rising up in the opposite lock, headed westward, still in commission, still looking gaunt and tubby, bound for some chore up the lakes. Probably scrapped long ago. R.I.P.

Getting to Ottawa was complicated. Louisburg is best described—as of 1943 anyway—as the hellangone. Little had happened there since Pepperell's Yankees captured it from the French a couple of centuries before World War II. It is a good seven hundred miles from Ottawa, and the war had fouled up whatever meager transportation was normally available. The details blur in my memory, indeed were pretty blurred at the time. I vaguely recall rattletrap trains through much low-grade winter landscape; and nothing to eat, for no comestibles were available at any stop we made. Late at night the cars were ferried across the Gut of Canso to the Nova Scotian mainland, and I was given to understand that somewhere topside in the hulking ferryboat's innards some kind of provisions existed. After getting lost several times among formidable machinery I finally found a cheerful if grimy woman in a small cubbyhole who sold me her last ham sandwich. Nova Scotian railroads proved no better supplied. On reaching Montreal I was really sharp set. But it was one in the morning, and not unreasonably, whatever sold food in the Montreal station was closed.

The next thing out for Ottawa was a milk train at 2:00 A.M. I settled for that. It consisted of a couple of moldering baggage cars for the milk cans, I assumed, and a vintage-of-1890 club car obviously back in service because of wartime shortage of rolling stock—a four-dimensional nightmare of booths, sofas, armchairs, writhing little side tables all in jigsaw-tortured golden oak with animal heads and implausible heraldry carved here and there. Lightheaded from hunger, I could easily have been persuaded I was dreaming it. And fittingly here was a porter—in wartime in that deserted station at that ghastly hour, a porter!—fetching in a lot of fancy luggage and a suavely plump lady in a coquettish mink cap and a really regal mink coat that had not gone to war. She said "Good evening" and with a sigh settled into an armchair, making no move toward taking off the coat, for the car was emphatically unheated. As we creakily trundled off toward Ottawa, however, she cast an ambivalent glance at a straw hamper on top of her heap of luggage and said: "That thing is really rather absurd. My family said I might get hungry. Would you care to help me keep some of it from going to waste?"

The contents of the hamper were no dream. Several kinds of elegant but substantial sandwiches. Cold roast chicken. Deviled eggs. Oranges, apples, shrimps in mayonnaise . . . I put away a good half of it and she, whose appetite matched her ample person, a third, I should say. We spoke little. I never learned who she was or why she was going to Ottawa in that catch-as-catch-can fashion—still the least probable thing in the whole affair. Then chilly-sleepy, we sank into our coat collars and slept like lambs until Ottawa at sunrise.

I covered half a dozen stories in Canada and was always well treated. Most particularly on that occasion.

My Canadian hosts' inability to flush me a submarine out of the Atlantic depths was frustrating, of course. Enjoyable as the voyage had been, constructive as my article on "Canada's Sheepdog Navy" probably was, a residue of illogical frustration stayed with me into 1945 when the European theater's war was obviously winding down. The Pacific Theater, though no longer as intractable as it had been looking, was still huge and problematical. Attrition was likely eventually to conclude it, however, and leave Uncle Sam willy-nilly responsible for much of what Japan had sought to overrun. That consideration was what had set me planning, as aforementioned, a postwar book on the South Pacific. So when the spring of 1945 brought an opportunity to go prowl that still war-infested region, I could tell myself that to do so would further the book project.

The public relations powers in Washington were assembling a troupe of a dozen or so civilian writers and such to go out there. I managed to get into the act, securing a nominal correspondent's sponsorship from the *Saturday Evening Post*. I found I'd have to wear a pseudo-uniform on the principle, apparently, that if the Japanese captured me they wouldn't shoot me for a spy as they would were I in civilian clothes. The shoulder patches on the shirts said "Correspondent" and so did the bronzed bars of lettering on the shoulders of the tunic. Whether the Japanese subscribed to it all was uncertain, but such formalities entailed officers' privileges in quarters, mess, and so on and conveniently high priorities in transportation. Fifty yards away I looked like an officer. Nearer at hand, my inborn talent for incurable mussiness was enhanced by the necessary lack of anything like laundry in most of the places I got to. I learned how to hang a shirt on a line to dry in something vaguely like recognizable shape. What I never learned to cope with was the badly worn zippers on the flight bag I had borrowed from Carl Carmer, who had been on such a junket into the European theater in 1944. Under any kind of stress they slid open. Time and again as I trotted across an airfield to board a plane that damn bag would begin to feel lighter and there behind me was a several-hundred-yard trail of shirts and socks.

Our party was curiously assorted. If it had a basis of selection I never understood it. It made some sense to include Frank Taylor, then a regular contributor to the *Reader's Digest,* and me with the Curtis magazines in mind, and Hugh Cave, a well-established writer of adventure stories, and George Harmon Coxe, veteran of whodunits, for one way or another what we saw out there might spawn fruitful stuff in print directly or indirectly. That probably also applied to our screenwriters, Herbert Lewis and Dalton Trumbo—that's right, the Hollywood Ten fellow. There was less reason to include an affable, red-headed young Communist to keep Trumbo company, I'd have supposed, only they fought shy of each other: on arriving in Manila, the kid managed to arrange to go upcountry somewhere to make contact with the Hukbalahap, to whom he had apparently adequate introductions. For that small number of Indians we had three PRO chiefs, a major and two captains—too many cooks, but it didn't spoil the broth; they handled contacts and logistics well. The major was our only casualty. He went along on a bombing mission over Korea in a plane that didn't come back.

We all got along well enough. I made good friends with

Cave and Taylor. Trumbo was amusing company; on our way home he told me that the one thing he had hoped to see and didn't was an atheist in a foxhole. His chief objective, however, seemed to be finding basket cases in hospitals, for he had written a pacifist novel called *Johnny Got His Gun* about one such and apparently he wanted to test his imaginings against reality.

In Hawaii, where we had a few days briefing on our way out, I almost supplied him with something of the sort through ill-advised greediness. With commendable and unusual solicitude, the armed forces there were committed to disrupting normal civilian doings as little as possible, importing all supplies and leaving local sources untouched. That meant, among other things, nothing better than canned orange juice for breakfast at Hickam Field, whereas I remembered yearningly the delights of Hawaiian papaya to start the day with. And outside my window in the Bachelor Officers' Quarters grew a fine, strapping papaya tree exhibiting a large fruit just reaching the butter yellow hue that meant voluptuous ripeness. There it was leering at me a couple of feet too far away and maybe twenty from the ground. I stood it for three days and then one morning sneaked out and round the building and shinnied up the tree. I was unaware that, though its trunk was as thick as a minor telephone pole, papaya trees are very weak and brittle; just as I was about to reach for my loot, bulging there beneath that circle of palmated leaves, the trunk broke off and I came crashing down. I weighed ten pounds less then, but why I didn't break my neck I don't know. In five minutes I had breath enough back to swear, shaky and utterly frustrated because the papaya had come down with me and was smashed into inedible fragments—and from the remains I judged it had been in just as toothsome shape as I had imagined.

Next day we were off for Johnston Island and points west and south. We had ample facilities for going off on our own. During a stretch on Guam I worked up a small piece on a crack battalion of black Seabees. On Tinian, with the book in mind, I made the acquaintance of its uncanny prehistoric ruins as well as of the huge airfield whence, in a matter of weeks, the *Enola Gay* would—only nobody knew about that yet—take off for Hiroshima. The climate of Tinian must be peculiar. It is the only place where I ever enjoyed getting up at 6:00 A.M. My walk to the mess hall for breakfast was softly breezy, subtly sunny, with a picture-postcard view of Aguijan, Tinian's three-tiered satellite islet looking like a piece of fancy pastry on a blue silk tablecloth. A few Japanese were still holed up on Aguijan refusing to believe occasional attempts to convince them that their war was over. Tinian had some such too. They often sneaked up back of the projector to enjoy the frequent show-ings of open-air movies. I think it was also on Tinian that I was poking into the ruins of a Japanese pillbox and found the forward half of a light rubber shoe of that Japanese model with a separate sort of thumb for the big toe. It picked it up and then wished I hadn't. It contained the rattly separate bones of a Japanese foot picked clean and dry by ants, I suppose.

So far, that was as near the enemy as I had got. On rejoin-ing the boys in Manila I learned that General MacArthur, sa-trap of that part of the Pacific Theater, had plans for us. It seems that when they asked his leave to let us visit, he testily said something like: "If they want to see war, make sure they do." So we were booked for ringside at a forthcoming com-bined operation, objective unspecified.

They flew us down to an anchorage called Tawitawi at the southern tail of the Philippines—a South Seas lagoon right out of the movies with coral islets; a baby mountain obviously made of amusement-park plaster; palms wherever one looked; gently rippling, tender-hued waters a few miles wide; and scores of slender canoes paddled by extremely picturesque natives. Only the effect was marred by numbers of gray-painted ships of various sizes and shapes in which unpicturesque U.S. Navy personnel were waiting to join the attack convoy on its way down from somewhere else. This was the Sulu-Islamic end of the Philippines that had recently specialized in piracy and the scowling little brown men in those canoes looked as piratical as their grandfathers ever had. Many brandished short swords and long knives with grisly-wiggly blades like the Malay *kris*. Their purpose was not intimidation, however; they wanted to swap homemade cutlery and other odd artifacts for navy skiv-vies, cigarettes, and canned stuff. Each ship had a tenuous raft of canoes clustered round it: "Hey, Joe, you want . . ." The prevalent headgear was a properly piratical knotted handkerchief or a straw cap colored mustard yellow with the dye-based atabrin (antimalarial) tablets, a bottle of which stood on every mess table to be taken regularly as prophylactic. Nobody ever did so, for word had gone round that prolonged dosage would turn one as yellow as springtime's first dandelion. But the stuff did become a lively trade item all over the South Pacific, the peoples of which prized its gaudy effect.

They shipped us in a navy landing-craft infantry (LCI) the size of a seagoing tug, square-bowed, low freeboard, unprepossessing to look at—but then war-useful ships often are so. She behaved well enough in the favorable weather we encountered but—had MacArthur gone so far as to order wartime squalor for us?—I do hope and believe she was the dirtiest ship in the navy. What the two Australian correspondents who joined us and our Australian liaison officer thought of her they were too tactful to mention. One had to take toilet paper and wipe the soles of one's feet after showering. And the chow was memorably terrible, far worse than the poor stuff we were used to in various military messes. We learned that just before she sailed her cook had been taken ashore sick. No time to whistle up a replacement, so the galley was left to the pot-walloper. He was too frightened by the assignment even to read the book to any purpose. What he put on the table was seldom recognizable. Indeed some of the crew got up a sweepstakes: Each put in a quarter, the pot going to him who guessed correctly what was on his plate. They gave it up because nobody ever guessed right.

Our skipper, a lieutenant junior grade, seldom left the bridge. Details were handled by a show-off chief petty officer who thought it was funny to pose as a Communist running things Stalin-style. But the engineer must have made some sense—anyway the engines kept running, and the bridge maintained station well enough when we joined the convoy. Our objective had soon ceased to be secret. On the bulletin board was a large map of Borneo, the huge island noted for oil and headhunters, plus a high-detail map of Balikpapan, its oil port that the Japanese had early captured to be an important source of fuel for their war machine. Our mission was to oust the Japanese. Part of the U.S. Navy's Seventh Fleet was to cooperate with the redoubtable Australian Seventh Division, who had the grim task of going ashore. (It would be the last amphibious operation of the war, but nobody knew that at the time.) Our Australian briefed us on how tough it would probably be. The garrison was known to be large, the defenses elaborate, including a sort of moat filled with oil to be set ablaze as a Wagnerian barrier against attackers.

The idea was a tight-security surprise, but it was highly likely that the Japanese were expecting us. For instance, the day before sailing our LCI went alongside a navy tanker for fresh water for the voyage. A dozen or so of the canoe hucksters paddled along and clustered round as usual. The tanker's bridge hailed that they had to know whither we were bound. Our bridge roared back "Balikpapan!" in full hearing of a few dozen Sulu tribesmen likely to gossip ashore for the convenience of Japanese intelligence.

So, full of fresh water and bellyaches from bad cooking, off we sailed, rather thoughtful about what was awaiting us. Even so my chronic love of being at sea let me actually enjoy those few days in convoy with the spray splattering from our square bow and the sparkling Pacific at her queenliest and ahead and astern all sorts of ships, baby flattops, escorts, transports, tankers, PT-boats that, seen head-on from a distance, looked like bathtub-toy battleships. Eventually Borneo—a dim, smudgy line on the horizon—hove in view. Cave, at my elbow on the rail, said: "So that's Borneo. I've written a dozen yarns about those headhunters and now I'll see what it looks like."

The little fellow in the galley sent us ashore for our baptism of fire on corn flakes and overwatered evaporated milk. By the time our launch had cast off the rocket vessels had already set most of the settlement afire and the Seventh's first wave had landed and was pushing inland where, thank God, the hellfire moat had failed to materialize. A heavy cruiser standing well offshore was still lobbing shells into the brushy slopes back of town. The pale yellow smoke from her guns went daintily well with the robin's-egg blue of the sky. It was a beautiful day there, half a degree south of the equator. As I waded toward the beach I reflected that at home in New Jersey on July 1 in latitude 40 degrees North the weather was probably horribly sultry-muggy.

The Japanese resistance did not live up to its billing. Obviously they had had ample warning and withdrawn, leaving only a token force to put up a show. In view of the U.S. Navy's presence between Borneo and Japan, Balikpapan must have ceased to be a serious source of oil supply. On thinking it over I have to wonder why MacArthur, a general noted for economy of means and casualties, bothered to knock the place off. Left alone, its garrison would have withered on the vine—only I suppose that would have been rough on the native population. Anyway, as I plodded along the beach hoping the water would soon squelch out of my boots, and finding my steel helmet just as uncomfortable as I had expected, I was grateful to the Japanese for deciding to cut their losses.

Ahead and to the right were sporadic explosions and small-arms noises. Quantities of black smoke were rising from the oil installations. I remember saying to myself: "Well, why wouldn't warfare look and sound like a newsreel calamity?" (This was before TV, so "newsreel" was the reference.) Here and there the Australians were busy, much like an experienced construction crew starting a new project. One group handling a couple of miniature field guns had the exact air of a road gang laying asphalt. Whereas we civilians wore helmets as we'd been ordered to, these professionals took pride in going into action in those up-on-one-side felt campaign hats that Australia goes in for. Soon after landing, however, they spoiled that jaunty look by a small frivolity: The beach had been a Japanese storage area of pole-and-palm-leaf shelters. The thatch had quickly burned off, laying open to the sky a surrealistic array of incongruities—a mass of miscellaneous rusty nuts and bolts neatly piled; another of white teacups, Western-style with handles, not merely by the gross but by thousands in a heap five feet deep, five wide, and ten long; another such of small gray sake jugs, whence MacArthur's orderly, I suppose, got the one he gave me (as previously described); yet another of garishly colored pottery teapots. Why on earth was Balikpapan stocked with dime-store chinaware on such a scale? But there it all was, taking the Australians' eye. Tea is a passion Down Under, of course, and Australian soldiers were known as even more acquisitive than American GIs. So practically every man was going into battle with a gaudy teapot strapped to his belt—a really curious effect.

Casualties were light. Among them, however, were our two Australian correspondents, killed when caught in crossfire in the valley.

So far my desultory effort to get closer to what Robert Louis Stevenson called "the bright eyes of danger" had not got far. MacArthur's seminar up there on the ridge had come to little more than showing me that I did not share young George Washington's pleasure in the whine of passing bullets. Unharmed and hungry after lunching on a candy bar in a half-destroyed building in midafternoon, I made the beach rendezvous in plenty of time for the launch back to the old LCI.

Six of us were to fly to Manila next morning in a courier flying boat (PBY). And that was where the danger part saw fit to develop, maybe on the principle of better late than never. To take us to the plane appeared an LCVP—an undecked, self-propelled barge rather like a huge sugar scoop with a motor where the handle should be—towing a steel dinghy. One youngster in dungarees stood forward staring round him uncertainly, another tended the motor and steered. In apparent charge was a U.S. army captain, a detail that I still find as puzzling as that heap of teapots. Of the three it was soon plain he knew most, though it wasn't much, about what to do when afloat.

The motor roared and off we went, slapping through the brisk chop that was kicking up its heels in the wide Strait of Makassar, where our armada lay. Within a mile or so the dinghy had swamped. Only the painter slanting stiffly into the wake showed it was still there. The captain had already warned us that in this sea it would be unsafe to go alongside the PBY seaplane, so the dinghy would be used to ferry us on board. How to manage that with the dinghy underwater was a problem the dungaree boys seemed not to have grasped, but the captain recognized it and made them seek help from a transport that lay ahead. Her crew swung out a tackle, hooked on to the painter, hauled the dinghy up to drain endwise like a preposterous fishing trophy, and set it back again nicely afloat in the ship's lee. "Don't go so fast!" they shouted.

Our seagoing farmer boys did manage to find our ungainly aircraft. Her Australian crew watched our approach with justified uneasiness, for she was irresponsibly swooping and heaving as the breeze freshened and the chop heightened. The farmer boys had no notion how to get a line on board, but we landsmen worked it out by trial and error and got into the dinghy to haul it along the line to the plane as though operating a backwoods ferry. In calm water it would have been simple. This water was not calm. Most of us were beyond the age of optimum agility and wearing heavy boots. As each of us tried to scramble on board we found the fuselage slippery wet, the handholds poorly designed, and the aircraft's unpredictable antics inhibiting. The best we could manage was not falling in. The pilot, a massive, fair-haired, unbelievably sunburned Australian, would watch each series of failures, then lean out of the open bubble and ask searchingly: "Are you chaps sure you want to go to Manila today?"

Herb Lewis, who was watching from the LCI through binoculars, said later it was a funnier bit of slapstick than anything Mack Sennett ever thought of. Anyway, the Australians and we found it so absorbing that we failed to notice that the plane was sailing gently crabwise downwind, right into the whole anchored convoy. At very nearly the last moment the pilot apparently sensed something was wrong, looked up and round, said something emphatic to the copilot, and they both scrambled out on the plane's high wing, which was aimed at the broadside of a large gray ship. The two of them sat on the wing end with their legs stuck out like buffers on a British locomotive and walked the plane sidewise until the wing cleared the ship's stern. I hope they were promoted and decorated for it. It sounds impossible, but both were very, very husky and the plane was drifting broadside to, hence not briskly.

When the pilot was back in the fuselage again, we heard once more: "Do you chaps *still* want to go to Manila today?"

The sane answer would have been "God no!" but it was too late to make it, for the farmer boys had taken alarm and were half a mile away, looking on but obviously with no thought of returning. Renewed attempts to board were our only recourse. The weather was briskening further and once the dinghy filled, she would sink like a stone and we had no oars to keep her head to the wind with. None of us knew—though nobody cared to mention the issue—what the shark situation in the Makassar Strait might be. No doubt the Australians would try to rescue us, but seven encumbered men take a lot of rescuing under such conditions. In any war game with competent umpires we'd have been ruled already dead. We flinched and cursed and clutched and sloshed and floundered ourselves on board.

Then it came out that the pilot's recurrent question had only partly come of solicitude for our safety. He was uncertain whether in the kind of sea that had built up he could get the PBY off the water. He made us all crowd forward to shift the center of gravity toward the nose; we resembled one of those how-many-can-get-into-a-telephone-booth stunts. As he gunned the engines and she tried to get "up on the step" the waves no longer slapped her bottom familiarly; they made crashing impacts that felt as though the next one would open her seams and hello Davy Jones! We did get airborne, of course, or I wouldn't be writing this. But dubious as it looked for a few minutes, none of us regretted having got clear of the dinghy. Only now, forty years later, does it occur to me to wonder what became of it.

Before heading homeward I spent a while with the Thirteenth Air Force at their base on Morotai, a Dutch East Indian island whence their bombers were working over the remains of the Japanese presence in that area. After submarine hunting, bullet dodging, and risking drowning, I rounded out my war, such as it was, by going along on bombing missions. During one the bombardier suggested that I could watch the bombs all the way to the target if I lay on my belly and hung my head over the edge of the open bay. I did so and had an excellent view. But that torrent of cold air gave me a magnificent head cold that so fouled up my chronically vulnerable Eustachian tubes that I got home deaf as a blue-eyed white cat and had finally to make myself consider hearing aids, for some of the new damage proved permanent. So, though I never heard of a civilian Purple Heart, if there were such a thing, I might have a claim to a very pale lavender one.

A few days after I got home they dropped the bomb on Hiroshima. On the train platform that morning I agreed with my good neighbor, Walter Dorwin Teague, the eminent industrial designer, that atom splitting had come just in time to solve the world's impending energy problems. Maybe we were essentially right. Probably not.

Inadvertently, no doubt, World War II had already contributed constructively to my education. Early in 1942 Dr. Millet, the psychiatrist for whom I had handled Scotty, telephoned to say a colleague of his needed help on a project that might interest me. It did. The colleague was Dr. Richard M. Brickner, a well-established neuropsychiatrist who was working on a book about the emotional significance of Hitler's Germany. Dr. Edward Strecker, a very eminent psychiatrist, and Margaret Mead, then already well on the way to becoming America's den mother, had agreed to write introductions based on their respective disciplines. What I—and my wife, who worked even more closely than usual with me on this—were needed for was to get Brickner's ideas into a shape that would be read widely enough to help the nation understand what it was dealing with. The J. B. Lippincott Company was interested in it.

Brickner proved to be an outgoing, solidly bright bundle of mental energy and clinical insight with whom my wife and I were much taken. He had worked out maybe twenty thousand words on paper. As was likely from so good a brain, much of it was usable sentence by sentence, but it needed organization and was too often confusingly elliptical. His thesis was no one-sentence affair. In brief: Using the evidence in Nazi propaganda and its ancestors in Germany's intellectual and military past, he identified her institutional behavior over several generations as manifesting the syndrome of classical paranoia—a term now so abused and irresponsibly applied that it should be abandoned. Properly, of course, it then meant a distinctive psychosis characterized by delusions of grandeur, persecution fantasies, retrospective falsification. Brickner refrained from diagnosing Hitler as an individual, saying no diagnosis without personal examination was worth anything. Nor was he saying that all Germans, or even a large majority of them, were paranoid. He was saying that the gradually developed cultural-emotional bent of a critical mass* of Germans bore a sin-

*This useful double entendre was not employed in Brickner's book because before Hiroshima "critical mass" was not part of the language.

ister and probably significant resemblance to the paranoia pattern. He suggested that the incidence of individuals tending toward that pattern was enough higher in Germany, though not at all unknown elsewhere, to give her national behavior the distinctive flavor that Nazism manifested in action. A tenable hypothesis, and I think as well of it now as I did then.

This all owed much to the sociocultural-psychiatric assumptions familiar in the 1930s from the anthropological work of Ruth Benedict, Margaret Mead et al., assuming that particular emotional patterns can be found in the behavior of particular cultures in contravention of the liberal assumption that all human beings act alike under the same standard stimuli. In order to handle such materials I needed, and gave myself, a cram course in that school of anthropology—a discipline with which I had too little previous acquaintance.

Working closely with Dick Brickner, my wife and I midwifed him into a clear, cumulatively impressive text. It was very seriously considered by the Book-of-the-Month Club. Indeed their interest was warm enough to lead us to revise a couple of chapters to meet their suggestions as to what would heighten its chances. But finally, while I was out in the Midwest on an article, I had a telegram from my wife: "BOM FINALLY SAYS NO HAVE A DRINK." When she filed it, the Western Union operator objected that wartime regulations forbade telegrams of congratulation. "This, my dear," said my wife, "ain't congratulation."

There had been obstetrical difficulties, of course. Dick was innocently given to nervous insistence on unnecessary small revisions that my wife deplored in strong terms. Dr. Mead, five times worse as nitpicker, often threatened to withdraw her endorsement-introduction unless . . . At one point my wife told Dick: "You're supposed to be a psychiatrist. Persuade her to simmer down." "My God," he said, "I can't handle either of you women. Why can't both of you keep your ovaries out of this?" But he and we stayed good friends.

Without the BOM the book did only so-so. Reviews were mixed. Psychiatrists tended to shy from the notion of mass behavior cognate to patterns known in individuals; anthropologists were more receptive. For me it was an invaluable catalyst. Working with it put me elbow deep in a heady kind of thinking and data handling. The one part that was predominantly my work was a midsection on the anthropological background. I enjoyed doing it so much that it came over me that for the previous ten years most of my writing, though sound, often useful journalism, had employed only the upper-layer, tactical part of what brains I had. Half deliberately I began to hanker after tasks of wider dimensions. One result was the plan to write that book for postwar briefing on the South Pacific, preparation for which now took me farther and farther into anthropology of several schools. The eventual consequences over the years were my two books on the background of America's race problems and my triptych informal social histories for Putnam's.

The South Pacific project also led to a small but prickly sequel to my misadventures with Harvard. My quondam roommate, Foss, after doing very well in newspapering had secured one of Harvard's Nieman Fellowships that provided chosen journalists with a residential year of seminars and courses and presumably an informal, catalytic immersion in a stimulating, academic-intellectual culture medium. He had got on well with the Nieman committee and suggested that I follow his example, with him midwifing my application. It was a welcome thought. A year in Harvard's strong anthropology department? Yes, indeed. And the Nieman process sounded interesting. I applied and Foss lubricated. Here, it occurred to me, though I said nothing to that effect, was Alma Mater's chance to recompense me in some degree for that disgraceful negligence in 1926. The scenario was: spring-summer in the Pacific theater; fall 1945 to summer 1946 Niemaning; then off to prowl the postwar subject area for a year.

When I took off for my homeopathic dose of war in the spring, the omens looked very good. On my return in August the Nieman committee had me up to Cambridge for final determination. The major hurdle was an interview with a committee member—in my case Professor Arthur M. Schlesinger of the history department, brilliant father of a brilliant son soon to come to fame. My application had duly mentioned anthropology as the field I would use the fellowship to work in. But Schlesinger wanted details, so I described my project. He had spotted my hard-of-hearing trouble and barked at me that it would be no good attending lectures on anthropology when I couldn't hear them. I replied, maybe not as suavely as might have been, that I had a hearing aid on order and would sit in the front row. He said: "Why not just go to a good library and read up on anthropology?" I said that was just what I had been doing. I did not ask, though I wish I had, why, if no more than that were indicated, did Harvard bother with lectures on anthropology? He grumped at me in apparently arbitrary distaste and in a few days the Nieman staff let me know that I was rejected because, if I remember correctly, I was overqualified, too far along in journalism for a fellowship to be pertinent.

It did not add up. My impression was and remains that the fat was in the fire before I entered the room. Foss had got his award the year before though he was my elder and equally experienced. If the Nieman people had changed policy since then, they should not have countenanced my application down to the wire like that. Schlesinger certainly had no personal reason to behave thus; he had never laid eyes on me before. Gradually I came to understand that he as well as I was up against Alma Mater. He was under the unrealized influence of her subliminal whispering that I was still her stepchild.

In a way, however, his position proved up. My undirected reading paid off. My *Anatomy of Paradise* won the 1948 Anisfield-Wolff award for nonfiction best advancing interracial harmony. Professor Ralph Linton, chief of anthropology at Yale, ascribed to it "the rare quality of combining scientific accuracy with humor and charm." Professor Douglas Oliver of Harvard told me it showed I was a better anthropologist than most academics with anthropological union cards.

13

Footnote on Writers

RECENT LITERARY FOLKLORE is rich in writers'
woes. Ever since the craft of authorship was upgraded to the
status of romantic obsession, say circa 1800, its emotional hazards have been notorious. Merely to pick up the pencil or sit
down at the typewriter is occasion for tooth-gritting self-disci-
pline. At cruelly unpredictable intervals "writer's block" smothers
creativeness for days or weeks of introspective torture. Editors
and publishers are negligently numb to the twitchings of the
writers whose fragile skills they exploit. We know nothing of
the miseries of Chaucer, Vergil, or Rabelais, and of Shakespeare's little but that line about "the poet's eye in a fine frenzy
rolling." Our time, however, prefers Melville spinning *Pierre*
out of his gut like a harassed spider to Trollope extruding the
Palliser cycle like toothpaste out of a tube.

This confession may be damaging. My experience—pay due
regard to inadequate quality of product—has been nearer
Trollope's than Melville's end of the spectrum. I like to write
just as I like being at sea. There have been unnecessary exas-
perations and occasional need to command myself to get at
that project now instead of after lunch, but never revulsion
against writing as such. My craft has been intrinsically euphoric in effect—not as Byronic ego trip or solipsist Joycean
rope dance but as a means to joy in manipulating that nobly
exacting medium, the English language. Hence the only unfavorable passages in reviews of my books that ever really
troubled me were those—not many, thank heaven—objecting

not to what was said but to how it was written, causing me uneasiness lest I had not done my tools justice.

A minor dividend, sometimes flavorsome, has consisted of personal contact with writers. Not that I am one of those gregarious "men of letters," expert in the best and worst of their peers, the sort of data acquired at writers' watering holes and in Yaddos, symposia, and professional organizations. Twice well-meant but unwise judgment put me on literary boards: the Authors' League's and the visiting committee of the Harvard University Press. Between diffidence and impaired hearing, to the first I contributed nothing; to the second only a brief reply to a direct question whether *Uncle Tom's Cabin* had ever been out of print.

Somebody—Arthur Koestler, I'm told—once said that wishing to meet an author because you like his writings is like wishing to meet a goose because you like paté de foie gras. True, true; but he should have added that contact with authors, whether close or casual, can sometimes be rewarding because their behavior illuminates quirks of human nature less clearly manifest in craftsmen in less demanding trades. For instance, something about writing seems to betray a minority into assuming one or another kind of false face or feathers. In certain cases where some of the following are still living, names or identifying contexts, not essential facts, are altered.

Consider Vera Haraszth, author of successful "suspense" stories remarkable for ingenious organization and workman-like handling of what was not her native tongue. She was a blond version of the French *gamine*—thin but not to emaciation; hospitable, generous, and talking the topics of the day in a vivacious paprikash accent. Her trouble was addiction to the long bow. For months her social prattle about the carefree 1920s in Central Europe and her career as footloose reporter for both Continental and British magazines passed readily as genuine legal tender among us. Her freewheeling experiences had obviously inspired the kinetic plots of her books, rich in action but saved from implausibility by ample reenforcing detail. There was the personal account of how she and a boyfriend had won an amateur skiing contest in full evening dress when they had impulsively left a dinner party and driven all night to breakfast at a mountain resort where they found a ski meet going

Footnote on Writers 279

forward. Another about how, as guest at the Argentinian consulate in Dar-es-Salaam, she had gone to bed naked because of the heat, walked in her sleep, waked to see herself in a full-length mirror in the drawing room, and wondered for a few seconds how the consulate's chambermaid had managed to turn white overnight.

Our neighborhood had a scare. On a Saturday afternoon a psychotic drifter in Pennsylvania stole a car, kidnapped a girl, was spotted crossing into New Jersey, known to be armed, heading our way. Little else was talked about at a dinner party that included my wife and me and Vera. A few weeks later at another party with most of the same cast the episode was harked back to and Vera launched herself: That night she had been alone in her rather isolated house. The radio report sent her looking for her revolver. It was unloaded and she had mislaid the ammunition. For hours she ransacked the place, getting nearer to hysteria. She began telephoning friends; none answered. She called the state police and they said, Lady, all our men are out looking for that car, we got nobody to send, you lock all your doors and windows and pray. Then—oh, joy!— the radio bulletin that the psycho had driven off the road, turned the girl loose, and shot himself dead. Vera drank three fingers of cognac and turned in and slept until eleven the next morning.

She told it half comically, half chillingly, altogether brilliantly. Nobody interrupted, but those outside her line of vision were looking bleakly at one another. For during the entire evening of the panic she had been not trembling at home but at the party we had all attended. During her remaining stay among us she was treated no differently. But she may have sensed something, for we got no more tales of sprightly adventure. The strange thing is that in other respects she was no phony. When she claimed a well-known So-and-so as old friend, it proved up. Once, when we were going to Europe, she gave us notes of introduction to a Dutch politician and a Swiss novelist, both important; each talked and talked affectionately and respectfully about her. Apparently she just couldn't resist when some conversational cue prompted a fantasy to be embroidered so engagingly that she came to believe it herself. She may have deliberately yielded to this quirk as she found herself making a good living with printed fictions. But basically it was a specialized form of the Walter Mitty complex—no harm in it even if it did make one wonder how reliable were the details in the articles she had sent back to those magazines.

Indeed maybe mere incidental entanglement in writing for print can carry this hazard. A good while ago we had as house guest a close friend, Professor Pundit of Oxbridge, scholar-critic. The other guests at dinner were a physician-novelist, Dr. Paragon, and his clever journalist-wife; and Professor Protean, eminent psychologist at a famous university—not primarily a writer but he had written for the general reader several beguilingly lucid and deservedly popular books on human behavior. Over preprandial drinks we got into TV broadcasting, and Protean stuffily made it clear that figuratively as well as literally he had no time for television. Over long drinks after dinner Pundit and he talked academic old times in Britain, where Protean did much of his early work, and there developed one of those wonder-what-happened-to-him dialogues as in the Noël Coward song. For some twenty minutes: "Oh, yes, Henry Smith! Dear Henry, he finally blotted his copybook and the last I heard, he was still clinging to the shreds of his reputation at Weissnichtwo." "Remember Jacky Jones at the London School?" "Yes indeed, worked with him for a while on a cross-discipline thing. Brilliant, easygoing chap. We're rather out of touch now."

Many such short rallies went back and forth across the net. It was poor manners, for it left the rest of us out. In Protean, one of those presentable egocentrics, it did not surprise me; but it was unlike Pundit's usual considerate behavior. After Protean and the Paragons left, I said to Pundit: "You and Protean have a wide common acquaintance." "We do," he said, "but not that wide. He kept being so knowing about everybody I mentioned that I tried him on a number who never existed—and he knew them just as well." There was more to come. Next morning Mrs. Paragon phoned: "Turn on your TV, channel X." It was an interview-phone-in-consulting-expert program of advice on emotional problems. And the house expert, obviously a longstanding fixture, was Protean, the man utterly walled off from and contemptuous of anything to do with television. This still puzzles me. His actual achievements were such that he needed no Saint Peter–like denial of involvement with popular media and no self-aggrandizing pretense of knowing people he never heard of.

Twenty-odd years ago J. K. Galbraith, dean of gadfly economists and author of a couple of dozen books, including several of high general interest, decorated his autobiographical *The Scots* with a scene from his boyhood back on the farm in Ontario. Barely adolescent, he was sitting on a fence with an attractive neighbor girl when his father's stud bull in the pasture beyond mounted a cow. After a bit young Galbraith said: "I think it would be fun to do that." "Well," said the girl, "it's your cow." Doubtless the canons of obscene humor are much the same both sides of the U.S.-Canadian border. My narrower point, however, is that I met that one sixty-odd years ago in the state of Indiana and several more times elsewhere long before Galbraith printed it in 1964 as something that actually happened to him. His foreword did warn: "Here and there, as the reader will guess, I have . . . contributed one of the folk tales of the community." But that caveat cannot apply here, for he gives the exact location of the pasture, the kind of fence, and the name of the bull, though, chivalrously, not of the girl. Pretty good as such jokes go, only not good enough to account for such a lapse of judgment in so canny a man when the risk of detection was so high. He might as well have told how he, benighted far out in the country and seeking lodging in a farmhouse, was told: "All right, stranger, but you'll have to sleep with the baby." Such indiscretion must be a sporadic side effect of printer's ink on the susceptible.

The most striking case of the Mitty complex is recent and understandably conspicuous: the affair of Lillian Hellman and "Julia." It invented an original and much more serious form of literary sharp practice—plagiarism of the unconsenting personality, hijacked because Miss Hellman wished her autobiography to make her out a gallant heroine in an accepted good cause. The ensuing hullabaloo did not end as dramatically as it seemed to promise, but it will long remain a curiosity in literary history. And since I had a tiny, peripheral part in it, let me add my two cents worth.

First the victim: Dr. Muriel Morris Gardiner, close friend of the Furnases. We first met through her; in later years her country headquarters in New Jersey were only twenty miles from ours. Chicago-born, she inherited a more than considerable fortune from her parents, whose marriage had combined the Morris and Swift meat-packing interests. About being so rich she was far more graceful and conscientious than attractive girls in such circumstances usually are. At Wellesley she developed scruples about disproportionate wealth in a catch-as-catch-can world. As graduate student at Oxford she "read English," but her radical drift strengthened. The rest of her life she subsidized and otherwise abetted those engaged in what struck her as worthy causes. But as far as I know she remained an informal, occasional volunteer. She was not the joining sort.

After Oxford she settled in Vienna to explore Freudianism, was analyzed by Anna Freud, took a medical degree, and became a respected psychoanalyst. In the 1930s she became acutely aware of the gathering storm that culminated in *Anschluss* and the Nazification of Austria. She began to take part in the underground resistance under the code name "Mary" and was soon a much valued courier, safehouse keeper, and financial angel. Her continuance in her profession, known affluence, and U.S. passport all helped her to do a great deal without rousing crucial suspicions, though she had close calls. There was small symbolism but some irony in her donning a corset for the first time in her untrammeled life in order to conceal bootleg passports smuggled across frontiers.

Toward the end of her underground career she made a second marriage—to Joseph Buttinger, chief of the far-left wing of Austrian socialism. We seldom talked politics with her and never asked questions, so we knew of all this only vaguely. Once, however, things surfaced explicitly: She asked me to lend her my passport to help her get somebody out of Austria, which had got too hot to hold him. He had blue eyes, the same given name, and, like me, was getting bald up front. Unquestioningly I handed over. Actually it was never used but eventually returned to me without telltale Austrian rubber stampings on its pages. I never knew how she got Joe out otherwise, but he arrived with her in America, played an important part in the International Rescue Committee, and became a scholarly expert on Vietnam. For their anti-Nazi activities, the Austrian government decorated both Muriel and Joe.

After the war Muriel was mostly in America practicing her profession, writing books on psychoanalytical problems, but also much on the go, often to Europe, particularly Austria, keeping up with former colleagues and making new friends, for which she had a vast talent. It was late in the 1970s when she first consulted us about "Julia." Every day, she told us, she had a phone call or letter from Washington or London or Hong Kong or Boston: "Muriel dear, I've just read that book [or seen that movie]. You are Julia, aren't you?" She was half amused, half vexed, altogether perplexed as to what, if anything, to do about it.

The book was *Pentimento*, second item in Lillian Hellman's triptych autobiography. The movie version was titled *Julia* for the heroine character of the "Julia" segment of the book, played with a sort of witchy glow by Vanessa Redgrave. The subsidiary heroine, played all shapely vigor and pluck by Jane Fonda, was given no disguise name but called outright Lillian Hellman, famous American author. Her first-person account of "Julia" and her own doings in that connection were a suspense story owing much to Miss Hellman's experienced skills as Hollywood screenwriter and made both book and movie rousing successes. But it was the preliminary handling of the "Julia" character that put the fat in the fire.

Miss Hellman's "Julia" was depicted as a very rich American whose parents raised her in marble halls. Her girlhood chum was Lillian Hellman, who became a famous writer. Over the years, though in different spheres, they kept their friendship warm. "Julia" studies at Oxford, then in Vienna, gets into the anti-Fascist resistance, is wounded in a shooting affair, and loses a leg. Lillian comes to see her in the hospital. A good while later Lillian, in Paris en route by rail to the USSR on literary-political business, gets a phone call from "Julia" in Vienna. Will she please run a highly hazardous and crucial errand for the good cause? smuggle a mess of badly needed dollars into Germany by breaking her journey in Berlin, where "Julia" will meet her and relieve her of the money. Dauntingly risky—but for "Julia" Lillian loyally consents to become deputy heroine. The money is concealed in a huge, wedge-shaped fur hat that made Jane Fonda look like a Cossack princess— well calculated to make her inconspicuous. But ten or a dozen

successive underground spooks whisk Lillian through to the
Berlin café where "Julia" awaits, and a quick finesse in the
ladies' washroom transfers the hat. Then off to Moscow as per
invoice. Never mind the rest about Lillian's trunk and her devoted efforts to find and succor "Julia's" missing baby daughter. Whether Muriel saw the movie I don't know, but she did
read *Pentimento,* for she was scornful about the hat trick and
the rest of the blatant Hitchcockery. "If we'd done things as
complicated and foolish as that," said "Underground Mary"
Muriel, "we'd all have been arrested and shot."

The damningly close parallels between "Julia's" and Muriel's biographies left no room for claims of coincidence. When
the archivists of the Austrian resistance and its surviving participants were asked whether any second rich American woman
had had a hand in their ranks, the unanimous answer was no.
Early in the proceedings Muriel had written to Miss Hellman
saying people keep telling me I must be "Julia," have you anything to contribute? At first Miss Hellman denied getting the
letter, then telephoned Muriel suggesting they lunch, then never
followed it up. She did play the one card available, pointing
out that, as Muriel agreed, they had never met. But then an
adequate connecting link was found—Wolf Schwabacher, a
lawyer, long since dead, who was well aware of Muriel's underground career and had been a close friend of both women.

Most understandably, even before Muriel published her
modest autobiography, *Code Name "Mary,"* the literary Rialto
was buzzing with it all. It was unimpeachably clear that Miss
Hellman, operating from hearsay through Schwabacher, had
coolly borrowed and hardly bothered to fictionalize the iden-
tity of a genuine heroine in order to make herself look like
another. For nothing in *Pentimento* is represented as fiction. It
is all I-Lillian-Hellman-in-person knew a real "Julia" inti-
mately and did that perilous thing in her behalf. When asked
who the obviously pseudonymous "Julia" really was, she could
only plead that to tell would imperil persons still living. As for
Muriel, bothered but dispassionate throughout, she never said
yes when asked if she thought she was "Julia." It may have
helped there that I amused her by pointing out that it would
be absurd to claim to have been a person who had obviously
never existed.

So far as I know there was no question of legal steps. Neither common nor statute law recognizes copyright for one's life story. Maybe the currently assumed constitutional right of privacy could have been invoked, but litigation was not Muriel's style. Miss Hellman's volatile temperament probably ruled out what was her only recourse—a public statement: "Very well, I apologize to Dr. Gardiner and admit I've been a self-aggrandizing fool like King George IV of Great Britain, who insisted he had led a cavalry charge at Waterloo when everybody knew he'd never been near the place; like Shelley's friend Edward John Trelawney (sometimes John Edward), whose best-selling account of his wild adventures after he deserted from the Royal Navy was erased when, generations later, research showed he hadn't even deserted to begin with. . . . At least I put an original twist on it." There were practical considerations against that anyway. Such an admission, her advisers may have thought, would enable Muriel to ask a share of the thumping sums, whatever they were, that Miss Hellman realized from *Pentimento* and *Julia*. If so, they should have realized that that would never have been like Muriel even had she needed money.

More cogently: Miss Hellman was already ill-advisedly enmeshed in suing Mary McCarthy for calling her a liar on Dick Cavett's TV program, and such a confession would have ruined her chances of establishing her credibility in court. That inevitably would have been a hotly pursued issue. The defense would have put Miss McCarthy on the stand; and probably Martha Gellhorn, Ernest Hemingway's second wife, who had already charged in public that practically nothing in Miss Hellman's published account of Papa and the Spanish Civil War was truthful. And very probably Muriel would have been asked to testify about "Julia." It would have made a memorable literary courtroom battle royal. But I'm glad Muriel was spared it.

Hellman versus McCarthy never came to trial. Miss Hellman died before it could, and Muriel too a few months later. Miss Hellman's partisans showed on PBS a miniseries of adulatory interviews with her. Very recently a family-sponsored hour about Muriel called "The Real Julia" was also broadcast on PBS; properly it pretty much let the controversy roll to the outfield. Meanwhile zealous magazine article research and two

conscientious biographies of Miss Hellman have left little doubt
that the hijacking indictment is a true bill. What still puzzles
me is that so little heed was paid to the last line of a smaller
segment of *Pentimento,* wherein Miss Hellman autobiographiz-
ing in person as usual tells of going to Germany on family
affairs around 1930–31 and getting strong whiffs of developing Nazism. The segment ends: "I never went back to Germany because it was the time of Hitler." Was it in Berlin,
Connecticut, or Berlin, Oregon, that Lillian Hellman gave "Julia" that precious hat?

Horace's calling practitioners of literature likely to be *irrit-
abile* is as sound as most stereotypes. Though treacherously
unreliable guides, stereotypes nevertheless often have something in them, as Nathan Glazer once noted. Regrettably often,
for example, writing-for-print leads to literary controversy. In
that respect I verge on the atypical, having been thus involved
only three times in sixty years, once in re "Julia," twice as principal.

In the matter of my skirmish with the late Ian Fleming one
might object that his works, basis of those absurd, flashy movies, do not qualify as literature. But let's not be finicky: When
it became known that among John F. Kennedy's engaging traits
was an addiction to James Bond, curiosity sent me to *Live and
Let Die,* a Bond item laid partly in New York, about the ambience of which the writer obviously considered himself mighty
knowing. Its many errors of detail stirred up my longstanding
irritation (see Horace) at British authors' inability to get details
about America and Americans right. While writing about
something else to the literary editor of the *New Statesman,* I
incidentally grumbled that in my declining years I might earn
a modest living by vetting such details for British novelists at,
say, half a crown per blunder. As it happened, at the time the
paper was organizing a special issue about America; it was
suggested that I contribute a piece to be called "Limey Howlers."

My lovingly assembled examples of misbegotten dialogue
and distorted folkways came from H. G. Wells, Alec Waugh,
Nicholas Monsarrat, Agatha Christie, Peter Cheyney, old Uncle Tom Cobley, and all. I tactfully admitted that, for all I

knew, the British characters in Henry James's novels were just as guilty the other way round; I even mentioned a few commendable exceptions among British writers: Wodehouse sometimes; Aldous Huxley ditto; Graham Greene, whose Americans tend to talk the same nonspecific, dry, and trenchant idiom as all other ethnic breeds; and David Divine, then military correspondent of the London *Sunday Times,* who saw much of the U.S. Navy during World War II and wrote a light novel about it in which officers and men actually talked good United States. In fact I had written Divine to congratulate him on his expert ear. I enjoyed myself dwelling in particular depth on Fleming's mistakes, beginning with James Bond's "soaring across the breath-taking span of the Tri-Borough Bridge into the heart of Manhattan." He went on to reproach American men with consistently suffering their womenfolk to usurp the driver's seat of the car. The items he ordered from room service at the St. Regis were so curious that I went to the trouble of asking the staff there how they would react if a customer ordered espresso with cream for breakfast. They were shaken. So was I on learning that James Bond's Martinis must be shaken, not stirred.

I was unaware that Fleming as well as Divine was on the staff of the *Sunday Times.* I rejoiced to hear from Divine that "Ian is darkly suspicious that I put you up to it. . . . I am encouraging the suspicion." Fleming took it so hard that he wrote the *New Statesman* a long letter that was delightedly passed on to me for reply. I kept it short, saying I thought it best just to let Mr. Fleming stew in his own espresso with cream. There was another nice repercussion. Francis Brown, then in charge of the *New York Times Book Review,* liked "Limey Howlers" and asked me to contribute occasionally to its "Speaking of Books" department, which I enjoyed doing. But I should have known of the Divine-Fleming connection. Score a transatlantic error against me. Still, sometimes it pays off in fun *not* to know the score.

For a while forty years ago I was involved in controversy about my zestful demolition of Robert Louis Stevenson's mistress-whore-fiancée. A pity to treat an attractive girl so ruthlessly, but my exorcising her gave me not only great pleasure but also my chief claim to scoring a coup in scholarship.

At Stevenson's death in 1894 a mass of his unpublished writings and certain accumulations of his letters became accessible. The bulk of the letters, heavily edited by Sidney Colvin, his mentor sponsor, were soon published. Most of the originals—the unedited pieces of paper—were deposited in the National Library of Scotland under a fifty-year embargo, many others went into private hands. The embargo expired just as I was beginning work on my biography of Stevenson. That gave me the benefit of significant details in the numerous excisions that Colvin had made. Many of the unpublished manuscripts, including much early verse, were explored by George S. Hellman, an American scholar-dealer. He and a colleague or two published most of the verse. He deserves posterity's gratitude for the great care he took of those papers. But his imagination was overeager.

A few of the manuscript verses were obviously addressed to women—not indecorous but erotically warm. On the margin of one of them Stevenson had penciled: "Claire." On their extremely vague content Hellman built an edifice of surmise, deducing that as a youngster in Edinburgh Stevenson had been wildly in love with "Claire," a girl of inferior social status, wanted to marry her, was harshly forced by his family to break it off and go abroad ostensibly for his health. When Hellman published this finding he got from Stevenson's stepson's wife, a rather unstable lady, corroboration: Yes indeed, Claire had been a "beautiful, fair-haired lassie . . . a blacksmith's daughter . . . as innocent as Louis himself."

But soon a competing version appeared. John A. Steuart, a Scottish writer with an imagination as powerful as George Hellman's, had gone prowling Edinburgh gossip from Stevenson's time and pieced together a different Claire—no blonde innocent but a dark-haired, Highland-bred prostitute of the sort Stevenson was known to have patronized when he had a few spare shillings—which wasn't often. And a fresh mention of "Claire" turned up in a Stevenson letter. So, dark or fair, innocent or fallen, thenceforth those writing about Stevenson—a couple of novels and innumerable biographical and critical things—took Claire as a sordidly significant fact in his life. When embarking on my research I had small reason to doubt that, fuzzy as most of the data were, glibly as Hellman,

Steuart et al. had obviously abused the scholar's privilege of exegesis, Claire had some substance. But I also hankered to chase away enough of the clouds to determine just who and what she had been and how much she actually meant in Stevenson's life.

Now the second thread: Colvin's hostess-consort, Mrs. Frances Fetherstonhaugh Sitwell, estranged wife of a dissipated clergyman. She was cultivated, beautiful, very close to Colvin—nothing carnal, however—and made a career of inspiring promising young writers. Stevenson's many and lengthy letters to her are suffused with genuine if somewhat cubbish devotion. He apostrophizes her as Madonna, Consuelo, Mother, and dwells with voluptuous grief on what agony it is to be away from her glowing presence. Yet both the adoring passages that Colvin put into print and the less discreet ones that he suppressed make it clear that though the youngster tried at least once to seek privileges, Mrs. Sitwell was delicately skilled in keeping things noncarnal. This sounds preposterous today. But this was five generations ago in another moral-cultural climate, and certainly for Stevenson, probably for Mrs. Sitwell— her letters to him do not survive—the relation was as here described and valuable to both.

Now the third thread: When my wife and I were in Britain on the Stevenson research, a second, privately held lot of letters came on the market at Sotheby's. Their content was known to have been mostly published by Colvin, but I needed to comb them, as I had those in Edinburgh, for significant excisions. I went to the sale and saw them sold to a representative of Scribner's for an unnamed American client. Neither in London nor in New York would anybody involved break confidence and tell me who now owned them. I had to put that issue on hold and take the next step in research—approaching Edwin J. Beinecke, the affluent Yale man whose collection of Stevensoniana was reputed to be uniquely rich.

I wrote a persuasive letter and got invited to Beinecke's Greenwich estate. Over lunch we talked Stevenson. I told of the small but indispensable bits I had gleaned from the Edinburgh letters and asked whether he knew who had bought the Sotheby lot. "I did," he said. "They're in the next room. Want to see them?"

The next room was a lofty, elegantly equipped library stiff with Stevensoniana—not only the Sotheby letters but also the bulk of the materials that Hellman had worked from and much else. All of it, with later accretions, is now in the great rare book library that Beinecke gave to Yale. At the time he actually insisted on our piling items that we needed to examine thoroughly into our car to take home to Jersey, trip after trip. I had strong misgivings. What if my house caught fire? "So might mine," Beinecke said. "It's all insured wherever it is." He was thoughtfully generous to the *n*th degree. He wouldn't even let me leave him a list of the irreplaceable things we were taking.

By then, however, the startling consummation had already occurred. Though Beinecke was an adept Stevensonian, he had not yet been meticulously through the Sotheby letters. They were, of course, my first concern. Letter after letter to Colvin with some interesting excisions but largely already familiar from published books. . . . Then suddenly! misfiled for half a century! a letter from young Stevenson *to Mrs. Sitwell* and well along in it an excised sentence: He has been wandering through Edinburgh streets and dreaming of "showing all these places to you, Claire, some other night."

Never mind the blacksmith's innocent daughter and the raven-tressed Highland whore! "Claire" was merely the earliest of those romantic sobriquets that Stevenson lavished on Mrs. Sitwell. And eventually Beinecke's collection turned up two more bits of evidence to that effect.

My wife, working at another desk, thought the worst when I screeched, jumped in the air, and began to whoop. When I calmed down enough to explain, she danced a sort of cross between the tarantella and a Highland fling. If you seek Claire's monument, look in the bowels of the Beinecke Library or, more conveniently, on pages 462–63 of my *Voyage to Windward: The Life of Robert Louis Stevenson* (New York: William Sloane Associates, 1951). It's out of print even in paperback, so this is not an advertisement.

Sometimes a writer's life has its moments. I can, however, understand why George Hellman was highly displeased with my page 463: "when biographical ingenuity gets astride of a hint, it is perilously easy to conjure up spirits from the vasty deep."

* * *

"Julia," "Claire," Galbraith's neighbor girl, Protean's wide acquaintance, Vera's exploits, and Fleming's bogus New York were all in some degree ill-advised excrescences. For the honor of writers generally, let me tell of evenings with a very eminent member of the craft walking a slack wire, so to speak, between two contexts, both characteristic of his personal world, I understand.

No need for pseudonyms here. All the participants except me have been some years gathered to their fathers. Donald Klopfer of Random House, long our neighbor in the country, was one of William Faulkner's publishers and close friends with him. That weekend we were dining the Klopfers and Dick Pratt, architectural editor of the *Ladies' Home Journal,* and his collaborator-wife Dorothy. Late on Friday Pat Klopfer, Donald's wife, phoned that Faulkner was to be with them next day, could they bring him along? Yes indeed. On Saturday afternoon she phoned again very anxiously: Faulkner seemed to be working up toward one of his periodic alcoholic disasters, a prospect even worse than usual because he was on his way to Egypt to work on a Howard Hawks movie. Would I make sure he got only one drink before dinner and very little wine? I said I'd ration him as far as being a host would permit. Further would I tell my wife and the Pratts on no account to mention his writing, for that made him nervous and his mood was fragile enough already?

Klopfers and Faulkner were prompt. Having seen only publicity pictures of him, I was startled by his smallness. He was tiny—not disproportionate but all in miniature. His wistful handsomeness made him look like a French colonel seen through the wrong end of a telescope. As I kissed Pat she slipped me a note: "He's already had two. Please!" When drinks were broached, he asked for straight bourbon. I filled him a two-ounce shot glass and wondered what I'd do next round. But during the hour or so while the others had a couple each, he sipped daintily at long intervals, occasionally complimenting me on the quality of what was, after all, some merely passable standard brand. He still had a drop to knock back when dinner was announced.

Indeed from the moment he arrived he was as gentle, courteous, and otherwise as well behaved a guest as ever crossed our threshold. Those were the stormy hangover-from-Mc-Carthy times. During dinner political issues were broached and fur began to fly. Nobody threw anything, but vocabularies heated up and sore spots were zealously probed. Faulkner stayed not aloof but sympathetically concerned. He sat there by my wife listening solicitously, using every opportunity to throw in mollifying considerations, maybe contributing a folksy anecdote to take the edge off some wild accusation—the perfect gentleman peacemaker. And when the wine came round the second time his glass had hardly been touched.

Things were quiet after dinner. My wife and I gossiped with the Klopfers and Dorothy while Faulkner and Dick discussed something absorbing at the other end of the room, Faulkner barely visible in a huge chair, Dick, twice his size, leaning over him. After the Klopfers' party left, I asked Dick what Faulkner and he had talked of. He was apologetic: "I couldn't resist the opportunity. It was all about his writing. I told him he was for me Mozart and Bach in one."

For once anticlimax was welcome. A few days later, however, Pat was phoning again: "I was right all along. Bill got as far as Paris and then dropped out of sight, probably on one of his toots. They haven't found him yet, but they will. They always do." It was a week or so before they did, got him dried out, and shipped to Egypt.

Years later we were to dine with the Klopfers in New York and again Faulkner turned up unexpectedly. We had a pleasant, low-key sort of evening highlighted by a bottle of miraculously old Madeira that Donald opened in Faulkner's honor. Afterward we shared a taxi downtown, Faulkner in front with the driver. Over his shoulder he said he was sorry the Klopfers had sold their New Jersey place where he had known such enjoyable times. A big change, he said, and "I don't like change. I suppose I'm getting old." "Come on, Mac," the driver said, "you ain't old yet. You get in this cab good as you ever did." All the way down Fifth Avenue they discussed practical geriatrics in pithy monosyllables. I yearned for a tape recorder.

In a matter of weeks Faulkner fought his last round with Bourbon and lost, dying in reaction to the measures the doctor took to bring him out of it. So he never had to get much older.

14

Horse and Buggy Modern

LIVE FORTY OR fifty years in the same house and it becomes a sort of noncontiguous skin. To have raised the place from a pup intensifies that intimacy.

The 1930s saw a strong back-to-the-land movement among trendy Americans. Ralph Borsodi's *Flight from the City* and a determined how-to manual, *Five Acres and Independence*, were as much on people's minds as *Your Money's Worth* and *The Coming Struggle for Power*. Every other week one heard that the So-and-sos had found a delightful little old farmhouse in Fairfield or Rockland County, twenty acres and a never-failing brook, and were planning milch goats and an orchard. Most such Good Life projects still depended to some extent on jobs in or persisting connections with decadent Manhattan, automobiles, telephones, radios, and often a thousand or two a year from the trust fund set up by Uncle Henry's will. But even some root-hog-or-die schemes succeeded, and many such arrangements proved permanent.

Now, "trendy"—a useful label not yet available then—did not describe the Furnases. For some years their position was that, while others might pursue such hopes if they liked, cutting away from asphalt and Heymann's Sixth Avenue meat market was not for Helen and Joe. Yet so much yeasty talk among so many we knew was bound to rub off obliquely. I was devoting seven days a week and some evenings to magazine work and enjoying it. But my wife thought I was overdoing and maintained that returning from strenuous journalistic

missions to a cramped, noisy New York apartment was less
than my due. Why not something quiet and more relaxing,
yet with Manhattan readily available by rail or highway?

We had saved up enough to underwrite such a change.
But we declined to act precipitately. With about the right
amount of hesitation we rented for experiment with rural
amenities a fine old rambling white clapboard house (circa 1750)
far across the North River toward the northwestern corner of
New Jersey, an area decaying, yet still not suburbanizing; bought
a car (first I ever owned) and set out to learn whether magazine free-lancing would go with bucolic joys. If it didn't, we
promised ourselves, back to Manhattan, maybe sadder, certainly wiser, no bones broken.

It worked temptingly well, soon decisively so. We hedged
by securing a Village pied-à-terre, a furnished top floor on
Tenth Street above the Enrico & Paglieri restaurant. It had
only a two-burner kitchenette but shouting down out of the
window to Joe, the E&P doorman, to fetch up a menu produced admirable meals. Rail service on the New York Susque-
hanna & Western (it had never been built farther than the
Delaware River) was dingy but reliable. We found highway
traffic to and fro tough, but that congestion was nothing like
today's. Our landlady, who lived in a sort of dower house across
the road and did her gardening with a tall Scotch highball set
between the rows, was genially obliging. And the old house
itself was a charmer—on a pretty little river set in wide mead-
ows manicured by the Jersey City water department; refresh-
ingly roomy; fine old fireplaces; the landlady's family's worn
but hospitable turn-of-the-century furnishings; and a huge
swimming pool that, in consideration of two cases of beer, the
local volunteer firemen regularly drained and filled from the
river as their required equipment testing. In token of tenancy,
I once dived into one end of that pool and threshed my way
to the other.

Soon, however, we learned the grim truth about old houses.
Our incomparable black housekeeper, Minnie Pinkney of
Brunswick, Georgia, put up with the three-burner kerosene
stove as good-naturedly as she did everything else. (Housekeeper? Kerosene stove? Yes, a long time ago.) But the an-
thracite coal furnace was majestically inadequate. In Indianapolis

I had learned the rudiments of wrangling a coal furnace, and Eddie, the landlady's henchman-factotum, stoked it when we were away on jobs. But the old building's walls and window frames were sieve-leaky. After the first two winter months I needed another fifteen tons of coal. "Yup," said the local storekeeper when I ordered, "You can hang your hat on them drafts in the old place." It had three plumbing systems, probably installed generations apart, all temperamental and so mysteriously connected that even Eddie, who knew the house as well as his own, was sometimes baffled. In other departments, about twice a week something broke, jammed, carried away, rusted out, disintegrated, or leaked.

A summer and winter showed us that we liked our two-ply life. Friends came out weekends, and weekdays we saw as much of New York as we needed or wished to. Minnie came in with us to keep up with her folks in Harlem. The house was a good place to write in. Jitters, the fox terrier, loved it. But we also learned that, in view of my lamentable shortcomings as handyman, for permanent commitment to the country we needed something new-built and crammed with brand-new, guaranteed-by-the-maker, reliably automatic, modern conveniences. Otherwise, I'd soon be writing a sequel to the piece that Paul Gallico had recently done after trying the same arrangement: He called it "Hell Hath No Fury Like a House in the Country."

We had occasionally spent a weekend with the Carl Brandts at their country place in central New Jersey—an august freestone mansion sixty miles from Manhattan in Hunterdon County, then just beginning to be infiltrated by prosperous urban seekers for peace and quiet. Rolling hills, black-and-white cows in lush green pastures, lots of woods, tree-shaded county seat—the only thing that had ever happened in Flemington was the Hauptmann-Lindbergh trial—still sleepier villages, yet excellent rail service into New York on the Lehigh Valley Railroad. Carl was benignly aware of our liking for the county and encouraged us to buy one of its handsome, old-timey farmhouses for reconditioning. We remained firm about building from scratch.

Every available weekend that second summer we combed Hunterdon for a suitable building site. It took time and pa-

tience. Local real estate agents were bored with us, for commission on mere acreage at prices then prevalent would hardly
be lunch money. Eventually we found what we wanted: thirty
acres, mostly thriving second-growth hardwood forest, but the
front ten acres open and growing up in baby red cedar, dogwood, and sumac sloping steeply down to a county road; a
moribund apple orchard halfway up; a never-failing brook a
hundred yards farther on; a ten-mile view across the valley of
the South Branch of the Raritan. (The Lehigh runs along the
river near enough for its whistles to waft sociably across in
damp weather; only today's it's Conrail and the whistles have
become diesel hoots.) The owner, a sharp old fellow living over
the way in a tumbledown cottage with a huge red barn whence
he sold antiques—no extra charge for the quaint background—balked at selling only the front ten acres we wanted.
All or nothing—so we paid twenty-one hundred dollars for
much woods and enough open hillside, seventy an acre. Going
price thereabouts now is five to six thousand dollars an acre.

Our tract had never known any structure except a rough
bridge across the brook for firewood hauling. In 1939 new-
house design on any price level was somehow traditional—Dutch
Colonial, Georgian-Federal, Cape Cod saltbox, half-timber
pseudo-Tudor, or for real pretentiousness pseudo–Mount
Vernon or pseudo-Tara, which is pseudo indeed. "Modern
design," *machine-à-habiter*-minded, was widely discussed and as
trendy as back-to-the-land but as yet applied only gingerly and
very seldom to private dwellings. My wife and I had come to
feel that derivative designs would be anomalous, and aside from
such considerations, we were aware that "modern" jobs, simpler to construct, could give more house per dollar. I looked
up a promising young architect of my acquaintance and delighted him with a proposal to do an unpretentious "modern"
country dwelling.

Most of the details were handled by his still younger partner—call him Kurt—a lanky, well-spoken German fresh from
study at Harvard under the great Walter Gropius of Bauhaus
fame. We got the full Bauhaus treatment, representing the
bulk of what we wanted. When Dick Pratt first saw the elegant
pole-and-riserless stair that I climb up to bed every night, he
said, "Pure Gropius!" Some years ago we visited the model

house near Lincoln, Mass., that Gropius built for himself, embodying his ideas about simple design using only readily available materials. We were right at home. The elevations differed, but the interior treatments were hospitably familiar.

At the time Hunterdon County's only example of "modern" was a sound if stodgy specimen of what my wife called "filling-station modern," all heavy concrete like a military pillbox with corner windows. Our architects prescribed an austere complex of wooden rectangles with a slightly sloping roof, the severity somewhat relieved by curves in the toolshed-garage element and a sinuous, freestanding brick wall. The sheathing was of wide clapboard western white cedar left untreated to weather silver-gray. Second-story balcony clear across the front with bedrooms opening on it. Much of the furniture was built-in of heavy plywood, which saved us money, for even with my wife's few heirlooms, we had nothing like enough beds, chairs, and so on for a three-bedroom, large living-dining-room layout. The south windows were designed large-to-huge to take advantage of heat from winter sunshine, summer sun to be curbed by a high, overhanging "eyebrow" calculated to the proper angle. Northern and western windows compensatorily small and few. It was all radical then.

Though our hoard of U.S. Savings Bonds covered most of the cost as it was incurred, toward the end we needed to borrow. Hunterdon County banks were unprepared to lend a dime on any such structure. It was woundingly clear that, if we could find a mortgage officer willing to risk five thousand dollars, the effective collateral would be the land, the driveway, the bulldozed site, the foundation excavation, and the 180-foot well. In case of foreclosure, any potential purchaser would, it was assumed, demolish and begin again. Hearing of this problem, Bruce Gould volunteered to try Curtis leverage on some Philadelphia bank. But just then a bank connected with the local lawyer who had handled the land purchase said in effect "Well, all right," and we had our five thousand dollars. Carl told me that the antique-dealing previous owner was furious when he saw what was being built; he had counted on selling us antiques for a traditional house. The neighbors up and down the road called this gaunt, grim thing looming up among the apple trees "the chicken coop," and the resemblance was there.

As soon as we moved in, there was a trickle of inquisitiveness on one pretext or another. We showed them round, inside and out, and on leaving they usually said: "Well, it ain't half as bad as it looks from the road."

They'd never know the place now. The house is no longer visible from the road, for reforesting over forty years, part spontaneous, part our plantings—state-supplied black locust, red oak, Austrian pine, Japanese larch—has turned those open front acres into high woods. The four-foot sycamore sapling that I asked the bulldozer man to spare is now eighty foot tall and thirty inches through at chest height. (The sycamore is the Hoosier totem.) It is both gratifying and disquieting to contemplate a sixty-foot black locust put in to check erosion in 1941 and recall the windy, cold spring day when you planted it, a measly-looking seedling ten inches tall. Trees have blocked our view, but cutting a vista through would expose the place to the noise and bustle of today's intolerable traffic on the road. For the eye shrubs, lawn trees, and modifications have tamed the chicken coop, that architectural interloper, into a well-entrenched homestead.

Just dues now: This building project was no Mr. Blandings affair. The architects' self-conscious inquiries about their clients' ways of doing—"life-style" in today's cant—were, for all I know, duly incorporated in design. Certainly their use of internal space was all we could ask. Each cubic foot counts without any cramping effect. Within a few years the two small servant's rooms and bathroom off the kitchen would be anachronistic, but neither the architects nor we knew that at the time, nor that Minnie would go home to Brunswick to look after ailing family; and those rooms proved indispensable for storage— "modern" means no attic. The best of Kurt's good ideas was in choice of builder: He advised taking the highest among several bids because that particular firm was locally renowned for excellent work. We did so and never regretted it. Forty-odd years later not a creak; only one crack—in the fireplace brickwork because I asked the bricklayer to change the pattern; one other flaw, the floor under the stove is half an inch out of plumb. Another sound notion was to cook with gas instead of electricity, for otherwise the occasional power outage, less frequent now than then but still a hazard, would mean impromptu cold buffet for dinner and no coffee. For ornamental planting, Kurt wisely chose native red cedar, dogwood, and rhododendron; they still flourish.

Soon enough, of course, as with the old house, difficulties bobbed up, too many of them irritatingly reflecting Kurt's failing to allow for the New Jersey climate. Through those huge living-room windows the winter sun blasted in, raising the temperature above 85 degrees Fahrenheit while the thermostat, taking Fahrenheit at his word, kept telling the oil burner to lay off, so the rest of the house froze. We had to shift the thermostat into my relatively windowless office. And those large windows are fixed. Only a few sets of slender casements can be opened. Kurt was unaware that in Jersey summers far more cross-ventilation than they afford is necessary.

Opening doors was inadvisable because they had no provision for screen doors, meaning no recognition that Jersey is a summer insects' paradise. (The heating ducts were designed to take air conditioning if we wished it, but back then it was crude business.) Grumbling, Kurt designed Rube Goldbergish screen doors. The carpenter shook his head over them, but they eventually filled the need. Further Kurt had to add a horizontal trellis across the big windows with wide planks slanted at what he calculated to be the right angle to keep the summer sun off. It was ineffective until we planted vigorous vines to climb all over it and leaf out.

The bedrooms also had heat problems. The subtly slanted "eyebrow" did not keep the sun's heat from reverberating up from the balcony deck. We had to install awnings—those old pull-up-and-down canvas affairs with steel-pipe frames that gusty thunderstorms loved to take apart. Again and again a house wren insisted on starting to build a nest in the folds of the dining-room awning. When I dropped the awning before breakfast to block off the sun, her early morning's work with twigs would fall down. Understandably she was outraged. Nobody dared go near that end of the house for fear of this twittering termagant, the size of my thumb and weighing only a few ounces but scolding like a feathered fishwife.

Then there was the Jersey sun's effect on the cedar sheathing. Theoretically it would need no care, but after a year its surface was so parched that to run a thumb across it left a mark. Kurt sought remedy and came up recommending oiling it. We oiled it. Next year the same trouble led us to oil it again. Third year the same. The fine old-line paint company that made the oil sent us a new kind certain to solve the problem. It didn't. Eventually these successive frustrations made me turn to conventional paint, never mind the elegant weathered effect we had been promised. The oil impregnating the wood came bubbling out under hot sun and ruined the paint job. The problem was insoluble until clapboard-faking aluminum siding appeared, phony as the proverbial three-dollar bill, of course, but following the horizontal lines of the house as suavely as the cedar ever had and never needing paint. At about the same time fixed aluminum awnings came along and we joyfully substituted them for the canvas-and-steel hair shirts.

With such improvisations we eventually got the place well and truly into shape. Thus correcting Kurt's miscues was expensive and relations began to fray at the edges. I haven't heard from him since he married a pleasant girl with some money of her own, bought acreage up in North Jersey, and built on it much the same house as ours, only correcting what was wrong first time around.

So we never learned what he would have thought of our later modifications. Actually the aluminum awnings' emphatic and sturdy downward slant ties the house to the ground admirably and the heavy vines on the front trellis wonderfully informalize it. After thirty years my wife called the basic design "horse-and-buggy modern." Ten years later still we became fully aware how time turns the strikingly new into the taken-for-granted. When we went to visit that Gropius house at Lincoln—contemporary and prototype of ours—it had recently been taken over as an aesthetico-cultural landmark by the Society for the Preservation of New England Antiquities.

15

And I Hope to Travel More

IN THE ACCEPTED distinction between "tourist" and "traveler" tourists go a-traipsing in order primarily to see things that have been impressively talked up; secondarily they may more or less enjoy locomotion with its promise of get-away-from-it-all. Travelers go places for economic or social or professional reasons; but they too may come to share the tourists' pleasure in putting miles and static ties behind them. Thus W. Somerset Maugham kept moving so widely because it paid him as sententious fictioneer to immerse himself in the relation between Western man and exotic circumstances; yet he was obviously also addicted to the direct stimuli of alien places and the process of reaching them. I have been and still am both traveler and tourist in all possible combinations.

The ancients seem to have thought major travel an onerous chore, as no doubt it was on foot or on horseback—no saddles, mind—or even in a litter along the famous Roman roads. And the joys of rough weather on the wine-dark sea in a so-called ship smaller than a modern harbor tug readily escaped them. Postmedieval England sent its gilded youth across the Channel to make the Grand Tour not so much to show the lads *Sehenswürdigkeiten* (though the worthiness-to-be-seen of Versailles and St. Peter's was recognized) as to enable them to learn French, maybe Italian, and get the hang of fencing and dancing while sowing their wild oats away from home. Later, however, cultivated Britons and Germans, having swallowed romanticism whole, suffered severe seizures of rapture

301

ın the presence of an Alp, a waterfall, a ruin. Through books and pictures that sort of thing filtered down into simpler social strata. Hence, in the fullness of time, Cook's Tours and *The Innocents Abroad,* and the essential tourist, guidebook in one hand, postcards in the other, camera slung baldric fashion, luggage crammed with souvenirs.

Such tourism, as governments fondly call it, was largely the child of steam. The convenience of railroads begat Cook's Tours. The Innocents Abroad went junketing in a steamer and used railroads freely. For the century or so dominated by those two means of transport, traveler and tourist often found enjoyable for its own sake the process of going somewhere. To lunch at leisure in the diner of the Lehigh Valley's old Black Diamond while the scenic intricacies of the Appalachians streamed past the window! To lean on the corridor rail in springtime savoring the joyful-green pastures and white cattle and blazing-yellow mustard fields of Burgundy! To pace the deck of an unpretentious steamship yielding good-naturedly to a rolling sea on a smiling-sunny day! Nowadays at sea one has only the cruise ship, a floating resort-casino-cum-shopping-cart-cum-house-of-assignation. On land American rail travel, what's left of it, is a subsidized public charge. In spite of engineering advances, it is ominously dwindling in Europe. The Autobahn-Interstate has made driving oneself a boring nuisance. So now traveler and tourist typically fly. They get nothing of that salubrious sense of gradually, if temporarily, changing *coelum* and, with luck, *animum* that long-distance trains give and, in the seagoing version, makes certain landfalls memorable wonders. The legendary typist on the London bus asks her seatmate where she spent her holidays. "Majorca." "Where's that?" " 'Ow should I know? I flew there."

My chronic bookishness permeates the tourist aspect of my hither-and-yon past. Among my mother's purchases of books was a set of fourteen tall, slim volumes with gilt letters on their leather-bound spines: STODDARD'S LECTURES. In one sense the many, many miles I have logged in my time represented checking up on Stoddard.

John Lothrop Stoddard was an amply mustached Williams man who had two years in divinity school, taught briefly at

Boston Latin, then earned fame and fortune by supplying vicarious touristing to the places that respectable America circa 1900 yearned to visit. Season after season, in lyceum halls and minor theaters, he combined unctuous patter with lantern slides of Rome tonight, or Switzerland; the Rhineland Wednesday, next week Scotland, Venice, the Holy Land. . . . As his public developed, he included China, India, Mexico, California, the Grand Canyon. But the emphasis, following the cultural slant of the day, was on Europe. His personal favorite was the Austrian Tyrol. In his sixties, replete with dollars and renown, he retired there. During World War I, he alienated American admirers by writing apologetic propaganda for the Central Powers. Mark Twain said his pictures were good but the lecturer should have kept still or "died in the first act."* The only remaining vestige nowadays is Fitzgerald's mention of a set of his books among those on the shelves of Gatsby's library.

Those printed lectures were generously rich in two to three-inch halftones of the slide photographs: cathedrals and castles, cascades and cafés. Recently I visited them on my basement shelves and was overwhelmed by instant recall and subsequent sightseeing. For time and again since I first went to Europe in 1934, I have accidentally or purposely rounded a corner and run plump into a Stoddardism. My first sight of the Paris Opera detonated instant memory of volume 5, page 50, upper left margin. Much later, crossing Switzerland by train on a moonlight night, I wakened and raised the window blind—and there whisking past was a precipitous waterfall, a dead ringer for the halftone of the Giessbach, volume 1, page 146—maybe only eighty feet instead of a thousand or so, but its spirit untamedly wild, association immediate. Edinburgh Castle, the temple of Olympian Zeus in Athens, Santa Maria della Salute . . . all DEJA VU in caps. If I ever visit Ireland, my first round tower will afford the same blend of "Damned if it hasn't been there just like that all the time!" with a flash of suddenly being eight years old in a stuffy house in Indianapolis. Such things pack emotional clout. Only ten years ago I felt resentful because the interior of Hagia Sophia no longer

*Robert Sattelmeyer and J. Donald Crowley, *One Hundred Years of Huckleberry Finn* (Columbia: University of Missouri Press, 1985), p. 410.

sported the extravagant hangings that Stoddard pictured. My first view of Ely Cathedral was, however, all it should be, just like Stoddard's standard photograph, the one with sheep grazing in the foreground. When the Pullman porter pointed out to me (nine going on ten) a forest-shaggy hump in the distance as a mountain called Pilot Peak, I felt cheated. My first mountain should have looked like Stoddard's snow-swathed Jungfrau or, better still, his savage, naked Matterhorn.

The lecture texts that went with the pictures were stiff with historical and literary references such as cultivated literacy might value in 1900. That all Stoddard's paying customers were so well read was unlikely, but no doubt his assuming they were was flattering. Thus his lecture on London—a place that rather daunted him—took it for granted that the whole house knew about Newman Noggs and Mr. Jingle. His Scotland was awash with Burns—liberally quoted—Scott, and a hard-breathing defense of Mary Queen of Scots. As to Byron, he actually carried *Childe Harold* in his luggage for ready reference. In Greece he gave his audience most of "Maid of Athens, ere we part" with a photograph of a plump Greek soubrette, and the deathbed scene at Missolonghi like this: "No woman's hand was there to smooth his brow or give him the countless little comforts which only woman's tender thoughtfulness can understand . . . with a weary sigh . . . he sank into that peaceful slumber in which his spirit gradually loosed its hold on earth and drifted outward into the Universe." Switzerland naturally called for chunks of "The Prisoner of Chillon." In Venice, Faliero's head duly rolled down the Giants' Steps. On pilgrimage to the Holy Ground of Newstead Abbey, Stoddard practically took his high-buttoned shoes from off his feet and did eleven pages (volume 9, pages 189–200) about Byron as handicapped archangel more sinned against than sinning.

To supplement Byron, he often burst into his own impeccably rhyming and scanning verses. No, "burst into" is inaccurate. Confronted by some surefire tourist lion like the Venus of Melos, he professed to be "inclined to murmur"

> O goddess of that Grecian isle
> Whose shore the blue Aegean laves,

> Whose cliffs repeat with answering smile
>   Their features in its sun-kissed waves

and so on and on through fourteen stanzas that I hope his audience enjoyed as much as he must have in reciting them. Or in a jolly open-air café in a park in Vienna "on a scrap of paper, in the midst of innocent merriment and delightful music, the following lines were traced":

> The sun will set at day's decline.
>   *Qu'importe?*
> Quaff off meanwhile life's sparkling wine.
> Of what avail are tim'rous fears?
> Foreboding sighs and idle tears?
> They hinder not the hurrying years.
>   *Buvons!*

and four more stanzas of similar tenor with the same anomalous French instead of German tags. Nor was his muse always smiling. In India "the following lines were, in a moment of reaction, inscribed":

> I'm weary of the loin-cloth,
>   And tired of naked skins;
> I'm sick of knavish, filthy priests
>   Who trade in human sins;
> These millions of the great unwashed
>   Offend both eye and nose;
> I long for legs in pantaloons
>   And feet concealed in hose . . .
> Goodbye to whining mendicants
>   Who show their loathsome sores!—
> I'm glad to take the steamer now
>   And sail for other shores.

It occurs to me that reading Stoddard's verse over and over may have had a share in my aforementioned early distrust of all but narrative poetry. For another likely side effect, though I'd have gone to India had some writing job required it, I've never felt inclined to experience the subcontinent for its own sake.

As observer Stoddard sometimes did fairly well. His Madrid bullfight was better than Hemingway's swung-from-the-floor account with its curiously kittenish tone. Around 1894 Stoddard brought away from Berlin and Vienna dismayed awareness of what was likely to happen in consequence of headlong militarism; and from Belgium a commonsense certainty that, in case of war, the international guarantee of neutrality would be the first casualty. The squalor of London's East End appalled him as much as Stoke Pogis churchyard, complete with quotation, delighted him. Yet nobody could have mistaken him for a liberal. He was cordially respectful about Napoleon, Bismarck, and Porfirio Díaz. Though he decried German anti-Semitism, his admiration of Gladstone owed much to the Grand Old Man's contrast with Disraeli's Jewishness as Stoddard implicitly defined it. That is, he was a nonintellectual steeped in the terms accepted in his day, talking to stay-at-homes in their own language. That reflects my recent rereading. When I was seventy-odd years younger, it was the bits and pieces that kept drawing me back to those fourteen volumes. I got from him not only the Japanese for "Good morning" but the knowledge that the color orange had a special significance in Ireland; the nature of Turkish baths; what *Complet* on a Paris omnibus means; how to spell Iztaccihuatl; vignettes of Maria Theresa, Peter the Great, William Wallace, the Empress Eugénie . . . hooks of reference for a boy to hang further data and references on.

I felt no affinity with this pompous guide; and my subsequent touristing, though valued, has played second fiddle to travel. Yet I still sympathize with a bit he tucked into his account of Belgium: "I [Stoddard] am profoundly grateful for the irrepressible longing to visit the Old World that made my childhood one long dream of history and travel."

That attitude is outmoded now. So are most of his data, for he took one into countries that long ago ceased to exist. In view of what has happened to its Mediterranean coast, it is amazing to read his paragraphs (circa 1895) about how nobody goes to Spain, how primitive its facilities and communications are; you'd think he was talking about today's Albania.

In his London, the subway system, though an efficient way of getting about, was a smothering ordeal because of its coal-burning locomotives; electric traction power had not yet been applied to a drastic need. More striking still: Ninety years ago, rhapsodizing about the Himalayas as seen from Darjeeling, he called the great snow peaks "Forever virgin to the touch of man . . . unapproachable as the moon, nearer than yet as inaccessible as the North Pole." North Pole. Mount Everest, K-2 et al. The moon. All conquered in my lifetime. What price virginity now?

Stoddard never worked the South Seas, not even Hawaii, though the Pearl of the Pacific became American territory well before he hung up his lyre and walking shoes. The combined influences of *The Bird of Paradise,* Tin Pan Alley, and the movies had not yet made the hula tourist bait as seductive as bagpipes and the cancan. How he would have liked a lei hung round his neck we shall never know, nor how poi and kava would have struck the man who found pulque dreadful. But the South Seas have bulked large in the hither-and-yonning into which Stoddard incited me, supplying rich examples of how enjoyably a typewriter, locomotion, and sightseeing can blend. In view of his influence it is curious that among some twenty volumes, I have never written a "travel book." No *Beyond the Mexique Bay* or *Old Calabria,* even supposing I could write like that. One reason may be that nobody ever asked me to try such a thing. It may be just as well.

As to highlights of travel-with-a-purpose in the South Seas, the chronological way may be best: Lord Howe Island in 1936; Fiji, Tahiti, and the Aitutapus a dozen years later.

You never heard of the first. Few, even in the Southern Hemisphere, ever had. It is a crescent-shaped scrap of land maybe three miles long in the middle of the Tasman Sea, the waste of waters between Australia and New Zealand. From a distance it probably still is the most beautiful bit of topography I ever saw. And it also was—unhappily is no more—the nearest thing to a harmoniously organized social paradise that ever existed.

When I got there, I was ten years away from my introductory course in geology but retained enough to make the volcanic origin of the place obvious, as it is in so many of the South Pacific's "high islands." The southern end of Lord Howe is a mass of dark basaltic rock rising sheer two thousand feet out of the surf-heavy sea—twin peaks, one still conical, the other squared off, probably by a cataclysmic explosion many millennia ago. The younger northern end is a harsh jumble of volcanic detritus and a few cones. Chordwise across the inner curve of the crescent, betokening the lack of chill in the local waters, what is reputed to be the world's farthest south coral reef protects a Hollywoodish lagoon. Debris from mountains and reef forms the low-lying middle of the crescent, most of it charmingly shaded by the interlacing tops of girlishly slender-trunked palm trees. One walked beneath them over silently sandy pathways while up aloft the persistent breeze rustled confidentially among their fronds and let sunlight sift through green and gold. Here was a vivacious, all-alive stillness.

One walked. Lord Howe Island had no wheeled vehicles. Local transport went no higher than a few horses and the kind of stoutly made sledges that my grandfather called stone boats. They slid easily, with just a subtle hiss, over the gray sand. Through the palm boles came on one hand the blazing blue lagoon, on the other maybe a small pasture for local livestock. But the palms dominated the whole midsection as a glass roof dominates a greenhouse—and by creating the local economy made it the unique paradise that it was. There were a few severe storms, for the Tasman is no millpond. But heavy damage was rare and as to other weather, the temperature seldom went above 75 degrees Fahrenheit, seldom below 65. Fresh water was a problem, but as on Bermuda, with a little care rainwater catchments were adequate.

My wife and I owed awareness of Lord Howe to the late Freeman (Doc) Lewis, an early father of the paperback industry, who had read about it somewhere and, learning we were off to Australia the winter of 1935–36, adjured us to go there and let him know whether it was as wonderful as it sounded. It was.

To get there from Australia required the only thing, except radio, that linked the island to the mainland three hundred miles away—a venerable little ship, the *Morinda* of the Burns-Philp trading and shipping company, whose checkered funnels and shore depots stocking anything from tobacco to typewriters were well known anywhere within a thousand miles north and east of Sydney. Eldest of the company's by no means new fleet, she was so old her plates were of iron, not steel—an advantage, they said, for iron was less likely to crack when she came foul of an unmarked coral horsehead in some tropical lagoon. Every month or so she grunted and thumped her way out through Sydney Heads to Lord Howe, on to Norfolk Island (once a high-security penal colony, later home of some descendants of the mutineers of H.M. Armed Transport *Bounty*), on into the steamy New Hebrides, then reversed the route homeward bound. On her and her alone Lord Howe depended for fetching textiles, hardware, tobacco, whiskey, reading matter, kerosene for lamps, gasoline for launches, basic medical supplies for the resident nurse—no doctor—everything the islanders could not work up for themselves. To pay for that perpetual shopping list the homeward bound *Morinda* took to Sydney in season the bulging sacks of palm seed that supported the whole shooting match.

Tiny for a seagoing steamer, the *Morinda* looked absurd lying at her Sydney pier. Her upper deck was far below the stringpiece. My wife remarked on the strangeness of going *down* the ladder when boarding. The passenger saloon, bisected by the boardinghouselike dining table, and the dollhouse staterooms opening off its gallery smelled glumly of fifty years of mutton fat. The only nonfrowsy items onboard were the adequately clean crockery and sheets. The captain, an elderly, gray-headed Scot, was rated ranking curmudgeon of the Sydney waterfront. The *Morinda* was hard to love. But her doughty behavior out in the middle of the Tasman in some of the screechingest weather I ever saw at sea was ingratiating. Weeks later we returned in her so short of cash that how to tip the stewards was a problem; the captain lent me ten pounds on my face. Next day, when I went to the company office to repay, I had trouble convincing the staff that Captain Perry, rest his grumpy, solid soul, had done anything so far out of character.

Topographical description could not convey the wonder of one's Lord Howe Island landfall. The logistics can be filled in. The lagoon being much too shallow for even the *Morinda*, she had to lie off and lighter in the Lord Howe part of the cargo, us included, in small boats. The sea was choppy, the ship was rolling grandly, and making it into a boat from the foot of the ladder took quick timing and resolution. "This place is well named," my wife said. "Lord, how I land!"* A local launch towed us through the gap in the reef to the spindly little pier on the beach. Paradise, radio-alerted by the Australian government tourist agency in spite of their seeming never to have heard of the place, received us cordially.

Why paradise? Not because of the exquisite climate or the unmatchedly lovely topography, but because this was the only Western-flavored polity I ever heard of where three weeks work a year would afford all the native-born a pleasant living. There was nothing against doing more if you liked. Most of the islanders did to some extent go beyond gardening and fishing—superb fishing—to supplement the basic income; some were substantially enterprising. But mere local birth did virtually exempt one from the curse of Adam. The automatic basic livelihood was rather like the "vagabond wage" that Bertrand Russell envisaged to palliate the paternalistic harshness implicit in collectivism. Here is how this phenomenon came about:

Unlike the South Sea paradises of tradition, Lord Howe Island never had any preliterate, lusciously brown "natives" to be corrupted and so exploited that vicious scars came of the consequent acculturation. When it was discovered two hundred years ago its only inhabitants were seabirds. Dauntless explorers and colonizers though the old Polynesians were, else they'd never have reached New Zealand or Hawaii or Easter Island, they never found this scrap of land in the middle of nowhere. It was the whalers of the early nineteenth century—mostly Americans, some Australia- or New Zealand–based Britons—who settled it, at first merely coming ashore for leg stretching, water, and firewood, then leaving a few men, maybe invalids, ashore to grow green stuff to supply the ship next time around—hence a permanent tiny colony. Among the few women soon involved were Polynesian "wives," so technically

---

*Actually it (and a confusing group of atolls much farther north) was named by Royal Navy officer-discoverers for Richard ("Black Dick") Lord Howe, Britain's most redoubtable admiral of the late eighteenth century.

many of the 150-odd islanders probably had a dash of brown-skin genes. You'd never guess it. To us they looked just like their American, New Zealander, and Australian cousins. It fitted their American background that the local cuisine traditionally included fried chicken and pumpkin pie. Very tasty too.

As kerosene took over from whale oil for lamps, whaling dwindled world over. But eventually somebody learned that Lord Howe's palms, growing by countless thousands and producing annual millions of seeds, were of all the palms in the world best suited for decorating hotel lobbies, restaurants, conservatories, and so on. Well into my time "potted palms" signified an earnest elegance and, among musicians of the 1920s, the "In a Chinese Temple Garden" sort of thing was known as "potted palm music." It was an exacting assignment implying no natural light, intrusive cigar smoke, negligent watering. Mortality ran high until Lord Howe's palms demonstrated how doughtily they could survive all that. And better still it turned out that nursery men could not propagate Lord Howe Island palms in captivity, so to speak. Only cozily back home in latitude 31.33 South, longitude 55.09 East, would these popular vegetables grow fertile seed. Apparently Mother Nature had decided to rehabilitate this whalers' depot by giving it a worldwide monopoly on the potted-palm industry.

The adaptable islanders began harvesting palm seed to meet the consequent demand. But they were unreliable about gathering and processing and inexperienced at bargaining. New South Wales, the Australian state that had nominal sovereignty but never bothered much about it, stepped in to set up a cooperative agency to supervise and market the seed on a monopoly basis, insisting on a quality product, sharp bargains, and fair distribution of profits. The eventual arrangement was: During the annual three-week seed harvest all hands and the cat would gather, dry, sort, and bag seed to meet government standards. In return every islander-born got a share in the cooperative; off-island spouses, of whom there were a few, got half-shares. Each share paid dividends proportionate to the year's net—sums far higher than previous catch-as-catch-can marketing had ever secured, indeed so ample that thus to be born on the place afforded a workable livelihood. One needed no heating fuel, only inexpensive kinds of clothes and not much of them; one could live on fish, poultry, dairy stuff, and green stuff without cash outlay—and all this in one of God's most beautiful and healthful environments. It delighted me then, and still does, that this unique, beneficent economy came about because New South Wales' Socialist-minded, arbitrary government thus created and exploited a classic capitalist-type, get-rather-more-than-the-traffic-will-bear monopoly.

Yet with a caution rare among governmental paternalisms, New South Wales pretty much let the islanders do things their own way as long as they observed the terms of the monopoly. An early bit of friction served as lesson on how not to play guardian. Government learned that the island had no jail—intolerable in a civilized community. Without consulting the islanders, it sent over a knockdown two-cell jail—timbers, bars, locks, doors, irons all complete. In all past history the island had seen only one homicide, three generations back; and the tightly knit nature of their society had kept other publicly punishable iniquities practically unthinkable. In the islanders' view not only did they need no jail, to suggest they did was insulting. They refused to land the stuff. Government sent it back with peremptory orders to see it got ashore. So they used it to build a nice shelter for their cricket ground. And Government wisely let it go at that.

As the monopoly took hold, a curious problem led to a bizarre currency. Men were not the only alien creatures to come ashore from the old whalers. Rats, mankind's invariable companions, not least in ships, also knew a good thing when they saw it. Presumably swimming ashore, they soon flourished because palm seed proved admirably palatable and nourishing. They took to living altogether up among the palms, sleeping there and feeding on the seed clusters. Nobody minded for a while, but as the rats' numbers grew, their inroads on the seed supply began to look serious. A bounty was set. Traps and poison failed, for the rats seldom set paw on the ground and were too well fed for poisoned bait to tempt them. The remedy was the .22 rifle. Whenever there was nothing more urgent, the islander set out among the palms with rifle and fox terrier (to spot the game up there and finish off the wounded) and whiled away an hour or so shooting rats out of the trees.

Their tails, cut off as bounty tokens, were preserved in a jar of alcohol at home. In payment for items at the cooperative store—cigarettes, sewing thread, or whatever—accumulated tails were accepted as a medium of exchange. Thus paying the bounty slightly reduced the annual dividends, but the islanders had the common sense not do overdo it, so the supply of rats and that of palm seed achieved a rough equilibrium. When moved to tell about Lord Howe Island I always get instant attention by saying I knew a place where the rats lived in the treetops and people lived on three weeks' work a year. It all made a fine article for the *Post*. I was actually well paid for having visited somewhere so enjoyable.

The island's isolation need not be exaggerated. Radio kept the islanders in touch, as much so as they wished, with the turmoil of the 1930s. Most households had wind-up phonographs and ordered records from Sydney, including waltzes and fox-trots for dances in the community hall. The ladies went in long dresses but barefoot, donning their dancing slippers on reaching the scene. Some young islanders were sent to Sydney for advanced schooling; of those a few stayed away to make their lives on the mainland but more were happy to come home. Each trip of the *Morinda* probably saw an islander or two going to and from Sydney, but that was not locally considered a pleasure, for, though never seasick in their own small craft among the Tasman's great swells, the different motion of a ship in a seaway made them miserable. A few mainland vacationists, usually ardent fishermen, came to stay over a voyage at one of the small boardinghouses that a few island families kept for supplementary income.

I recall an elderly Australian politician, William Hughes, telling us, on hearing we planned to visit Lord Howe, that it was the pleasantest place he had ever seen—only one warning: Take along an electric torch with good batteries; you'll need it to find the outhouse after dark. In the island's serene, faintly breezy, temperate nights even that was a pleasure.

What a research sociologist would have made of the place I cannot surmise; it's too late now. We had over three weeks there because the *Morinda* went aground up in the New Hebrides and it took a while to get her afloat again. Meanwhile we had got to know many of the local population and learned of the several loosely cohering clans formed round family ties, as though recalling their remote Polynesian forebears. No edged rivalries were discernible. Had the place had a coat of arms, the motto would have been "Live and let live." Yet there was nothing Quakerishly bland about those we saw most of. They were salty as well as easygoing, handy with rifle and small craft but never overbrisk; slow-spoken but quick on the uptake. We made good friends with the middle-aged couple who put us up and kept in touch with them while they lived, as I still do with their son in Sydney. When old Mrs. Kirby, a local matriarch, and her daughter visited us in New Jersey, her very presence in the room—all bright-eyed style and relish for good Scotch—left the place feeling aired out and tingly.

When the *Morinda* radioed that she was on her way back to Sydney and would pick us up in a few days, my wife wept.

People sometimes ask: "Of all the places you've seen, which do you want to visit again?" I answer: "I know the place but I can't go back. It isn't there anymore." No doubt much of that rustling canopy of sun-gilt palm fronds survives. But between the Wright Brothers and the botanical tinkerers the Lord Howe Island we knew has been erased. Soon after our visit, somebody found a combination of fertilizers and environment that would produce fertile seed elsewhere. That broke the seed monopoly. Then after World War II the monopoly held by the *Morinda,* that seagoing slum—forgive me, old girl—that had kept outside infiltration down was broken by a tripper-transporting flying-boat service. When my wife and I were in Australia in 1981, we learned that an airport for regular-scheduled planes from Sydney was operating briskly where part of the palm grove had been. We hadn't the heart to fly over and see how much things had changed.

Soon after World War II we met a second Burns-Philp vessel that made the *Morinda* look stylish—"vessel" because the silhouette of M.V. *Yanawai* had little in common with that of a seagoing ship. She had practically no freeboard, being a sort of self-propelled barge with hatchways and deckhouses casually strewn fore and aft. Where she kept her Diesel engines I never knew, though one was all too aware of their rumbling vibration—not the kind of ship where the chief engineer invites well-considered passengers to take a tour of the engine room. (The only stranger craft I ever met was the cross between a backwater ferryboat and an outdoor café, with some touches of a railroad handcar, in which, breakfasting on flapjacks and maple syrup, we once ascended a Liberian river.) The *Morinda*'s staterooms had doors; the *Yanawai*, chief recourse of passengers for the outer islands of the Fiji archipelago, had only scanty curtains blowing in the trade wind. Her cuisine was slightly better and, being so breezily constructed, she smelled better. But her drinking water tank lay next to the fuel bunkers, and a certain osmosis had developed. The only booze on board was Australian gin—potable but the necessity for diluting it with the ship's water added a kerosenish taint.

Lest this sound patronizing: The *Yanawai* well and truly did her duty of transporting supplies, about the same inventory as the *Morinda*'s, to the minor islands and taking back to Suva, Fiji's chief town, copra (dried coconut meat) for shipment to the British soap, cosmetics, and cooking-oil industries. In those shallow and relatively protected waters, she needed little freeboard and could not afford the draft of water that conventional design would have implied.

For the first half of this low-keyed voyage, our traveling companions were an engagingly outspoken couple, members of the local oligarchy (white), returning from Suva to their coconut plantation on their private island some two miles square. They had most helpfully arranged us passage in the *Yanawai* and otherwise been thoughtful friends. And it wasn't in all circumstances that Nora Palmer (which was not her name) succeeded in being helpful. During the ship's hither-and-yonning, she grew anxious about getting home to see what crimes of slackness her domestic staff had been up to in her absence, hence was apprehensive lest faulty navigation lead to delay. Several times I found her on the bridge giving the captain peremptory advice: "Now Bill, I'm sure you're headed too much to starboard. Remember you stuck here three days last year because you were too close in to the point. I tell you, if you don't ease her off . . ." while the captain, a rotund, good-natured little fellow in white shirt and shorts, grew redder and more apoplectically silent because he couldn't tell the wife of one of the company's good customers to shut her face and go below or he'd put her in irons. Sorry about "go below." In the *Yanawai* there was practically no below to go to.

Whatever it has turned into, as we saw island after island with its hair down, Fiji was then classically colonial. Thus, when we made the island principality of a prominent family who were still dallying in Suva, Nora escorted us ashore in a ship's boat and took possession of their large, cool, airy house as though she owned it—as, of course, the owners would have done vice versa on the Palmars' island. She walked in clapping her hands for all-hands-on-deck, ordered the Fijian servant who came panting in to go fetch us tea: "Mind now, wash your hands before you touch anything and see the cook does it too." He said, "Yes, sir." The Fijian's English wots not of "ma'am"; "sir" is the courtesy-deferential handle for both sexes of highly placed whites. In Samoa, our host's cheery Fijian orderly invariably greeted my wife: "Good morning, sir!"

For me another such landing off the *Yanawai* was disastrous. No landing stage or pier, and the grounded prow of the ship's launch left several rods of waist-deep water to negotiate. It was customary for servants to wade in and carry visitors in dryshod. For Nora, nippy little Scotswoman, and my wife, at a slender 120-odd pounds, that was all very well. Ashore they went as if playing Sabine women. Conscious of my 165 pounds and awkwardly long frame, however, I mistrusted the lanky-built, grizzle-bearded, rather elderly Hindu (Fiji has a majority population of imported East Indians) who waded out to waft me ashore. The boat's crew insisted it was done all the time, no hazard, I mustn't think of wading. Overruled, I let the old fellow collect me—not piggyback, which would have made some sense, not fireman's lift, which would have made more, but child-in-arms style. After a few blundering steps, down he came and me with him, both souse over ears. It wasn't the first time I had got soaked in line of duty. But my deafness had developed far enough to make a hearing aid advisable. And you've no notion what a brief soaking in tepid Pacific saltwater does to the insides of a hearing aid. For the several months before we returned Stateside I had to get along without it—a decided handicap on the job. To avoid that I'd have waded ashore twenty times.

Otherwise, life as the *Yanawai* snored her devious way

through far-flung Fiji, was low-keyed, peaceful and rewarding. Indeed Fiji generally was rewarding. In Suva the deep-
verandaed Grand Pacific Hotel, with its view of the furry-green
hills across the harbor (including "Joske's Thumb," an implausibly shaped peak), was old-timey comfortable. Sir Alexander
Grantham, governor of Fiji and High Commissioner of the
Western Pacific (later governor of Hong Kong)—forty years
ago the British Empire still had some substance—was candid
about the complexities of the thousands of square miles of his
bailiwick and of the ethnic trouble between Fijians and the
local East Indians. Our quondam host in Samoa, Colonel Francis
Volcker, took us along on his tour of the Fijian villages whence
had been recruited the battalion that he had commanded in
the Solomons in World War II. Those Fijian units, you may
not recall if you ever heard, were the troops the Japanese
dreaded most. Now demobilized and settled back into their
wickerwork *bures*, no longer required to persuade their bear-
paw feet into military boots, they came flocking, hulking and
genial, coffee-brown, half grinning, half tearful, to dance
and sing, make speeches and present gifts to their white
chief, the more delightedly because they had expected never
to see him again. Volcker's operational eye—he had lost the
other in World War I—was wet much of the time.

The cultural sponsor and home commander of those Fijian
troops was one of the cannniest and most prepossessing men
I ever met—a high-ranking chief from the eastern group of
Fiji, Ratu Sir Lala Sukuna. (*Ratu* means "chief" more or less;
Lala Sukuna was his name; the "Sir" was a well-deserved British honor.) Most South Seas patricians are, as previously noted,
tall and bulky. Sukuna, not royal but next thing to it, was maybe
only five foot seven but made it up in the brawny bulk of an
eighteenth-century sedan chair man in a Rowlandson cartoon,
heavily muscled all over, with the legs of an old-time square
piano. His skin was the color of a black olive, his small eyes
were jewel-bright, his facial expression conveyed depth on depth
of ironic shrewdness. Traditionally Fijians wore their frizzy black
hair teased out into medicine-ball-size globes that make an
"Afro" look like baldness; in the wild old days they treated it
with lime to turn it henna-red or lemon-yellow. But soldiering
required going close-cropped, so Sukuna's bullet-shaped skull

enjoyed its own shapeliness. In Suva he stayed in uniform—regulation British army tunic and a just-below-the-knee *sulu* (a khaki version of the native kilt) with a sawtoothed lower hem. A few years later when he came to New York in the British delegation to the United Nations, he wore well-tailored lounge-suit jacket, shirt, tie, all very Savile Row, but instead of trousers a same-fabric kilt showing plenty of his formidable black calves and huge feet in leather-thong sandals. Inez Robb, the Scripps-Howard columnist, meeting him at some UN press doings, wrote he was Anthony Eden from the waist up, Dorothy Lamour from the waist down.

At Oxford he had acquired a wonderfully sententious, dry, clear British-English speech like that of a specially comprehensible British actor. Sukuna's experience in the Western world had further included service in the French Foreign Legion in World War I. As soldier and particular representative of the Fijian people on the governor's council, he was chosen to supervise recruiting and training of the Fijian troops in World War II. When we met him, the war had wound down and he was devoted to putting the social and cultural pieces back together among his people. His watchful, serene good-humor would, I'm sure, have been a good omen for our first meeting. But I think it helped that, with the merest hint of maybe applying a test, he asked me whether I'd tried the notoriously powerful local tobacco. I said no, I'd heard of it and would like to. So here was a sample black as a Labrador retriever wrapped cigar style in a dried banana peel.* Luckily I was then a very heavy cigarette smoker steeped in tars and nicotine. I finished the thing able to say sincerely as well as convincingly that I had enjoyed it. From then on Sukuna and I got along.

Setting the date well ahead to make sure of the right size and kind of turtle, he gave us a Fiji-style dinner in his spacious house in Suva. We sat on the floor with palm fronds for tablecloth. Fingers were needed, for traditionally Fijians used a fork only for *mbokolo*—the man-meat that our host's not-so-distant ancestors greatly relished. We were served no *mbokolo*, but the

---

*I recalled this when in the 1960s Youth tried smoking banana peel in the belief it had something in common with marijuana.

turtle was excellent and I recall pleasantly the crunchy, salty seaweed eaten as salad. The most striking thing was the service. In many prewhite South Sea cultures under no circumstances did a member of a lower social stratum dare raise his head higher than his superiors' heads. That was why, to the bewilderment of the white discoverers of Hawaii, if a chief visiting the ship went belowside, his retainers on deck immediately jumped overboard. As Sukuna's guests, my wife, as well as I, was a chief by courtesy, so we could sit heads up, but his Fijian servants came in and out on their knees with heads bowed to make sure of not transgressing. And Andi (or Lady) Maria, Sukuna's wife, with whom we had spent pleasant hours, could not sit down with us at the actual feast.

A few years later, when Sukuna was at the UN, we had him out for a few country weekends. He was the only guest I ever drove the 120-mile round trip into New York to fetch. That was partly real respect; but also, to some extent, precaution lest his unusual appearance stir up some fool passenger on the train. The problem wasn't simple. In some ways, he was well advised to keep to a costume that emphasized his exotic origin. West African blacks told me that in America they had far less chance of difficulty with headwaiters and such when they wore gaudy headgear and swathy garments. But I dreaded an ethnic-minded humorist confronted by a husky black man garbed in what looked like a woman's dressmaker suit. Remember this was forty years ago. Wishing to get Sukuna a guest card at a New York club, I wrote to the secretary, making it clear that he was as black as he was distinguished and his costume was helpfully distinctive. Back came a damping demurrer: A card would be issued if I wished. But had I considered that my distinguished friend might be cruelly embarrassed if some oafish member in his cups got funny about his complexion or his clothes? And who could guarantee something like that might not happen? I thought the point, though possibly casuistic, unfortunately valid and dropped the matter.

Actually the man was so solidly impressive, skirt or not, that the risk might have been small. Apparently he had no trouble at the Men's Bar (long since erased by feminist agitation) of the Roosevelt Hotel, where he was staying, even when it was full of Republican delegates to some convention. "Those

Republicans!" he said one evening to our guests. "Remarkable the things they say to one another! And they wear the most extraordinary clothes!" Nobody batted an eye. I was proud of them. They had seen enough of him to gather that several flavors of irony were likely to underlie much of what he said. Once he got discussing the West's curious folkways, British/ Colonial division: "Now there's that official visitors' book at Government House in Suva." This isn't verbatim but pretty close. "The proper kind of new arrival knows all about it and goes up in a taxi and writes down his name and where he's stopping. Then the governor's aide-de-camp makes inquiries and if the fellow sounds tolerable, he's asked to tea to give them a look at him and if he behaves well enough he's asked to lunch and eventually to dinner. . . . And nyether he nor the governor sees anything out of the way in the man's saying in effect, Here I am! I want to be asked to dinner! Among us Fijians that would be unthinkable. What about here in America? Would one do anything like that?"

I didn't get to know him well enough to call him "Joe," as his closest Western friends did. But I did risk a personal comment on his capacity for alcohol—which must have stood him in good stead at the Roosevelt bar. The occasion was a lordly luncheon given him by our good neighbors in the country, the Klopfers. Ten or a dozen at table; the only other guest I recall was the late Glenway Wescott from the other side of the county. Martinis. A sort of antipastoish first course, a delicate cold soup, sherry. With the main course, whatever it was, a magnum of wonderful red Burgundy from Donald Klopfer's capacious cellar. With dessert (chilled fruit compote, I think), champagne. Sukuna paid due homage to each and every glass and rejected no refills. With coffee excellent cognac. The postprandial talk turned to drinking—as well it might—and specifically to the lore of Bourbon whiskey. Asked what he thought of Bourbon, Sukuna said he had heard of it but had yet to try it. Donald broke out a bottle of something 100-proof bonded. Sukuna tried it straight; then with a splash of branch water for tradition; then on the rocks, discussing each version with grave attention and eventually pronouncing Bourbon indeed a splendid institution.

I had fallen out, even refusing brandy, because I had

homeward driving to do. But as I drove, I made bold, as I'd not have done after a cold-water lunch, to remark to Sukuna that, of all the workmanlike drinkers I had known, he showed least effect per ounce. I meant it. So far as one could tell he had ingested nothing but rainwater for a month. (I was reminded of Robert Louis Stevenson's account of the prowess of another South Seas dignitary, Kalakaua, king of Hawaii: "What a crop for the drink! a bottle of fizz is like a glass of sherry to him; he thinks nothing of five or six in an afternoon as a whet for dinner.") "Ah," Sukuna said, "there was no cause for uneasiness. At Oxford I was widely known as omnibibulous Joe."

When we had people to dinner to meet him, their party phone calls next day usually rated him the most delightful weekend guest we had ever shown them. I vividly recall Sukuna in a large chair in our living room talking with pithy charm about heaven knows what with four or five assorted lady admirers in bright-colored dresses sitting round him on the floor—crimson, blue, gold, whatever, just as decorative as they were fascinated.

I felt touched as well as honored when, not long after Sukuna died at home in Fiji, his friends there asked me to come down and write a biography of him. Previous commitments made it impossible. In any case I lacked adequate acquaintance with the lush, harsh, unique environment whence he had sprung—so far, yet never for a moment losing his roots or his balance.

Sukuna's impressiveness owed much, of course, to his skill as amphibious partaker in both Western and his native worlds. Soon after meeting him down there, I spent a memorable afternoon with a middle-aged Polynesian of a different kind of impressiveness who had never been away from his native environment in a group of South Sea islands that, since he may still be alive and I'd rather not risk annoying him, we'll call the Aitutapus. And call him Motu, which means "island."

He was a physician-warlock specializing in venereal disease and a Polynesian version of psychiatry but well grounded in general sorcery and island medicine, which are closely intertwined. He occasionally killed people by magical remote control but only on rare occasions and for special, defensibly constructive reasons. Cautiously he made it clear that he never did so for personal purposes.

I met him through the local government doctor, Western trained, half Polynesian. Motu had come to him saying that familiar spirits had told him I had arrived seeking knowledge of the Aitutapus and he wished to help me. Down among the islands, what they call "coconut wireless" operates with remarkable speed. When the doctor took me to see Motu at his home up a half-overgrown back road, there was little ceremony, but I felt expected and welcome. The familiar spirits had evidently endorsed me, at least tentatively.

All he wore was a pair of beat-up chinos and an olive drab undershirt, relics of the American occupation of a neighboring island. His short, curly dark hair showed a grizzle of gray, his skin was getting leathery, but he was as smooth-muscled as a young man and moved springily, with easy balance. He laughed a good deal, usually at his own remarks, in a high, percussive chuckle with a suggestion of gloating; it was probably more for social lubricant than out of amusement as such.

His dwelling, set among coconut and papaya trees, was a run-down example of the local style of perpendicular poles for siding and coconut-frond thatch; on the main road the roofing would likelier have been the more admired corrugated iron. We met his ten-year-old daughter, who sat peering over his shoulder most of the time; and his twelve-year-old son, skinny and fierce-eyed, whose occult power to make diagnoses was indispensable to his father's practice. In old times Motu would have had no offspring, for celibacy was then required of healing wizards. But that old usage, like so many others, had crumbled away, and apparently having been incelibate had not interfered with development of his powers.

At one point the clairvoyant son brought us some papayas as presents; at another he fetched drinking coconuts that the doctor opened with the household cutlass (South Seas for machete). A pair of kittens, a nondescript dog, and a hen and chickens were in and out of our group in the shade. But the feeling, though informal, was businesslike, say, a press interview with a dignitary sure enough of himself to feel relaxed. I sat on a packing case that the daughter brought. The doctor, as though expressing his halfway ethnic position, sat on the ground with his legs out and his back against a palm. Motu sat cross-legged, as is polite in Polynesia, with flies coming and going on his bare feet. I admired his garden—the best kept I had yet seen in the islands—and then we settled down to questions. I asked how Polynesian physicians were trained. This is the gist of what I learned:

Doctoring—and witching—were dynastic matters. An incumbent practitioner chooses a close relative, usually male, for saturation with the family's exclusive lore of herbs, spells, massage, surgery, the full battery of therapeutic techniques handed down through the generations. This may start at the age of twelve and continue for twelve years in an on-the-job apprenticeship. Motu had a twenty-six-year-old son graduated and practicing on a sister island. Specialization also goes dynastically: Group A owns the cure for yaws, say, Group B for rickets. Park Avenue style, a physician-warlock sends patients to colleagues depending on what ails them. Motu's island had ten practitioners whose specialties pretty well covered standard indigenous ailments. Diseases that came with the white men, for which local treatments were lacking, were consistently sent to the doctor's government hospital—after all, white men naturally have a handle on their own complaints. Pneumonia, for instance, for which Motu's likes had no procedure, called for the new sulfa drugs. Motu conceded great virtue in many white men's methods. But the mere mention of antisepsis made him laugh in amiable scorn.

Contrary to the usual notion, he said, gonorrhea afflicted Polynesia long before whites arrived, and his cure for it came from the legendary island of Hawaiki, whence his people originated. He went off into the brush and brought back the crucial ingredient, a two-leaved herb with a gnarly, whitish root. The right number of the right-size roots are crushed and steeped in the milk of ripe coconuts along with the right number of leaves—it goes by fives—from three particular trees, two of which he pointed out nearby. The patient drinks the mixture, after which he gets only the thin contents of drinking coconuts and is forbidden to urinate until he absolutely cannot stand the torment. Frantic urination completes the cure. It hardly needs saying that while the mixture is preparing, proper spells have to be recited in the group's graveyard or other environment rich in associations. Under missionary influence, Motu said, some of his colleagues might omit the spells when preparing prescriptions. He was noncommittal about possible loss of efficacy but did insist that his cure for gonorrhea would be useless without a full set of spells.

It was better to gather herbs wild as needed than to cultivate them. All were specifics: A poultice of this plant ripened ulcers; another checked the general infection that might otherwise develop a new ulcer elsewhere. It would have been rude to ask whether, if herbs sometimes worked without spells, spells sometimes worked without herbs, but Motu obviously relied on spells alone for some physical effects. One of his incantations would sterilize a married woman who wanted no more children. It would work whether or not she knew it was being applied. When he thought his family large enough, he had worked that spell on himself without diminishing his libido. Anthropologists have long acknowledged that Polynesian magical killings, sometimes called "praying-to-death," sometimes "Maori bullet," work well when the victim is aware or suspects he is under attack. Motu insisted that his lethal techniques worked regardless. Zestfully he described a case of a victim gradually succumbing under successive paralytic strokes.

He often resorted to massage where a Western doctor wouldn't, to hasten the knitting of a broken limb, for instance. He treated prolapsed uterus with a wide belly band of braided coconut fiber. We didn't go much into surgery, in which Polynesians are traditionally handy with shark teeth or the razor-sharp edges of bamboo splinters for scalpels. He did show me a tool for treating dark bruises—a flexible stick a foot long with a tiny, needle-sharp shark tooth lashed boathook-fashion to one end. One held the tooth over the bruise and tapped with the other hand so the point bit lightly and rapidly into the discolored area. Gaily he demonstrated on my trouser leg, making popping sounds to accompany the vibration.

He and his colleagues had little economic reward. Gifts from patients, yes, but seldom of substantial value even in the elementary local terms. Motu, like his less formidable neighbors, depended on his own coconuts, papayas, taro, sweet potatoes, and chickens with some cash from desultory crops of tomatoes. His reward was the prestige due his skills and the satisfaction of carrying on the old folks' traditions.

Like certain other local physicians, he was a deacon in the local church, a massive edifice of coral blocks attesting that Christianity had been on the island for over a century. He seemed to feel no inconsistency between a diaconate and eminence in the black arts. Indeed, he admitted being mostly heathen still and resenting the cash contributions that the church exacted. He had little use for the Christian God anyway, impishly pointing to the sky and saying that god up there was too far away to be of much practical use; far better the old Polynesian gods who knew local ways and, the lesser ones anyway, aided physicians. He thought that the local missionary, a brisk little Briton, was jealous of warlocks like himself. But he went along and deaconed partly because it fitted his social standing, partly because he approved of Christianity's success in suppressing the petty but destructive civil wars that had formerly kept the Aitutapus in chaos.

He really went out of his way to interest me. He gave a mock-up demonstration of how, in the old days, a warlock would take possession of the powers and body of a rival. He gathered a couple of small red fruits locally used for necklaces; turned his battered straw hat upside down to represent a vessel for steeping certain herbs in water; into it popped the fruits, chose one for use and, using me as dry-run target, threw it in a clean hit on my breastbone. It was essential, he said, that I should have been unaware of his intent before the throw. Given that, provided nobody had been allowed to witness his preparations, from then on my spells and daily life would be hopelessly at Motu's command. I said that might lead to bad feelings. With an amiable grin, he said in its time that sort of thing had caused many a bloody little war.

His assurance, brash in fact but not in manner, made me think of some young physician holding forth on psychosomatics. What about dentistry? Until whites' alien foods came in, his people had had no tooth troubles. (That needs qualification, but there is something in it.) He did not sound like a quack. Quacks usually run down both established medicine and their rivals in quackery. Later he took me to see relics of the old prewhite culture—great stone platforms of black boulders hidden away in the rank, breathless bush farther inland. Those old stones had carried great magic. I was struck with Motu's being so jaunty about them, resting a casual foot on the edge of a platform or a casual hand on the standing stone on which the great chief had sat for some ceremonial purpose. Clearly he was well at ease with such things, like an engineer familiar with the switchboard of a high-voltage power station. In thanking him I said I supposed no other man in the Aitutapus would have known those places so well. No, he said in thoughtful disclaimer, at least one other, maybe two.

Next day the missionary alleged to be jealous of Motu confirmed for me with a sigh that many of his flock still took too much stock in witching and magic.

My only other contact with the black arts—so far—came in a TV broadcast in Chicago of Bob Cromie's excellent *Book Beat* program. Aware I'd be out that way, Cromie asked me to come on the show, and I didn't notice that the date was October 31. When I arrived at the studio, Cromie was his usual genial and astute self, but I was startled to find that my fellow guests were a sort of convention of the occult arts apropos of Halloween— a couple of practicing warlocks, a connoisseur of classic voodoo, a veteran water dowser, a learned astrologer, with me cast, apparently, as contributor of pertinent American folklore. Feeling rather fish-out-of-water, I kept as low a profile as politeness permitted and came out scatheless. Nor did anything really bone-chilling come from the others. Cromie apologized about that. He said he had hoped to have Sybil Leake, the nation's premier witch, as headliner, but when he finally learned how to reach her and gave the invitation she had wired back that Halloween was her annual religious festival night and she always spent it communing alone with her guiding powers, black or white she didn't say. Cromie kept a straight face. I don't think I quite managed it.

What we were doing in the South Seas, meeting Tugi, Sukuna, and Motu, may need explanation. Early in World War II I signed with a publisher to do a book after the war about that part of the world because the United States, long potent down that way, would be more or less in charge when shooting stopped. In the intervals of war-connected writings, I read intensively on the history and cultures of the region. And in late spring 1946 my wife and I sailed from San Francisco in the old *Matsonia* (we had first known her in 1935 as *Malolo*, a.k.a. *Marollo*, Matson Line), just taken off transport service and refitted to resume passenger service to Hawaii.

Awkwardly titled *Anatomy of Paradise,** the eventual book did well. It was a minor Literary Guild selection and, as aforesaid, won an Anisfield-Wolff award. But that finished product in print necessarily left out the shaggy details of our legwork consequent on the South Pacific's being most deplorably out of whack so soon after the war. Hence our absurd problem— our Old Man of the South Seas—of *how to get to Tahiti.* For a year and a half of diplomacy, legwork, fretting, and frustration we lived, slept, and ate that question. And Tahiti was a must. Thanks to two hundred years of popular balderdash, a book on the South Pacific lacking some account of Tahiti would be like a book on Thanksgiving unaware of turkeys. Yet for two reasons, with both of which we grew miserably familiar, the place promised to be inaccessible.

First, transport, along with almost everything else, was badly fouled up. That hampered us throughout our year among the islands, but as to Tahiti things were really black. There was no air service whatsoever into the Society Islands, of which Tahiti is focus; and in early 1946 the only shipping line calling there was a New Zealand outfit that wouldn't book women. All we could do was keep on prowling the rest of the region and hope that as things shook down, some means of getting there would somehow materialize. Second, the French government, in charge of Tahiti, didn't want to let us in. It was nothing personal, just that the French colonial authorities had thrown in with Vichy and now could not forgive Americans, any Americans, for the United States' share in having turned that into a calamitously bad bet. Their tempers were specially edgy because the U.S. Navy had built an air base on Bora Bora, one of Tahiti's sister islands. After V-J Day, the navy invited the French to buy the installation at a reasonable price to be negotiated. The French,

---

*Some weeks before publication, but when it was much too late to change, the publisher's advertising agency came up with, and used as headline, the phrase we should have used as title: *Both Sides of Paradise.*

scenting a necessitous bargain, offered some derisible amount, something like twenty-five thousand dollars if I remember rightly.* Understandably annoyed, the navy dismantled the base right down to the coral, removing Quonsets, radio and radar, fuel tanks—the runways would have gone too if the Seabees could have managed it. No other island in the group had an airfield, which explains Tahiti's lacking air service for us or anybody else.

Our first glimpse of how sticky getting there would be came when our New York travel service, arranging pertinent visas, reported that, after some weeks of runaround, an understrapper at the French consulate-general had warned them privately that they were wasting their time. Between policy and bad feeling, visas for Americans, let alone writers, were out of the question. Dead end. We bemoaned our predicament in the hearing of a good friend who happened to be doing business with a French industrialist who was close to a highly placed French politician. Pressure applied through him was zealously followed up, step by molasses-slow step. Cable costs came to some sixty dollars (say, three hundred dollars now). Eventually word from on high reached the consulate, for here was a note in the mail: If M. Furnas cared to pay a call there, matters could be arranged.

Only . . . At the consulate I was handed a mass of papers to fill out—the most elaborate nonsense I ever encountered. For each of us there was a questionnaire four pages long. Then each had to procure from our local police—the French hadn't thought of the IRS and the FBI—a certificate that no criminal charges were pending against us. Then each had to supplement the questionnaire with a five-hundred-word statement— in French—of why we had to visit Tahiti. And several other paperwork absurdities that I've forgotten. Except for the police certificate, where triplicate was enough, it all had to be in

---

*Just before we left the South Pacific, the French reopened the matter, trying to get at least the basic equipment returned. How it finally worked out I don't know. But my wife, whose French was far, far better than mine, was asked by both the French aviation colonel sent out to negotiate and the U.S. Navy four-striper commanding the base at Pago Pago in American Samoa, to act as interpreter between them. Neither she nor I had the faintest idea what was the French for *windsock* or *runway*. Gamely she did what she could with me cheering from the sidelines; and at the end the Frenchman kissed her hand and said: "Ah, madame, la France est bien redevable."

seven copies, no carbons accepted, every page signed. I still suspect that some of those details were dreamed up specifically for us by some vice-consul sulky because Paris had overruled him.

We had our little essays vetted by an expert in the language and got all the typing done. And here I was at the consulate handing the sheaf of papers over along with our passports for the well-earned visas. No, no, nothing so precipitate. Monsieur evidently was not aware that no visas would issue until he and madame had each deposited in the Tahiti branch of the Banque d'Indo-Chine three hundred dollars in French francs to make sure we did not become public charges and could be deported at our own expense if we proved undesirable; *and* showed the New York consulate-general receipts witnessing that the money was well and truly there. I had the devil's own time finding a New York bank that would undertake such a transaction. One after another expressed surprise that the Banque d'Indo-Chine was still in business in view of the recent Japanese occupation. But eventually some bank did ascertain that a Paris address was available and remitted six hundred dollars to same with instructions to forward it to Tahiti by any surviving means (it must have been radio) and cable acknowledgment to me. It sounded impractical, for postwar communications down that way were utterly discombobulated. It proved to require only a couple of weeks, however—and cable tolls toward three figures. When I turned up again at the consulate with receipts in hand, the sound of grinding teeth behind the counter was plainly audible. But the visa stamping—involving fees, of course—got done with triplicate copies of some of the original papers given me to show the Tahitian authorities. For the next ten months that sheaf of costly obfuscation—it should have been on platinum foil—never left my righthand inside jacket pocket.

Now all we had to do was get to Tahiti. It was more trouble than Dorothy had getting to the Land of Oz. All the while we were busy in Hawaii, Micronesia, Fiji, Samoa, the Cooks, New Zealand, and so on we had to expend extra time and energy on trying to find out how to manage that. We couldn't afford to charter and otherwise there was nothing available, nor would there be for a year or so. After months and months, however, one momentous day we learned that the French were restoring the Messageries Maritimes' prewar service round the world by way of Suez, Saigon, New Caledonia, thence to Tahiti!—and home via Panama. The first ship in the service had already been assigned—an elderly cargo liner of limited passenger capacity that was unlikely to have room for way passengers Tahiti-bound. Every other French *colon* stranded by the war would be pulling wires to get a passage home in her. The best we could hope for was what the Islands then called MOF—mattress on floor. Okay, we had to get to Tahiti if we slept on deck. Early in the war, New Caledonia (the large mineral-rich French island northeast of Australia) had been an important staging area and the New Zealand Air Force was still running a courier service of C-47s thither. To New Caledonia we went to hope for the best, and meanwhile to learn about the island.

After naggingly numerous weeks the ship reached Saigon, New Cal next . . . sailing from Saigon postponed . . . rescheduled . . . then promised so definitely that we packed up. Tahiti actually began to sound substantial instead of an abstraction invented to plague us. The ship arrived, but with her came disquieting rumors that she would scrub Tahiti and go home via Suez . . . No, the Tahiti *escale* was restored, only a few days now. . . . Then defeat. The crew had left a number of lucrative black market deals unconsummated in Saigon and refused duty unless the ship returned there and home via Suez. The home office gave in and ordered her home the wrong way, leaving us as many hundreds of miles as ever from Tahiti. We were too depressed to get much comfort out of having been spared what certainly would have been a hell-ship voyage. Quarters unspeakable probably; officers certainly in bad humor; crew half mutinous . . .

Being thus marooned was less enjoyable because Nouméa, New Cal's metropolis-port, was a dispiritedly feckless place where the United States was unpopular for three reasons: One, it had, as aforesaid, helped pull the Vichyite rug from under the colonial French. Two, after flooding the island with heavy-spending, easy-mark GI's, Washington had repatriated most of those golden-egg-laying goslings—end of bonanza. Three, assuming that eventually Japan would win and take over New Cal for its minerals, many *colons* had buried their hoards of

U.S. currency. Now exhumed, the paper used by the U.S. Bureau of Printing and Engraving had so rotted and mildewed that it was no longer acceptable.

The *colons* and the government bureaucracy were in turn deservedly unpopular with most of Nouméa's population—indentured labor, mostly male, some female, recruited from Tonkin (now North Vietnam) before the war to work the mines, hew the wood, draw the water, cultivate plantations, and perform all the other drudgeries that the native, very black Melanesians could not or would not buckle down to. Such exotic labor had always proved a headache when resorted to in Fiji, Samoa, Queensland. In New Cal consequences were specially dismal because the indentures of most of these woebegone, slender exiles had expired during the war. They were entitled to be sent home as per invoice and theoretically would be replaced by other Tonkinese banishing themselves for a few years to obtain some hard cash. Only times had changed. The fortunes of war had undermined whatever respect for France Tonkin had ever had. Few fresh recruits would be forthcoming. And suppose some did consent, where were the planes or ships to fetch them and take their predecessors home? Anyway, to fulfill the agreement would deprive New Caledonia of its indispensable dishwashers, pick-and-shovel brigade, crop hoers. The situation had its own realistic logic but not of a sort to reconcile the Tonkinese to this flagrant breach of faith. The only things distinguishing them from slaves were that they were paid one way or another and could not be sold from one employer to his neighbor. None could blame them for bitter resentment.

We knew them chiefly as servants at the hotel where we spent weeks of vain waiting. Their surliness and sloppiness, however understandable, did not enhance whatever charm they normally possessed. They mopped the dining room at lunchtime because that enabled them to slosh the mop over the guests' feet. They had to be bribed to make up the room, let alone find clean linen; a pack of cigarettes (valuable there and then) a day was only a beginning. Expostulation was difficult because we had had no previous need to learn Tonkinese and their French was the baby-talk pidgin of France's Oceanic possessions: "Moi nettoyer chambre," that sort of thing. Complaint to the manager was fruitless. He was a hard-eyed *colon* with no use for any of his alien guests, who, being Australian, New Zealander, American, Dutch, and Free French, had all been on the wrong side of the war. Or maybe he was just a constitutional misanthrope. He snarled at one for paying the weekly bill, and to remark that a certain dish was noticeably palatable made sure it would never reappear. Between him and his staff his was the second worst hotel in the world. (The worst will be described later.)

Fortunately most of the guests, semistranded like us, were very pleasant. Our two Australian couples were good company; so were the RNZAF representative and wife; so was the sweet-tempered, matronly French lady who had consorted with an American colonel, now gone home, and was cherishing his handsome collie, whom she called Tedd*ee* and consoled when he mourned his departed master. The U.S. consul, Bob Brown, a compact, able, and obliging young fellow, knocked himself out to be helpful. Three of the above-mentioned couples became keep-in-touch friends whom we have visited in their various eventual homes, and vice versa.

What finally blasted us out of limbo was word that the U.S. Air Force, the only available eastbound transportation, was closing its New Caledonia base. Never mind Tahiti, we had better be on its final flight to Fiji. And no sooner had we left the baleful atmosphere of the Nouméa hotel than our luck changed. We were hardly unpacked in Fiji when we learned that Tahiti had suddenly became accessible. The French were sending it a new governor. The RNZAF was providing a special plane to take him, his wife, and a French Colonial Service inspector to their new posts via Fiji, Samoa, Rarotonga (refueling stops), and on to that stripped-naked airfield on Bora Bora, thence to Tahiti by interisland mailboat—and the RNZAF, whose flight crews and ground personnel we already knew well, would be charmed to take us along. Better still, the French party were to stay overnight in Samoa with our very good friend, New Zealand's governor there. That made sure our relations with M. et Mme. Haumant and M. Lasalle-Serré would be cordial.

One vestige of the hotel's hex popped up, however. At Rarotonga Dr. Tom Davis and Lydia, the local chief medical officer and his nurse-wife, a handsome and hospitable couple whom we knew from a previous stay, put us up overnight. After dinner that evening came the local RNZAF manager in a dither. All our luggage except our overnight gear had been missent to New Zealand. Oh, yes, it would be retrieved eventually but to wait for it in Rarotonga would mean that the special plane for Tahiti would go on without us and God only knew when anything else would be flying to Bora Bora. So far as the RNZAF was concerned, probably never again.

There went all our clothes but what we stood up in *and* all the notes, rough drafts, crucial reference books, and typewriter essential for work on the book. We were aghast but probably would have been even more so had not our months and months in the South Pacific broken us in to the way things down there were always more or less out of sync—like that ship's movements being governed by the crew's black-market deals. The Davises, old South Sea hands and then some, barely tut-tutted. They assumed that we'd naturally go right on to Tahiti considering ourselves lucky to have toothbrushes and shaving tackle, cosmetics and night things. They got out a large suitcase and put into it some spare clothes for me, mostly the ragged white ducks that Tom used in the operating room, and for my wife several dresses of Lydia's easily spared because she was rather too pregnant for them to fit. Fortunately we were respectively much of a size. Off to Tahiti in the morning!

We found Bora Bora memorable not only for how lovely it looked as we banked to land on that notorious airfield—it is in my view the most beautiful island in Polynesia—not only because it meant the unattainable was actually attainable, but also because it afforded us an unforgettable experience of another sort. The Bora Borans, alerted by radio that the new governor was coming, had set up a great feast for him. That evening the French party, the RNZAF flight crew, and the Furnases were superlatively speeched at, sung at, danced at, and fed to bursting on local delicacies—a first-class Polynesian "do." We were all particularly taken by the delicate texture and exquisite flavor of a local shellfish, new to us, resembling a prehistoric trilobite six or seven inches long.

Next morning the mailboat sailed with us for Tahiti by way of Raiatéa. She had begun life as William Wrigley, Jr.'s yacht—

smallish but comfortable, for she still had most of her million-aire-fashion fittings, albeit neglected, but was skittish in a sea-way. It was soon clear that our French friends were poor sailors. But *mal de mer* was soon overlaid by a devastating counterirri-tant—the momentous consequences of that Lucullan feast the night before. It was the second worst case of food poisoning my wife and I ever knew. (The worst was in St. Rémy-de-Prov-ence due not to *fruits de mer* but to a cheese that had developed a most original flavor.)

Wrigley's yacht builder had shamefully scamped the plumbing. There were tense moments as three French and two American sufferers sought to combine courtesy with ur-gency. The captain, unaffected because he had not attended the party, had a sound explanation for our misery. Delays en route had kept our plane from arriving on the day set. Un-aware of that, the Bora Borans had everything cooked and ready twenty-four hours before we arrived. Naturally reluc-tant to discard all that good stuff and start over, they had kept the fancier items—unrefrigerated, of course—and in all inno-cent hospitality served those shellfish crawling with cataclysmic Bora Boran microorganisms.

Swimmingly, however, the old yacht made her rounds. Fortunately the population of Raiatéa had not planned a wingding for the new governor, so we just delivered the mail, shook hands, and went on. At about 2:00 A.M. the final night, we came alongside at Papeete, chief town of Tahiti, prime fo-cus of the South Seas legend.

It should have been a great moment. Presumably the ghosts of Fletcher Christian, Herman Melville, Robert Louis Steven-son, Pierre Loti, Henry Adams, Paul Gauguin, and W. Somer-set Maugham (only he was still alive then) hovered over the feebly illuminated quay. If so, they were invisible in a dismal dimness inconsistent with a welcome for a new governor. It was a ghastly hour to begin with, and though one might have expected at least ceremonial music to brighten things up, not even a bugle weighed in. The only honor guard was a loose group of a dozen or so white-clad officials. Apparently the bu-reaucracy of Tahiti saw small reason for fulsome courtesy to usurping interlopers sent by Free France.

Down the yacht's ladder came M. Haumant, Mme. Haumant, M. Lasalle-Serré, Mrs. Furnas, Mr. Furnas. As Mr. Furnas touched ground, a white uniform popped up to ask had he permission to land, a matter that Haumant had never bothered to bring up. Gloatingly, triumphantly, Mr. Furnas flashed his sheaf of papers. But Haumant heard the question, turned, flapped a hand at the questioner, and uttered a highly idiomatic French word best spelled "Ptttttt!" Anticlimax! The officious official turned away. After all those costly, exasperating goings-on the year before, the hard-won papers never saw use.

Obliging members of Papeete's expatriate colony lent us more clothes. That was necessary because local stocks of wearables had vanished during the war. From a Chinese shop I bought the only pair of cotton slacks available.

The view of Moorea across the water from our thatched-hut hotel colony up the shore was almost worth all the trouble. And beyond that our stay was remarkably educational. For instance, when a French medical officer told us he was eager for a supply of penicillin (then just coming into general use) because the VD rate among Tahitians was known to be 80 percent, we asked what about the other 20 percent? He said they had yet to be tested. And as though doing his duty by the stereotypes in books and movies, the U.S. consul was shacked up with a local Polynesian belle, and anybody needing a document validated had to get there before noon while he was still sober enough to sign his name.

To Tahiti I owe my only claim to persisting literary fame. Now and again still another gargly article or book about Tahiti mentions disapprovingly the curmudgeonly journalist who once wrote that it was "Tobacco Road with palms." That was me. Only proper credit is never given.

It was our privilege to be visiting Tahiti at the first time in the two hundred odd years since it first charmed white interlopers that it could have been described as "off the beaten track." Only a few years later it was back on every travel agent's agenda. Nowadays practically all tracks are at least potentially beaten. That may be just as well. The connotations of the phrase were sniffily snobbish. Invidiously one spoke of "places where tourists never go," "where you never find Americans or Germans." There the rose-hip strudel still had the traditional crusty-

tender texture and the perfect beaches remained innocent of
two-legged life except the *opukaikai* birds working out their
pecking order in their idyllic fashion. I have followed a few
such recommendations. My first visit to Venice—tourist-rid-
den but the most admirable thing in Europe—began woefully
in a tucked-away *locanda* guaranteed to be frequented by only
genuine Venetians. There they were too, taking in stride the
obscure local canal where sluggish currents concentrated all
the decayed oranges, worn-out brassieres, empty sausage skins,
deceased fauna, cigar butts, and less identifiable flotsam collected by the Queen of the Adriatic for several months. The
plague of flies in that unspoiled little beach village on the Côte
d'Azur circa 1934 was thicker than what Moses inflicted on the
Egyptians.

Such mishaps reenforce the commonsense principle that
usually, not always, the track to Upper Barataria is unbeaten
because the country is damned uncomfortable or ugly or dull
or unhealthy or dangerous or any combination of two or more
of those attributes—anyway nowhere anybody would go without pressing necessity. Forty years ago the towns on the right
bank of the Rio Grande were cases in point, probably still are.
I visited them not in quest of exotic amenities but because of
reporting assignments. At about the same time I went to Nicaragua, not because it was obscure and sounded romantic but
because I was interested in the Nicaraguan Canal scheme, then
temporarily reviving, and in William Walker, the "gray-eyed
man of destiny" whose paranoid capers down there more or
less pioneered the Latin American filibustering industry. The
Nicaraguan consul in New York refused to accept any such
grounds for granting me visas. He was almost candidly explicit
about his assumption that since I represented no government
or industrial agency, I must be up to something clandestine,
probably revolutionary. In his view, business or revolution were
the only two conceivable motives for visiting his fatherland.
Fortunately a Nicaraguan I had recently had a drink with in
Detroit had given me a note of introduction to his cousin, one
of Nicaragua's oligarchy. Only the sight of that persuaded the
consul that I was not one of Walker's great-grandsons hoping
to take up where the old gentleman left off.

Apparently the management of Managua's hotel alerted the

government tourist office. It consisted of a diffident little man who brought round a bundle of leaflets poorly printed in Spanish and significantly yellow on the edges. We were, it developed, the only tourists he had ever dealt with. The hotel's small swimming pool contained no water. Managua was uniformly dusty, discouraged, run-down, and so poverty-stricken that my Detroit acquaintance's cousin never let his chauffeur buy his black Packard limousine more than a gallon of gas at a time, for any left in the tank was sure to be siphoned off. We called on the American minister, Meredith Nicholson, once a best-selling Hoosier novelist—I knew his sons as fellow members of the Corpse Club in Indianapolis—to whom we had a letter. He was miserable with malaria, whispering heavy apologies for being unable to entertain us because his wife was even worse stricken.

Another hazard "off the beaten track" is the curse of Babel. European schools are deservedly admired for their effective teaching of foreign tongues, but even mildly adventurous travelers often have reason to mistrust glib assurances that in Paris, Amsterdam, or Florence "everybody speaks English." To say that convicts the speaker of never having strayed beyond the concierges of high-ticket hotels and the headwaiters of expensive restaurants. Outside the Ritz circuit, things can cloud up in grotesque ways.

An Englishman once told me that one could go round the world knowing the local words for only two things: W.C. and beer. I saw that tested during a very pleasant and fertile day in Helsinki. My wife and I went into a handsome café to rest our feet. A buxom young waitress appeared exuding Finnish goodwill and saying what we took to be the Finnish for: "What would you like?" English puzzled her. French, German . . . we were running out of languages and she was winsomely distressed. The Finnish tongue, beautiful as I'm sure it is, is about as way out as Basque. Then up from subliminal depths where it had no right to be—the only Swedish I know is *smorgasbord*—came swimming the Swedish for beer: *öl*. I pronounced it with, I hoped, due value on the umlaut and victory!—good beer too.

As for the W.C.: That evening after we boarded the train for Leningrad, it was demonstrated how nearly useless sign language can be. Never mind those early explorers who learned through the big chief's signs that the Sacred City of the Seventh Sapphire was five days' journey away through heavily wooded mountains; they were either clairvoyants or liars. On the train was a clever young fellow passenger who had missed his dinner. For ten minutes he beleaguered a patient railway guard with signs of great ingenuity meant to convey "I'm hungry." All they got him was a glass of water politely tendered. Luckily he was standing near the washroom door, which had the usual VACANT/OCCUPIED sign above the knob—in Finnish, of course. Bright Boy opened the door, pointed to the visible word "VAPO," then to his belly. The guard laughed for five minutes, went away, and returned, still laughing, with a sandwich. There it is if you ever need it: *Vapo* must be Finnish for empty: God knows how it's pronounced. These things can be important: On that Volga steamboat our chuckle-headed Harvard junior used the ladies' washroom for two days before somebody saw him coming out of it and corrected his erroneous impression that ДАМСКАЯ meant "gents."

In Cadiz science came to my rescue. We needed hydrogen peroxide, why I can't recall. In a quaintly cool and darkish Spanish pharmacy we led with our two polite phrases, got courteous smiles, and began trying to pronounce "hydrogen peroxide" as a Spaniard might. To no avail. I tried to write it down but my handwriting is difficult for all, me included, and the absurdity of the situation did not improve it. High school chemistry to the fore! In large letters I wrote H_2O_2 and in two minutes it was all *Muchas gracias.* Later in that voyage I spent sodden hours on a savagely rainy day trying to acquire more than a tiny pinch of sodium perborate from each of a succession of pharmacies in Thessaloniki. Only in one place did I get anywhere with gestures meant to mean yes, thanks so much, but I want a lot of it, not just a pinch. Here they sent out back for Uncle Henry, who had been in the States but he had forgotten what little English he had ever acquired and the end product was a half-liter green bottle full of a slightly oily liquid that, when I opened it in the stateroom, smelled like dilute sheep dip. It went overboard in the Aegean Sea on the way to Istanbul.

Athens actually is well supplied with local citizens with

American or Australian pasts whose English is good and helpful. Less so in Thessaloniki. We needed a bank. *Taxi* is one of the very few reliable international words, but the waterfront afforded no such thing. Away we trudged, soon spotting a pleasant-looking, raw-boned woman whom we asked if she spoke English. "Nein, nein." My wife said ah, and went into competent German. Good-natured bewilderment, knowledge of German obviously very slim. "Geld wechseln," I said; it worked. "Ja! Ja!" she said, "Trapeza!" and, beckoning us to follow, set off at some four miles an hour. We scrambled after, wondering what a trapeze could have to do with our needs. Now and again one of us put on speed, drew alongside, and remonstrated: "Geld wechseln!" but that elicited only a firm: "Ja! Ja! Trapeza!" A mile or so farther on she halted and pointed triumphantly to a solid-looking building across the way displaying large white letters with her justification: ΤΡΑΠΕΖΑ, and below, much smaller, the names of a couple of British and American correspondent banks.

Explanation: We assumed, probably correctly, that she owed her minimal German to the Nazi occupation in World War II. As for why the modern Greek for "bank" is so like the term for the contraption that spangled creatures disport on at the circus, that is too complicated to go into here. For a hint, *bank* derives from the medieval Italian for a low table. Take it from there in the largest dictionary at hand.

The beaten-track rule is certainly worth heeding, but exceptions can occur. Only recently I read in the Sunday paper an account of one of the few places to which "off the beaten track" still applies: It might well be called St. Hellangone—a small island out in the middle of the South Atlantic eight hundred miles from the nearest land, of volcanic origin and so confusedly rugged that there is no place to build an airport. The only way to get there, unless you have a private yacht, is by a small (three thousand tons, eighty passengers, one class) British ship from England six times a year. Cruising speed fourteen knots, hence three weeks at sea with only two intervening ports. A week or ten days ashore while the ship goes off on local errands. Population very pleasant, mostly brown-skinned. Local history a compendium of old-timey colonial problems topped off by St. Helena's having been where the British sequestered Napoleon for safekeeping after his escape from Elba and the bloody sequel at Waterloo.

I reached for the telephone, nickering like a proverbial firehorse smelling smoke. In spite of a long waiting list a single stateroom soon turned up. RMS *St. Helena*—the only blue-water vessel still entitled to the "Royal Mail Ship" flag once flown by *Mauretania, Homeric,* and so on—was a seagoing joy. And her namesake island was a unique, sea-girt charmer more than worth the subsequent ordeal of twenty hours in the air flying back from Capetown.

Sometimes long shots do come home.

16

Down to the Sea
in Ships

WELL AFTER WE ARRIVED in Tahiti, Volcker radioed from Samoa that the RNZAF had retrieved our luggage and he was holding it, so we'd have to come back there to get it. We had vastly enjoyed our previous several weeks with him at Vailima, his official residence, built by Robert Louis Stevenson for his final years.* But logistics again! Getting out of Tahiti for Samoa or anywhere else began to seem as difficult as getting there in the first place. We joked bleakly about doing something for which the government would have to deport us, which would force them to whistle up some kind of outward-bound transport. Then came word that a Norwegian shipping company had assigned a passenger-carrying freighter, *Thor II,* to a service San Francisco to Papeete to Samoa to New Cal. Through a friend who knew her captain, we got booked. It took blasting to recover our six hundred dollars from the local branch of the Banque d'Indo-Chine. Had Haumant not intervened, it would probably still be there. But the bank disgorged, we finished our job, and we said a travelogue-style farewell to beautiful Tahiti and were off for another month with Volcker.

---

*Our long stays there set me planning the biography of Stevenson (*Voyage to Windward,* 1951) that followed *Anatomy of Paradise.* I had long contemplated writing about him, and breakfasting, lunching, and dining in the room he died in seemed to me to be telling me something. As much by luck as judgment the book drew on much previously unpublished material illuminating and clearing up many aspects of that most interesting man.

He died long ago. No doubt *Thor II* is also dead, sold to some fly-by-night flag of convenience or scrapped. She was our first freighter—a form of locomotion to which we grew addicted, pursuing it under nine or ten different flags for a large part of the ensuing thirty years. We were already ship-happy, of course. Fair warning here: there will be a lot about ships for a while. And it will be the trouble with Lord Howe Island all over again: Ships of the sort we delighted in will never be readily available again.

No more cozy little cargo liners or elegant all-first-class small liners or genial all-tourist-class liners. Even the great gilded three-class, five-day *Queen Mary* and *Ile de France* sort of thing that we had no time for is gone,* and the *United States,* the most cunningly designed merchant hull that ever propelled itself through saltwater, lies gathering barnacles in Norfolk. Only the *QE2* maintains something like that tradition for only part of the year, and once Britain tires of subsidizing her, she will never be replaced. Worse than all those deprivations, the break-bulk freighters that we valued so highly have been almost entirely superseded by container ships built without passenger quarters. Nowadays about the only way to cross the Atlantic (or the Pacific for that matter) is to huddle in the stuffy equivalent of a stalled over-the-road bus while females in uniform treat you as though you actually are what you feel like— a peevish convalescent in an overcrowded hospital.

My low opinion of airplanes persists in spite of my having learned a few years ago that the Wright Brothers' earliest experiments in successful heavier-than-air flight were zealously abetted by one of their Dayton neighbors, a certain Charles Furnas. Anybody with that surname spelled that way from the southwestern corner of Ohio is unquestionably somehow a relative of mine.

---

*In the mid-1930s we had booked a return passage from England in the old *Minne-waska,* all-tourist, of the Atlantic Transport Line. Arriving in London we learned that the International Merchant Marine (J. P. Morgan's shipping conglomerate), which owned Atlantic Transport, had scrubbed the operation. The IMM office explained that, under the circumstances, they owed us a top-class passage in their next sailing, meaning first-class, no extra charge, in the U.S. Lines' *Leviathan.* They were utterly startled when I said: "No thanks. What's available afterward that's not so fancy?" So we came home in Red Star's all-tourist plodder *Westernland* and enjoyed every shabby minute.

That ships have personalities is known. One morning on the fantail of the *Scythia,* when she and the sea were cutting capers for each other, I heard a deckhand doing some nautical chore remark to himself: "Why, the old girl flirts her arse like a duck!" The reader is already aware of the deep affection that the unlikely *Morinda* and *Yanawai* inspired in my wife and me. But did you ever hear Him say to Her anything like: "Honey, do you remember that dear old 767 that flew us to San Clandestino?"

It has taken me just twenty minutes to remember and list the fifty-eight ocean-going ships ranging in size from the *Queen Mary* to the *Morinda* in which we sailed between 1934 and 1981.* Who could pick outstanding favorites among so many? There was—it's all in the past tense—the Oranje Line's all-first-class *Prins Willem van Oranje* (eight thousand tons, Rotterdam to Montreal), maintained like a plutocrat's yacht by the owner. He personally chose her wines, and though she could take 120 passengers, he forbade booking more than 80 to make sure that everybody had solicitous service and lots of room. There was Cunard's all-first-class *Media* (nine thousand tons), a post–World War II fine lady with all her big sisters' elegance without white tie nonsense. Not that we regarded elegance. Just as much of a maritime charmer was the Royal Netherlands' *Oranje Nassau* (New York to Rotterdam via the Dutch West Indies and Madeira). She could exceed eight knots only with a following wind and her bottom was so foul that the captain deliberately ran her slightly aground in the mud coming out of the Paramaribo River in hopes of scraping off some barnacles. But we were in even less of a hurry than she was. Indeed we very seldom disembarked from any ship not feeling that the voyage was too short. The *Oranje Nassau's* East Indian cooks did a toothsome *nassi goren.* The first officer taught us to have a drop of Dutch bitters in our *jonge genever* before lunch. Her West Indian cargo-handling deck crew sang im-

*The list omits Norway's *Vistafjord,* a cruise ship in which we once made a convenience crossing of the Atlantic, and the coastwise ships, once numerous, that we used from New York to southern ports in the 1930s. History remembers those rather scruffy services for two things: Ira Gershwin's "boat dat's leavin' fo' New York" in *Porgy and Bess,* was one of the Ward Line Clyde-Mallory ships; and so was the *Morro Castle,* which burned disastrously off the Jersey shore in 1934.

promptu calypsos forward, one with the refrain "I goin' home an' tell my maw / About my trip in the *Oranje Nassau*." She shipped a deck cargo of dairy cattle at Port-au-Prince, which gave us the unsettling experience of waking to find a cow leering at us through the open porthole of our forward stateroom. After unloading the cattle at La Guaira, she went on eastward to a tiny port called Corinto where she was the first ship to call in years; the municipality threw a party built round the local rum, so old it poured like molasses.

Yet I always think of my first crossing of the Atlantic as essence of shipboard. Our fellow passengers at the *Pennland*'s doctor's table were all good company and one became a lifelong friend. The ship took eleven days to cross, with a well-chosen variety of weather. So good a time was had by all that nine days out we had drunk the bar dry of Amstel beer. She had no slot machines, health-spa facilities, Catskill-style entertainment, swimming pool, or bridge lessons. That *Pennland,* single-stacker, elderly, somewhat hen-shaped, was strictly a workhorse with a sound disposition accommodating people who had good reason to cross the ocean at moderate expense.

Appropriately my key memory of her is prosaic. Midmorning on a day of light fog and sporadic rain, I went forward into her bows, where anchor chains, bollards, winches, and the ship's bell were huddled together in damp half-light. The bell sat like an unpended mushroom, its edge dripping condensed fog. The foghorn's blatting set up intermittent and curiously pleasant quiverings underfoot. A lower than "moderate" sea was causing a merely tentative, dreamy roll. At half speed we were slipping ahead with just enough swish under the forefoot to show, in spite of poor visibility, that we were still progressing toward Bishop's Rock. It was all various shades of wet gray and though not silent, quiet . . . quiet. A shiny-wet seaman came plodding forward, tapped the bell ting-ting, ting-ting, and went aft again. For landsmen ten o'clock but at sea four bells. Ships no longer ring the old four-hour-watch bells. I last heard them in 1960.

When I think of being at sea, as I often do, the sound of the *Pennland*'s bell and those fifty-year-old circumstances are the essence of it.

* * *

After our propitious experience with *Thor II,* freighters—Norwegian, Dutch, American, Canadian, Swiss, French, Belgian—became the locus of an intermittently amphibious life that delighted my wife and me. We both loved just being at sea and luckily were both good sailors. Once the ship is off soundings, my nervous system gets a sort of blossoming lift. And since my head works better, much of my writing has been done on a card table in a stateroom or in the dining saloon between meals; or once in quarters so cramped that I worked with my feet in the bunk and the typewriter on my thighs. In a freighter a writer can expect regular hours, no telephone, no gussied-up distractions, fresh air ad lib, exercise ditto, and occasional ports for now-and-again breaks.

Many people tended to think in pulp-magazine terms of Tramp Steamers—the legendary, obsolescent, rusty half derelicts all cockroaches and smuggling, skipper seldom sober, accepting cargo, no questions asked, wherever offered. Such ships existed, probably still do under dubious flags in the interstices of the shipping world. But the vessels that served us so delightfully were usually well maintained, sizable (say eight to twelve thousand tons), more or less recently built, booked by responsible owners on regular runs from their home ports into the Mediterranean or down the west coast of South America or round the world—anyway on definite trade routes. Their passenger quarters ranged from adequate—somewhat hospitalish staterooms all steel panels and two-story bunks, private shower and toilet, usually built in World War II—to staterooms as ample as average first-class on the North Atlantic with very comfortable fittings. The cooking was, in American freighters, hearty and decent; in Europeans often admirable. Under whatever flag, nine out of ten officers were unostentatiously capable and pleasant, some very fine fellows indeed.

Even on the short North Atlantic runs, one was never sure when the ship would sail. A day or two late was normal. I recall frantic exceptions when she cast off a day or two early and we had to scramble half packed to Montreal or Norfolk. And once she sailed, anything might happen. At the U.S. consulate in Accra (Ghana) I had a casual chat with the captain of a Farrell Line freighter outward-bound down the West African coast; he said he understood we were going home via Farrell and he looked forward to picking us up when he came back homeward-bound in a few weeks. I said thanks but that would be too early, we had a lot to do. So, delays in West African ports being what they were, it was his ship we came home in over two months later. In Monrovia (Liberia) I had had a cable from Carl Brandt in New York, who knew little about freighters, saying a certain magazine editor wanted to see me, please return, cable exact date arrival. I cabled back something like: "Landing New York some Thursday between May Day and the Fourth of July." And our eventual sailing from Monrovia was, of course, put off several times. Each time the friends we had made during our stay came to see us off again, which used up most of the liquor supply we had laid in for the voyage,* and then she sailed in a hurry before we could replenish. All the way across we had to ration ourselves to one small snort per diem. A pleasant voyage even so: The captain played Monopoly earnestly and the chief engineer raided a shipment of movie films returning to a New York distributor and projected them on a screen rigged between the after king posts. No movie palace was ever like that: One sat facing aft in a deck chair with a blanket when needed, enjoying a gentle roll and a scrap of new moon and here was the garbage-collecting gondolier's song that opens *Trouble in Paradise* rolling out over the Sargasso Sea.

And when we did make port, it wasn't New York, of course, but Fall River, Mass. The experienced freighter addict took it for granted that she wouldn't make all ports on the original schedule, for throughout the voyage the home office, the shore agents, the busy radio, and the vagaries of international trade collaborated to revise any and all arrangements. What one heard at breakfast about the next destination was even money to be changed by dinnertime. One of my last freighters was scheduled for Rotterdam out of New York, but at the last minute was sent first to Baltimore. So off down the coast. Eventually I was wakened early by the familiar noises meaning we had come alongside at Baltimore. When I came on deck, there half a mile away lay the poor old *United States*, towering particolor

---

*In freighters bottle goods are usually sold by the chief steward at lower-than-shore prices; not in this ship, I forget why.

funnels and all. Overnight Norfolk had become our destiny; we never made Baltimore. These unanticipated shifts sometimes took you to places you had never heard of. Had the *Great Republic* not been diverted to Iskenderun, I'd never have known that is the Turkish name for classic Alexandretta and never have seen the amazing Hellenistic mosaics at Antikya that alone remain visible of what was Antioch, the Paris of the Near East, two thousand years ago. Had the *Export Agent* not made Ceuta, I'd never have seen General Francisco Franco's footprints preserved in bronze like the footrests of a shoe-shine stand to commemorate where he stood just before leaving to start the Spanish Civil War. I wonder if they are still there.

Freightering is best defined by extended example. Late in 1952 we were bound for West Africa from England in connection with a book on the history of American blacks. First Sierra Leone, then still a British colony, founded in the late 1700s as a refuge for freed slaves. The occasional small liners putting in there were booked solid for months and months. We booked on a Dutch freighter. But when we were on the verge of crossing to Antwerp to join her, her sailing was canceled. Have no uneasiness, said her London agent, go on to Antwerp and our agent there will take care of you. We felt plenty of unease but, lacking other recourse, went to Antwerp.

There a harried little man in a shipping office said yaw, yaw, on Tuesday you sail for Sierra Leone in the *Maloja,* new Swiss freighter, very good. Sternly I mentioned that we had paid for a private shower and toilet and meant to get them. It hurt his feelings. "Oh, sir," he said, "you have a suite." And so we did: little two-bed bedroom, a neat if cramped bathroom, and a tiny, cozy sitting room under the starboard corner of the bridge. What was Switzerland, the most landlocked country in Europe, doing with a merchant marine? With the lettering on the counter MALOJA/BASEL? She could never have been anywhere near her sponsor city half a mile above sea level and hundreds of miles up the too-shallow Rhine? Why, during World War II, the belligerents, for strategic, economic, and political reasons careful of Switzerland's interests, allowed her a few freighters under her own flag to fetch critical supplies from the outside world to Genoa, thence by rail. After the war that operation fused with the Swiss barge lines down the Rhine to Rotterdam so successfully that it was worth while to add this new, German-built *Maloja** to the fleet and put her on the profitable if headache-ridden West African run. Lucky for us.

Her deckhands were Swiss barge men already skilled in water-borne maintenance, line handling, and so on. But Rhine barges afford no blue-water experience, so her captain was Belgian, chief engineer German, first officer Dutch, chief steward Latvian. We passengers added to the United Nations effect: a Swiss consular officer and his Italian-reared Russian émigré wife taking up a post in the Belgian Congo; the consular dog, a black Spanish poodle; a Belgian Colonial Service officer returning from leave; we two Americans; and in Casablanca we acquired an Iranian bound somewhere down the coast. About him I recall only that he had long black curly hair controlled by a hair net. As to the others, the Swiss was a quiet man of goodwill; his wife a doe-eyed charmer; the Belgian all right as bureaucrats go; the mate and the chief genial but not chatty; and the captain a chunky, bullet-headed, black-eyed, terrier-nervous salt-of-the-earthling whom our three weeks on board made into a solid family friend.

His style of abrupt thoughtfulness emerged when we were well off soundings and he could relax, so far as he ever did. At breakfast he looked down the table at me: "Tomorrow is one of your holidays." I blinked, my wife looked blank. "Yes," he said, "something about thanking the good God. It is on my American calendar."† Ah yes, next day was the last Thursday in November; we had forgotten about it. "Thanksgiving!" we said. "What does one do on Thanksgiving?" "Well," my wife said, "mainly we eat too much turkey." The captain looked troubled, said he doubted the chief steward had a turkey in the freezer, summoned him. No turkey but an amazing variety of other things to become a most original Thanksgiving dinner washed down with champagne on the house somewhere at sea between Finisterre and the Canaries. Later, after we had

---

*I had never heard of Maloja either. My large atlas identifies it as the name of a minor Swiss mountain pass and the adjunct resort between Switzerland and Italy.
†His English was workably good, even better than is usual among ships' officers out of northern Europe's narrow seas. Indeed English is almost a lingua franca for master mariners, pilots, radio operators et al. throughout the blue-water world—happily for me, the poor linguist.

bunkered at Las Palmas, he took the ship an expensive number of miles out of her way to show his passengers the majestic cone of Tenerife with a fat tutu of cloud round its middle.

In time we learned—not from him—that he had been a leader in Antwerp's waterfront resistance to the Nazis. Several times, when we went to Antwerp to pick up a freighter, we had the luck to find him in port—by then he was skippering FINA tankers on the Persian Gulf run—and dined with him. And we stayed well in touch by mail. I recall one letter explaining the advantages, chiefly monetary, of tankering but ending with a pen-and-ink wail: "But not like being on the bridge of my beautiful *Maloja!*"

The dog was the best-behaved animal I ever knew, testimony from one who owned and highly valued dogs for fifty years. The name was Pye; we never made out why Manya Solberg thought that fitted. The other puzzle was why Pye, manifestly female, was "he"—something to do with hyperlogical application of the rules of gender in German? Anyway, the ambiguity had no warping effect on the animal's cheerful but dutiful disposition. "He" never barked out of turn, never made messes even under exigent circumstances, never strayed more than ten feet from master and mistress going ashore. When we went sightseeing in Dieppe and Boulogne on our way down-Channel, Pye led us down the accommodation ladder with such assurance that no French functionary on the quay, whether from customs or immigration, ever asked questions. Weeks later that quality stood us in good stead when we inadvertently infiltrated the French naval base at Dakar, Senegal, West Africa.

"He" and we five humans had taken the municipal ferry—a shabbily informal open launch—to the nearby small island of Goree, now a sort of park-resort, once a focus of the wicked old slave trade; the barracoon is preserved intact and that we had to see for the book. On our return to the landing at the indicated time, there was no sign of our ferry, instead a smaller and better-kept launch with a neater two-man crew. The Belgian persuaded us that the other craft had probably broken down, which seemed not unlikely, and this superior job was the replacement. So we embarked, the crew cast off and put-putted for shore. No word exchanged. Soon perplexities arose. Why did they steer well to eastward of the ferry landing? And why did they wear not the usual grimy skullcaps but clean white berets with red pompoms? Such headgear, we recalled, was part of the French naval uniform. This was a navy launch and we were being silently helped ashore smack in the middle of the French naval base. Obviously we had been mistaken for some party of navy-sponsored picnickers whom the launch was sent to fetch home.

Security! It took no morbid imagination to envision awkward consequences, not least because it might be the commanding officer's wife and cronies who were thus stranded on Goree. Shrinkingly we followed the old principle: When you have no notion what to do, do as little as possible. We said "Merci!" to the pompoms and set off, Pye ten feet ahead as usual, along a roadway leading straight inland. Its vista showed the main gate with a small guardhouse and an armed sentry. Sharing an unspoken sense of "Here goes nothing," we followed Pye. The sentry presented arms—in honor of Pye apparently—I unlimbered my Shortridge High School ROTC hand salute, Solberg and de Belder supplied Swiss and Belgian equivalents, and there we were safe on Dakar's dusty streets. We agreed that we owed our immunity to Pye. "He" so obviously had every right to do just what he was doing. Besides, would any conceivable spies or saboteurs take along not only two elegant ladies but also a middle-sized black dog? Not even James Bond.

We had already been to Casablanca—twice. The first time, as we anchored to await a berth, the ships shore agent came scurrying out in a rowboat shouting emergency instructions through a megaphone. He could not use radio because a strike had shut down most of the port facilities, radio included. We were to up anchor and go run our errands farther down the coast until things cleared up. Off we went to Agadir. Ninety years ago Agadir was in the headlines as scene of an aggressive demonstration by some of Kaiser Wilhelm's nice new men-of-war. These days, I understand, it is afflicted with high-rise tourism. In 1952 it was a sleepy, sloppy aggregation of skinny men in burnoose gowns, secretively walled-in dwellings, the odd camel—but all camels are odd—and up the hill the old walled citadel, a formidable, festering slum. It proved memorable because, though it did have a branch of a Casablanca bank and its staff spoke a crippled French, they had never heard of travelers' checks. There was a French-flavored beauty shop where Mesdames Solberg and Furnas had their hair done, but nobody in the whole settlement had ever heard of American Express (don't tell Karl Malden) or Cook's or Barclay's or was even aware that such negotiable instruments had been invented. We had stepped right out of the twentieth century. It made one understand how Ulysses must have felt when, obeying the oracle, he walked so far from saltwater that the Scythians, or whoever, took the oar over his shoulder for a threshing flail.

Then farther down the Moroccan coast to Safi, which nobody has ever heard of yet, a discouragedly minor version of Agadir. But it needed the myriad bags of cement in the *Maloja*'s forward hold, so we waited there several days for the rain to stop and we could unload them. Then the agent radioed that the strike was over, all is forgiven, come back to Casablanca. Never mind the movie, Casablanca was not only harsh but also dull. It was a relief to unload whatever was consigned there and be off southward round the legendarily perilous shoulder of Africa for Dakar and Freetown, Sierra Leone. Note now that whereas the *Maloja* was scheduled to get there in two weeks, what with dawdling in the Channel ports, leisurely bunkering, Casablanca's strike, and the hit-or-miss weather at Safi that inhibited unloading cement, we had been on board well over three weeks when we sighted the mountain back of Freetown that gave Sierra Leone its name. Had it been five weeks, we'd have been delighted.

Yet some unpredictable delays sometimes work out badly. The *Maloja*'s were what got us acquainted with the promised "worst hotel in the world." The British Colonial Office's public relations man there had been alerted about us, but by the time we arrived he had to take off on a leave that could not be postponed. The governor was away visiting other West African colonies. No U.S. consul to consult with. Whatever arrangements anybody had in mind for us had disintegrated in the hands of inexperienced local understrappers. We had nowhere to lay our heads but the local hotel.

It was the hotel that readers of Graham Greene's *Heart of the Matter* will recall; his description is a masterpiece of grisly detail. My wife and I had read *Heart* in preparation for Sierra Leone. As the ship eased into Freetown harbor, I reassured her about what we would be up against: This stepchild of a country would be no pleasure. We'd just have to put up with confusion, harsh reactions, chiselings, as necessary for getting the job done; but things probably wouldn't be as bad as Greene's account. After all, I reminded her, the succinctness necessary in writing telescopes situations, and novelists are entitled to put a special edge on their materials.

Some years ago a letter from Greene asked me for some details about his distant cousin, Robert Louis Stevenson, that I could supply. In answering, I wrote that I had long owed him an apology and had misled my wife—for the hotel was half again worse than his description. Only in one respect had it improved: Bedbugs were not as ghastly plentiful as the book said, which probably meant that since World War II DDT had reached Freetown. Beyond that, well . . . The beds in our room were decrepit and grimy and swathed in mosquito curtains that gave out clouds of ancient dust when touched and were rendered useless by numerous rents ineffectively repaired with safety pins. The carafe of water on the rickety little table had tiny bits of God knows what floating in it and as for its having been boiled—a precaution necessary thereabouts—it was soon clear that the very notion was absurd. Even when we persuaded the scrawny lad in charge of the rooms to supply fresh water we dosed it with Halazone brought along for such purposes and hoped it would work. For other liquid intake the beer at the bar was bottled, thank heaven, but the bottle necks had had lots of handling and the glasses were nicked around the edges and cloudy outside with the accumulated fingerprints of ages.

The bathroom window looked over the corrugated-iron roof of the cook shed. Its ridge pole was always crowded by a dozen or fifteen of the vultures locally depended on for scavenging. Theoretically they should have been out on the streets competing with their fellow birds for dead rats and decayed orange peels, but the odors welling up from below, where our food was cooked, kept them hopefully fascinated. That made sense, for English lacks the vocabulary to describe the hotel's cuisine. Our first dinner made it clear why the center of each table carried a great clump of all the world's most emphatically flavored bottled sauces—several brands of Worcestershire, A-1, tomato ketchup, walnut ketchup, several mustards, several versions of Tabasco, half a dozen others of which we had not been previously aware. Each of the other guests, mostly alien technicians installing things for the government, had his own formula for an eclectic condiment cocktail of half a dozen ingredients enabling him to choke down what appeared on his plate. What the original materials were was inscrutable. The house supported a large number of cats of various sizes and colors. We counted them before each meal. We survived only because the local general store run by Lever Brothers, the British soap firm then big in West Africa, stocked a few marginal comestibles, the most helpful being fancy biscuits and tiny cans of Gail Borden's condensed milk, the baby-formula stuff. After a few days of semistarvation, my wife literally lived on that.

One evening on the hotel veranda we were chatting over beer with a new arrival, a British supervisor of the chain of West African newspapers (so-called) operated by the *London Mirror*. We mentioned our eagerness to board the promised Norwegian freighter that would take us to the Gold Coast (now Ghana), our next objective. He asked where we were staying in Accra, the capital. We said we'd heard it had a hotel. "Yes," he said, "I was there a week ago. It'll make you think these were the good old days here." A bad moment, but no report on it because in Accra the U.S. consul and his English wife, bless their hospitable souls, put us up.

Eventually the Norwegian ship rescued us from Freetown. She was no spandy-new lady like the *Maloja*; sunk during the war, she had been raised and though rehabilitated, showed her age. Nevertheless please imagine what a shock her clean, roomy quarters and excellent food were. The most beautiful sight ever seen was the luncheon smorgasbord waiting for us when we boarded that memorable morning. The stewards were all women, squeaky-clean and smiling; the chief steward had once been landlady of a seamen's boardinghouse in Singapore, weighed at a guess three hundred pounds, was broad as the stateroom door and could have licked any two men on board. She didn't need to. The captain ran the bridge, the chief engineer kept the engines oiled, and Helga or whatever her name was bossed that ship Bristol fashion, good-naturedly but with in-depth authority. And her galley! That lunch was only a teaser. We joined the ship late in December but had a few days to acclimatize before her Christmas dinner, which otherwise would have been a really dangerous shock. It was as toothsome as the *Maloja*'s Thanksgiving effort and twice as copious, washed down with aquavit with beer chasers. Nobody stinted. I don't know who had to stay on the bridge. I still marvel that we didn't knock the continent of Africa slaunchwise.

For freightering under our own flag: In 1960 I had a novel half written. We booked ourselves out of New York for the maiden voyage of an American Export freighter for Naples, Leghorn, Genoa, round through the Strait of Messina to Venice, where we'd leave her, drive round for some weeks, and pick up one of her sister ships to go home in. Inevitably, at the last minute we learned she was coming into not New York but Norfolk, and never mind Naples, she was going straight through the Mediterranean to Port Said with eight thousand tons of wheat. Great scramble to procure Egyptian visas and off by overnight Pullman in the middle of a blizzard.

A fine ship she was. Stateroom no. 9, forward under the bridge, was the size of our living room with windows, not ports. The lounge for passengers and upper officers ran the width of the superstructure, all deep carpet and deeper armchairs; its glittering self-service bar had commodious lockers for one's supplies. A friend of ours in the shipping business in Norfolk came down to see us off with a case of Gilbey's gin out of bond. We had only four other passengers. One couple, of whom more later, had shipped a case of champagne and preferred that by themselves in their stateroom; the second couple were pleasant as could be but no confirmed tosspots, so our gin floated us and the officers nicely to Port Said; only about the time we sighted Cape Trafalgar the slop chest ran out of dry vermouth. The chief engineer took it on himself to go ashore at every port to hunt down Noilly-Prat or equivalent. Mrs. Pleasant and the purser proved to be demon Scrabble players, and my wife played the game brilliantly though not by the book.

In the old break-bulk freighters, one soon came to value the entertainment of watching unloading and loading, which beat sidewalk superintending all hollow. One hung over the forward or after rail while right and left local longshoremen manipulated electric winches that miraculously coordinated interminable wire cables and fifty-foot booms into obeying unspoken orders. Unspoken, not silent, for the winches kept up intermittent, nonverbal dialogues of noises between a whinny and a growl that dramatized the course of every slingload as it came swooping up out of the open hatchway. Far below in the hold a gang of ten or a dozen other experts juggled cases of canned tomatoes, bags of cement, crated small motors, kegs of beer, huge boxes of pork bellies, barrels of molasses, depending on where the ship was and whither bound. It was always a breathless moment when the new slingload took off from pier or hold, cleared the hatchway edge by inches, soared up or eased down before settling with anomalous gentleness. There is some fun in watching the Brobdingnagian shore equipment that handles containers off or on, but except for their colors of paint, all containers are alike.

Bulk wheat meant different handling, of course, of a striking sort. Presumably it had been loaded out there on the West Coast through a grain elevator's giant chute. Port Said had no such dehumanized gadget. Its unloading machinery consisted of a weak platoon of sparely made brown men standing up to their ankles in wheat and using metal scoops, the kind grocers used to keep in the coffee barrel, to fill gunnysacks. Even had they worked at a good clip, it was obviously going to take a while to bag those billions of golden grains. Observing their gracefully leisurely pace, the captain gloomily predicted we'd be there ten days. Actually it took twelve, costing God knows what in payroll, supplies, insurance, amortization, and so on. Yet in all fairness I should mention that the scoop-and-bag crew never wasted their employer's time by climbing out of the hold to seek a latrine to answer nature's calls. They just did it where they stood and resumed work. Never eat bread in Egypt.

Port Said is the northern terminus of the Suez Canal, and for further study we had a daily parade of most sizes and all kinds of shipping under half the world's flags. The dominant motif was tankers riding high and empty on their way to the

Persian Gulf or coming back wallowing deep to build up the western world's calamitous dependence on Mideastern oil. These were not yet the monsters designed to go round by the Cape of Good Hope but biggish girls for all that, the more striking because for some strange reason they were mostly painted in coquettish pastel shades. The sight of thirty thousand tons of tanker with a light apple-green hull and apple-blossom-pink superstructure is hard to believe; the variations, none plausible, included beige and baby-blue, lavender and deviled-egg yellow.

Within a few days it was so clear that the captain's pessimism had undercalculated that it was moved, seconded, and voted that we six passengers could apply for shore leave to go touristing in Cairo, only a hundred-odd miles away. This took some deciding. Lumumba had just been assassinated, and rumors implicating the CIA had warmed up anti-American sentiment. American cars were being burned in the streets of Cairo and so on. At the captain's suggestion, we three male passengers consulted the U.S. consul in Port Said. He said that if we went in a body with a guide he could recommend, used common sense about not making ourselves conspicuous, and didn't stray from the others, there was no grave risk. So off we went in an antique Cadillac war wagon in charge of a fez-wearing, voluble, and venal but on the whole reliable ornament of the Port Said tourist industry, such as it was.

"We" were, of course, Mr. and Mrs. Pleasant and the middle-aged couple who preferred to drink their own champagne. They had every right to, if they liked; and Mr. Backhoe—a highly affluent midwestern earth-moving contractor—was well enough behaved in a dim way. Mrs. Backhoe was the problem. An egg-shaped brunette who had been her husband's right hand in building up the business, she was soon known to the whole ship as the Queen of Diamonds. She wore them from breakfast to bedtime in her ears, round her neck, in rings and brooches and doubtless on her toes and in her navel, though we had no opportunity to check. As the trip to Cairo was shaping up, Mrs. Pleasant suggested to her that in view of the consul's advice, she should leave her pretty toys back on the ship. Mrs. Backhoe replied: "Oh, these are just my old diamonds. My good ones are in the purser's safe."

A memorable woman. The purser, Mr. Levy—not his real name but stet the connotation—was an obliging, capable young fellow who annoyed Mrs. Backhoe by not obeying dietary laws. She had been reading one of Herman Wouk's books calling American Jews to come home to Deuteronomy, so, though she was no more Jewish than she was a Parsee, she hounded him daily about eating bacon for breakfast. On the question of where to stay in Cairo, the Backhoes wanted the Nile-Hilton, but its prices were pretty rich for others' blood; we let it go at lunching in its dining room overlooking the Nile, which strikingly resembled the lower Mississippi, and Mr. Pleasant was delighted to find (it was Tuesday) that he could there attend the weekly powwow of the Cairo Rotary. Mrs. Backhoe, condemned to a French-flavored, dismal but decent hotel without a view, decided it was filthy, which it wasn't, and that she wouldn't undress for the several nights we slept there.

Her idea of keeping the party inconspicuous as we went sightseeing was to toss small coins, of which she had laid in a large supply, to the ragged children rife on Cairo's streets. The inevitable result was juvenile mob scenes joined by adults; and anybody remonstrating with her was reproached for hardheartedness. When we visited the pyramids, I had good reason to believe she had kept her word about sleeping in her clothes. Only Backhoe, Pleasant, Mrs. Backhoe, and I, in that order, climbed to the alleged royal burial chamber in the apex of the Great Pyramid. The interior ramp is very steep, a good 45 degrees, and the lady's looming proximity so close ahead of and above me wafted back unmistakable evidence of the firmness of her resolution. I was helpfully distracted, however, by the hazard she represented. Her idea of appropriate footgear for pyramid work was spike-heeled sandals. At a chivalrous guess she weighed 160 pounds. The steepness of the grade, the inadequate cleats for footing, and the height involved made a menacing combination; and each time the lady's foot slipped, which it did on every fourth or fifth cleat, I was sure she'd come blundering down and send us both helter-skelter down the ramp a few hundred feet to the solid granite bottom. A horrible way to die. I was almost hysterically relieved when she made it to the top and I could follow, no bones broken, into the dim chamber. It contained only an empty, built-in sarco-

phagus of dark stone like a bathtub for Beelzebub and an unmistakable odor of stale urine, doubtless human—what other
animal would have made that climb? I thought of the grain
scoopers back in Port Said and reflected that in some respects
Egypt had changed little through the centuries.

After visiting Tutankhamen's utterly astonishing treasure
in the Cairo Museum, we returned uneventfully to Port Said.
The ship was at last on the verge of emptying. Off we sailed
riding high, because eight thousand tons lighter, for Naples,
Leghorn, Genoa . . . On the way we encountered a curious
saltwater folk custom that may still persist: As we transited the
Strait of Messina between Italy and Sicily, locus of the classic
perils of Scylla and Charybdis, several skiffs came out from
the Sicilian shore, each with a man shouting and waving in the
bow. Briefed by the officers, we were ready. Each of us had a
tightly stoppered bottle containing a dollar bill and a letter
addressed to oneself at home. Each bottle was tossed overboard and the skiffs rowed frantically to get there first. It was
understood that the boatmen would buy an airmail stamp, mail
the letter, and keep the change. They faithfully did it too, net-
ting the equivalent of eighty cents. Since each skiff contained
two men going to all that trouble in hopes of eighty cents between them, it was obvious that in Sicily in 1960 things were
tough, maybe still are.

At Naples our first acquaintance with Pompeii and Hercu-
laneum. At Leghorn a side trip to Pisa that decided me that
the interior of the baptistery is the world's loveliest bit of architecture. At Genoa the news, not unexpected, that the ship
had no reason to go all the way down and round Italy again
to take us to Venice; the line's agent, all deferential apology,
sent us across to Venice by rail first class on the house. In
Venice I learned that the local seasonal dish of *bacala* (dried
cod) stewed with spices and served with diamond-shaped chunks
of yellow cornmeal mush, a specialty of nearby Vicenza, is a
masterwork worthy of Palladio in another idiom; and that one
of the very great pleasures is to get lost in the old city's irresponsible maze of narrow alleys and tiny squares. A month
later another export freighter picked us up in Venice and took
us home by way of Thessaloniki—visit to watch them oh-so-
carefully excavating Pella, Philip of Macedon's old capital; Iz-

mir; visit to Ephesus; Barcelona; incredulous look at Gaudi; Cádiz. That was freightering. I finished the novel two days out of New York.

Conventional travelers hearing about freighters used to assume that, with passenger lists so small, the presence of a clinker or two would be an unbearable calamity. The risk was there, of course. The sure preventive was to be the only passengers. On two blessed trips we had that privilege, for, though freightering was increasingly popular, a given ship seldom booked the legal twelve maximum.* In any case it was odds of nine out of ten that our fellow pilgrims would range from tolerable to highly companionable. For in its heyday, freightering did not appeal to fat cats and stuffed shirts. The Queen of Diamonds was highly exceptional. Then there was the bad luck of which I was inadvertently the cause for an innocent boy: At a dinner party I met a woman who, catching my name, accused me of having written a magazine article about freightering and went querulously on about what it had done to her son. It had made him yearn to try it, so his parents' high school graduation present to him was a freighter passage New York to India—no ports except the Panama Canal, an uninterrupted five glorious weeks at sea. And the eleven other passengers proved to be missionary nuns.

Maybe to punish me for that, we soon had a voyage to show just how bad things could be. Of the six of us in a beautiful freighter on the Scandinavia–New York run, three and a half were wildly unbelievable. She was a fast ship, but that transatlantic voyage seemed five times as long as usual. The captain, whose mother had obviously raised no foolish children, had one look at us, went topside, and we never saw him again the whole trip. He took all his meals in his own quarters.

The tolerable "half" was a Scandinavian student of hippyish flavor on his way to an exchange scholarship at an American university—harmless but skittery, dull company. The centerpiece of the bouquet was a Scandinavian nobleman

---

*The legend was that twelve was the limit because above that number the ship had to carry a doctor, meaning added expense. Not so, I learned on looking into it. More than twelve would mean she had to have round-the-clock radio watch, requiring at least two Sparkses, also expensive.

domiciled in Hong Kong, returning thither from the old country where he had cashed in a substantial family legacy. He had a new Volvo in the hold and dozens of gaudy-colored slacks and tops and enough hashish to last him twice round the globe. Long, straight yellow hair, metallic bright blue eyes in a sharply handsome but chronically peevish face, and competent English with an improbable but clear accent. When only slightly high he talked and talked about how washing machines would be the ruin of civilization, which did not keep him from half monopolizing the passengers' washing machine for his fantastic rig-outs. When somewhat higher, he made passes at the student. There would be a knock at our door— young Holgar saying: "He's at me again"—and we'd grant sanctuary. When higher still, Goldilocks would writhe on the floor of the lounge wailing and twitching in agony because he knew he could never be as great a man as Dag Hammarskjöld. One had more than enough of him in a few hours. Holgar besought me to persuade his admirer to let him alone. Several days out I had a try at it—result only a haughty freeze-up, no respite for Holgar. But the day we landed Goldilocks warmly embraced me and said he'd never forget me, I'd been like a father to him.

One such apple in the barrel would have been more than enough. Add our witchy, chunky, middle-aged cosmopolite who represented herself as half Basque, half Polish, and long resident in Hawaii though she never made it clear whether she was headed thither. Under indirect examination that she was too stupid to detect, she proved to know less about Hawaii than a new-landed tourist. She had sartorial problems too: At first she dressed—and looked—like the grim lady who presides over the cash drawer of a third-rate French café. But soon she was changing her dress four or five times a day, for she had half a dozen U.S. Army footlockers stuffed with clothes—mostly those trailing, dull-hued, often beaded creations that your Great-aunt Genevieve called tea gowns. Not only were these creations weirdly outmoded but slightly tattered, sporadically stained—Count Dracula's daughter turned loose in his grandmother's wardrobe. Had the purser been at all accessible (which he wasn't, wise man) we might have learned what kind of passport she carried; probably Ruritanian and forged at that. She got thick with Goldilocks because she wrote and carried with her sheaves of what she thought was poetry in English—for ordinary purposes her English was passable—for him to declaim in the lounge. Other times they quarreled violently and she accused him of secreting illegal drugs in her footlockers so she'd be arrested on landing.

Inmate number three was so unmistakably round the bend, poor thing, that it was a scandal she was allowed to travel unescorted. Slight, elderly, evanescently fair, dead-panned, she could have been the half-mummified ghost of the Little Mermaid, only she was Icelandic and spoke nothing else. The only one who could communicate with her was Holgar, whose native Danish is close akin to Icelandic. Though she had a good deal of luggage, she wore only one dress the whole voyage—a full-skirted, square-necked brocade affair shot with gold thread that my wife called a cocktail dress that had seen better days. In calm weather she merely sat in the lounge occasionally thumbing her nose at the Polish-Basque poetess to whom—her one rational reaction—she had taken a violent dislike. But rough weather, of which we had a good deal in this midwinter passage, went to her head. With the ship swinging and prancing hazardously, she would dart out on deck to do a kind of off-to-Buffalo dance step, bare-headed, bare-armed in driving rain or snow or whatever precipitation offered. It was ghastly likely that a sudden roll would toss her overboard or throw her down to break a hip or two. Holgar would sigh, shake his well-meaning head, go out and talk her into returning to the lounge to resume cocking snoots at her she-enemy. Reading Isak Dinesen can be a pleasure but living her stuff in person . . .

And thanks to freighterish complications, we had an extra day of our seagoing asylum. The longshoremen of the Atlantic coast went on strike. That scrubbed our landing in New York and sent the ship to Baltimore, her nominal home port, to lie up till the strike ended. Down to the Capes of the Chesapeake for ours and all the way up the Bay; for once we did not welcome prolongation of a voyage. Even when we came alongside, the port was so tightly tied up that for some hours it looked as though we wouldn't be able to disembark. Lowering the accommodation ladder was not permitted; the customs and immigration officers were swayed on board standing on a loading pallet swathed in a cargo sling. By afternoon, however, common sense relaxed restrictions. Though no cargo could be landed, passengers and luggage could go ashore.

To what became of the Icelandic woman we had no clue. The line was legally responsible for her, so the captain can hardly have just turned her loose. Presumably whoever had shipped her on the European side had arranged to have her met. Goldilocks and the poetess went off together, not in the Volvo, which was stuck on board, of course, but in a huge rented station wagon that Goldilocks ordered up by phone; its springs sagged under all those footlockers. They said they were going to Florida. After some weeks we began to wonder what on earth did become of them. But at the time we were too happy to see the last of them to feel curiosity. Some years later we sailed in a long-voyage container-freighter, the second engineer of which had been third in our Ship of not Fools but Grotesques. He recognized us and laughed his young head off recalling how entertaining the ship's personnel had found their glimpses of what went on in passengers' country that voyage.

His amusement was understandable. A pretentious playwright would have based something speciously titillating on that strange voyage. But at the time my wife and I found it less and less amusing to have to cope, as we necessarily did, with those emotional derelicts, cajoling, reproaching, snubbing them lest they get unendurably in our hair or damage one another. The line's agents had no business booking that clot of mental invalids, and its officers badly neglected their responsibilities. That voyage was a dismal mess. Yet contrast is part of good portrayal. Let M.V. *Multipsycho* show the dark side of freightering.

Strange experiences with ships, particularly freighters, need not be as pathological as Goldilocks' capers, just cockeyed. Once, finishing a magazine assignment in Jamaica, we arranged to return in an ore carrier taking bauxite to Mobile. On her way to Trinidad to load, she was to pause off Ocho Rios to ship a replacement cook and pick us up. It sounds nothing notable until one learns that she lay offshore several miles to signal to a small launch to fetch the cook and us—at three in the morning on a very black, moonless night. As we chugged off toward where the ship's lights would, we hoped, still be when we got there, the launch seemed smaller and smaller. On reaching the ship we found not the usual accommodation ladder, all substantial steel and wood and little platform and plank steps and handrails, but a primitive, dangling rope ladder, mere ropes and sticks. The ship was large and, being utterly empty, rode ungodly high. All we saw of her was a perpendicular cliff of freeboard a trifle blacker than the night and the silly-looking ladder slatting back and forth.

I had had some experience with such contraptions and knew how tricky they are. As my wife studied the situation, she looked even graver than I felt. The launch danced and skipped, the ship rolled unpredictably, the boatmen struggled to keep our end of the ladder accessibly taut. A fall from it would mean either tumbling down into the launch to break any number of bones or a solid risk of drowning. "Next time," Mrs. Furnas said, "I wear slacks," swung up on the ladder and went up and up as though trained in a circus. She never faltered. I was proud of her. The chief steward hauled her over the rail and said: "I think you need a drink." She agreed. It should have been VSOP Courvoisier.

Only once did I see her back away: I did a piece for *Esquire* in the role of nostalgic traveler celebrating the worst eating he ever encountered. The piece is missing from my files—which are unreliable—so I am unsure whether I included Henry Ford's soybean banquet. Venezuela's broiled iguana lizard was cited, however, as not half as bad as it sounds. Star billing went to breakfast in a far-back-in-the-bush Samoan village. Our hospitable hosts had some idea of what *papalagi* (*n*-sound before the *g*, please—it means "white outsider") want early in the morning, and they did their best. Tea (recognizable); scones (British for baking-powder biscuits), only of very high specific gravity and stone cold because baked the night before; and fried eggs, yolks still runny, also stone cold because fried the night before. My wife said we just couldn't hurt their feelings by not eating everything. Reluctantly I agreed. She then let me know that with all the will in the world she was physically incapable of even one stone-cold fried egg—I'd have to take care of all four. I objected that there wasn't even salt and pepper to help them down. She was firm. I ate all four. It proved a good investment. Thenceforth, whenever there arose some question of which of us would take on some distasteful or onerous duty, usually some social chore, I reminded her of what she continued to owe me for my heroism in the matter of Samoan eggs.

The chief steward on the ore carrier was a polite but whacky young fellow hipped on calligraphy and reading personality from handwriting. The captain's hobby was taking photographs of sunrises from the bridge. The captain of one of our Farrell ships, an ardent student of rope knotting (a robust and seamanly sort of macramé), had loaded every interior handrail on board with intricately matted specimens of his imagination and skill. Then there was the genially loony skipper of the Dutch freighter that took us up and down the Saguenay River and out through the Gulf of St. Lawrence to Rotterdam via Rouen. We began to wonder about him in the Gulf when he anchored so the whole ship's company, himself included, could spend the rest of the day fishing with hand lines overside. Not that we objected. It lengthened the voyage, and the fish we dined on that night showed that pristinely fresh cod has virtues that customers of fish markets wot not of. And it helped prepare us for the freewheelingness of this captain's hobbies. He was an ardent correspondence-school student of Rosicrucianism—a sort of dilute theosophy with headquarters in San Jose, California—and was learning to play the mandolin, also by correspondence.

The bulkhead between the captain's quarters and our stateroom was very thin, so we could follow his progress with the mandolin. In the almost three weeks we listened we could detect small improvement, but we could usually tell what tune he and the exercise book had in mind. "Home on the Range" was readily identifiable. His best rendition of that came when, after three pleasant days up the Seine at Rouen, the ship went back downriver under a glorious full moon. The French pilot being altogether in charge, the captain's duty was merely to stay available. So he got jolly-drunk, took his mandolin up to the bridge, turned on the bullhorn, and sang "Home on the Range" al fresco all the way downriver, over and over again. Half of Normandy was treated to his booming, overpowering craving for a home where the buffalo roam. What the local peasantry, let alone their cattle, made of it we never knew.

As previously stated, the decline of freightering came with the rise of containering—securing cargo in huge metal boxes stacked in ships' holds or on deck and on arrival swayed ashore to be hauled off tractor-trailer fashion. One sees specimens being whisked along Interstates or piggybacked by rail, marked SEATRAIN, HAPAG . . . They are here to stay. They reduce losses from dockside pilfering and stow or off-load a given cubage of stuff faster than break-bulk work ever could. But this very efficiency entailed losing the virtues of the good old days. A generation ago one could look forward to two or three days in a given port. The container ship bustles in and out in eight or ten hours. Her full loads stack so high that they block one's forward view from anywhere below the bridge. Worse, few are built with the traditional passenger quarters. The extra cubage, plumbing, furnishings, steward, and so on, one is told, rule out the old system. And even the few container ships that do take passengers lack some of the elder ships' charm. Their superstructures are so high that the passengers' quarters might as well be on the boat deck of the *QE2*. Deckspace is stingier; no more constitutionals to and fro on a few hundred feet of forward well deck with the sea swishing and lifting beyond the bulwark at one's elbow. The new facilities equipped to handle containers are usually well away from the traditional ports. No more leaning on the rail to enjoy the local tugs, skiffs, launches, ferries, all the old-timey bustle of Antwerp or Istanbul.

Even before containers took over there was a canker in the bud. Whereas forty years ago captain and chief engineer played host to the passengers at one or two large dining tables, family style, passengers came to be assigned to tables separate from officers. This blunted one of the pleasures of freightering— being in on all that happened to the ship and crew. Then the per-diem cost climbed far above the contemporary rate of inflation. Time was one could go round the world in a Norwegian—the best freighters afloat—for six or seven dollars a day. No longer. Maybe in consequence, as word of mouth reached the wrong ears, there was an infiltration of cruise-type passengers looking for a quaint variation on their annual infestation of the West Indies and assuming that anything that expensive was worth looking into.

Ah well, it was lovely while it lasted. At one juncture we almost made it our way of life. We greatly liked the maroon-

hulled, admirably handled freighters of the Belgian Line, New
York–Antwerp. They were named for Flemish painters—
Breughel, Rubens, and so on—had excellent Flemish cooking
and commodious quarters, particularly one stateroom with a
huge bathroom: shower, tub, *and* bidet, the only one I ever
saw at sea. Twenty-odd years ago, the Port of New York Authority, impelled as much by empire building as by congestion
at Kennedy, La Guardia, and Newark, decided to build a fourth
jetport. Its first choice of site, the Great Swamp area in New
Jersey's Morris County, was bitterly opposed by Jerseyites within
thirty miles, us included, for nobody wanted the threatened
blessings of unbearable noise, traffic congestion, and crassly
regardless development. Affluent and weighty persons in Morris
County raised seven figures' worth of dollars and frustrated
the Port Authority by buying up the Great Swamp and giving
it to Uncle Sam for a perpetually inviolable wildlife refuge.
Nice too for the snakes and owls. Only at that point the Port
Authority said very well, our second choice is a level spot in
the middle of Hunterdon County—where the western end of
one of the proposed runways was to be within a mile of our
house in the woods.

The odds against successful resistance were appallingly high.
Hunterdon lacked Morris's kind of money and clout; and once
their difficulty was resolved, though Hunterdon had done its
bit to help them, the Morrisites gave us no support. For reasons best known to themselves New York's press and TV went
slavishly along with the Port Authority's blather about how,
unless that fourth jetport was built at once, grass would grow
on the Long Island parkways. (That not only sounds like nonsense, it was; but NBC actually did a half hour of it, culminating in a shot of an entrance to Kennedy with a sign: "AIRPORT
CLOSED.") Hunterdon's shrill squeals succeeded only in putting
the catastrophe off for a year or so.

Many Hunterdonites, us included, determined to go elsewhere when the blow fell. I had a scheme: We'd sell our house
and thriving woodland, take a small apartment in New York
for occasional business or pleasure, but make our regular
domicile one of those remarkable Belgian Line staterooms back
and forth across the Atlantic voyage after voyage. The line
might well make me a pretty fair rate on a yearly basis. And

when we needed or wished to stay ashore over a voyage or two in New York or on the Continent, I'd pay the line a 20 percent commission to sell our room. My wife foresaw minor complications in some contexts, as did I in others. But we agreed it was basically a sound and potentially enjoyable *pis aller.*

Before we could open negotiations, however, the line dropped its New York–Antwerp service and put the ships on the West African run, which suited us not at all. Then a recession-occasioned falloff in airline bookings and the advent of larger planes carrying more people per takeoff cooled the Port Authority down. They suddenly proclaimed what disinterested as well as disgruntled people had told them all along, that no fourth jetport was needed. Had the dice not rolled that way, however, Mr. and Mrs. Furnas might well have become the Flying Flemings of the North Atlantic. And they'd probably have loved it.

17

The Privilege of Hearing

IF YOU MUST have a handicapped sense, choose impaired hearing. To agree we hard-of-hearing need only imagine ourselves blind instead. Most of us twelve million Americans often saying "How's that again?" are not as young as we once were and are consequently losing acuity in the auditory nerve that transmits sound from ear into brain. Many escape this penalty of aging, but so many do not that it may be regarded as, like wrinkles, a normal result of the wear and tear of time. Thanks to today's too-loud music that impairment will probably be appearing earlier among those now in their teens to forties. All such lowered efficiency muffles the higher frequencies of sound. Music gradually changes quality, women's voices lose clarity. My own auditory nerves have been getting duller and duller these past thirty years and there isn't much to do about it.

My case, however, had already involved other kinds of hearing loss. By far the most severe was otosclerosis, a gradual buildup of calcium-based stuff that clogs the chain of tiny bones, smallest in the body, that carry sound from drum to nerve. That condition caught up with me in the mid-1930s. Even in my late teens I was aware that others picked up the lyrics from phonograph records more readily than I. Otosclerosis is genetic, hereditary, a Mendelian recessive like blue eyes, affecting millions to some extent, maybe a million seriously. It was very probably the cause of extreme deafness in my mother and her father.

369

It first forced itself on my attention at a summer theater performance. I was missing so many lines that, though seated well up front, I had little notion what the play was about; whereas the people with me were having no trouble. Other such experiences began to pile up. I was reluctant to try hearing aids because they had not helped my mother much and were still cumbersome—a mike the size of my hand and packs of heavy dry cells in the hip pocket. Handicapped hearing fitted ill, of course, with the interviewing that my magazine work required. You'd better be sure just what your man said in reply to a loaded question. And having grimly to concentrate on word-by-word distracts one's attention from the tactics and strategy, the poker-playing cut and thrust, of question and backpedaling answer. For ten years, however, I managed without aids. By the time that congestive head cold caught over the Dutch East Indies in 1945 forced me to change my mind, aids had become more efficient and less cumbersome.

Off and on I had gone to otologists—ear specialists. One of the most eminent, Dr. Edmund Prince Fowler, Sr., welcomed me as a classic datum in his research on otosclerosis. Back then remedy did not exist. But gradually wonderfully clever surgery under high microscopy culminated in "stapes mobilization," a procedure that oh so delicately enters the middle ear, clears the bones of obstruction, and reattaches them. A marvelous advance—only the half a dozen otologists who examined me over the years agreed that my otosclerosis was inoperable. That verdict was worth regarding because failure can mean complete loss of hearing in the ear concerned.

So I went along with hearing aids, which were improving more or less in sync with the gradual loss in my auditory nerves. Luckily I was shifting from magazines to hardcover books based primarily on library research, hence little interviewing. Yet I often still had negotiations to juggle with publishers, librarians, government officials with whom understanding all one heard was indispensable. One otologist offered me a counsel of despair—better learn lipreading.

That proved unnecessary. I now get by with a stepper-upper on my business phone and sporadic use of aids for social and business occasions. Even with aids, however, I get dismally little dialogue in either stage or movie theaters. I last visited a live theater a dozen years ago and then only because a friend was in the cast. But in my own house and for radio, much of TV, and shopping, I manage without aids. Some of that relative freedom depends on skills that most of the hearing handicapped develop in self-defense—unconscious lipreading, reflex concentration, bluffing ad lib. In my case much more credit goes to a wildly improbable series of events that probably exhausted whatever credit I had with whatever gods of chance may be. And none of this shamelessly implausible story would have happened had I not been a writer.

My wife and I were in Edinburgh dining with the Marryat Dobies. Marryat, retired head of the National Library of Scotland, had been a good friend ever since he had nobly helped us in research on Stevenson. We mentioned that we were on our way to have a look at France between the Rhone and the Catalan border. The Dobies said Ah, a neighbor of ours has just done a book on that region; come to tea tomorrow and we'll have her in. She proved to be an elderly, peremptory, and obliging Scotswoman who strongly advised us to visit Lamastre, a little place on the eastern slope of the Cevennes, and stay at the Hôtel du Commerce using her name. In Lyon ten days later we rented a Hertz car with Lamastre our first stop.

On the way we followed our usual procedure, consulting the *Guide Michelin*. The Hôtel du Commerce was there right enough, but its rival Hôtel du Midi cost little more *and* its restaurant was starred. Guiltily, greedily, we chose it. It was off-season; we were the stately proprietress's only guests. She laid herself out to give us the house's best—exquisitely good—and after dinner had us into her sitting room for *digestifs*. When she heard whither we were bound she opened a campaign: Dramatically she tapped her left wrist with her right index finger and said that down in that country we must consult the great Dr. Causse in Béziers, for she saw monsieur wore a hearing aid and Dr. Causse had operated on her deaf ears so successfully that she had kissed him. See here on the wrist the little scar where he had taken a bit of tissue for the repair.* He was overwhelmed with patients, but we must write at once and mention her—he was sure to remember her, and of that

---

*Causse's technique in stapes mobilization. Dr. Shambaugh (who will be discussed later) uses such shreds taken from just over the ear. So I have tiny scars there as though I'd had a face lift.

I was certain—and when we were down that way he might be able to spare time for an examination. And so on and on, all courteous, kind insistence.

My wife was longingly impressed. Not I. I had heard "No, inoperable" from so many ranking otologists that I was disinclined to take my hereditary hair shirt to a provincial French doctor. For politeness, however, I agreed to write. Mme. Barratero produced stationery and made me do it then and there, read it, approved, and doubtless suspecting I might not mail it, kept it to go to the post office in the morning. Frenchly frugal, she advised making it clear to Dr. Causse that this was only consultation. If he advised operating, we should wait to have it done at home where our insurance would apply. She thought of everything.

After breakfast we bade her a warm farewell, loaded the car—and it wouldn't start. The local garage man jump-started it but said those people in Lyon should be ashamed—this car was whatever the French for rattletrap heap would be. Go to the nearest large Hertz agency and demand something better. And don't turn off the ignition till you get there. Nîmes was handily on our way south. We rolled into the local Hertz place with me indignantly firing bad French from my window and my wife far better out of hers. In a mood of good-humored *zut alors!* the staff calmed us down, saying yes indeed, those Lyon pirates, it's their fault, not ours. A brand-new Peugeot is coming in tomorrow morning, stay overnight and it's yours. Then the boss mechanic, a massive, bright-eyed, swarthy type in a black beret and a blue smock, pointed to my hearing aid, tapped his left wrist with his right forefinger, and said monsieur must go see the great Dr. Causse in Béziers, he operated on my ears and now . . .

That shook me. Was something trying to tell me something? As we neared the neighborhood of Béziers, I allowed my wife to telephone Dr. Causse's office. Yes indeed, the doctor has seen your letter and is interested, can you be here on Wednesday?

Béziers is an austerely charming little city with a horrible history as the scene of one of the worst massacres in the medieval crusade against the Albigensian heresy. Dr. Causse's clinic consisted of himself, two disciple-colleagues, a cadre of nurses and technicians, and a mob scene of patients from all over France. By afternoon they worked me in for an audiology test. It had to be in French, of course—that baffling tongue that I read fluently, write recognizably, speak atrociously, and because of lack of auditory presence of mind *and* poor hearing, find largely incomprehensible—so I had small faith in its accuracy, none in its turning up anything promising. Hours later we saw the second in command, an impressive clone of Raymond Massey, who discussed my case considerately and warned us not to be too cast down if his chief's verdict was unfavorable. Go have your dinner and come back this evening.

Well after nine o'clock we saw Dr. Causse, still in his operating-room whites. He had practically no English, so my wife got the brunt of his finding. Had we come some years earlier, my otosclerosis might have been operable. Now it was too late; about that he was regretfully firm. We asked about my nerve trouble. He could offer nothing there himself, but at a recent international medical meeting, he had met an American doctor who had a promising new approach. We should consult him. He couldn't recall the name but would look it up and write to us. We thanked him, paid his very reasonable bill, and went away. The obvious high caliber of the whole outfit had so raised my wife's hopes that she was even farther down in the dumps than I.

Neither of us was sure that we'd ever get that name and address and, suppose we did, that said American doctor would be any help. A month later we received a large, elegant envelope containing Dr. Causse's best wishes and the name of Dr. George E. Shambaugh, Jr., of Chicago. My wife prodded me into writing to him describing my case and the circumstances; I added that Dr. Causse was probably unaware that Chicago was a long way from New Jersey, would there be a colleague in New York or Philadelphia employing this new approach? The reply was prompt: Dr. Shambaugh could suggest nobody; all his diagnoses depended on new X-ray methods developed by a Chicago specialist, Dr. Galdino Valvassori. I'd have to come to Chicago.

For me that tore it again. Having written dozens of magazine articles on a wide range of medical matters, I could recognize the quack's usual prattle about new, esoteric techniques that only he employs. But still hanging on, my wife phoned her half-brother, a well connected Chicago lawyer: "John, do you know anything about a Dr. Shambaugh?" "Yes indeed. Went to him a few weeks ago. One of the best ear men in the country." Shaken again, I did what I should have done before—reached for *Who's Who*. My putative quack was former head of department at Northwestern University Medical School, former editor of the *Journal of Otorhinolaryngology*, etc. My wife said: "Shambaugh . . . Yes, that was the name of the man who took out my tonsils when I was small." Later in Dr. Shambaugh's office she mentioned that, and he pointed to a portrait of his father hanging on the wall behind her. Again coincidence had joined hands with happenstance.

Dr. Shambaugh's technician's audiology test was in English. Then to Dr. Valvassori's office in the same Michigan Avenue building and a brisk three rounds with his see-all and know-all gadget, a precursor of today's tomology. One lay supine, head wedged in a box to prevent movement, while overhead a complex of stainless steel snakes slithered, writhed, shimmered, and grunted in wild convolutions obeying the signals of a chipper lady trainer. The thing was obviously brainchild of a Hollywood mad scientist. (The only other one then in use in America was used as a prop in *The Exorcist*.) We were sent away to lunch and spent some hours at the nearby Art Institute while the results were evaluated. Having renewed acquaintance with *La Grande Jatte* and *The Song of the Lark*, we returned hoping that the devil-machine had something constructive to offer about nerve deafness. Nerve deafness wasn't even mentioned. Dr. Shambaugh was all professional joy: "Your ears are operable for otosclerosis." My wife burst into tears.

The devil-machine's pictures had shown the clogging in both ears to be ripe for surgery. Otologists who had found them inoperable were wrong but largely because they lacked this new diagnostic tool.

Dr. Shambaugh's obliging leaflet of preoperative briefing set the odds of success in my case at ten to one. I'd have settled for even money though I did mistrust its warning about a "probably temporary postoperative" loss of sense of taste. "Probably"? Hm-mm-m. The operation on the right ear was a brilliant success; all at once I was hearing things I had forgotten existed. The only sour note came with my first postoperative meal, the old "liquid diet" of fruit juice, bouillon, Jell-o. My wife urged me to try something even though I didn't feel like it. I took a spoonful of bouillon and said: "It's happened. My sense of taste is gone." She tried a spoonful: "My boy," she said, "this is hospital food. It has no taste." So I tried the Jell-o and for once was delighted with that substrawberry flavor as strong—or as weak—as ever.

Standard practice was to wait a year on the other ear, but I persuaded Dr. Shambaugh to make it six months. Success again. Were it not for the irreversible nerve damage inflicted on me by the calendar, my hearing would now be, though undeniably subnormal, not inefficient under favorable conditions. And Dr. Shambaugh's capsules of calcium combined with fluoride—the treatment that Dr. Causse knew of—do seem to have slowed down the nerve problem.

This hands-across-the-sea referral made Shambaugh and Causse friends on a sort of otological pen-pal basis. They have collaborated on a book on ear surgery. All because Furnas wrote a book about Robert Louis Stevenson. Or because greediness sent the Furnases to the other hotel. Or because Hertz rented them a dog. Or because Mrs. Furnas's half-brother had ear trouble at the right time. Or, harking back to travel, because the Furnases, for no particular reason, wished to have a look at the old province of Rousillon. And basically, of course, because Furnas went into writing.

Indeed I have been lucky. And indeed my universe—only mine, not yours, not anybody's else's—kindly as it has treated me, doesn't make sense.

18

A Profession?

WHEN A QUESTIONNAIRE asks: "Profession?" I put down "writer" with misgivings. My *American Heritage Dictionary* defines *profession* as: "An occupation or vocation requiring training in the liberal arts or the sciences and advanced study in a special field." That takes in doctors, lawyers, engineers, architects, the bulk of the clergy, and is loosely pertinent to painters and sculptors, most of whom have attended some sort of art school. And before formal training in such fields was available, various *ad hoc* apprenticeships had developed. I doubt, however, whether writing is or needs to be or should be considered a profession; and suppose it is, whether worthwhile formal training for it is possible.

Literary history strongly supports such doubts. Chaucer, the radiant, uncannily skilled founder of our literature, was not primarily a poet and yarn-spinner but a courtier-diplomat-civil servant. Shakespeare was an actor doubling as company staff writer. Milton was a scholar inclined toward holy orders, then a Roundhead civil servant: Congreve a gentleman-pensioner of government; Defoe a London businessman; Swift a beneficed clergyman dabbling in politics; Fielding a fledgling lawyer; Richardson a bookseller; Byron and Shelley patricians of private means. Granted, a starveling Grub Street eventually appeared, composed largely of hacks writing-to-live but few Samuel Johnsons came out of that substratum. Jane Austen, Maria Edgeworth, and the Brontës had family-household livelihoods. Strange as it now sounds, most of the significant elder

writing in the English-speaking world's birthright was fruit of
a minor hobby of the educated classes. Their manuscripts might
indeed get printed but had no purpose more pressing than
self-prescribed respite from practical affairs.

   Those were, in fact, Sunday writers whose products turned
out better than Winston Churchill's landscapes. An important
point! Henri Rousseau, Gauguin, Grandma Moses . . . few
Sunday painters attain the museum galleries, whereas in literature until *c.* 1800 the reverse was true. As American literature struggled into the light, the story was the same. Few
significant writers wrote for a living. Hawthorne tried it and
had his ups but also his downs relieved by long dependence
on government posts. Melville tried it, met disaster, and survived only through family subsidy and dreary years as a customs inspector. Cooper was a landed patrician with an early
career as a U.S. Navy officer, Holmes an eminent physician.
Longfellow's professorships floated him until he made national icons of Paul Revere, Hiawatha, and Evangeline. Bryant
and Whitman were newspapermen. All those except Whitman
came of prosperous-or-better upper-class families. Housewife
Mrs. Stowe did her hobby scribbling for pin money until Uncle Tom spun her into orbit as career writer. Emily Dickinson
was a family-supported crypto–Sunday poet. Henry James was
the first important American example of an uninterrupted career of serious fiction—and it was inherited means that enabled him to try it.

   Since writing as cultivated hobby so long dominated literature, it follows that one's ancestors' nephews, when asked what
they planned to do, seldom replied "to be a writer." For back
then it would rarely have occurred to youth, still less often to
youth's parents, to rank that among "professions in which men
engage,/The army, the navy, the church and the stage . . ."
Youth might choose the law and take to Sunday writing that,
getting into print, gradually became the major concern, as
happened to Fielding, Irving, Arthur Pendennis, and Edgar
Lee Masters. Joseph Conrad and William McFee were ship's
officers whose offwatch writings got taken seriously enough to
suggest writing careers ashore. Young Joyce Cary served awhile
in Britain's West African colonial government before concentrating on writing. William Carlos Williams kept up his physi-

cian's practice. Wallace Stevens remained a high-echelon insurance executive.

It hardly matters whether it was caution, habit, or divided affection that persuaded such renowed figures to keep on with their original callings after Sunday writing proved a springboard. It may matter that, in this respect, as in several others, writing seems to differ from the other arts—also from the professions because of the number practicing it. Even now that telephones and tapes are smothering the letter, more people still occasionally organize words on paper than ever try to practice law or medicine. Hence, until our century, writing lacked the dictionary-mandated facilities for that "advanced study" in its "specialized field."

That neglect certainly led to no shortage of writers of all degrees of competence. Nevertheless, Academia, finally mindful of having been bred out of literature by pedagogy, set about filling the gap by inciting colleges to offer courses in "Creative Writing," a label that did distinguish their beneficiaries from freshmen in courses meant to harass them into heightened literacy. But the phrase not only sounds at first like oblique reference to the first chapter of Genesis, its wistful windiness was and remains ominous: A class of a couple of dozen undergraduates abetting one another in a common yearning "to be a writer," reading their things aloud for comradely criticism under the Creative smiles of a writer-in-residence hovering over their family mutual-admiration society. Mark Twain and William Dean Howells did well without ever having gone to college, let alone one listing "Creative Writing 8" in the catalogue; add Ernest Hemingway and John O'Hara. In your grandfather's time, writing-minded students at Limbo University managed to find and abet one another without curricular auspices, and if some genial faculty member wanted to gather under his wings a little group of aspirants on his own time, nobody stopped him. But hours-under-the-elms now devoted to credit-earning writing courses would be better devoted to gaining elementary acquaintance with disciplines—for starters, biology, anthropology, psychology—likely to form nourishing compost for young writers' sympathies and scope of vision.

While Creative Writing was still only endemic, our culture tried to make the newspaper city room an incubator for writ-

ers. The precedents were the careers of quondam newspapermen Mark Twain and Rudyard Kipling gradually reinforced
by those of Stephen Crane, Theodore Dreiser, David Graham
Phillips. . . . Enter a new literary role model—the debonair,
growingly cynical, shrewd young reporter getting by on a
meager salary while pecking away nights on the novel that will
send him airborne into fame. Maybe because newspapers were
too few to handle the crowd of aspirants, Academia saw fit to
step in again. Following the lead of the University of Missouri
in 1908 and then of the Pulitzer bequest at Columbia University, schools of journalism proliferated coast to coast and have
blithely survived the scorn of Abraham Flexner's *Universities*
(Oxford University Press 1930): " . . . [They] do nothing for
undergraduates that is worth their time. . . . Does anyone really
suppose that Harvard, having no school of journalism, will . . .
furnish fewer editors, reviewers and reporters than Columbia
will?"

The problem of whether one can teach what is learned only
by individual, trial-and-error experience is at least addressed,
if not entirely met, by arranging periods of actual newspaper
chores for journalism students. Add that the deans and other
faculty of such schools are often retired managing editors or
TV anchorpersons who can recommend promising graduates
to former colleagues on the old paper or network. It remains
regrettable, however, that the very existence of these pre-
sumptive academic counterparts of schools of medicine and
law heightens the illusion that journalism—and by association,
"being a writer"—is a profession. Suppose a keen freshman at
Limbo U does well in Creative Writing, enters the School of
Journalism, graduates into a cub's berth on the Zenith *Bugle*,
earns his salt there while still intent on "being a writer" and
eventually has a solid career with novels about the seamy side
of a midwestern city—is he more or less a professional than
Dashiell Hammett, who never had an Alma Mater and never
yelled at a copyboy? Flexner again: "[Such] questions answer
themselves." Yet as I write this, New York's well-considered
New School is advertising in its "most extensive writing program in the country," a course in "Creative Journalism," presumably blending both of Academia's pointless attempts to
oblige.

Maybe the definition of "professional" should require "deriving primary livelihood from the chosen activity." That would allow for the author-beneficiaries of today's zillion-dollar advances on anticipated best sellers; also certain less-than-blockbusting novelists whose loyal publics can be counted on to buy x0,000 copies of each successive job; and the handful of nonfiction stalwarts uncannily shrewd at covering subjects likely to catch the public eye of the moment. Yet that criterion is too narrow. Seven years ago the Authors Guild asked its members how they were doing. The average annual income from writing reported by 2,239 dues-payers, even though fattened, of course, by blockbusters, came to less than $5,000. Allow for relatively inactive elders and youngsters still damp behind the literary ears, yet writing with revenue at all in mind remains what it was eight generations ago—except for a special few, nothing to rely on. Even in the reputedly well-paid field of screen-writing, a high-salaried member of the Writers Guild recently reported, ". . . 85% . . . work sporadically and cannot support themselves as writers." (*Newsweek*, August 29, 1988.) No wonder the run of accepted writers remain the Sunday kind, gaining eating money by other means, often academic posts. This is a profession? More like an occasionally remunerative recreation.

Yet it will continue to attract certain temperaments. Their nature stays hard to define. What psychologist's pigeonhole can accommodate both Henry David Thoreau and Guy de Maupassant?

Practicing writers, part- or full-time, understandably shy off when a bothered but doting parent confides that Jason or Jennifer is entering Limbo U and plans "to be a writer" and could you . . . The easy reflex is: "My advice is *don't!*" in a voice like Noel Coward's adjuring Mrs. Worthington not to put her daughter on the stage. That does no harm. If the kid has what it takes, he'll probably hold that course somehow; if he doesn't, he probably never had it. Yet he may steer better if cured of thinking of "being a writer" as solid. So one should stroke the beard and utter some such wisdom as this:

Don't waste time in Creative Writing or a School of Journalism. *Cf.* Flexner as above. But if you can manage the opportunity, get some newspaper experience.

Don't major in English. Academia neglects the aspects of

literature that will bring out the best in you—that caused a wise man (I wish I could remember who) to say its chief mission is "to delight"; presumably not to provide grist for Ph.D. mills to grind exceeding small, or yet vehicles for self-conscious ego trips. Never forget that though writing is very important, writers are not.

Do take the academic opportunity to learn your way around in at least one foreign language—French, German, Italian, Spanish, in that order of preference. Goethe said nobody knows his own tongue until he is well acquainted with another. Choose language courses entailing wide reading, not intensive analysis of a few idolized masterpieces.

Read, read, read! as Professor Medoff so brusquely recommends. Yes, read the current stuff that gets conspicuously reviewed. Most of it will, to be polite, look watery by the time you are middle-aged, but such slippage is built into any literary period and you should have the feel of your time. Concentrate, however, on what the trendy will regard as archaic—the riches between 1580 and say, 1940. The savory virtues of your elders and betters will sink in now better than later. This is your time to imbue the marrow of your bones and the fluid in your spine with the endogenous pungencies and synergisms of the mother tongue that you hope to be privileged to use. Read the King James Bible, Shakespeare, *The Pilgrim's Progress*, Thoreau, and *Huckleberry Finn* over and over till they come out of your ears. For further guidance take a survey course in English and another in American literature; but pay little heed to the lecturers' comments; read the plums you choose as though they were written yesterday just for you. Or to save wasting time in lecture halls, invest $3.25 in one of those *Cliff Notes* pamphlets that predigest literature from *Sir Gawain and the Green Knight* to Kurt Vonnegut for students boning up for exams. Its back cover lists some two hundred standard items thus vandalized because likely to be "taught" in literature courses—which amounts to an admirably handy roster of reading that your word-faculty will find enrichening. Those books' vocabularies, materials, and footwork will never be yours but, if you are lucky, their infiltrating essences will endow you with a feel for words and their marshaling as intimate as that of a fish with water.

When Flaubert, say, or Virginia Woolf or Ring Lardner gives you a special glow, absorb pretty much everything they wrote but without chaperonage from Academia. Flaubert *in French*, mind. Eschew translations almost altogether. The few exceptions should include the masterful warmth and rumble of Cotton's Montaigne and Urquhart's Rabelais. For unless you become a linguistic prodigy, your contact with Homer, Sophocles, Ibsen, the giant Russians must come through translations ranging in quality from the vapidity of the Putnam *Don Quixote* to the lamentable flabbiness with which the aforesaid Russians are fobbed off. Those shortcomings were probably what made Gertrude Stein, when Garson Kanin showed her an academic list of one hundred must-books for students, throw it down in disgust and snort: "Good God, they're hardly reading anything in English!" So postpone practically all translations until after your thirtieth birthday, since more than minimal contact with them while your word-faculty is still cartilaginous may stunt its growth and warp its shape. I first met *Candide* in a standard translation. The content plainly had a vivacious bent but the insipid English embodying it muffled everything. Some years later the original French was a burst of sunshine. I was shocked a while ago to learn that a certain Ivy League college (name withheld out of possibly misplaced deference) was listing an undergraduate course in "The French Novel" using translations throughout.

Take to heart the implications of that overwhelming ratio of Sunday writers. Put aside the modern notion of "writing" as full-time, monolithic, sole-resource career. Trying to make out on occasional small checks among rejection slips seldom improves one's product. It leads to wild swings or misbegotten imitations of what seems to sell. Instead after college or during summer vacations, learn a skill or trade that will support you (doubtless modestly) while leaving you spare time and energy to fumble toward learning to write. Maritime radio operator would be fine—good pay, board and room thrown in, and Sparks usually has more off hours than Charles Lamb's India House clerkship ever afforded him; but American ships are scarce these days. Enter community-college courses in such things as dental hygiene, lab technology, TV- or Xerox-servicing—anything legal that, without heavy labor, brings a basic living and won't stay on your mind after hours. Take advantage of the growing spread of the four-day work week, leaving a nice bloc of three-Sundays-in-a-week as in Poe's story. Part-time jobs too are getting more numerous.

But beware of that berth in a literary classroom to which the writing-minded often resort. Your bread-and-butter occupation should have nothing to do with words and books. A weekly change of idiom and atmosphere will keep both fresher, and the necessary contacts with benchmates, customers, supervisors will help preserve your sense of objective reality—for writing is insidiously solipsist. And negatively, the classroom's entanglement with current fashions in criticism necessarily dulls one's verbal antennae. As for teaching Creative Writing, listen to Walter Tevis (successful novelist, *The Hustler,* for instance) celebrating his escape from that: ". . . Teaching hurt. . . . I was a professor of English . . . trying to write at the same time. . . . I found myself leaving my enthusiasm in the classroom. I enjoyed the students, but, as long as I had a live audience, I didn't have a second need for an unseen reading audience. . . ." Nor are editorial jobs advisable. The talents of Dickens, Thackeray, Howells, and Hawthorne survived extended editorial responsibilities, but all of them were well into stride before risking such attrition from others' words and awkwardness.

I can recommend all of the foregoing because so little of it—chiefly the avid reading and the foreign language—comes out of personal experience. Had anybody given me such counsel sixty years ago, my path might have been smoother. Yet I was a wrongheaded, stubborn youngster and probably wouldn't have taken it anyway.

Index